THE
BLUE BOOK
OF
BROADMINDED
BUSINESS
BEHAVIOR

THE
BLUE BOOK
OF
BROADMINDED
BUSINESS
BEHAVIOR

Auren Uris

THOMAS Y. CROWELL COMPANY
Established 1834/NEW YORK

Designed by S. S. Drate

Manufactured in the United States of America

Library of Congress Cataloging in Publication Data
Uris, Auren.
  The blue book of broadminded business behavior.
  Includes index.
  1. Business etiquette. 2. Business ethics.
I. Title.
HF5386.U69 1977   395'.52   76–54769
ISBN 0-690-01422-8

10 9 8 7 6 5 4 3 2 1

Dedication

To all those on the workscene who understand that one's job is a crucial part of one's life experience, and accordingly strive to make it as constructive, harmonious and rewarding as any other part of life.

Acknowledgments

In a work of such broad scope as this, a great many people are necessarily involved—colleagues, friends, generous experts in many fields willing to share their views and experience. Gratitude to all has been expressed by me on an individual basis. While it is impossible to mention every collaborator formally, public appreciation is due those whose help has been extensive and continuing. This group includes—

Colleagues at the Research Institute of America: Grace Barrett, Rick Blake, Jane Bensahel, Leo Cherne, Joseph Cowley, Raymond Concannon, Ken Dobrer, Patricia Durston, Eugene Epstein, Beth Harding, Mary Jollon, Domenica Mortati, Marjorie Noppel, Tom Quick, Trevor Thomas, Louise Trenta and Barbara Whitmore.

For library services and guidance: Inese Rudzitis and Joy Elbaum, of the Research Institute library.

For outstanding help with the physical preparation of the manuscript: Winifred Mathie, Doris Horvath, Lesley Lull, Lisa Goldsen, Louise Ligato, Ellen Taylor and Fay Rossi.

To Ruth Burger, Directing Editor of Executive Membership, Research Institute of America, particular appreciation for assistance in the early planning and development stages of the project, and help in resolving some of the knotty problems of organization and treatment.

To Suzanne Nixon, for original and enlightening views on aspects of behavior that represent major breaks with the past.

To Doris Reichbart, for helpful discussions about fine points of procedures, to the end of maximizing their usefulness.

And finally, to my children, Mary, Victoria, Bettina and Daniel, who help keep me young and open-minded.

Contents

INTRODUCTION

The simplest forms of etiquette in business require sending one's secretary a card on his or her birthday, knowing how to put a visitor at ease, and so on. But problems tend to arise in situations that are less cut-and-dried:

- A male employee falls back on the old gallantry in his treatment of a woman executive, and makes her thoroughly uncomfortable.
- A subordinate's unthinking behavior in a meeting slights his boss.
- A sales manager takes a colleague to dinner, fails to provide the clear signals that she is assuming the role of host, and precipitates a stupid squabble over the check.

There is considerably more to business etiquette than courtesy and the use of proper forms. True, these may not be neglected. But the fact is that there are *several* purposes to business etiquette. We can start with the matter of common courtesy—greetings, farewells, handshaking, and so on—but must immediately add to the list:

- the minimizing of uncertainty and strain in personal encounters;
- celebration of nonwork elements—anniversaries, birthdays, and other organization-related events so as to enrich the work experience;

1

- adoption of policies and procedures that make the organizational climate harmonious and more rewarding to the individual employee, from mail boy to president.

Clearly, in the alternatives between a narrow view and a broad one of business etiquette, this book adopts the latter. It is my purpose to provide ideas, information, and insights that not only promote gracious conduct but also aim to improve the health and spirit of organizations both public and private to the end that they become better places to work. A worthy goal. A formidable challenge.

HOW ETIQUETTE ENHANCES

In society, the solecism is usually punished by a loss of social status or the shattering of a reputation. At work, reactions may take on immediate and specific forms: demotion, loss of opportunity, loss of standing in the organization. Typical instance: the employee who takes advantage of the proximity created by an office party to tell the boss off, or to discourse on what's wrong with the organization, and finds employed status does not survive the night.

Happily, the person whose behavior reflects courtesy and consideration for others is rewarded by the respect and esteem of colleagues. There's no case on record of anyone becoming a top executive because of good manners—but it's always a strong facilitating factor. And of course organizations must build into procedures and policies a sense of etiquette to enhance the corporate personality and image.

The plain fact is that business is seldom "strictly business." Every organization observes rites and rituals that complement the purely functional procedures. And these observances add a special élan, a wonderful vitality to organizational life.

THE UNIQUE REQUIREMENTS OF BUSINESS BEHAVIOR

Etiquette embraces a wide variety of means by which the personal concerns of the individual and the collective good of the organization are furthered. It encompasses the do's as well as the don't's, the things that should be said and those best left unsaid.

In keeping with the broad view of etiquette adopted here, it is possible that some subject matter to be found in these pages will prove unexpected. For example, you will find the subject of discipline discussed (see Chapter 4, "Discipline," page 178) at some length. The reason for this inclusion is that in terms of workscene behavior, discipline—understanding it and knowing how to apply it—is essential to maintaining peace and harmony. And without a stable climate, the finer points of day-to-day behavior become irrelevant. What is the point of talking about proper forms of address in a milieu made unstable by disorderliness and insubordination?

RULES THAT GUIDE RATHER THAN BIND

The world of business creates its own kinds of relationships. Therefore, it requires its own rules of behavior suited to the unique situations that develop in the business setting. The organization —and employees at all levels—who want to operate effectively must follow codes of conduct based on business values and attitudes.

Many people balk at the idea of "rules." They equate them with restraints—and no one likes to feel boxed in. But no rigid codes of conduct are implied in the concept of business etiquette. Conformity for its own sake is not recommended here. On the contrary, flexibility and an awareness of what is involved in terms of feelings and the organizational realities are the bases for action.

Common sense, that great problem-solver, is only partially useful in the area of human conduct. On the business scene, the complexities of the human psyche are further complicated by the intricacies of organizational life in such matters as status, privilege, and authority. The material in this book provides guidance for the entire spectrum of people in business—from the file clerk who wonders if it is O.K. to buy her boss a birthday present, to the top policymaker wondering what to put in the company handbook under the heading "Proper Attire."

ETIQUETTE, YOU, AND YOUR ORGANIZATION

There are three questions people have about business etiquette that are worth examining because they clarify the nature and viability of manners as they pertain to the individual and the organization:

IS BUSINESS ETIQUETTE THE SAME AS THAT OF SOCIETY AT LARGE? There are situations and factors at work that have no parallels elsewhere. For example, the outside world has no ceremony quite like the office Christmas party or the company picnic. And the intimate working relationship of boss and secretary is unique, as are the relationships between colleagues. Therefore, the idea that the etiquette of the outside world can be transferred *in toto* to the business scene doesn't quite work—even though some customs from the larger milieu, introductions, for example, can be applied.

ETHICS AND ETIQUETTE—ARE THEY TWO SEPARATE AREAS? In business, ethics and etiquette overlap. Take the expense account (also known as the "swindle sheet" and "gyp slip"). The actions and prohibitions that constitute good etiquette also lead to good ethical conduct—and vice versa. Ethics and etiquette always require the same behavior—even though the *reasons* for that behavior may differ.

ETIQUETTE AND GOOD MANAGEMENT—ARE THEY THE SAME? Surprisingly, yes. Surprising, because one *might think* that the objectives of etiquette and effective management do not coincide. Behavior undertaken in the cause of etiquette might seem to suggest inefficiency—wasting time for reasons of sentiment. But consider:

An employee is fired because of redundancy. Etiquette suggests that he be treated with consideration—an exit interview that shows the organization cares about his feelings, his future, and so on.

Is this inefficient, coddling behavior when seen from a "strictly business" standpoint? Not at all. It's simple good management to seek to maintain an attractive image in the public mind—and considerate treatment of separated employees is an important factor in organizational public relations.

Some actions are both *bad management* and *poor etiquette*. For example, favoritism is unfair, inequitable, and therefore undesirable etiquette, which opposes mistreatment of individuals. And favoritism is also undesirable from a good-management standpoint because it results in a deserving person's losing out to one who is well connected—eventually demoralizing to personnel. (You'll find the subject of favoritism discussed in connection with status in Chapter 5. See especially the heading *"Special Problems of the 'Boss,' "* page 231.)

What has been said above suggests the impossibility—or impracticality—of considering matters of etiquette without due regard to the overlapping matters of ethics and good management. Accordingly, where considerations of etiquette impinge on these two adjacent areas, they will be discussed so that you may take action with full knowledge of all the basic considerations involved.

THE NEW ETIQUETTE

Today's etiquette is not yesterday's. The social upheavals of the late 1960s left their imprint on our attitudes and values both at home and at work. One simple way to describe the nature of the revolution is to say that stuffed-shirtism is dead. Everything from personal dress to the basic relationship between the sexes has changed drastically. And, inevitably, life at work is different today as a result of basic factors like these:

• *Women.* Not just their "liberation" but their presence in growing numbers. If you grew up in a time when it was considered impolite to precede a woman out of an elevator or to use off-color language in a woman's presence, you've got a new set of rules to learn.

• *Broader horizons.* "After all," says one newcomer to the executive suite, "good manners in business is just a matter of common sense." Perhaps much of it is. But the best intentions and the clearest logic are not enough to guide a person's behavior in the broader boundaries, geographic and emotional, that exist in business today. Should you take a visiting Japanese businessman to lunch at a Japanese restaurant? Chinese? Russian? What do you say to an ex-boss you detested who has fallen on hard times? Should you ask your secretary to do your Christmas shopping? Subtle considerations are involved in questions like these, and we need considered and insightful thinking for satisfactory answers.

• *The new informality.* Take the simplest expression of the new relaxed attitudes—styles of dress. For men, the white shirt and the gray-flannel suit were once taken to be official executive garb. Now, in many offices, a man wearing pants and jacket that match would be considered square. And offices that a few years ago might have frowned on any departure from staid blouse and pleated skirt for women, with a conservative hairstyle to match, now are reluctant to set any rules for dress for fear of the charge of "invasion of privacy" or sex discrimination.

• *Decline of authoritarianism.* It is an exaggeration to say that might on the workscene no longer makes right. Most organizations are still hierarchical, and a boss packs more clout than his or her subordinates. But in recent years more informal methods of relating between people at different echelons have become common.

As a result of forces such as these, much behavior once expected and accepted would seem archaic today. Just a few years ago, a large corporation (here nameless) fired a young executive who was seen taking his secretary to lunch. Today, in the same company, an affair between the two would arouse less attention. No one seems to care much, one way or the other.

THE GROWING IMPORTANCE OF CODES OF CONDUCT

Despite the relaxation of some standards, it would be terribly wrong to conclude that business has arrived at the stage where anything goes. On the contrary, the rules that govern acceptable behavior are as important as ever—in many ways, more so. But there are a greater number of choices, with a correspondingly greater need for guidelines.

Business could never operate smoothly against a backdrop of anarchy. Thus, the qualities that give etiquette importance are very much present on the workscene—the sensitivity of people, the need to avoid painful oversights or insults, the benefits of treating others with perception of their individual feelings.

In addition to considerations of feelings, people have been preoccupied for years with the questions of efficiency, productivity, and profitability of business behavior. The subject of etiquette in business has gotten considerably less attention.

But now the increasing importance of the human element has been emerging as the solution to key problems of our industrial society. And there is greater awareness of the role of human interrelationships in motivation, job satisfaction, and individual productivity.

In a world where the wrong word can displease and lose a customer, an inappropriate manner alienate an employee, and a badly worded announcement infuriate an entire staff, etiquette takes on new importance and new interest.

More positively: in a world of rapidly shifting values, one must update behavior and the policy that guides behavior, the interaction of people at all echelons. It is the new world created by recent social upheavals that has made us aware of the need for reconsideration of what goes and what doesn't go in the way of business conduct. And it is to the satisfaction of this complex and urgent need that this book addresses itself.

1

Your Company and the World

CORPORATE IDENTITY AND ETIQUETTE

The title "Your Company and the World" that heads this chapter makes a key distinction. It is that there are two entities: your organization and everything else. The coexistence of an organization and the "everything else" that constitutes the world outside is both a useful symbol and a practical reality.

Every organization devised by humans becomes a mini-universe. This world develops its own internal rules, values, and procedures. It has a population—called employees. And from the day it is created, it develops a character, a personality that reflects everything from the nature of its business to the way its employees comport themselves.

While the exact process by which an organization builds its character and image is subtle and intricate, there are three elements that are relevant here:

• *The organization's designation.* "The name," said Friedrich Nietzsche, "is what first makes a thing visible." Organizations rightly are concerned about their names. One corporation—Exxon—recently spent millions of dollars to change its name in order to unify and simplify its many activities. What an organization wants to be called—after all, the A&P isn't just your neighborhood supermarket, but a link in a vast chain properly designated as the Great Atlantic & Pacific Tea Co. Inc.—is a factor in its public image. (For more on names, see Chapter 3, "The Written Word.")

• *Presentation to the public.* Whether the organization has its own public-relations department or hires an outside agency, the projection of its activities to the public at large paints in another aspect of its image.

And the face that an organization presents to the outside world is by no means the sole result of public-relations ploys. There are a large number of contact points, mostly human, at which the public meets an organization—salesmen, service people, telephone answerers, for example. When properly briefed, these can do a great deal to make the organization seem attractive to people on the outside. (For more on these "public" people, see "Your Company's Ambassadors," page 16.)

• *Internal climate.* Some people who are sensitive and experienced can walk into the reception room of an organization and tell at once what its working atmosphere—and character—are. Cues for this appraisal are anything from the receptionist's smile—is it really friendly, tight, or nonexistent?—to the texture of the carpet underfoot. One of the major contributing factors to organizational climate is management's ideas about the worth of an individual, any individual; management's willingness to make the effort to keep the human as well as the mechanical aspects of corporate operations in focus; and, finally, its observance of ceremonies that show its interest in sentiment as well as profit.

In all these factors influencing organizational climate, etiquette offers helpful guidelines. (Of special relevance to the matter of climate is the section on "Establishing a Code of Conduct," page 11, and Chapters 5, 6, and 8, on "Status," "Appearance," and "Parties.")

YOUR COMPANY'S VERSION OF ETIQUETTE

Hand-kissing is getting to be a thing of the past in the United Nations. According to one observer, the practice started to disappear as foreign delegations comprised fewer titled aristocrats and the Third World members increased. These latter, of course, lacked the European tradition of which hand-kissing is a part.

To citizens of the world of business, this development in the social observances in the U.N. suggests two pertinent facts:

• *Etiquette tends to be unique in each organization.* This means that what is "good" behavior in one organization may be unacceptable in another across the street. The reasons for this individuality are essential to the understanding and practice of etiquette.

• *The social behavior we call etiquette is not fixed and unchang-*

ing. As an organization grows, changes, develops, its etiquette—that is, its mode of acceptable conduct—tends to do likewise. A number of key factors shape the modes of conduct that are acceptable and desirable in your organization:

1. *Formality and Informality: How Much for You?*

Dun's Review editor Thomas J. Murray describes the greeting he got from William Moore, Jr., president of Golden State Foods, whom he was meeting for the first time: "Hi, Tom. I'm Bill."

That's the way it is on the West Coast, Murray says, and adds: "Compared with the frenetic pace and double-breasted conformity of executives in the canyons of Manhattan, everything in California is casual and loose. You see it in the way executives dress and even how they do their hair."

No judgments need be made here as to the desirability of formality versus informality. For example, let no one tell you that formality is bad and informality is good. That's a little like arguing about the "goodness" of water. Even of that precious liquid, if you have too much you've got a flood; too little, a drought. Both extremes are bad.

The degree to which convention and tradition limit behavior— the amount of decorum and ritual you find in interpersonal exchanges—has as its eventual purpose the ease and comfort of individuals. Generally we feel most at ease with the kind of behavior we're used to. That's why an individual accustomed to a somewhat formal atmosphere must go through a perhaps painful course of adjustment to be able to live in an informal milieu. And, of course, the opposite is true. If you are used to informality, the rules and procedures of a more formal system take getting used to. Generally, the degree of formality arises from three elements:

• *Community manners.* Thomas J. Murray's description of the informal breeziness of West Coast executives comes down in specific cases to the town or area in which a firm is located. Every organization exists in, and is part of, a community. The location, the history, the size, the ethnic makeup of a community tend to create a level of acceptable behavior. Small communities tend to be friendlier, breezier, those on the East Coast tend to be more conservative in manner, and so on. Your company reflects an amalgam of these community factors.

Seldom do community standards create organization standards to which the average person cannot adapt. Even the switch from the "formal" East to the "informal" West didn't faze editor Murray for long. We quickly adjust to a board chairman in an open-necked sport shirt, a millionaire in jeans, or a corporate male president in shoulder-length locks.

But there can be exceptional influences not easily put aside. A recent dispatch from Isfahan, Iran, described problems of behavior and morale interfering with operations of some American aircraft companies there and causing American pilot-instructors to rebel and many to leave. Local factors—everything from the Iranian-style squatter toilets to a disregard for American concepts of safety—put pressures on employees that made it difficult for them to adapt.

• *Requirements of "the business."* Different industries tend to have different levels of formality. The basic reason for this is the need of individual industries to project a particular kind of image to the public at large. For example, banking organizations tend to be more formal places than firms in the entertainment field. Visit the offices of a toy company, for example, and you'll find employees more immediately friendly and open.

This doesn't mean that banks tend to recruit individuals who are more reticent. It does mean that banks make a favorable impression on their customers and the public by giving an appearance of stability, solidity, and careful regulation.

An art agency or other creative service will impress its prospective clients by offices that are decorated in a far different manner, by employees who dress in extreme styles and indulge in uninhibited personal behavior. The same behavior that would be perfectly acceptable in the art agency, if displayed in a bank would be likely to persuade a potential depositor that his or her funds were in the hands of questionable characters.

• *The personalities of top executives.* There is considerable truth in the old concept that an organization is often the shadow of its top people. Certainly the climate of an organization is affected by the tastes, preferences, standards, and behavior of the people who run it. Accordingly, if the top people in an organization prefer informality and like to swing a little themselves, this tendency will take hold down through the echelons.

2. *Permissiveness: How Tolerant Should Your Company Be?*

An executive was recently fired by a company for displaying unacceptable behavior. The behavior: he was seen out on a date with a young lady a few weeks after his wife had died.

This case demonstrates the sensitivity of some organizations to the private life of its employees. One of the interesting aspects of the situation above is that the company didn't act because its name was linked in some public way with the event. It was simply felt that the behavior was unacceptable from an employee at the executive level —even though it was in no way related to his job responsibility.

But, for the most part, permissiveness in the organizational context involves behavior on the workscene itself, in such matters as:

• *Dress, and so on.* What should people be permitted to wear? Should any attempt at all be made to define limits of acceptability? Who should decide the limits of sexiness a young woman may exemplify in what she wears, or the swinginess of a man's garb—or his hairstyle, for that matter?

• *Interpersonal relations.* A basic question here is the degree of friendliness that will be acceptable between the sexes. What that phrase "degree of friendliness" comes down to, in practical terms, is whether men and women will be discouraged from eating together in the company cafeteria; whether a male executive can take his secretary out to lunch without risking a reprimand from his boss (or she from her boss); whether a man and woman can stop in the corridor for a chat without anyone's giving it a second thought.

• *On-premises rules.* How rigid should regulations be about matters like smoking or eating? Some companies permit neither. Others may not be delighted over it, but will even tolerate an employee's heating a bowl of soup over an electric ring.

Considerations like these, which have to do with on-the-job behavior aside from immediate job activities, are also usually related to the nature of the organization's main business.

All considerations of this kind eventually end up becoming part of the set of rules by which the organization is run. . . .

ESTABLISHING A CODE OF CONDUCT

Every organization has a set of policies or rules that act as guidelines for operating behavior. Everything is included from how to handle the employee who is guilty of excessive absenteeism to how to observe employees' twenty-fifth anniversaries with the organization.

However, personnel executives and executives in policymaking positions know that policies may be both written and unwritten. How does management decide what its policies should be? There is a vast number of organizational matters involved—in addition to a code of conduct, such operating areas as pay, hiring policy, firing procedures, discipline, and so on must be considered.

One personnel expert points out that there are five principal sources for determining the content and meaning of policies:

- past practices in the organization;
- practices prevailing among other organizations in the community, the industry, or, indeed, the nation;
- the attitudes and philosophy of the board of directors and top management;
- the attitudes and philosophy of middle and lower management;
- the knowledge and experience gained from handling countless personnel problems on a day-to-day basis.

This last item suggests a pragmatic basis for policy formation: learning what works, what will be accepted. It is this last point that implies that the attitudes and philosophy of the rank-and-file are also factors.

Some policies are not put down on paper because executives feel this gives them latitude and freedom of action in touchy or controversial areas. Of course, it's possible to compromise. A policy stating that "Employees are expected to be suitably attired" can be condemned by no one. Its looseness ensures flexibility and the freedom to deal with cases on an individual basis.

THE RELATIONSHIP BETWEEN EMPLOYEE AND ORGANIZATION

Most people understand that a person affiliated with an organization has, in effect, an unwritten contract. Aside from the ordinary and obvious commitments an organization has to its employees—to protect his or her health, provide satisfactory conditions of work, provide a fair compensation, and so on—there are other commitments less obvious that generally prevail in the world of work. For example, organizations are interested in the general welfare and well-being of employees. This doesn't mean that they will not be fired for cause, that they will not be reprimanded for wrongdoing, or otherwise disciplined. Most companies still have a paternalistic attitude toward those on their payrolls. For many companies this is an old tradition and persists as a part of company policy. In other organizations the paternalism is very much attenuated and not so obvious as the turkeys that such organizations used to give to employees at Christmas. And most employees identify with their company—despite occasional fault-finding with management.

INFLUENCES ON EMPLOYEE-ORGANIZATION ATTITUDES

Most organizations have the interests of employees at heart and try to avoid acts that damage employee–management relations.

That's why the process of firing employees as an economic necessity—rather than the occasional firings that are done for wrongdoing—are so traumatic for companies and their top executives. The methods and procedures recommended for firing employees should be made as painless and constructive as possible. (For more on the subject of firing, see pages 133 and 150.)

But here our concern is to sketch out the basic understanding between employer and employee, of which good etiquette requires full observance. Everyone is aware of the preferred attitudes of employees toward their organizations. A simple demonstration of this fact: "I work for a lousy outfit," a disgruntled employee says. "It's run by a bunch of knuckleheads. How they've stayed in business I'll never understand. . . ."

We've all heard this kind of diatribe and experienced a sinking feeling or revulsion. Why do we react negatively toward an employee who badmouths the organization? We do so for the same reason that we respond with dismay when someone speaks ill of his or her parent. Even though the facts set forth may be true, we dislike the idea of vilification of what basically should be a beneficial relationship. Certainly in theory the employer-employee relationship should be mutually rewarding. The company benefits from the employee's activities, services, contributions. The employee benefits possibly from the challenges and involvements of his work, but certainly from the material reward of a paycheck. We are aware of a pathology, a kind of ugly sore that's being exposed, when a partner in what should be a good relationship says or does something that reveals a rotten subsurface.

The rules of etiquette that emerge from this discussion and this relationship are simple and to the point:

• *Top-echelon executives who set company policy should avoid doing anything in devising policies, procedures, company rules that demean, intimidate, or violate the integrity of employees.* The worker is worthy of his or her hire.

• *Organizations, in the persons of the executives who guide them, must be aware that the employees on their roster didn't get there by chance.* A person of responsibility somewhere along the line made the decision to hire. With this decision went the implicit commitments mentioned earlier.

And the employee has an obligation to his or her employer. Any behavior or acts that contradict or nullify these obligations violate the foundations of acceptable business behavior and conduct. For example, the individual in accepting employment is committed not only to delivering "a fair day's work for a fair day's pay" but also, in general, to furthering the well-being of the organization. If for any reason the employee develops ineradicable antagonisms toward the employer, he or she does have the option to look elsewhere for a paycheck. One of the indicators of the nature of the attachment to an organization by an employee is the readiness with which most of us identify with company objectives and fortunes. We speak of "my company." People who watch intercompany athletics see that individuals have no difficulty at all in rooting loudly, even wildly, for their organization's team.

THE LIMITS OF LOYALTY

Yes, there are loyalties that are exchanged between employer and employee, but neither's commitment is total. As has already been pointed out, a company cannot continue to suffer an economic loss by keeping redundant employees on the payroll. And, of course, sometimes judgments to fire do not involve extremes and an organization may let an employee go for less than extreme reasons. Behavior, while not destructive, may be unacceptable.

And from the employee's angle, there are very few of us who would subscribe to the slogan "My company, right or wrong." If we feel the company is "very wrong," guilty of acts or policies that are unacceptable, we will generally leave it.

One of the things that happen on the workscene: sometimes there is a clash between an individual's personal interests or values and those of his organization. In such a case problems are created that require specific moves.

In the ultimate situation, the move becomes literal: out of the organization. When for one or a combination of reasons an individual feels he or she can no longer continue a present job affiliation, quitting is the logical course. One's first loyalty must be to one's self, one's own career and future. Such thinking is sound psychology, good business, and does not conflict with the tenets of etiquette. Just as an organization may terminate an employee for the good of the organization, the employee may leave for good and sufficient personal reasons.

WHEN PERSONAL AND ORGANIZATIONAL GOALS CONFLICT

From time to time, employees—at any echelon—may find that their views, values, or goals differ from those of their organization. While the problems that stem from such a divergence tend to be ethical and relate only peripherally to etiquette, it is incumbent on management to try to assist the employee in what is surely an uncomfortable position—and may even be untenable.

There are several ways in which personal and organizational goals may differ. A firm may want to change its physical location. The move, beneficial to the organization, might be inconvenient or unacceptable to some employees for reasons of their own situation or preferences.

Sometimes the difference between organizational and individual goals may lie in the area of philosophy, feelings, or values. A company may want to stay with traditional manufacturing procedures that environmentalists say are detrimental to the local ecology. An environment-sensitive manager or employee may side with the opposition.

In some cases, the result can be devastating, but even a mild reaction can mean upset and demoralization. People who are susceptible to this threat of goal uncertainty and seek to resolve the situation might consider steps like these:

1. *Accept the Dichotomy.*

Employees—particularly top executives—have a blind spot. Usually identifying with the company, they are puzzled by the contrary views of others. The company president, for example, is surprised and hurt because his secretary isn't as zesty as he is about doing catch-up work on Saturday.

It's realistic to expect people to have a selfish and hardheaded view of things. Don't expect them to put company interest ahead of self-interest. It isn't natural, and it may not even be desirable.

2. *Stress the Overlap.*

When discussing the subject of personal versus organizational goals with subordinates—the subject might arise in the course of a performance review, for example—agree freely to the divergences. But once you've done that, you're in a strong position to make the point that there are vital areas in which personal and organizational objectives are identical. For example, the company is interested in an employee's growth, advancement, health, personal and family welfare.

3. *Reduce the Gap.*

"I've been here twenty years, but the organization doesn't give a damn about me personally," says an embittered employee. "The bottom line, that's all that counts." The sally stems from the employee's upset over a reorganization seen as detrimental to his situation. His superior had two points to make, and made them:

• *Reassurance.* "I can tell you in all sincerity, Jim, that your standing and reputation here are of the highest. We're all fully aware of the outstanding job you've been doing. . . ."

• *Reasons.* Then the executive went over the change, explained its rationale, discussed the new opportunities created for the employee. The executive concluded, "Our organization, like most others, just can't afford to make major decisions without considering their effect on people. And you're one of the best. . . ."

A speaker at a recent management seminar said, "The thing that makes managers most effective is their complete identification with organization goals." That's true, in general. But when realities turn harsh, it's wise to acknowledge them and proceed from there.

To sum up: both employees and organization representatives must comport themselves in a manner of mutual respect. Even when there are differences—of opinion or interest—nothing should be done that slights the other.

YOUR COMPANY'S AMBASSADORS

It's obvious that every organization has a whole range of contacts with the world at large. These representatives of your organization play an important part in filling out the image of your organization. In order for favorable impressions to be made, it's desirable to do two things: first, to spell out all the groups that officially or otherwise represent your company to the public; and then, consider the preparation these ambassadors should get that will be most helpful to the company.

AMBASSADORIAL GROUPS

The headings below indicate individuals and groups who, one way or another, become company spokesmen and representatives because of their interaction with people on the outside.

SALESPERSONS. The men and women who sell your company's products and services represent your organization to a particularly vital group—customers and potential customers. Aside from the question of whether or not they're effective salespeople, their behavior when calling on customers tends to be translated almost directly into company attributes. If the salesman is warm, friendly, and helpful, these qualities tend to be taken as typical of the organization. On the other hand, if the salesperson is loud, perhaps overly extroverted, these qualities also, rightly or wrongly, are attributed to the character of the company.

SERVICE PEOPLE. A mechanic or repair person who turns up on the customer's premises to service or repair equipment or to explain some aspect of your company's operation may do so in a courteous, helpful way that will redound to the credit of the organization, or less so if the behavior is unattractive.

KEY EXECUTIVES WHO REPRESENT YOUR ORGANIZATION TO THE MEDIA. Of particular importance are the organization officers who are official spokesmen. These are the ones who are photographed, interviewed, appear on radio and television to give your organization's official views, explain developments, make projections about the industry, and so on. (For more particulars, see Chapter 2, page 87, "When An Organization Representative Is Interviewed by the Press.")

EXECUTIVES AND PROFESSIONALS WHO SPEAK TO BUSINESS, MANAGEMENT, AND OTHER GROUPS. A middle manager in your research-and-development department may be invited to address a monthly meeting of an engineering society, or your treasurer may be asked to address a group of security analysts. Since these people are almost always identified with your organization ("And tonight our speaker is Mr. James Smith, Vice-President of Marketing for the T. C. Jones Company"), not only the demeanor of the speaker but also the content of the talk is considered to be right out of the horse's mouth.

That is, unless explicit disclaimers are made, it's almost inevitable that the speaker is taken to be not only *with* the company, but its spokesperson.

EMPLOYEES WHO PARTICIPATE IN COMMUNITY AFFAIRS. Particularly in small towns, people who are affiliated with an organization and clearly identified with it help flesh out the company image in the community. For example, in one small town in upper New York State, one of the foremen in a paper plant, the town's largest employer, was a member of the town board. His behavior obviously could reflect either well or badly on the company.

RECEPTIONISTS AND PHONE-ANSWERING SECRETARIES. To a large segment of the outside world, the first contact with your organization is either a receptionist or, in the case of a telephone contact, a phone operator or secretary. Their manner, if it's friendly and helpful, makes a favorable impression. Any negative characteristic, such as discourtesy, irritation, and so on, will have an adverse effect.

THE ENTIRE EMPLOYEE GROUP. To a greater or lesser degree, every employee is associated in an outsider's mind with the organization.

WHAT YOU CAN AND CAN'T DO IN BRIEFING YOUR "AMBASSADORS"

Having identified the groups and individuals that project your image to the outside, the question arises: What can you do to have these people so comport themselves as to do your company good on the outside? There are some helpful steps that may be taken, but first it's important to realize the limitations.

For example, an organization would have trouble trying to sell all its employees on the idea that "Everything you do and say in public will reflect on the company. Therefore you have to always be on your best behavior, mind your manners, and so on."

This type of instruction or suggestion might logically apply to some groups. For example, policemen are trained to understand that their behavior is always under scrutiny and must be shaped accordingly. Salesclerks and other people who represent a company directly to the public at large—this group also includes company guards, messengers, and so on—will accept as part of their training the idea that in addition to just doing their jobs they must so conduct themselves as to make the organization appear in a favorable light.

The point is that these people are "working" when they appear in public. But any attempt to influence the behavior of other employees when they are off company premises would be taken as a violation of individual privacy. This, then, is one of the limits of guidance or suggestions for employees who meet the public. But for other groups, such as those enumerated above—salesmen, and so on—these points are suggested:

1. *Increase Awareness.*

It seems so obvious, and yet it's often overlooked. Management must consciously inject into the orientation and training of salesmen and others that they will be regarded as representatives of the organization and should conduct themselves accordingly.

2. *Give Them a Picture of What You Want Projected.*

In cases where the organizational image is fairly well established, the qualities you want transmitted should be spelled out. Here are a few possibilities: "We're an old-line firm, and our strong suit is dependability. We get this idea across to the public when people who represent the company stress their reliability, keep their word, and so on, in their dealings. . . ." Or: "We're a young, growing organization. We want to give an impression of savvy, flexibility, eagerness to please. Now when you call on customers . . ." The instructor should then relate these qualities to the way the salesman, service person, and so on, conducts himself or herself.

The fact that an organization does in fact have a projectable image that is furthered by its employees is illustrated by a bit of journalistic lore. The point made shows how successfully *The New York Times* has been able to present itself as a high-class and prestigious entity: A business executive whose organization is about to announce its expansion plans is sought out in his home by the press. The executive's butler goes into the library to announce, "Sir, there are five reporters and a gentleman from the *Times* in the foyer."

3. *Monitor Performance.*

Without playing Big Brother, it's nevertheless desirable that there be some kind of follow-up of the guidelines you've established for your ambassadors. For example, a salesman who for one reason or other raises a row in a prospect's office because of some kind of personal exchange may do so for acceptable reasons—in one instance. But if such upsets multiply, the employee's problem must be investigated, and if it seems insurmountable, some change must be made to prevent the company representation from being damaged. At the same time, favorable behavior should be recognized and rewarded.

A SPECIAL GROUP: EMPLOYEES' RELATIVES

The spouses, kids, and other relatives of employees are a very special group. They have a special interest in you, and you have a special interest in them.

The thing that makes employees' relatives special is that there are many situations and points at which they have contact with your company. For example:

- when they come to visit on company premises;
- when they telephone;
- when there are interactions between the relatives and the employee's boss, secretary, and so on.

There are perfectly legitimate reasons why companies are interested in employees' relatives, and vice versa. For example, every youngster wants to see where "Daddy or Mommy works."

However, here are some of the situations that may cause embarrassment and related difficulties involving employee relatives:

- *The dependent wife* may check in too often.
- *The executive spouse* may think her husband's secretary is also her assistant.
- *The unexpected visitor.* The husband, wife, mother, sister of an employee may "just be passing by." The point is, there they are out in the reception room. Two things are obviously required. One is that they be given a friendly welcome. This is largely up to the employee himself or herself.

But that phrase "friendly welcome" is not necessarily satisfied by the employee alone. It's usually expected that the relatives will be taken around to be introduced to colleagues, subordinates, or the boss. Two recommendations are made in this connection. One is that these introductions be made in a relaxed and positive way, and then that the meeting be made as short as possible.

WHEN RELATIVES VISIT COMPANY PREMISES

One might think that visiting relatives would pose no special problem, since ordinary modes of proper conduct should see them through handsomely. As a matter of fact, one would expect the average visitor to be on his or her best behavior. But problems arise because some of them are unfamiliar with the work milieu.

So it's best not to take for granted that relatives are going to know how to behave when visiting your premises. And the problem is likely to be one of discomfort rather than misconduct. You want the guests to be at ease in unfamiliar surroundings. The suggestions that follow can decrease the chances of mishap and increase the pleasure elements:

1. *Apply the Rule of Reason.*

Employees should be informed tactfully that while the organization is not ill-disposed to having relatives visit, the rule of reason should be applied:

• *Visits should not be excessive in number.* An employee—whether a junior executive or file clerk—who has a stream of personal visitors turning up or too many visits by the same person, must be reminded that "After all, this is a place of business"—gently at first, more firmly if the action persists. An exception: a secretary in an insurance office had her daughter, who worked across the street, come in every day for a brown-bag lunch at an unused desk in a storeroom. This habit, developed gradually over a period of time, interfered with no one. As a matter of fact, it introduced a pleasant family note, and was completely accepted.

• *Visits should be of reasonable duration.* Even the nicest individual, lingering overly long, begins to get under people's skins. And, after all, there is work to be done. If the employee seems to have difficulty in terminating a visit, then his or her boss may take the initiative. "I'm awfully sorry to have to interrupt," says one experienced supervisor to his assistant and her visiting boyfriend, "but I do want to remind you, Linda, that these reports have to be finished by the end of the day."

2. *Limit Visits to Low-Pressure Times and Nonfrenzied Places.*

Every place of work has peaks and valleys of activity. Sometimes you can make the point for all on a single occasion: "Tom, I certainly enjoyed meeting your fiancée. You know, if she visits again, I suggest that you try to avoid Friday afternoons. Things are so hectic then. . . ."

And some areas on the workscene may be centers of activity. For example, it might be perfectly fine to have a visitor turn up in a company showroom, while in a place of frantic-paced production the visitor would represent both a nuisance and a safety hazard.

It's advisable to have an employee take time off from the job and see the visitor in a rest area. "Why don't you take your brother down to the cafeteria for a cup of coffee?" a supervisor suggests, both solving a problem of interference and showing an appreciated consideration for the subordinate.

3. *Children Can Be Special Problems, So Give Them Special Attention.*

People who have had the experience can tell you that few things are as disruptive as a couple of youngsters exhilarated by their strange surroundings, who respond by rampaging about.

Of course, ages and dispositions vary widely. But, speaking of the "dangerous age," in this case about four to twelve, consider steps like these:

• *Don't leave them alone.* This doesn't necessarily mean someone on constant guard duty, but it does mean someone keeping an eye on them to keep them out of trouble.

• *Satisfy their interests, if possible.* To maximize the pleasure of the visit, give them a conducted tour—of reasonable scope. Every place of business has places or things of interest. In some cases, the business activity itself can intrigue a young mind. Factories, of course, are ready-made for curious children, and if they are properly guided, the sights, sounds, and smells of production can be fascinating. Office operations, too, have their interest. Four- to six-year-olds will be fascinated by anything from a desktop stapler to the making of paperclip chains.

But older children capable of understanding some aspects of the business operation should be given simple explanations that, among other things, will give them an increased understanding and respect for what their relative does when he or she is on the job.

SHOULD EXECUTIVES' RELATIVES BE TREATED DIFFERENTLY?

It would be unrealistic to suggest that our democratic sense mandates equal status to the wife of the organization's president and the wife of a stock clerk. But acceptable behavior requires that even though the status of the employee *does* rub off, relatives of lower-echelon employees be treated with the same friendliness as those of executives. Such evenhandedness will win you a worthwhile benefit: while the considerate treatment of an executive's relative will be accepted as a matter of course, you make the lower-echelon employee and the relative feel awfully good.

GREETING AND INTRODUCING THE VISITORS

Let's say you're a young executive newly come to the Good-Fit Shoe Company. Your wife, who teaches in the local grade school, has been intrigued by the stories you've told her of the people you work with. A school holiday comes along and you arrange to meet for lunch. And she's going to pick you up at the office. To make the first visit as failsafe as possible:

• *Alert the reception desk.* Your visitor will appreciate the thoughtfulness of being expected by the receptionist. If she is welcomed with: "Oh, yes, Mrs. Blue, Mr. Blue said you'd be coming in," the visit is off to a good start.

• *Expect to have to offset self-consciousness.* Understandably, she feels somewhat at a disadvantage. It's up to you to be the gracious host and to take the initiative.

• *Smoothing the reception-room encounter.* Your wife enters and is greeted by the receptionist. Next, you get a call telling you that your wife has arrived. It's desirable that you not send a secretary or subordinate to guide your visitor but that you honor the occasion by appearing yourself. Then:

• *Introduce your wife to the receptionist:* "Ruth, I'd like you to meet my wife, Margaret." Then, a brief explanatory sentence eases the way: "This is her first visit to Good-Fit." Or perhaps in a lighter vein: "She's very curious to see the kind of swingers I'm working with."

• *Take your wife's arm and lead her toward your office, with a brief farewell to the receptionist:* "Thanks again, Ruth."

• *Avoid status lines in making introductions.* You don't want to seem snobbish or overly status-conscious in your introductions. At the same time, you don't want to buttonhole everyone you meet and go through the formalities. Of course, there are a number of "obligatories," the people you should have your wife meet. As far as others are concerned, make the introductions as convenient. Generally, it is desirable to add some explanatory phrase about the third person. For example: "Henry, this is my wife, Margaret." Then, to

Margaret: "Henry is very important around here. He's the paymaster."

• *Introducing your secretary.* Now you're approaching your office. Just outside your door sits your secretary. Since Miss Blake, of all the people in the company, is probably the one your wife will be in closest contact with, your introduction here should be the opposite of perfunctory.

In this situation, Emily Post herself would be hard put to assert exactly how the introduction should be made. Post lays down three rules for introductions:

1. A Man Is Always Introduced *to* a Woman:
   "Mrs. Harper, I'd like you to meet Mr. Woodward."

2. A Young Person Is Always Introduced *to* an Older Person:
   "Professor Higby, I'd like you to meet my niece, Ginny King."

3. A Less Important Person Is Always Introduced *to* a More Important Person:
   "Bishop Frost, may I present Miss Hinman?"

In the situation we're describing, let's assume that your secretary is female and about the same age as your wife. Who should be considered the "more important person"?

Of course, in a personal sense your wife is the more important. But in the work situation, where your wife is a visitor and your secretary is on her own turf, the latter qualifies as the more important. It is a gracious concession on your part—and, implicitly, on your wife's as well—that the introduction be made: "Jane, I'd like you to meet my wife, Margaret. Maggie, this is my secretary, Jane Wills." After the two greet each other, you have the opportunity to say to your wife: "Maggie, I've already sung Jane's praises, so I'm not going to embarrass her by repeating them now. . . ." Permit the two to chat as they will, then lead your wife into your office.

• *Use your office as center of operations.* There are a number of people you want Margaret to meet. Seat her comfortably—preferably not in your chair—then bring your colleagues in. This procedure is preferred to one in which you lead her from place to place. First, Margaret will probably feel more at ease in surroundings to which, however briefly, she has become accustomed. Second, if you show up at a colleague's door with Margaret in tow, it may be at an inopportune time for the other person. With your wife in your office, you can inform the people and invite them in. If they're free, they'll accept. If not, the meeting can be deferred: "Love to meet her. I'll be in in about five minutes."

• *Introducing your boss.* Bringing your wife and boss together may be a matter of special moment. Nevertheless, it should be done in as relaxed and pleasant a manner as possible. Obviously you want these two people to make mutually favorable impressions. But as eager as you may be to have them hit it off, it is best to make it a low-pressure situation.

Be prepared to keep a flow of conversation going. But if you find that the talk is moving along in a friendly give-and-take, let it continue under its own steam, with only occasional participation on your part. After all, the occasion is one in which these two people should be getting to know one another.

You may want to make some favorable comment about your boss or about your wife. Any extreme compliments about your boss might be taken as calculated flattery. Any statements of a similar nature about your wife, however, are free of the same taint. While your statement that "Bill Rich is the best boss a man ever had" would be fine if said in a jocular vein, the same statement said seriously would seem excessive.

But encomiums directed at your wife would have to be of a most extreme nature to be inappropriate. Consider one such effort: "As you know, Bill, Margaret teaches third grade. Well, her principal says she's the best teacher of that grade the school has ever had." Perfectly acceptable.

• *Try not to overlook any of the "obligatories."* Without intending to, it's possible to ruffle the feelings of a colleague by omitting him or her from the introductions. But obviously time or other considerations may interfere. If this is so, it will be an appreciated gesture if you seek out those who have been left out and explain: "Sorry there wasn't time to have you meet Margaret, she had to get home. . . . I hope we have better luck next time."

PROTECTING YOURSELF AND YOUR ORGANIZATION FROM PUBLIC DISPLEASURE

From time to time, an organization finds itself damned in the public eye. For example, during periods of gas shortage, oil companies are prone to feel the blast of public wrath. When utility companies raise their prices, citizens who feel they are helpless victims express their resentment, and any utility-company employee is considered a fair target.

And it is not only the large organization that comes under the cross hairs. In one small town, a local company bought up some old homes and razed them to enlarge its parking lot. The fact that the structures were rotting away and eventually would have become a hazard did not prevent an angry outcry from a group of residents.

Organizations generally have a public-relations apparatus that can be mobilized to offset such public reaction. But for the individual employee likely to have an immediate and personal problem in the community, among friends, and even in the home, more personal consideration and actions may be involved. You owe it to yourself as well as your organization to speak up against the attack. Consider:

• *Is silence the best course to follow?* Some people mistakenly feel that saying nothing or shrugging off any hostile or critical statements is in the long run the most effective action. Generally, this is not the case. Silence is most likely to confirm the adverse opinion.

• *Don't overreact.* An excessive response tends to damage rather than heal. In speaking up for your organization, present your case forthrightly. After all, there *are* two sides to most things. Reasonably, you want yours to be heard.

• *Get the facts straight.* Often, attacks against an organization are based on rumor, misinformation, and exaggeration. Just dealing with and nullifying these can be a strong move for you. Try to get to the bottom of the controversy. If possible, reach the people in your organization who are in a position to know the facts, the story behind the story. Even if some of the things you find out don't necessarily put your organization in the most favorable light, you can still make a stronger argument by presenting a more balanced and accurate account.

• *Provide the rationale.* Finally, offer the organization's reasons for its actions. Even if they don't change the attitude of your listeners, their feelings will be tempered. For example, consider a series of points that could be made to a resentful resident by an employee of the firm that eliminated an old house to make room for parking:

- While it is true that the structure was a kind of landmark, since it has been empty for years, it has gone to ruin.
- It has become a hazard for the local children who play inside on broken flooring.

- The company did try to get the community to take over the house and rehabilitate it, but there was little interest.

DEALING WITH CONTACTS FROM ABROAD

There is one circumstance in which your organization inter-faces—to use a currently popular term—with a world literally alien. This is the contact that organization representatives have with busi-nessmen and -women from foreign countries.

These international contacts may take place in this country or theirs. But in either case, questions of proper conduct and procedure arise: What does one do about possible language difficulties? What does one do about the other person's expectations? If the meeting is in the other person's home country, what should one do about local customs; for example, should one try to master the Japanese bow of greeting? And how should one handle the matter of social distance in face-to-face standup conversation? South Americans tend to stand close—uncomfortably so by American standards—Scandinavians at a greater distance than we are used to. Should we go along with the preference of the other person or attempt to follow the American way?

EIGHT RULES FOR INTERNATIONAL AMITY

There are general rules that can maximize the benefits and lessen the hazards of contacts with foreigners. Obviously, if your meeting takes you to a distant land, the specific situation into which you will be moving will create special requirements of behavior. But aside from the unique elements in specific meetings, here are some guide-lines that can help:

1. *Be Aware That Part of the Problem Is Psychological.*

If you're facing the prospect of a get-together with a stranger from another country, it's natural that you have doubts and questions about what is going to happen. The simple fact that you are a bit on edge because you're facing the unknown is in itself a problem. The cure is simple: relax, don't build up concern fed by the anticipation of dire consequences that may result from mistakes or misunder-standings. The other person is probably in the same frame of mind that you are.

2. *Prepare—As Far As Possible.*

Some moves you can make will ease matters. If the other person is a non-English-speaking Frenchman and you have had a few years of French in school, you may want to take a brief refresher course, dig out a text on conversational French, or practice with a member of your family who knows the language. Perhaps the problem is not so much one of language as of one-to-one behavior. If so, do you have a friend or colleague who has done business with nationals of the country with whom you will be dealing, who can brief you?

There is one kind of preparation that is mandatory—but simple. For example, if you have a proposal to make to the other person, you help matters by mastering the details. Perhaps some aspects of what you have to say may be illustrated by photographs, charts, or other visual material understood in any language. The more in command you are of *your* end of the conversation, the smoother the exchange is likely to be.

3. *Don't Try to Be a Roman.*

It is unwise to try to match or beat the natives at their own game. You may know a good deal about French wines, for example. Fine. Discuss these matters with a French host, but don't make a contest of it. Among other reasons, why deprive him of the pleasures of playing host?

To what extent should you attempt to pick up local customs? Answer: to the extent that you can do so intelligently. Take the matter of the Japanese bow. Should you attempt it? Yes, if you can find a Japanese who will teach you not only the physical movement but also the tradition that goes with it.

While it's inadvisable to "go native" in some cultures, in others people delight in a foreigner's attempt to pick up their ways. Italians, for example, will be thrilled by your use of even a few words of their language. (The French are likely to be dismayed.) How do you know when to attempt a foreign language and when to avoid doing so? The next point may guide you. . . .

4. *Get Help.*

When there are specific points of conduct you want to know about, look for assistance. But be sure you seek out a proper source.

A person who has done business in the country may be able to set you straight on a number of crucial points. For example:

An American importer wanted to write to a Chinese producer of animal pelts. How should he word his letter? He was able to get in touch with someone who had traded in China. This businessman explained that the best approach was a straightforward letter of explanation and inquiry sent to the appropriate national and regional Chinese trading corporations: "Be as explicit as you can, and send along as much technical data as you can." Finally, the American was dissuaded from trying to get his letter translated into Chinese. "They'll do a much better job of it in China than you can here," he was properly counseled.

5. *When in Doubt, Say So.*

If in the course of your contacts some question arises and there's no reason to hide it, don't hesitate to pose it to the other person. "In order to get a contract," said one businessman, "must I get approval from anyone else, or is your signature sufficient?"

You may apologize for your ignorance or for having to ask a question that conceivably seems to impugn the status of the other person. But your sincerity should make it apparent that no disrespect is intended.

6. *Watch Out for Social Missteps.*

When you're abroad, local standards of conduct may differ considerably from what you're used to. Anything from punctuality to sexual mores may be involved. Some countries have "local time" that is half an hour later than the clock indicates. To be "on time" is to be too early. Establish this point as soon as you can. As for social fun and games:

A recent traveler doing business in Poland was told: "Remember, you are here on business." The speaker, a representative of the trading company with which the traveler was dealing, referred to the presence in the café where they had met of a number of attractive young women among whom, according to another foreign visitor, "the hunting is very good." But the Polish business people made it clear that socializing with members of the opposite sex would be viewed dimly. The tendency in other countries might have been quite the reverse.

7. *Don't Be Upset by Surprises.*

Hiring a taxicab in the Middle East is not the same as hailing a cab in an American city. For one thing, a driver never gives you a rate. You are asked what you want to pay, then the bargaining begins. And hotel reservations may be made but not necessarily followed through. One traveler for a construction company returned to his hotel after a few days' absence to find that his room—which supposedly was reserved—was no longer available. In fact, because rooms were in short supply, he had to spend the night in the hotel annex—a shack with no water and no bathroom.

Expect that travel and practices will differ, count on getting the hang of things as your experience grows, and be prepared to suffer—a little.

8. *If the Meeting Is on Your Home Turf, Be a Guide As Well As a Business Person.*

Expect the foreign traveler to be friendly, and if unfamiliar with this land, to be interested in it.

And don't be misled with the now obsolete concept of the Ugly American. True, our popularity fell during the Vietnam War. But in most countries we have a large reservoir of goodwill. Depend on this factor to make business relations pleasant.

In entertaining visitors, don't be misled by national stereotypes. Avoid the "all x's are y" fallacy. Some Germans are *not* avid sightseers; they may prefer a quiet day in the American countryside. Some Swiss may get more pleasure from Disneyland than from the Morgan Library. Learn the interests of the individuals to whom you are playing host, and try to cater to these.

2
The Spoken Word

George Bernard Shaw, in *Pygmalion,* dramatizes the importance of the spoken word by showing Eliza Doolittle transformed from a flower peddler to the cynosure of admiring socialites as she graduates from common speech to the language of scholars and aristocrats.

The ear of the business world is no less sharply attuned to the nuances of what people say and how they say it. The educated, articulate individual is quickly set apart from his less well educated colleagues. And because of implications for "businesslikeness," the clear, forceful executive rates higher than the mumbler.

Elegance of speech is only one factor. The business world also sets store by the *power* of the spoken word. Individuals have leapfrogged rapidly through the echelons because they have been able to express themselves effectively. The executive who can get up before large audiences—trade associations, professional groups, and so on—not only gains attention but strongly advances his or her career chances. And what people say can soothe, give pleasure, or hurt and offend.

The spoken word can also be the culprit that causes on-the-job complications. Examples:

- The way an individual gives instructions and commands can determine whether he or she will have a smooth-running operation or a pack of discipline problems.
- The individual who understands the do's and don't's of interviewing—the one who doesn't can step on toes unwittingly—will achieve interview objectives.

- The effective use of the telephone—everything from the etiquette of saying hello to knowing how to interrupt—is crucial not only for efficiency but for good relationships.

Finally, there is an array of business ceremonies in which the spoken word determines the climate. The master of ceremonies at an organization event can set the tone and ensure the success of a company function. The introduction of speakers, the presentations that are part of anniversaries, retirements, and so on, also are keys both to the success of the event and the status of the individual speakers.

Clearly, there is an overlap between the spoken word and the written one (see Chapter 3). For example, one may express gratitude or apologize orally or in writing. One may communicate an involved idea face-to-face or in a written presentation.

By and large, the overlap between this chapter and Chapter 3 has been kept to a minimum, or, where spoken and written forms differ—as in traditional euphemistic language, for instance—both areas have been covered.

GENERAL REMARKS

"BUSINESSLIKE" LANGUAGE

There is a kind of language that is described as "businesslike." It implies directness, a crisp quality. Its major virtue is economy: it delivers the maximum message with a minimum expenditure of time and/or energy. An employee giving a verbal report to a boss would probably be looked at askance if sentences were long, rambling, diffuse. The brisk manner is not merely acceptable, it is both proper and desirable in many business situations.

JARGON: ITS USES AND ABUSES

Related to the matter of businesslike language is the use of jargon; that is, the terminologies or characteristic idioms of particular "in" groups. Every business and industry tends to develop its own specialized vocabulary that has to do with situations, processes, or materials specific to it. Here, for example, are a few sentences one might overhear in a printing or publishing operation: "Let's put that on thirty-pound stock, using two colors. A sans-serif type would be about right, ten-point, using a thirty-pica line. Of course, we'll have to watch that paper for show-through, and you've got to make sure the color doesn't bleed at the edges." To people on the inside, this makes complete and explicit sense. However, to those who are not, it's just so much gibberish. Two suggestions, then, about jargon as it may exist in your organization:

• *Avoid it as much as possible with strangers.* Where technical or special vocabulary *is* used, explain it to your visitor.

• *When training new employees, make the acquisition of the specialized vocabulary a specific part of job training.*

CHATTING WITH SUBORDINATES: YOUR PLACE OR THEIRS?

Informal meetings are an important part of organizational communication. Matters big and small are dealt with on the basis of a few words exchanged almost in passing in the corridor or during discussions over a lunch table.

But there are certain types of meetings a manager initiates with subordinates that may pose a question of place. Should you ask the person to come to your office, or should you go to his or hers? Both protocol and effectiveness are involved. For the most part, employees are expected to come to the boss's office. But there are circumstances where the boss would be well advised to drop in on the subordinate—either with or without advance word. Here are *five occasions when the subordinate's workplace is the better choice for a talk:*

• *To stress informality.* No doubt about it, a meeting in the boss's office, regardless of content, is a more formal—and therefore possibly more formidable—occasion.

• *To skirt the usual "boss's door" watchers.* Some executives, because of physical layout, have a circle of eyes that keep their door under surveillance every working minute. This group may include a secretary, assistant, receptionist, and so on. And sometimes just to avoid speculation—in some cases it might be anxiety or concern —you don't want to raise the question in the minds of the watchers: "Uh-oh, why is Mr. Lane seeing Joe Dooley?" Accordingly, the boss stops by Joe Dooley's desk to say what he has to say. Interestingly enough, there may be more witnesses to this meeting than there would be if Joe came to his boss's quarters, but the very openness of the contact of itself will minimize tensions.

• *To avoid closing your door.* The subject matter may be confidential, even secret. Your office, unless the door is closed, may be excessively available to the listening ear—even if people don't intend to eavesdrop. But for somewhat the same reasons just mentioned —avoiding tension—you don't want to close your door. If the person you want to talk to has a relatively isolated or eavesdrop-proof work-place, it may be a better choice for your meeting.

• *To keep it brief.* Quite simply, some people are hard to get rid of. Once they set foot in your office, you have to go to almost absurd lengths to get them out. When you use the other person's desk for your meeting, you find it much easier to wind up the matter and leave.

• *To show friendliness.* Some subordinates, for one reason or another, hesitate to take the initiative for up-the-line communications. You may have no working reason to ask them to drop in to see you, so your stopping by to see them, for some small or medium-size talk, diminishes the communication gap.

INTRODUCTIONS

WHEN ARE INTRODUCTIONS IN ORDER?

There are many situations in business in which an individual meets another for the first time, or finds himself or herself before a group of strangers. To introduce, then, as the dictionary puts it, is "to cause to be acquainted." In addition, introductions of individuals to others whom they may know very well are common for ceremonial effect: ". . . and so I give you our esteemed founder and the president of our company, Mr. J. G. Harding!" J. G. Harding can now follow with the next part of the ceremony, his talk—of whatever nature—with the applause and interest resulting from the "introduc-tory remarks."

Introductions, then, are in order to smooth those first bumpy minutes of people meeting each other for the first time, or for the purpose of putting the spotlight on a speaker.

WHO SHOULD DO THE INTRODUCING?

A combination of verbal fluency and status are the main factors that help mark the right or "best" person to handle an introduction. Here's how these two factors work with regard to a few typical situations:

• *Introducing a new employee.* An individual's first day on the job is always a special event. And the way in which he or she is ushered into the workplace and presented to colleagues figures large in how quickly and how well the fitting-in process takes place.

Company practices vary widely on how introductions are made, and, of course, the nature of the newcomer's job makes a difference: a new president in a small company might have the entire employee group assembled, with an introduction by the chairman of the board or the outgoing president (if he or she were leaving under happy circumstances).

A lower-echelon employee—a file clerk, teller, machine operator in a factory—is usually asked to report to Personnel to finish some details of actual enrollment, then is escorted to the workplace and turned over to the supervisor or department head—who may have done the actual hiring, or at least has interviewed the individual. Two courses are then open to the supervisor:

He or she will take the newcomer around the department personally: "Tom, this is [or, I'd like you to meet] Grace Liston, our new quality-control inspector. Grace, Tom Hewitt is one of our best lathe operators. You'll be working together to some extent. . . ."

A second acceptable practice: have a senior or respected member of the department escort the new employee around and make the introductions. If the department is large, it is suggested that introductions be made only to key individuals—especially those with whom the new employee will be working directly. A few words of explanation should then be given the newcomer: "Pete, I'm going to have you meet just the people in your accounting unit this morning. You'll get to know the people in the adjoining offices in the natural course of events. . . ."

• *Introducing a colleague to an outside group.* A group of Company A's key customers has been invited to a meeting to be addressed by Edwin Wright, head of Research and Development, who is to describe a technological development of trade interest. To get the meeting off to an auspicious start, and to give Edwin Wright the benefit of a strong sendoff, John Henning, Sales V.P., introduces the R&D executive to the group, stressing Wright's experience, expertness, achievements in the field, and so on.

Henning has been selected to make the introduction for several reasons: First, he is of sufficient status in the company to warrant the respect of his audience. (Chances are, he knows several of them quite well.) Second, he is an effective speaker—fluent, enthusiastic, with a relaxed warmth that comes through clearly to his listeners. Third, and although not essential it can be helpful, he knows Edwin Wright and is even familiar with the findings Wright is going to talk about.

• *Introductions "within the family."* A common—and occasionally difficult—situation that calls for an introduction is an organization event in which the chief speaker or guest of honor is known to most of the assemblage. Let's say the president or other top executive is to address all or a large number of employees. Who should introduce him? (The question of whether he *needs* an introduction will be dealt with shortly. See "When Should You Introduce Yourself," below.)

Planners of such events have made their selections from all over the organization landscape, and to good effect. The essential criterion is that the introducer be at ease before the audience. Once that qualification is satisfied, here are some possibilities:

AN ASSISTANT. His or her opening can be: "I guess I know Mr. Smith better than anyone else in the place. . . ."

THE NEWEST EMPLOYEE. "I've only been here a few weeks, yet I can tell you this is a great place to work, and one of the major reasons is our president, Mr. Smith. . . ."

AN ASSOCIATE. "Mr. Smith and I have seen a lot of changes together, and I have seen some changes in Mr. Smith. When he started here, he was twenty years old, and a packer in Shipping. What he has become today is the result of personal qualities. . . ."

WHEN SHOULD YOU INTRODUCE YOURSELF?

You can end someone's discomfort or end an awkward silence by taking the initiative and introducing yourself. For example, you and the other person are waiting for an elevator. You say: "Pardon me. My name is Gene Blake. . . ." Then add: "I've seen you in the treasurer's office. Have you been working there for long?"

Or, for a person at a company get-together whose discomfort you may want to ease: "Hello, my name is George Rice. What's yours?" Then, on learning the name, use small talk—about the get-together itself, for example—as a bridge into a more general conversation.

If you're moved to help a stranger—someone you meet in the office corridor who seems to be lost, for example—you needn't give your name. A simple "May I help you?" covers the situation adequately.

SELF-INTRODUCTION BY A SPEAKER

In some situations, a speaker may find it proper and convenient to introduce himself or herself to an audience:

• *When no one else is available.* For one reason or another, there is no individual at hand to act as master of ceremonies—as might be the case if the person selected for that role has suddenly been taken ill.

• *When the occasion is informal.* Let's say a small subgroup in a business seminar has gathered for a discussion and the expected leader fails to show up. A member of the group may stand and say, "Ladies and gentlemen, my name is Ron Adams. If it's all right with you, I'll act as temporary leader, just to get things going. . . ." Or, in a small group where the assigned leader isn't known to the others, he or she may make a self-introduction.

• *For dramatic purposes.* At a fairly large gathering and on a somewhat formal occasion, a speaker who introduces himself or herself is doing the unexpected—which is always attention-getting.

A self-introduction should make these points:

NAME AND TITLE: "I'm Anne Vargas, vice-president of our association."

BACKGROUND: "I've been a member of our group for six years. Last May I was given the responsibility of member-relations chairperson."

PURPOSE: "In the next few minutes I'm going to report to you on our membership survey, the results of which, in my opinion, are truly startling."

"UNACCUSTOMED AS I AM. . . ."

INVITATIONS TO SPEAK THAT YOU MUST ACCEPT

Anyone in business, particularly individuals in the management echelons, must expect to be called on to speak in public. Even in a working meeting, it's desirable for an individual to be able to get up and say his or her piece.

For many people, regardless of the level of their public-speaking skill, if the call comes, it may be impossible to refuse. Of course, the better your skill the more at ease you'll be and the more successful your public deliveries. While the "how to" side of public speaking is outside the domain of this book, there are many questions of etiquette that are bound to crop up when you receive an invitation to speak.

The first question may well be "Can I back out?" Under certain circumstances you have no alternative but to accept:

• *When your boss makes the suggestion:* "John, I've been asked to give a talk on our sales campaign for our new product before the advertising group. It's a good opportunity for us to tell our story in a way that will get us some good notices. Unfortunately I'll be out of town on that day. I'd like you to take on the assignment. . . ."

• *When you're a logical choice:* "Adele, each department has been asked to give a description of its operations to the new group of salesmen as part of their background training. As head of the office operation I'd like you to be prepared to. . . ."

• *When a refusal puts you in a bad light.* Sometimes, despite feelings to the contrary, motives may be misinterpreted in an undesirable way. For example:

Andy Arnall, a highly creative and successful engineer, was moved from a production job to be assistant to the head of Research and Development. The production managers had formed a management group that met every month at a local restaurant for dinner and arranged talks bearing on some aspect of their work. Andy Arnall was asked to address one such meeting on a subject of his own choice.

He didn't particularly like the idea, felt he'd pretty much grown away from the group. But he correctly assumed that a turndown would be viewed as a sign of snootiness and his feeling that he was "too good" for his former colleagues. Accordingly, he accepted and tried to make his participation wholehearted and in the spirit of the invitation.

HOW TO TURN DOWN A SPEAKING INVITATION GRACEFULLY

Usually, when you're asked to speak, it's all in the line of duty, and you accept. However, there may be perfectly acceptable reasons why you cannot:

- You're just not available on the date or at the time given.
- Your health or a family situation doesn't permit (there may be travel involved, for example).
- You're insufficiently versed in the subject required.
- You expect a fee, which the inviting group is unprepared to pay.

When your reason for turning down the invitation is clearly acceptable, you express your regrets, explain why you can't accept, and, if you like, ask for a "rain check," hope for an invitation "at a later time," and so on.

There are other acceptable reasons you can't reveal:

- You question the nature of the group—for example, you think it's too liberal or too conservative or somehow you differ with its basic policies.
- You think little of the group and don't feel it's worth your time.
- You feel your reputation or status may be tarnished by publicity that links your name with the group.

When the real reason is of such a nature that it seems undesirable to give it, the rejection should be as diplomatic as possible. You can simply use some of the reasons on the first list: "Unfortunately, I have a previous engagement on the date you suggest. . . ." Or: "Personal matters of a critical nature are preempting all my spare time. . . ." Or: "I don't believe I'm sufficiently well informed on the subject of your interest to be able to make a worthwhile contribution. . . ."

Please note that the explanations suggested above fall into the area of the "white lie." In some situations this is an entirely approved-of device to avoid hurting feelings, saving face for another person, and so on.

If an invited speaker wants to refuse because he or she disapproves of the policies or tactics of an organization and if, in addition to refusing the invitation, wants to protest against one or another aspect of an organization, the situation may be used to register one's opposition: "I cannot accept your invitation because I am strongly opposed to the viewpoint you espouse on civil rights . . ." or whatever it is that you find offensive. Two things are advisable in such a case:

First, make sure you want to go on record on this matter. Second, word your disagreement in an open and courteous manner. After all, you've been paid the courtesy of an invitation. Even if you have strong resentments, this is not the context in which to express them with abuse or excessive hostility.

"JUST A FEW WORDS" FOR INFORMAL OCCASIONS

Almost every type of business ceremony requires that someone "say a few words." In formal situations, there's no question that the services of a speaker, toastmaster, master of ceremonies—call him or her what you will—are required. But informal situations, from the brief birthday-party-in-the-reception-room to after-hours drinks by a group of colleagues to mark a peer's promotion, also demand that *somebody* say *something.* Not to do so seems to miss the point of the gathering, gives the affair a "so what?" feeling.

• *A small birthday lunch for a colleague* requires that something be said that focuses on the special nature of the occasion. These two points lend themselves:

• *A toast.* If the group is having drinks—hard (cocktails), soft (Cokes, and so on), or medium (beer or wine)—someone, probably the person who has organized the party, should raise his or her glass and say, "Happy birthday to our esteemed friend and colleague," or, "To Pete Jones, the nicest guy a person could work with," or some such sentiment.

• *Before presentation of a gift.* Where a gift has been purchased to present to the guest of honor, clearly a few remarks are called for. In an informal situation, just a few sentences are best. Anything longer tends to be a burden on the guests and a dampener of the pleasant relaxation that the informal atmosphere happily tends to create.

The presentation typically should focus on the occasion, include praise for the virtues of the guest of honor, possibly a few words about the reason for the choice of the particular gift. Here is an example: "I guess some of us are wondering how it's possible to be hard at work one minute and a short while later enjoying ourselves thoroughly in these pleasant surroundings. Well, the reason is right here at my elbow, Sheila Baird. Eight years ago she had the good sense to come to work with us, and that's the anniversary we're celebrating today. And to show Sheila how grateful we are for helping to make our jobs more stimulating and for sharing her wit and wisdom with us, today we're presenting a token of our appreciation and gratitude."

The gift is handed over, and when Sheila opens it the "sharing of her wit and wisdom" phrase becomes clear because she's given the latest collection of *New Yorker* cartoons and someone in the group has succeeded in giving it special value by getting the signatures of some of the cartoonists inscribed on the flyleaf.

• *A large farewell party for a popular colleague.* It's common practice to honor a person who is leaving the organization, and in many cases the observance is held on company premises—lunchroom, conference room if it's large enough, or sometimes the office of the president or other top executive.

It should be the responsibility of the people planning the get-together to arrange in advance for the speaker and to give him or her the cue as to when the talk should be given and approximately how long it should be.

Again, the substance of the talk should focus on the occasion and basically should praise the qualities or contributions of the guest of honor.

Some key themes:

• *Friendliness and warmth.* "We'll always remember and value Julie's years with us because, on a personal level, she was always there when you needed her. If you felt down, you talked to Julie to get the brighter or more hopeful side of things. And if you didn't respond, she'd let you have it right between the eyes: 'Would you rather be dead?' "

• *Creativity.* "Take it from someone who was right there and saw it happen: Robbie set a standard for problem solving and practical imagination seldom matched in this organization. Why, I remember the time. . . ."

• *Personal integrity.* "Roger is one of the few people I know who never seemed in doubt on ethical or moral values. In his own calm and self-contained way, he always seemed to have a clear view of the rights and wrongs of a situation. . . ."

How should the person being honored respond? That's the next point to be covered. . . .

WHAT THE GUEST OF HONOR SHOULD SAY

Friends and colleagues of Alice Green have been invited to a party to celebrate her promotion to manager of the order department. During this event, her boss makes a warm speech about Alice Green's splendid service, her contribution to the company. This is followed by the presentation of a gift to Alice. Of course she's urged to open it, and when she does, it turns out to be a splendid pen-and-pencil set on an onyx base, just right for the new executive position she'll be in.

Someone in the audience calls out "Speech!" and others pick up the request. What should Alice say? Alice and all people in the same situation have a range of choices, and here they are:

1. *Version I.*

This is for people who are either overcome by emotion or don't like to speak in public: "I love you all. It's been wonderful working with you, and I hope it will continue that way for years to come. And thank you for the lovely gift."

2. *Longer Version.*

This is recommended for people who want to do a little bit more than just express their warm feelings toward coworkers and gratitude for a gift. In addition to the expressions of warmth and gratitude, you might want to add:

- some words about the organization as "a good place to work";
- expressions of thanks to those who have been of help;
- for an individual who has been of special help, special praise: "But of course it was Mr. Henley who encouraged me to get the training and technical background I needed to qualify for the management job. . . ."

3. *Version III.*

This is for the accomplished speaker. If the guest of honor is an experienced speaker who has the impulse to give the occasion full treatment, he or she certainly has that prerogative. The points made above all apply. But here are some additional ones:

• *Reminiscences.* The speaker may want to recall old times, the first day he or she started work, and so on.

• *Changes.* Of particular interest, particularly for newer people, are the recollections that old-timers may have of "the way things used to be," what's different today, and so on. This theme is particularly welcome if it avoids the suggestion that the olden days were the golden days that make the present seem depressing or otherwise undesirable.

There's one impulse above all others that a guest of honor should *avoid,* regardless of how justified it may seem. This is the voicing of old resentments, a "paying off of debts" to enemies, and so on.

There may be a certain irony in the eyes of the guest of honor to the smiles and cheers that in his or her mind cover over some pretty rocky and unpleasant incidents. For those people who have something to be bitter about, a perfectly practical suggestion: make the acid comments in privacy, to friends and faithful colleagues. That way one can ease the load on one's chest without blowing an audience and a pleasant event into smithereens.

• *Some clichés to avoid.* One way to make a speech sound fresh and spontaneous is to direct it to the immediate and unique aspects of the gathering. One might say, for example: "I doubt that any room has ever held so many people of goodwill. . . ." Or: "As Mr. Jones handed this wonderful gift to me, I must confess to feelings of bewilderment. I thought, *'They're* rewarding *me* for ten pleasant years working with the nicest bunch of people anywhere on the planet. . . .' "

As much as possible, avoid the clichés that are often dragged out on such occasions: "I'm happier than I can say. . . ." "I'm overwhelmed. . . ." "What can I say? . . ." Of course, experienced speakers sometimes use clichés to add a certain amount of camp humor. A veteran of the podium who starts off with "Unaccustomed as I am to public speaking, . . ." is sure to win a hearty chuckle.

The speech in response to a gesture of appreciation, whether a gift or a eulogy, does have one rule that supersedes all others: if you speak from the heart, anything goes (except the negative or hostile churnings mentioned earlier)—and, of course, it shouldn't go on too long.

MORE ON THE GUEST OF HONOR'S RESPONSE

Observing organizational celebrations over the years, it becomes clear that guests of honor—for example, the person about whom a speech has been made and to whom a gift has been given—have a unique opportunity to express their feelings in a way that will be pleasing to the audience and rewarding to themselves.

Typically, a guest in the position of having to respond accepts the gift, mutters a "Thank you very much," and the party continues. But such a response is often disappointing to the audience that would really like to feel the warmth of interaction with a colleague. And often the person being honored realizes in retrospect that an opportunity has been missed. Granted, if the individual is too overcome with emotion or intimidated by the situation (as a result of inexperience as a public speaker), the "Thank you" response will just have to do. But where the individual is sufficiently at ease to speak up, the situation is made to order for a talk that can add to the warmth and spirit of the occasion. Here's the way one guest of honor responded to an encomium addressed to her on the occasion of leaving for a better job in another organization:

"Dear friends, as you know, I'm leaving to accept what is generally called 'an offer I couldn't refuse.' It's an opportunity that I'm really looking forward to. But I can assure you that even if the job had ten times the appeal it has, I'd still be leaving with real regret.

"I've worked in this organization for eight years. To be altogether frank, I'd have to say that, as would be true of any job, there were ups and downs. For my part, I made some mistakes, and every once in a while things would happen that I could have done without. But almost every job is like that. And I want to assure you that the things I'm taking away with me are very fond memories and a strong sense of achievement in working for a worthwhile and mature organization.

"But best of all are the personal relationships I had in working with a fine bunch of colleagues. I know that my friendship with some of you will never end. I hope we'll be seeing a great deal of each other from time to time. But even with those people I didn't get to know well, there was always a pleasant and professional working relationship. By and large, people seem to like working here and take their jobs seriously. I can assure you that I never would have gotten the job offer I've accepted if it hadn't been for the excellent training and experience and, most of all, the high standards with which work is performed here.

"And so I want to thank you all individually and as a group for your help over the years. It's been a learning and maturing experience for me, and you've all contributed. For that, my thanks once again and continuing gratitude. I love you all."

QUALIFICATIONS OF A MASTER OF CEREMONIES

The qualities ideal for the person who is to do the introducing, make the sallies, and propose the wishes that are the duties of the toastmaster are:

- Preferably, he or she should be well known and well liked.
- He or she should possess a smooth and winning delivery.
- The person should have the wit of a Bob Hope or Johnny Carson.

And, strangely enough, many organizations have "naturals," people who are just cut out for the toastmaster's job. You know them because they've done it before and they've been howling successes. As a matter of fact, all they have to do is stand up and the audience begins to laugh and chuckle in anticipation of the amusing words they know they're going to hear.

But—your situation may be different. You don't happen to have a natural-wit-in-residence or a gifted orator who can hold an audience, make it laugh, cry, roar, or sigh on cue. What do you do then?

Here's how to take an ordinary mortal, with only limited oratorical powers, and help him or her carry the day adequately:

• *Modest expectations.* Don't give anyone—either the speaker or the members of the audience—the idea that there's going to be a terrific demonstration of the toastmaster's art. Many people tend to be nervous or self-conscious, and public speaking can be an ordeal. You ease the pressure on the individual and also get readier acceptance from an inexperienced speaker if you make it clear that the "few words" you ask him or her to speak will really be few.

• *Preparation.* Even if the introduction is going to be short, you not only dampen the speaker's worries but also increase the chances of success by taking care of these items:

DESCRIBE THE OCCASION. Tell the speaker the nature of the occasion: "It's Gus Peters's tenth anniversary. . . ."

WHERE AND WHEN. "We're going to have the get-together in the recreation room after work Thursday at five."

AUDIENCE. Give some idea of the size of the audience and mention key people who'll be expected. Make clear who'll be running things: "Helen Rogers will be in charge, and she'll tell you when to make the introduction."

SUGGEST CONTENT. Your "volunteer" speaker may ask, "What shall I say?" It's not an unfair question, as you may, and probably will, be more familiar with the situation. First, suggest that he or she read the paragraphs in the section titled "Just a Few Words" (see page 39). Then offer the following as a rough model:

- *Opening.* "As you all know, we're here to make a big thing of a big thing, namely, Gus Peters's tenth year at XYZ. . . ."
- *Praise.* "Those of us who have been lucky enough to work with Gus know him to be. . . ."
- *Assurance of esteem.* "Gus, your friends are gathered here to show our esteem and affection. . . ."
- *Conclusion.* "We wish you many more happy years. . . ."
- *If a gift is to be presented.* "As a small token of our feelings. . . ."

WHEN SHOULD THE CEREMONY START?

Let's take a typical case. There's to be a cocktail party in the organization's dining room to welcome a new top executive. People have been invited to show up at a specific time and actually begin drifting in a couple of minutes beforehand. Fifteen minutes after the scheduled time, practically everyone is on hand, including the guest of honor.

Should that be the signal to start the speechmaking? Generally the answer is no. The "speaking" part of the ceremony should start only after the "director," the person in charge of the event, feels that the "party" phase has gone on long enough for people to have had a drink, had a chance to chat among themselves, and so on. To a large extent, the best timing is a matter of feel. But consider:

TOO SOON. If the speaker starts the formal part of the ceremony prematurely, there's a feeling of perfunctoriness, that matters are being rushed, possibly in order to wrap it up as quickly as possible. This feeling obviously is not very flattering to the guest of honor and is certainly not calculated to accomplish the ceremonial purposes for which the audience has been gathered.

TOO LATE. If the speaking part of the ceremony is delayed too long, several undesirable things happen. People get restless. Some will leave. There will be a general feeling that the ceremony, when it starts, is almost an anticlimax.

Steer, then, between these two extremes for the best timing.

SPEECHES OF INTRODUCTION

The introductory speech—one in which you're called on to present an individual to a group—is a "set piece" in business use of the spoken word.

Introductions come in all shapes and sizes. Sometimes they can be extremely brief and yet quite adequate: "And now, ladies and gentlemen, I've explained the purpose of our getting together today. Let me introduce the next speaker, a person known to you all, our own Mrs. T. J. Bettley. . . ."

For small gatherings where the atmosphere is essentially informal, an introductory speech may consist of just a few sentences. However, despite the brevity of the remarks, they should include the following elements:

- the introducee's name, title, or affiliation;
- the title of the talk, or else a description in a phrase or two of the special matter to be covered;
- the reason why the speaker has been selected: "Since we're all interested in getting a firsthand report on how our branch is doing in Portland, I feel we could do no better than to have the situation covered by Bill Bridal, head of operations in Portland."

At formal meetings, introductions can be lengthy and detailed, and in many instances they are considered an opportunity for a tour de force. A speaker will go to great lengths to make an introduction that not only brings on the person introduced in an effective manner but also reflects on the wit of the person delivering the introduction.

Below are reproduced in full two introductions that are notable on several accounts—their humor, their use of anecdote, and the methods used to build a provocative and attractive picture of the person being introduced.

Admittedly, these talks are superior examples of the art, both written and delivered by individuals of international reputation. The expectation, then, is not that they will be used as direct models, but that they will serve to suggest the latitude this form can boast.

LEO CHERNE INTRODUCES DANIEL PATRICK MOYNIHAN

(Leo Cherne, executive director of the Research Institute of America, on April 12, 1975, introduced Daniel Patrick Moynihan, then U.S. ambassador to the United Nations, to an audience made up of members of Freedom House at City University, New York.)

Pat Moynihan is a most extraordinary man—so *extra*ordinary that identifying the precise nature of his uniqueness is itself a complex undertaking.

He has achieved a range of remarkable distinctions while still a young man—and yet this is not the hallmark.

He has time and again achieved notice because he has said or written something which is both significant and strikingly original. Ideas do not usually command attention in our media. Yet Moynihan has repeatedly compelled journalism to observe that an idea may indeed be far more newsworthy than an event.

I think the press has unconsciously understood that Pat Moynihan's ideas *are* events in the most important sense. They will almost always foreshadow action. Moynihan is not content to simply reflect on the world around him. His words, and they are often disturbing, produce the kind of discomfort which is an essential prelude to action.

He often invests his thoughts with a wit which makes the provocation deceptively acceptable. I doubt that that's his purpose. More likely, I think the wit is the barb which makes the seriousness beneath difficult to shake or forget. Pat has a great ability to enjoy life, to nourish fun—but playfully wasting an important idea is not his particular pleasure.

There is one thing about his ideas I regret and I'm sure others do, too. He has such an original way of understanding the world around him and of expressing his perceptions that there is no way for an idea scavenger like me to make his thoughts mine.

Edwin Land observed during a small meeting a week ago that a people who do not compel their leader to think do not have a leader. Pat Moynihan has spread pleasure wherever he has worked—but always at the price of compelling thought.

I think the most unusual aspect of Moynihan is the richness of those qualities one expects in a distinguished man of letters—or more still the creative literary figure—but not among those who take responsibility for action. Two centuries ago Sebastian Chamfort wrote of this dichotomy when he said "men of letters are often criticized for not going into society." "People," he continued, "expect them to be forever present at a lottery in which they hold no ticket." In the wagers of the last twenty years, Daniel Pat Moynihan's pockets have been filled with the winning and losing tickets. And he has in addition been oddsmaker, tout, jockey, even race horse.

During these twenty years of his public life, I'm delighted that I've known him for twenty-one years. It was in 1954 that we were both associated in the work of the International Rescue Committee—a year before he joined Governor Averill Harriman's staff. During the years that followed he was special assistant to the Secretary of Labor—then *the* Assistant Secretary of Labor. For three years he was Director of the Harvard-MIT Joint Center for Urban Studies. This in turn led to his being Assistant to the President for Urban Affairs, Counselor to the President, and member of the Cabinet; we invited him to do this first Mac Kriendler lecture when he was still U.S. ambassador to India.

And in each role it must be said of him as of few other men in public affairs—he has always been and in all respects, his own man.

His major works, *The Politics of a Guaranteed Income, Beyond the Melting Pot, On Understanding Poverty,* have each left an indelible mark on our understanding of our society. He is a member of the Editorial Board of *The Public Interest,* which at its origin was assisted by Freedom House.

The new *Encyclopaedia Britannica* describes this distinguished Irishman as poet, wit, critic, and brilliant political pamphleteer.

That could have been Pat but it *was* Jonathan Swift. And it could have been Moynihan, not Swift, who asked:

"How is it possible mankind will *take* advice, when they not-so-much as *take warning.*"

To give warning, offer advice, to share important understanding and above all to celebrate freedom I present someone I greatly admire—Ambassador Daniel Patrick Moynihan.

WILLIAM F. BUCKLEY, JR., INTRODUCES LEO CHERNE

(On January 4, 1974, William F. Buckley, Jr., publisher of the *National Review* and well-known television personality, introduced Leo Cherne, executive director of the Research Institute of America, to a meeting at the Waldorf-Astoria sponsored by the Sales Executives Club of New York. This was Mr. Cherne's thirty-fourth appearance before the SEC group, for which at its first meeting of the year he presented the major address.)

Mr. Chairman, ladies and gentlemen:

We are here to listen yet again to Mr. Leo Cherne—a tribute, rigorously analyzed, either to our charity or to our resolute faith in his prescience. Since there is nothing on the record that easily suggests that members of the Sales Executives Club of New York are specialists in charity, or indulgent lunchgoers, the presumptions are heavily in favor of the latter. This is the 34th consecutive year that Mr. Cherne has shared with us his vaticinations, and it is said that this year the call for tickets was even more clamorous than last year. Once again the disjunctive process. This means either that this year more than ever we feel the need to consult our clairvoyants: or that, this year we feel especially the need to patronize anyone who will risk his reputation—by making of himself a spectacle, in a world in which the flywheel seems somehow to have worked loose, leaving us without those gyroscopic road signs provided to us in the past by the prophets of the Old Testament, followed by Nostradamus, who passed the torch along, in 1940, to a young knowitall in New York, who has been telling us ever since what is going to happen spliced, in the spirit of the Old Testament, with some notion of what it is that *should* happen.

When Mr. Cherne wrote to me last November inviting me to impale myself upon this introduction, he felt, evidently, that historic reversals required him to submit to the punishment of being introduced by someone who has frequently disagreed with him. Thus he told me that, one year ago, the theme of his address here at the Waldorf had been, *"The Year of Returning Confidence."*

I recall an experience in my schooldays. Congressman Hamilton Fish was lecturing in the suburbs of New York. It was mid-afternoon and he was assuring his audience that the suggestion that the United States was vulnerable to attack in the Pacific by the Japanese Navy was nothing more than the war propaganda of interventionists, as we then called them. At this point the master of ceremonies was handed a note by a flustered attendant who came in directly from the wings and in turn the master of ceremonies passed along the note to the inflamed speaker, who took it in his hands but would not interrupt his peroration on the good intentions of the Japanese long enough to read it. It was only after he finished his speech and received his tumultuous ovation that he read the note informing him that at that very moment Pearl Harbor was being attacked.

Roughly speaking, Hamilton Fish was never heard from again. Though his son, also Hamilton Fish, performed an interesting public function a generation later. He fought a closely contested primary, and defeated for the Republican nomination to Congress a young lawyer called Gordon Liddy. Mr. Liddy was thereupon set free to apply his publicspiritedness to the benefit of the commonweal as chief security officer of the plumbers unit. One supposes that if he had neglected to bring scotch tape with him to the Watergate apartments on that haunted day, Leo Cherne might, at this point, be armed to tell us with pride that the year 1973 was as he had predicted it would be: the year of Returning Confidence. A synoptic way of putting all this is that if the Japanese hadn't bombed Pearl Harbor, Leo Cherne's predictions for 1973 would have been fulfilled.

Which suggests the difficulties.

It is, as we readily understand, a reckless game to play, that of predicting. I do not know why anyone attempts to do it. I could not imagine anyone presuming to do so who is less qualified on all counts than Leo Cherne. But then that limits the field pretty much to him. He is commonly thought of as the director of the Research Institute of America, a brilliant economist and analyst. To say that much about him is not incorrect, but one might as well have described Winston Churchill as a bricklayer. Mr. Cherne is far too restless to confine his interests to the morphology of getting and spending, and in any case he knows that much that affects that world is caused by movements undetected, and undetectable, by a narrowly-focused examination of economic trends. Accordingly Mr. Cherne is, as Churchill also was, an artist: if I may say so, a superior artist, whose sculpture hangs in the museums of the world. He is also a musician; and a lawyer; and a sportsman; and a philanthropist; and a freedom fighter; and an author; and a teacher—where does one stop?

Not, surely, short of acclaiming him as probably the most skilled polemicist in America. I have seen him in action, several times at my expense. He arrives at the television studio or at the lecture platform with charts, graphs, tables, encyclopaedias, balloons, firecrackers, bobby pins: just so you understand his point. His arguments are so neatly and authoritatively arranged as to make the mere thought of disagreeing with them somehow contumacious. I remember at one exasperated moment in the past observing that when the time comes for Leo Cherne to present himself to St. Peter, he will do so with a computerized log of all the arguments for his instant admission: not least among them, I hasten to predict—in the spirit of this session—the altogether unwarranted generosity with which he will, in just a moment, refer to me.

Whom he selected because—he said in his letter, given the, uh, circumstantial difficulties arising from the unfortunate theme he selected for last year's lecture, he sought, to introduce him, someone who—I quote him—"is both well known and renowned for his humility." On this theme he did not elaborate. I take it his point is to take public shelter by producing someone whose asseverations, by contrast, make his own appear to be exercises in ambiguity.

But of course we all see through him, and his charming attempt at humility. Leo Cherne could not wear sackcloth if Benvenuto Cellini stitched it on his frame. And we would not have it otherwise. Those who venture, inevitably stumble—and no doubt someday it will happen to me.

I give you our spirited, learned, venturesome friend, Leo Cherne.

HOW TO PREPARE FOR A FULL-LENGTH PRESENTATION

You've been selected to give the keynote talk at a company party to celebrate the tenth anniversary of a top executive. He's your colleague. You know him very well, as do a large number of people in the audience. He's the "man who needs no introduction," and yet you have to put the spotlight on him. He's "been a good friend to all of us," and yet you have to say some things that will constitute a pleasant surprise to his colleagues. Here are the steps you can take to prepare a talk under these circumstances:

• *Round up some factual data.* Get some of the basic elements of your colleague's history with the organization—when he started, what his original job was, the changes in his responsibility, and so on.

• *Note outstanding accomplishments.* By talking to his superiors and others who would know, note the outstanding accomplishments of his years in the company. In some cases this can be a simple matter. He may have developed a new product, headed up a new department, scored victories as the head of a task-force operation. Of course, the achievements may be less dramatic and therefore less easy to identify. If this is the case, you may have to content yourself with the particular qualities that the individual brought to his work—persistence, responsibility, imagination, enthusiasm, a general friendliness, and so on.

• *Collect anecdotes.* The nuggets of a talk of this type generally are the anecdotes—amusing, inspiring, or simply those that dramatize one or more virtues of your guest. Don't let yourself be limited by the incidents of which you yourself are aware. Consult with people who have worked closely with the guest, or those who have been particularly good friends. Usually among this group you will find recollections that will add substance to your talk.

Once you have the material, another question may arise. . . .

SHOULD YOU READ YOUR SPEECH?

An initial reaction might be "No." Generally, it's undesirable to read a speech, certainly not word for word. Such talks tend to be stilted and spoil the informality or spontaneity of the occasion.

This is not to say that a speech should never be read. As a matter of fact, in some situations where what is said is of extreme importance, a speaker will—and rightly—insist on reading from a prepared text to make sure that there is no misunderstanding and that there is a clear verbatim record.

Fortunately there are alternatives to reading word for word that are used by experienced speakers:

MEMORIZING. Some individuals have the gift of being able to read a prepared speech a couple of times and, by so doing, commit it to memory. If the speech isn't long and your memory is retentive, this may be a practical way of giving a fully prepared talk and yet seeming to be in direct and spontaneous contact with your audience.

USING NOTES. Most speakers use this approach. However, there is considerable variation in the completeness of what is put down on paper.

A skilled speaker can write half a dozen key words on a slip of paper or on index cards and with this slight assist develop a well-rounded half-hour presentation. For people who know their subject well, this is a practical and preferred approach.

USING AN OUTLINE. An alternative is to make a somewhat more complete outline. Here, instead of just a few key words to mark the main points, you develop a fairly comprehensive set of directions for yourself. Here's an example:

Title: The Future of the Production Department
Introduction: The need to look backward and forward in order to grow and achieve
  I. Brief history of the production department
     A. Size and operation when it started
     B. Growth factors
     C. Present capacity

II. Factors for growth
    A. Changing market needs
    B. Encouragement by top management
    C. Home-grown creativity
III. Plans and programs
    A. Appointment and operation of the "Future Development" group
    B. Liaison with Marketing
    C. Liaison with top management
    D. Specific projects: pretesting and finalizing plans

Conclusion: The future holds many uncertainties for all of us, but the best chance for resolving these favorably is a positive program that is practical and can be implemented with present resources.

HUMOR? YES AND NO

As everyone who has ever addressed or been a member of an audience knows, business groups have a low threshold of laughter. Perhaps business audiences love to laugh because much of their day concerns serious matters to which humor is a welcome change. In any event, they seem to have a heightened predisposition to the amusing word, phrase, or thought. The lightest comment can bring waves of merriment.

The speaker who feels a lack of the joke-telling gift can use this sensitivity to advantage by a relaxed, slightly humorous tack without trying to bring down the house—and yet may actually do so.

You needn't make excessive efforts to be funny. Light humor in good taste and inserted at proper points in a talk will get you the favorable response you want. You needn't be a "born humorist" to score. Avoid the old saws and stale jokes, and with reasonable luck your attempts at humor will be successful.

The best procedure is to use these guidelines before you make up your mind:

• *Is it natural for you?* Many people are lucky to have a built-in sense of what's funny, and can convey this feeling in what they say. Amusing anecdotes can induce laughter—when told by someone who has a "feel" for the particular story. But some people can't tell a punch line from a fishing line. People who have trouble with spoken narrative should eschew grafting prefab jokes onto their talks. One quick test: if the anecdote makes you laugh, you probably can communicate your feeling to others. But be sure you have it well rehearsed.

• *Is it appropriate to the occasion?* There are scarcely any circumstances in business or out when humor is completely inappropriate. A gentle bit of wit, if properly selected and delivered, can even enrich the eulogy at a funeral.

However, there are some obvious situations where the nature of the humor must be watched. It would be in poor taste, for example, in publicly welcoming a new executive, to poke fun at his or her predecessor.

• *Is it in good taste?* In addition to being suitable for a given circumstance, it's desirable to avoid off-color, suggestive humor, especially the category known as the "dirty joke." Also, so-called sick jokes may be fine for cabaret and nightclub performers, but they are risky in a business setting—as is ethnic humor.

Another category to avoid because of the risk of being in bad taste is the anecdote that ridicules or derides another person. The verbal cut-and-thrust aimed at putting down an individual, even if he or she is not present, is unwise. However, humor that pokes gentle fun at an individual is something else again.

The key here is the underlying motive of the so-called gentle poke in the ribs. If the sally hides a hostile dagger, no one will be fooled, but successful "ribbing" masks real affection. And, of course, as many speakers have discovered, the most effective humor, where people can join in wholeheartedly and without any reservations, is the joke the speaker tells on himself or herself.

A DISTINCTION THAT HELPS YOU BE AMUSING SAFELY

The question of whether or not to use humor falls into manageable perspective when you make a simple distinction. There's an important difference among these three approaches:

• *Telling jokes.* The humorous anecdote, particularly when it is of any length, requires the special skills of a raconteur. Speakers who have the ability to create suspense and keep a good story going have a great advantage and, keeping in mind the guidelines previously mentioned, should certainly look for occasions to incorporate humorous anecdotes into their remarks.

• *One-liners.* A type of humor that has gained particular popularity these days is the one-sentence gag, the throwaway line, a piece of wit that makes its point sharply and briefly. Some of our greatest comedians—Jack Benny, Bob Hope, name your own favorite—have worked their magic on audiences by judicious use of the one-line crack.

• *The light touch.* Finally, there is a kind of humor that doesn't depend on jokes or one-line gags, but rather on two other elements: a bantering tone of voice and an odd or unexpected word in an otherwise ordinary sentence.

On the business scene, the sales manager who starts a crucial conference with a sentence like: "Ladies and gentlemen, we are gathered here together to plan for the biggest damn profit we've ever made in any six months," has gotten his meeting off to a bright and dramatic start.

One executive recently won the approval and gratitude of an audience with these words: "As your chairman of the day, I plan to perpetrate no major crimes. And I hope you'll forgive me for my lesser ones. But as we plunge along through the demanding agenda that we've developed for ourselves, we must remember that we must treat ourselves as our own worst enemies. We cannot be willing to accept our first thoughts. We must bear down on ourselves until we either come up with practical ideas with real bite and impact or until we cry 'Uncle.' And my assistant has been instructed to shoot the first ten people who say 'Uncle' at any time during our deliberations. . . ."

You may or may not think the above opening particularly funny, but in the tense circumstances under which it was delivered—a serious need for the group to devise a successful program or see its survival threatened—the creativity of the speaker in avoiding the somber and using the light touch created a constructive and cheerful entry into the subject matter. And this is a most desirable outcome in any case.

HOW TO HANDLE A SLIP OF THE TONGUE

The verbal goof when speaking in public can be most upsetting. Your talk is going along smoothly, and suddenly you hear yourself uttering a phrase that's downright ridiculous. Some samples that people to their great discomfiture have heard issuing from their lips: "As the defectives on our police force know . . ." "As the brave people on our police farce know . . ." A speaker, intent on praising a colleague, says, ". . . and Pete's vast dearth of experience. . ."

Speakers have mispronounced names (Mr. Cockburn may be pronounced *Coburn*), substituted one place name for another (by saying Paris when meaning London), and twisted words or letters around ("After all," a sales executive says, "our main business is to get a customer's name on the lotted dine").

Whatever the slip, you have three possible courses of action:

• *Ignore it.* If the audience doesn't react, and there's no reason to go back—for example, if you say Paris instead of London and it really doesn't make any substantive difference in the idea you're putting across—just keep right on with your talk.

• *Correct yourself.* If you hear your mistake and it distorts a fact or otherwise misleads, simply say, "I'm sorry, I meant. . . ." and correct the statement.

• *Lead the laughter.* Sometimes the goof is sufficiently amusing to start your audience laughing. Join right in. Laughing at your own error not only erases the sting but makes the audience see you have a sense of humor—always a virtue.

The one thing a speaker must avoid if possible is a loss of poise. If you frown, are visibly shaken, the audience generally has a poor reaction. If you take the blunder in stride, the audience will go right along with you.

HOW MUCH TIME FOR THE SPEAKING PART OF A PARTY?

When people have been invited to attend some kind of organization function, there are rules of thumb that help you decide how much time should be devoted to speechmaking:

• *Nature of the get-together.* There are events that demand a certain amount of speechmaking but also suggest brevity. A Christmas party, for example, is such an occasion. Unless there is actual substance to be covered—for example, some organizations use the Christmas get-together as an occasion to report progress during the year—it is a good idea to be brief, to avoid trying the patience of the guests. They have come to celebrate and usually will welcome short speeches by top executives who can point up and heighten the warmth of the occasion. But once they have done this, the sooner the audience is permitted to return to celebrating in its own way, the better.

But when the occasion has a specific purpose other than celebration—for example, when it's to honor the accomplishments of someone in the organization—then due note of the occasion must be made. If the event covers twenty-five years of service of a valued employee, there must be sufficient recognition made of the individual's contribution. Perhaps more than one speaker should be permitted to add to the praise, encomiums, and so on.

• *Total time of the event.* There should be a reasonable ratio between "talking time" and everything else on the program. This ratio should also reflect the previous consideration, the purpose of the gathering. If the event is a company-anniversary party, a greater proportion of time should be spent on speechmaking, because there are relevant things to be said—recollections of the organization's beginnings, early growth, outstanding events, present prospects, and so on. A Christmas party or a picnic suggests less time devoted to speeches because the purpose of the gatherings—partying and picnicking—are antithetical to oratory. For an after-work cocktail hour marking some happy event that is to last an hour or so, the speechmaking should be held to five or ten minutes at most.

• *Ability of the speaker.* A rule of nature also affects the amount of time devoted to speechmaking. The rule: ten minutes spent listening to a witty speaker seems much much shorter than the same time given over to the company bore. If you're fortunate enough to have available a speaker who's a joy to listen to, then his or her presentation may be a highlight of the occasion rather than a necessary program item. In short, give spellbinders plenty of time, draw a tight rein on oral plodders. Tradition also plays a part in scheduling of talking time. Think back to similar events—or the previous celebration of the same event—for clues. If past practices seem to be satisfactory to all, stick with them. If there has been feeling expressed one way or the other, take these reactions into account in your program planning.

WHEN YOU MUST INVITE A PARTICULAR SPEAKER

It doesn't happen often, but there *are* situations in which, whether you like it or not, the finger of choice points at:

• *A person who traditionally has been the speaker for the occasion.* If J. B. Hustings has been delivering the keynote address for your anniversary party for the past five years, you'd better take the matter up with him before switching: "J. B., many of us would like to have you give your usual talk at the anniversary dinner, but the planning committee feels that as a change of pace it would be desirable to give some of the people from the other branches [or some of the parent-company executives, or whatever] a chance."

If J.B. is *the* top executive, you'll have to put it provisionally: "What do you think of the idea of giving Paul Retz the job? . . ."

If J.B. is a somewhat lesser light, you might make it more positive: "We're thinking of asking Paul Retz. . . ." Or: "Would you mind just relaxing and being one of the audience this year? . . ."

• *A "logical choice" because of the nature of the event.* If you're celebrating the sales department's great feat in scoring the "best quarter ever," the head of the department must be given an opportunity to speak up, no matter who else may be on the program.

Of course, in some situations there is doubt as to whether executive A. *is* the logical choice. For example: a big affair is being given on the occasion of a top executive's twenty-fifth anniversary with the firm. Who should make the speech that goes with the presentation of the gift? One person says, "His boss"—the V.P. Finance. Another says, "The president." A third says, "His sidekick, Fred Penny"—who is also his best friend. Where this doubt exists, it has to be resolved either by vote or by consulting with the highest-status person among the "possibles"—in the above case, the president. Suggestion: each person in a case like the above should be given some place on the roster of speakers.

THE SPEAKER AND HIS OR HER AFFILIATION

A speaker, whether he's a rank-and-file employee or president, will be seen by an outside audience as a representative of the organization with which he or she is connected. If all hands know that the individual is indeed a spokesman for his or her organization, then there is little room for misunderstanding. What the person says is taken to express organizational policies and viewpoints. However, there are occasions when the speaker affiliated with an organization is not appearing as its spokesman but in a personal capacity. Nevertheless, he or she will be identified with the organization if the affiliation is known—through a program note or as a result of common knowledge—and the audience will relate what is said and done to the organization. This fact has several vital consequences:

• *The speaker's dress, appearance, and manner will be identified with the organization.* What kind of limitation does this impose? Simply the awareness that the speaker is *not* a free agent. An individual on his or her own may veer from the norms of propriety—a man may show up unshaven, a woman in too informal attire. Criticism, if there is any, is directed against the individual, and it's entirely a personal matter. But nonconformity of the speaker with an affiliation may mean the organization also bears the brunt of possible unfavorable reactions. In these cases, the speaker should comport himself or herself in such a way as to avoid any negative impressions that reflect adversely on the organization. If in doubt, questions should be taken up with high-echelon executives or a public-relations executive if there is one.

• *What the speaker says will be taken as an organizational view.*
"It is my opinion," says a company treasurer, "that real-estate invest-
ments in urban properties are of a higher order of risk than was the
case five years ago." A local newspaper then headlines: X COMPANY
EXECUTIVE DOWNGRADES CITY REAL ESTATE.

"But I said it was *my* opinion," the treasurer protests to the head
of his firm who has called him on the carpet for espousing a view with
which the company definitely does not want to be identified.

"Not with the firm name printed on the agenda alongside yours,"
says the top executive grimly.

There are two devices that can protect the individual and his or
her organization: remarks made "off the record," and designated
clearly as such, or the speaker's making an explicit disclaimer: "These
are my own personal views, and not necessarily those of my organization." However, good sense, if not propriety, suggests that views
publicly stated cannot clearly retain the label of "Mr. X.'s personal
opinion." Reporters err, or a dramatic statement may be leaked
in such a way that its privileged nature is lost, and the damage is
done.

Sometimes the best compromise between your own strong personal feelings and the company's position is to delete any mention
of company affiliation from the program. Then—unless your position
is publicly known—you can feel free to speak for yourself and yourself alone.

SOME THINGS THAT SHOULD NEVER BE SAID IN PUBLIC

A figure high in public office recently made derogatory remarks
about past and present associates. He *thought* he was speaking in
confidence to a small group whose integrity he could trust. But
through a misadventure—a microphone hooked onto a public-
address system that was supposed to be dead but wasn't—his words
could clearly be heard by a group of startled reporters outside the
meeting room. Those words, nightmarishly, were sent out over the
news wires and made headlines throughout the world.

Of course, the official apologized to all the people of whom he
had spoken slightingly. But the damage was beyond repair. The
moral is clear: derogatory remarks about people or institutions or the
revelation of organization secrets should simply not be voiced *unless
there is a specific intent.* In February 1956 another political figure,
Nikita Khrushchev, delivered a secret speech to the Twentieth Party
Congress in Moscow revealing and attacking the excesses of Stalin's

one-man rule. It shook the Communist world—*but it was supposed to.*

A parent's old-fashioned advice to a teenager is: "Never say anything in private you'd be ashamed of in public." That's obviously overstating the case, but every person with an affiliation and a responsibility to an organization should be sensitive to the need to avoid statements or attitudes that might hurt that organization. And this awareness should best come from the individual's own sense of what's right and should not have to be imposed by any other person or organization. If the need for self-expression on sensitive matters becomes uncontrollable, then the individual should consider the moves that would divorce him or her from affecting the image of an affiliated organization. From time to time, people have severed their connections with an organization for the privilege of speaking freely, and their scruples should be considered proper and admirable.

HOW TO BE KIND TO AN AUDIENCE

There are a number of positive things the speaker can do that any audience will appreciate. Of course, the first thing is to make your talk as suitable and as effective as possible. In addition to this basic requirement, however, you should:

• *Stay within time limits.* Most speakers have an assigned period of time. Both they and the audience know the talk is to last a half hour, an hour, or whatever, because the program makes that point clear. But in other situations the amount of time is flexible. All other things being equal, it's usually best for a speaker's comments to be reasonably brief. The only exception to this would be an occasion when he or she is so obviously and effectively witty or attention-gripping that the audience wants more rather than less. With this one exception, brevity is recommended.

• *Consider the audience.* Every public speaker is obliged to himself and his audience to find out as much about the group as he can, well in advance. It can be painful to all concerned if the background knowledge or sophistication of the audience is miscalculated. A speaker can run into similar audience resistance if he attempts, no matter how subtly, to pull the wool over the audience's eyes.

Top management must be especially on guard when addressing rank-and-file audiences to avoid condescension or what is sometimes called "talking down." If either the manner or the content of what is said suggests that the speaker is communicating from a lofty height to a group of lesser mortals, the outcome can be catastrophic.

• *Respect age, religion, race, sex, and so on.* Also to be avoided: any references, anecdotes, opinions that are an implicit insult to any segment of the audience. A sexist joke, for example, even told with the best of good intentions, may antagonize someone in the group. And this may be true even if that particular quality is not an obvious characteristic of the group itself. For example:

A speaker, cued by the fact that his audience was all male, described what he thought was a hilarious anecdote in which a female secretary was being harassed by a male boss in terms of "being made a pass at." The audience laughed politely, but afterward one of the listeners said to the speaker, "You know, I considered that secretary story of yours sexist, and on behalf of my wife, my mother, and my two daughters, I want you to know I thought it was in bad taste."

• *Establish rapport.* The best thing that can happen to a speaker and to the audience is the quick establishment of a feeling of rapport. When both the speaker and listeners are on the same wavelength, the process of communication reaches a happy understanding and mutual appreciation. The statement that rapport is desirable may seem like the advocacy of peace, good health, or apple pie. But the fact is, the factors that help create rapport are not difficult to identify. In almost every case, a good audience relationship is established by a speaker when he or she is:

> *relaxed*—apparently at ease, even though suffering from a case of shaking knees, sweaty palms, and chest-thumping heart;
> *open*—leveling with the audience, communicating on a common level in an honest, direct way;
> *knowledgeable*—in two ways: comfortable with the subject, and familiar with the nature of the audience's interest in it.

CARE AND FEEDING OF GUEST SPEAKERS AND RELATED PREPARATIONS

As a courtesy, an obligation, and also as an indirect way of emphasizing the importance of an occasion, the people planning an event requiring the services of an outside speaker should pay special attention to his or her personal requirements:

• *Briefing.* The speaker should be given a comprehensive idea of the context in which the talk is going to be made. For example:

The management club of a large Southern paint company had invited a well-known management personality to address its annual dinner meeting. The subject of the talk, "New Ways to Achieve Management Effectiveness," had been agreed upon. To help the speaker tailor the talk to the special interests of the audience, the planning group sent him material covering the history and nature of company operations, a brief history of the management club itself, a printed program of the previous year's meeting. The size of the audience and a description of the dining hall were also included.

• *Liaison person.* A particular individual should be designated to establish and maintain contact with the speaker. If any unexpected developments take place or questions arise, the speaker knows whom to contact, and, similarly, the individual selected becomes the one through whom messages are channeled. (See page 64, on "Talking Paper," for a way to smooth this type of encounter.)

• *Query the speaker on special needs.* The speaker may have needs or preferences that range from special equipment for a presentation—for example, an easel chart or slide projector—to matters of diet if he or she is going to dine as part of the ceremony. Ask the questions that will elicit this information.

• *Travel.* In most cases, if considerable travel is required for the speaker to reach the site of the event, he or she will prefer to make the arrangements. But suggestions may be offered, particularly if you have experience that can be helpful: "We suggest that you take a flight into our local airport that arrives about four o'clock. This will give you plenty of time to check into the hotel. . . ."

It's a particularly nice gesture, where the trip involved is manageable by car, to provide transportation, especially if the speaker doesn't drive. In one case, for example, a university running a seminar provided a limousine for a speaker who lived about twenty miles from the campus. Of course, one of your group who has both the car and the time may perform a similar service. This arrangement also has the benefit of a "get-acquainted" chat between speaker and driver.

• *Accommodations.* If the speaker is from out of town, offer to reserve a hotel room or make whatever arrangement is preferred. How elegant the quarters are, and how expensive, depends on your own sense of what's appropriate. In a large city with a good choice of hostelries, one may avoid the unnecessary expense of a "big-name" establishment in favor of somewhat less pretentious quarters and still do very well by the speaker. Convenience to the meeting site, however, should always be a prime factor.

It is perfectly proper—indeed, may be preferred—if the speaker is put up for the night by one of your organization's people. But this choice should be made only with the speaker's advance knowledge and when you are certain the volunteer host can offer pleasant, relaxed surroundings and privacy for the guest if it's wanted.

• *Preparing the hall.* The responsibility for readying the room where the ceremony is to be held should be assigned to a single individual. He or she may have a staff to assist if this seems desirable—as it would obviously be, for example, if moving of chairs and tables were required. If the hall is rented for the occasion, arrange-ments should be made in advance with the management to have service people available when needed to assist your representative in getting the room ready.

It's important that the premises be checked a few hours in advance so that unsatisfactory situations may be spotted—poor lighting, ventilation, or room temperature, or failure of the hall's sound system to function adequately. Conditions like these if discovered in time can be remedied. If discovered too late, repairs may have to be made while the audience is beginning to trickle in or, even worse, may remain undone, so that your program is forced to labor under a handicap. However, if a problem is unavoidable:

• *Acknowledge inconveniences.* "Please bear with us" is an almost irresistible appeal. An audience will understand and sympathize with such a request. In the minds of everyone is the thought: "There but for the grace of God go I." And so a noisy air-conditioning system, a fixture that blows out at the last minute, a shortage of chairs for an overflow crowd—any such inconvenience—can be accepted and excused by people if you show your awareness of the problem and its consequences.

Of course, if the inconvenience is extreme, such as a broken-down heating system that condemns your audience to sit in chilly quarters, in addition to an apology, you may want to modify the program, curtail it somewhat, to lessen the hardship for the audience—whose attention and receptivity will be adversely affected in any event.

• *Just before the speech.* Let's say the audience is to gather in the company auditorium at three o'clock in the afternoon. Someone, preferably whoever is designated the liaison person, should have the responsibility of getting the speaker to the scene sufficiently in advance for him or her to have the time to take off hat and coat and look over the room in which the event is to take place. This is particularly desirable if there is a question about the facility or the equipment—the seating arrangement, the placing of an easel chart or blackboard, and so on.

A speaker sometimes likes to get the "feel" of a room by standing at the lectern, appraising sight lines, the placing of a microphone if a public-address system is to be used, and so on.

Washroom facilities are also an obvious requirement, as most speakers want a chance to freshen up.

• *Preliminary introductions.* If there is to be more than one speaker, it's desirable for them to be introduced to one another before meeting on the dais.

And, ideally, the person who is to introduce a given speaker should have met him or her in advance. Realistically, this is not always practical. What usually happens is that the person introducing the speaker to the audience has gotten the information needed either from a biographical sketch or other written material, or over the phone. However, the two people should be brought together as soon as possible—if it's a dinner meeting, for example, the introductions should be made as soon as both are present in the dining hall so that they can chat informally for at least a few minutes. This is not only a courtesy to the speaker; it also makes it possible for the introducer to say in his or her opening: "In chatting with our speaker earlier, he told me about the time. . . ."

"TALKING PAPER"

A practice used in government and diplomacy can smooth introductions and conversations between people who are meeting each other for the first time. This situation crops us when an outside guest speaker is to be met by a company representative or program chairman, for example.

The device is called a "talking paper"; that is, information that has been set down in writing that will make it easier for the host to greet and converse with the guest. A business version of the "talking paper" would include:

- the guest's name and title;
- highlights of his or her career;
- a brief account of his or her recent history;
- attitudes, ideas, and achievements in his or her present position;
- opinions, views, stands taken on public issues—partisan or advocacy positions on matters that might be touched on in conversation, or avoided;
- personal interests, hobbies, sports;
- suggestions for subjects that could be covered that might help or bear on his or her talk or the matter that brings him or her as a guest to your organization.

Preparing such a paper may be simple or difficult, depending on how well known the person is. If his or her activities are a matter of public record, enough information may be found in newspaper and magazine items. Otherwise, a discreet phone call to his or her assistant, spouse, or secretary probably will provide the needed data. No secret need be made of such a call. Its purpose is clearly well-intentioned, even admirable.

ORDERS AND INSTRUCTIONS THAT MINIMIZE UPSET AND HURT FEELINGS

One of the most common applications of the spoken word in business is the giving of orders and instructions that get the work done. You think you've made your instructions crystal-clear, and yet people keep coming back with questions. Or, worse still, they don't come back, they simply go ahead—and do it wrong. Injured feelings and fouled-up operations are twin consequences. Here are some of the reactions one hears to badly worded or badly posed directives: "Don't order me around," says a subordinate who resents a boss's needlessly authoritarian tone. "You were so vague, I wasn't sure what you wanted," an employee explains to a superior who's complaining about a foul-up. "I did exactly as you requested. You should have given me more leeway to change the procedure with the situation," an employee says, explaining a failure.

The fact is, order-giving must respond to several elements in the situation if exacerbated feelings and upset are to avoided. There is no one right way to tell people what to do. What's right in one situation may be entirely wrong in another. What's right for one person may be completely ineffective for another.

However, there is a right way to fit each and every situation and the people in it.

THE ATTITUDES YOU MUST WATCH FOR AND RESPECT

Some individuals have a built-in difficulty in giving orders. One group feels that it must "show who's boss." The result: an approach that may verge on browbeating and intimidation.

Another group has the opposite problem. It has difficulty in asserting authority or command. The result: ineffectual orders that often fail to register with the people supposed to act on them.

There you have the rub for people who give orders. Those who receive them also have attitudes that complicate the situation:

- *Oversensitivity.* An individual may resent the slightest show of authority as "bullying."
- *Dependency.* Some people find it hard to operate on their own. They require strong guidance in order to get things done.

• *Poor concentration.* Some people are poor listeners or don't "get" things easily. Orders must be spelled out and repeated.

Fortunately, there are ways to give orders that tend to neutralize or offset most of the obstacles, and so tend to maintain harmony and smooth the operation.

MAKING ORDERS ACCEPTABLE AND UNDERSTOOD

An essential first step in order giving is clarity. Here are some key points that help matters along:

• *Explain one part or a small group of related parts when the job is complicated, long, or unfamiliar.*

• *Explain larger chunks or the whole thing when the job is relatively simple, similar to procedures that are already familiar, or the person has a mind for detail.*

• *Omit needless details.*

• *Explain what* may *happen.* The hardest things to understand are those that are unexpected. So you'll always want to take possibilities into account: "If a long-distance call comes in while I am at lunch, will you have the call switched to Mr. Lee?"

• *Give the other person full opportunity to ask questions.*

• *Make yourself heard.* Seems silly, but lots of people don't like to ask you to repeat.

• *Make yourself understood.* To do so, use words that are familiar. If new words must be used, explain them carefully.

• *Show what you mean.* A lot of people can understand better if you show them. So, demonstrate when possible. A demonstration should be in three parts: first, a quick run-through so that the employee can get an overall picture of his goal; then, a step-by-step illustration accompanied by an explanation; lastly, emphasize the main techniques overall.

BASIC TYPES OF ORDERS

You have a variety of ways to give an order or instruction. Knowing the range of possibilities minimizes the chances of misunderstanding:

1. *The Flat Order.*

This comes straight from the shoulder, keeps the initiative in your hands. It works best when:

an emergency exists;

an assignment is simple and its urgency is obvious;

earlier instructions have been understood but not followed.

There are people who are totally immobilized by direct orders either because they resent a display of authority or because the feeling of urgency that the direct order conveys throws them into a panic. Therefore, whenever possible, try to soften the direct order in dealing with such people. While a manager may have every *right* to issue a direct command, the enlightened person is willing to ease up on his or her so-called rights in order to get things done.

2. *The Detailed Direction.*

This allows more leeway than flat orders, is explicit about details, spells out objectives as well as methods, may leave room for initiative. It works best in these situations:

tasks that must meet definite standards;

assignments involving a number of steps;

unusual assignments.

Detailed instructions often get under the skin of a particularly bright subordinate. The person with initiative who knows enough to check back should he or she hit a bottleneck also resents overelaborate instructions. The experienced order-giver will take the time to get to know each subordinate and adjust methods to the individual whenever possible.

• *Plot your presentation in advance.* Instructions must be logical. That means you have to think them through ahead of time. Think in terms of the other person's ability to understand.

Make them as *concrete* as possible. Employees will "get it" much faster if you can make your points in terms of their everyday experience. To make them concrete, use comparisons: "Follow these mixing instructions just as you would a recipe in a cookbook. . . ."

• *Once is not enough.* Repetition can be boring and even a little patronizing. As you go over and over the same material, you can often see the employee's attention wander. Yet it is frequently necessary. The trick is to schedule a refresher session at a later date—the next day, perhaps. This enables him or her to pick up and incorporate fine points or details missed the first time around.

3. *The Request.*

Most people react better to requests than to direct orders. As a result, the requests frequently get more done more easily. Use them when:

- you really want to know whether it is possible to comply;
- the time element is such that a discussion of pros and cons is feasible;
- you are requiring something over and above the call of duty.

Requests can backfire unless they carry enough authority to assure compliance. It's important that:

- *They don't seem to indicate a casual attitude toward the job.* Because the phrasing is low pressure, you must be careful that the urgency of the deadline or the caliber of the work is clear.
- *They are delivered from a position of strength.* Your voice, manner, and bearing all affect the reception that your request will receive. A "hat-in-hand" attitude on your part greatly weakens the request. It should be made in a firm voice by a person who expects compliance.

4. *The Suggestion.*

This approach uses a guiding hand rather than a dictated procedure. Use it in these situations:

- to get countersuggestions;
- to tap in on another person's ideas;
- to get individual or group participation;
- when you want thinking as much as action.

The suggestion form works well with these people:

- those whose initiative you want to develop;
- people with sound judgment;
- employees whose confidence needs a lift;
- people who tend to have open minds and will evaluate the idea willingly;
- people who though committed to one approach can adapt to a new one.

5. *The "Result-Wanted" Assignment.*

This tack centers on the end result, so it omits many and some-times all the details and places the initiative almost wholly in the hands of the employee you're talking to. Use this approach in these situations:

- volatile situations in which constant change precludes definite instructions;
- you know the end result you want, but can't anticipate all the steps on the way;
- you yourself have less well rounded knowledge than the person you're directing.

Tips on giving "result-wanted" assignments:

• *Set outer limits within which the person should keep.* Even though you expect the person to have judgment, allow for the fact that he or she may become overinvolved in the assignment. Give definite limitations: time, budget, priority.

• *Give as much of the thinking about the established goal as you can.* The more background you can give the person on the why's and wherefore's of the assignment, how it was arrived at, and how the work will finally be used, the better able the subordinate will be to employ that intelligence and initiative for which he or she was se-lected.

These days, subordinates are less likely to be passive in relation to their superiors. Accordingly, a person receiving orders in an unac-ceptable way can act to improve matters—ask for more detail or less, request a boss to take some of the pressure off: "I get what you mean, Mr. Hunt. You really don't have to push that hard." And as for order-givers, you have the benefit of a somewhat repetitive situation; that is, you tend to give your orders to the same individuals. You can modify your manner in keeping with the results you get.

SPECIAL TIPS ON INTERVIEWING

THE INTERVIEW: WHAT IT IS, WHAT IT ISN'T

Interviewing, though it resembles other types of communication, has rules and proprieties all its own. It is a face-to-face, one-to-one form of communication, but what sets it apart from ordinary conversations, chats, consultations, is that:

• *Of the two people involved,* one is the interviewer, the person who guides the conversation; the other, the interviewee, who generally goes along with the line laid down by the other.

• *The subject,* the purpose of the conversation, is known, agreed on in advance. Examples: a reporter interviews a business executive to get his views on a supply situation; a supervisor interviews an employee to get an explanation for a poor attendance record.

It's the relationship between the two people, one in charge, the other the follower, that creates the situations that require special handling by both. And since there are many specific types of interview situations—in addition to the two above, for example, there is the hiring interview, exit interview, information-seeking interview, and so on—and each makes its own special demands on the people involved, there are many nuances that should be considered.

The basic interview situation is one in which one individual "exposes" himself or herself to the probing and questioning of another. The limits of what can be asked and the manner in which responses should be made are crucial. And since the interview is widely used in business, it is important that violation of either party's integrity, privacy, or feelings be avoided. In addition, in employment interviews, there are legal restrictions. The interview is one of the many situations in which good management and etiquette coincide.

LEGAL LIMITATIONS: QUESTIONS YOU MAY NOT ASK A JOB CANDIDATE

Passage of antidiscrimination laws by the federal government means that there may be legal consequences for executives who ask questions that suggest a bias because of race, sex, age, religion, and national origin. In certain types of interviews, such as those for hiring or promotion, for example, questions that used to be asked regularly are now prohibited. It used to seem perfectly natural, for example, to ask a female applicant whether or not she was married, had children, and so on. Now interviewers asking questions like these (and their firms) could be brought up on charges of discrimination by the Equal Employment Opportunity Commission (EEOC) or the Department of Labor's Wage-Hour Division.

The guideline here is simple: if you wouldn't ask a man this kind of question, you may not ask it of a woman—and don't ask either sex a question *unless it has some special relevance to the job.*

Similarly, questions about a person's age, race, or religion suggest that these factors may be used as a criterion for hiring—and thus could be used as evidence in a discrimination suit if the applicant were denied a job.

Many state laws also expressly prohibit these kinds of questions. The best course—if setting or reviewing overall company policy—is to check with legal counsel for guidelines and specific do's and don't's in your own locality.

SHOULD YOU LEVEL WITH THE INTERVIEWEE?

Let's say you're interviewing a candidate for a supervisory job. You know a great deal about the job, you may even have had it at one time yourself. Some of the things you know won't make the candidate more eager for the position—on the contrary. What should you do? For example:

Executive Art Jonas is talking to a young man he feels will make a good department head for one of the manufacturing operations. Jonas knows that in the normal course of events it may be necessary for the supervisor to work odd hours—an occasional Saturday or Sunday. This is a likelihood he should definitely mention. If he doesn't, the candidate would be justified in complaining after he got the job and was asked to come in on a Saturday or Sunday, "But why didn't you tell me about this before you hired me?"

It's not merely good business, it's considerate behavior to tell candidates, especially those whom you are seriously considering for the job, as much as you possibly can about the *objective* aspects—everything from salary to working hours to the details of across-the-board responsibilities.

On the other hand, some reactions are purely subjective. For example, Clara Rogers is interviewing a young woman who she feels will make a good file clerk. Problem: Not only does Rogers think the job itself is boring, but in her opinion the present filing rooms, without windows, make an impossible place to work. Is she under a moral obligation to tell the candidate what she thinks? No.

The rule is: don't expect people to have the same values and make the same judgments you do. Your best move in these circumstances, which will satisfy not only the moral question but also the practical one of telling the candidate as much about the job as is necessary for a clear and accurate picture to emerge, is to take her to the workplace, show her around, let her make her own judgment. If the job candidate is a homemaker, for example, whose nerves have been worn to a frazzle taking care of a house and several kids, the comparative order, peace, and quiet of a file room might seem like heaven.

In general, be sure not to misrepresent. If you give an opinion, label it as such: "Yes, we start early here, eight A.M. But I find I prefer starting early and finishing early. It cuts down on rush-hour traffic, and you have more daylight hours for your own use."

If there are negative aspects to a position, you owe it to applicants to mention them to prevent disappointment or resentment later on; if you don't, the person may quit and the oversight simply leads to going through the hiring all over again. Experts in the personnel field will tell you it's best not to oversell a job. If a candidate comes along who seems to be particularly desirable, by all means stress the good points—everything from "This is a job with a future" to your company's being a good place to work, with a generous major medical plan and so on. But don't let your eagerness push you into presenting a lopsided picture. It's neither fair nor good management nor proper business behavior.

PREPARING FOR THE INTERVIEW

It's up to the interviewer to make the preparations that assure the smoothness and worthwhile results of the meeting. If it is run properly, you end up with two unruffled people who have been through a constructive experience together. Here's what a desirable outcome depends on:

• *Prethink the objective.* Pin down, in your mind or on paper, the basic points you want to cover. Let's say you're about to undertake a counseling meeting with a subordinate, one in which you want to review his or her work situation, find out the hangups or obstacles that interfere with performance, and then conclude with a plan or program aimed to help progress toward a goal.

To make sure you actually touch all bases, you might make a few notes:

Review present work situation.
Ask for his or her views on progress.
Check for problems, obstacles.
Together, work out a program.

In some cases, executives find that jotting down key phrases or sentences that they want to use in the conversation also ensures saying everything that's on their minds.

• *Physical setting.* For the ease and comfort of the interviewee, some thought should be given to the time, place, and circumstances of the meeting.

Privacy and an absence of noise and interruption are vital for the interviewee to feel he or she is getting your full attention. The physical comfort of the interviewee should be encompassed by a comfortable seating arrangement, good lighting, someplace to put hat, coat, bag, and so on. If the individual smokes, provide an ashtray. If you'd rather no smoking take place, a "Hope you don't mind if we don't smoke during our talk" should cover it.

The timing of the meeting generally should be mutually agreeable. If your schedule is badly overloaded, give the person a choice of two or three periods when you're available. It's the interviewer's preferences that should take precedence. An exception might be: "You're going to be out of town next Monday? Well, in that case I may be able to shift an appointment and see you at two on Friday. How would that be?"

In addition, the matter of the *amount* of time you spend is a factor. A ten-minute meeting to cover a matter of some scope—for example, for you to listen to and evaluate an idea a subordinate has been trying to explain to you for weeks—is bound to disappoint the individual. To avoid the feeling of a brush-off, the best approach is to make sure that the other person has had the chance to say everything that's on his or her mind.

There's one situation that may come up for which you should be prepared. Your secretary puts her head inside the door and says, "Mr. Greene [he's the Big Boss] would like to talk to you at your earliest convenience." Now the interviewee is sitting right across from you. If you seem to be wrapping up the dialogue prematurely, no matter how big the Big Boss is, it's a direct put-down.

Your best move is to avoid anything like "Say I'll get back to him in five minutes" or any other specified time. That suggests to the interviewee that he or she is getting short shrift. An imprecise phrase prevents the other person from the feeling that win, lose, or draw, he or she will be out the door in a specific number of minutes: "Tell Mr. Greene I'm in a meeting and will contact him as soon as I'm finished here." Or: "Tell Mr. Greene I'll be in touch with him shortly."

Then, if you resume the talk in an unhurried manner, you can wind up the meeting in acceptable fashion. (Some executives use this type of interruption as a means of concluding an interview. We'll cover that point shortly under "Wrapping Up the Interview").

CONDUCTING THE INTERVIEW

Here are additional points that can guide the interviewer's behavior:

MANNER. The interviewer's behavior is the key to the mood of the meeting. If you're brisk and to the point, that's what the meeting will be. If you're relaxed, pleasant, these qualities will dominate.

Your interview style is your own, based on your personality and your feeling of what the meeting requires. If you tend to be direct and refuse to use two words when one will do, don't expect to be able to put on a casual, hearty manner.

Of course, you must be yourself. However, be aware of the state of mind and the sensibilities of the other person. Seasoned interviewers know that in almost every case the interviewee tends to be on edge. Even a subordinate you've seen every day of your working life for the past ten years is likely to develop some anxiety if your secretary says, "Gladys, Mr. Hunt would like to see you in his office. Can you make it in about five minutes?" If Gladys doesn't know the reason for the meeting, curiosity will certainly be tainted by some uneasiness: "What's it about? Will he want to bawl me out because I left early last Friday?"

Anticipating, then, the defensive attitude of the typical interviewee, alleviate this feeling at the very outset:

THE START. The opening of the interview sets it on track. If there's any doubt about the purpose of the meeting, clear it up quickly: "I asked you to come in, Margaret, so that I could get to the bottom of your complaint about unfair assignments. . . ."

If the interviewee is a stranger, be sure to get his or her name straight, and use it at the first opportunity: "I'm pleased to meet you, Mr. Czerny. Did I pronounce it properly? It is the *ch* sound, not *z*? Thank you. Won't you sit down? . . ."

Small talk? Of course. Use it, if only a single sentence, to ease the conversation along, put the other person at ease.

Of special importance, especially when the personal stakes are high, as in a hiring interview: try as much as possible to give the other person the feeling that you have all the time in the world and it's all to be devoted to him or her. You accomplish this by:

AN UNHURRIED MANNER. Don't rush your questions or push for answers.

PERMITTING PLEASANTRIES AND BRIEF DIGRESSIONS. Without adding any appreciable amount of time to the meeting, you can inject a lighter note by asking a question somewhat outside the area of direct concern, particularly if you feel it will give the interviewee the chance to expand on a favorite subject: "I see by your résumé that one of your hobbies is fishing. Have you ever? . . ."

Although the point has been made that the reins are in the hands of the interviewer, in some cases key judgments and decisions rest with the other person. For example, in a hiring interview, the candidate should be assessing the company and the job at the same time he or she is being evaluated.

This does not mean that the interviewer must do the equivalent of "scrub up and look good." It's already been said the best guideline is "Be yourself." Even affability in excess has its negative effect. It often gives the interviewee an erroneous impression of future working relationships and/or diverts the interview away from more serious and more job-related avenues of exploration.

WRAPPING UP THE INTERVIEW

Your meeting should end with a definite understanding, a clear-cut conclusion. Of course, this may mean something like: "Then it's agreed, Tess, that we will get together again next week at this same time to continue our discussion of your proposal."

But if there is not to be a follow-up meeting, the interviewee should not be in doubt as to where matters stand.

FOR A DISCIPLINARY MEETING. "I'm sorry, Alex, but I must tell you that I agree with your supervisor. I think he's been fair, and in my opinion his revoking your lunchroom privileges for a month is fully justified. But thanks for coming in and discussing this matter with me. . . ."

A GETTING-ACQUAINTED MEETING WITH A NEW EMPLOYEE. "I've enjoyed our chat, Miss Pell, and although I don't get around to the department you'll be working in half enough, I'm sure we'll be seeing each other from time to time. You have a fine supervisor, one of the best in the company, so I'm sure things will work out. And if there's ever anything you'd like to discuss with me, let Mr. Cawley know and he'll arrange a meeting." (Note the effective way the executive has created a feeling of his availability, at the same time reinforcing the position of the employee's immediate superior.)

A HIRING INTERVIEW. Three possibilities:

Turndown. "I'm sorry, Mr. Jones, but although you have most impressive credentials and skills, I'm afraid the position we're trying to fill is just not suitable to your particular qualifications." The onus should never be put on the applicant, but on the mismatch between person and job.

Still being considered. "Miss Haley, we're still assessing candidates, so we can't commit ourselves at this stage. But you're definitely in the running, and you'll hear from me in about ten days. . . ."

They're in. "You're hired. When can you start?"

EASING THE TENACIOUS INTERVIEWEE OUT THE DOOR

The interview has come to an end—you think. You've given several signals—"Well, that's about it," you say, but the other person still persists in small-talk irrelevancies. "Glad we had this chance to meet face-to-face," you say, and the other person uses that wrap-up as the start of a little talk on how you were so different in person from the impression gleaned from your correspondence.

In some cases, the interview lingers on simply because the visitor overlooks your gentle hints and is unable to make the break himself or herself. For whatever reason, when you want to end the conversation and somehow that moment of "mutual consent" that both people tacitly recognize as a conclusion doesn't arrive, here are some moves to consider:

• *Make a closing statement about which there can be no misunderstanding.* No matter how unaware a person may be, there are some sentences that definitely end a conversation: "Well, that about covers it. Thank you for coming in."

• *Stand up and move toward the door.* If you talk as you do this, the act can seem quite natural. The other person will follow.

• *Use your secretary.* An assistant or secretary can, in a number of ways, help you terminate an interview:

AS A GUIDE TO THE ELEVATOR. You can call in your assistant and say, "Please take Mr. Root to the elevators [or the lobby or the reception room]." You might want to add: "Some people have a bit of trouble finding their way. . . ." for the interviewee's benefit.

BY PLACING A CALL AT A SPECIFIED TIME. Although it's generally undesirable to set clear-cut time limits, for the really tenacious visitor you pick up the phone and say, "We'll be through here in a few minutes, Grace. Will you please put my call through to Mr. Jones?" Or if a subordinate has asked to see you, the message can be: "You can tell Bill I'll be available shortly."

BY PLANNING THE TERMINATION. If you actually have another item on your schedule you want to honor, you can ask your secretary to interrupt at a specific time: "Remember, Mr. Jones, you have a meeting at eleven o'clock." The same tactic can be used if you know your visitor tends to overstay.

SHOULD YOU TAKE NOTES?

In the course of a typical interview, the person you are talking to will say things you want particularly to remember. An obvious recourse is to jot down notes. But—should you?

The problem with note-taking is that it may discourage the free flow of information. Most people find it difficult to talk casually if they're talking literally "for the record." Thus, weigh the advantages of note-taking against the potential disadvantage of introducing an unwelcome element into the conversation. However, there are procedures that can minimize the difficulties:

• *Brief notes are O.K.* If you intend to put down a word or two—a name, an address, a date—such brief notations can usually be taken in stride.

• *Ask permission for extensive note-taking.* If your notes are going to be lengthy, at the very least they will represent some kind of interruption or interference. You can minimize the damage by saying, "Do you mind if I put down on paper some of the things you're saying? I want to check back on that later. . . ."

Invariably the permission will be granted. But then it's up to you to observe whether your note-taking is bogging down the conversation. If it is, you'd be wise to suspend the writing, except possibly for a key word or two, and depend on your memory for the rest of it.

And of course there is a related problem that's not so common but that may arise:

SHOULD YOU PUT IT ON TAPE?

For certain types of interviews, it's desirable and helpful to have a complete record. Thanks to the improvement of small tape recorders, excellent ones are available at a low price. As a result, there are few offices without at least one, and people doing professional interviewing—reporters, for example—routinely carry them along on an assignment. The proper use of tape recorders hinges on the answers to these questions:

• *May you record secretly?* The answer is definitely "No." Unless you're working for the FBI or doing some kind of undercover work, recording an interviewee's words without his or her knowledge is completely unacceptable from an ethical as well as an etiquette point of view.

• *Can you record with permission?* Of course getting the interviewee to agree to speak while your machine is recording the conversation is perfectly acceptable. There is one practical consideration, however. Some people tend to develop mike fright. If you find your interviewee is freezing up and you are not getting the kind of free-swinging answers you hoped for, the recording process may be the reason.

In most cases an experienced interviewer can press ahead with naturalness and assurance in such a way that the presence of the recorder is soon forgotten. However, if despite your best efforts the recording process is obviously making the other person uncomfortable, discontinue it and either resort completely to memory or use handwritten notes to cover key points.

THE COURTESY INTERVIEW

From time to time, every manager or executive is asked: "Please see my friend ――. He [or she] is very talented . . . experienced. . . ." In some cases the request may be reinforced with a personal appeal: "She needs a job badly." Or: "He has been out of work for several months, and I would appreciate it if you could help."

The reason such interviews are called "courtesy interviews" is that usually you have no job available. The "courtesy" is obviously being extended to the friend or acquaintance.

In some cases interviewers will be holding the equivalent of a courtesy interview not because of the intercession of a third party but because an application or a request for an interview has been made that recommends itself to the interviewer. For example, the résumé of a well-qualified job applicant may cross your desk and you're sufficiently impressed by the qualifications to agree to the meeting even though you're sure there's no likelihood of an immediate job opening. In this type of interview, you avoid the complications of disappointment and hard feelings by:

• *Clarifying the situation.* Disabuse your caller at once of any idea that there is a job opening.

• *Lending a sympathetic ear.* Obviously courtesy and pleasantness would be expected in a "courtesy interview." Knowing the uncertainties and difficulties of job-hunting, you understand that sympathy and the willingness to listen can be both welcome and helpful, in that it gives the job-hunter a chance to rehearse his or her presentation.

• *Being as helpful as you can.* Even though you have no job vacancy, there may be other forms of assistance you can offer such as leads to other companies or situations in which there may be a position of interest to the interviewee.

Or you may discover in the course of the conversation that your caller has not covered some areas of the job market that you feel might be worthwhile, for example: "With your experience in retailing, I feel you might be highly attractive to people in chain-store operations. Have you considered trying companies of that type?"

The special point to remember about the courtesy type of interview is that job-hunters need all the encouragement and considerate treatment they can get. Job-hunting can be an upsetting, bruising experience. Your consideration as well as your help represents thoughtfulness with a worthwhile purpose.

WHAT SHOULD BE DONE ABOUT AN INTERVIEW THAT IS GOING NOWHERE?

In some cases an interview has scarcely begun when you reach the conclusion that it's a waste of time to continue. It may be a hiring interview, for example, and the job applicant is clearly unsuitable. Is the cause of courtesy helped by your continuing the interview situation, or should you bring it to an abrupt halt?

The most considerate course is to permit the interview to proceed for an acceptable minimum of time. For example:

Joan Bradley is interviewing for a copywriter for her staff. Within seconds after the start of the interview, Bradley realizes that, despite a promising résumé, the applicant lacks experience in essential areas. Bradley continues to ask questions for about five minutes and then says, "Miss Payne, you have a very interesting résumé and a good deal of valuable experience, but I realize now that there are certain qualifications described in my ad which you don't have. I'll be happy to continue our conversation if you like, because I think that sometime in the future I might be able to use someone with your experience. However, I can tell you that the job I'm trying to fill now is not right for you." The choice of continuing or not continuing the conversation has now been given to the candidate, who at the very least would have to agree that the interviewer has been open and candid.

WHEN THERE IS A COMMUNICATION PROBLEM. In some cases the difficulty in the interview is not that the interviewer has made an evaluation or decision that precludes further conversation. Something like the following may occur:

Manager Tony Lee has called a subordinate into his office to try to find out the reasons for poor attendance. After several minutes of conversation, Lee realizes that whatever the reasons for the absences, the employee is not going to reveal them. Questions are eliciting one-word answers or evasive replies clearly intended to reveal little and to obscure as much as possible.

Here the interviewer should terminate the conversation. While you might not want to hurt the interviewee's feelings by suggesting that he or she is not telling the truth or is being evasive, it's probably desirable to make clear your dissatisfaction. Here are two ways to do it:

"Helen, our talk doesn't seem to be accomplishing very much. I don't know whether I haven't been asking the right questions or whether there is some trouble at your end. One way or the other, we don't seem to be getting anywhere. I suggest that we postpone this meeting until another time when perhaps we can communicate better. . . ."

"John, I've tried to explain that the purpose of this conversation will be helpful to both of us. Unfortunately what's been said so far doesn't seem to be getting us anywhere. I would suggest that you think some more about this problem and we'll get together tomorrow. Perhaps if we make a fresh start, we'll get better results. . . ."

WHAT IF THE INTERVIEWEE LIES?

You're talking to a job candidate and you ask, "How long were you with the X company?"

"Five years," the person answers.

You happen to know the answer is untrue. The job the candidate claims he had at that company just happens to have been held by someone you know up until three years ago.

Then the applicant shows you copies of some publications. You ask, "Are these feature stories of yours edited versions of the original?"

"No, I did all the final editing of my own copy."

You know that is not true, since you know the managing editor of the publication and how he works.

One or two other answers of the candidate suggest that you're getting a lot of misrepresentation and some outright lies. What is your best recourse?

In different types of interviews, the facts you get have different value. If, for example, your interview is essentially an investigation, actually a hunt for facts, lies usually have to be pinned down immediately. For example, a manager talking to an employee about a grievance should not permit a misstatement to go unchallenged: "Well, Ken, you said that your supervisor has kept you on that clean-up job for the past two months. I have checked the record and find you've only been on it for two weeks. Is the record incorrect?"

However, in a job interview you would probably want to proceed more cautiously. Here are two suggested courses:

• *Give the interviewee a chance to correct the record.* It's perfectly possible that the person you're talking to has unintentionally misstated a fact or misrepresented a situation. If it's a minor matter, you may decide to overlook it for the moment and check other sources later. However, in certain circumstances it may be possible for you to present the question in another way and give the interviewee an opportunity to clear up the misunderstanding. Of course, if he persists, you must be guided accordingly.

• *Say nothing.* In some cases the simplest course—the one leading to the least complications—is to seemingly accept whatever is said at face value. Of course such misrepresentation is of itself a major reason for ruling against the job candidate, and so you mentally take the candidate out of the running, conclude the interview at some appropriate point, and end with the usual "Thanks for coming in." And, to make clear chances are slight, you might add: "I don't want to hold out any false hopes. Several candidates have qualifications that are almost exactly what are needed. . . ."

OUT-OF-HAND EMOTIONS DURING AN INTERVIEW

There are some interviews in which considerable emotional stress arises. A supervisor investigating a feud between two employees may find himself confronted by high levels of anger, indignation, or perhaps a mixture of emotions that ends in tears.

What can an interviewer do when confronted by excessive emotionality? The first order of business may have to be a temporary shelving of the original purpose of the meeting. If possible, try to help the individual regain control and composure. If necessary, postpone the balance of your questioning for another time.

Sometimes, of course, it is not practical to discontinue your interview. In that case you want to reduce the emotion so that the business of the interview can go forward constructively. Help the individual control runaway emotions so that displays during the interview will not become an obstacle to a future good relationship. Often an employee who bursts into tears at what is considered the abuses and injustices of a supervisor will become so embarrassed that never again can he or she feel comfortable in the presence of the manager who witnessed this weakness.

It is a fairly reliable rule-of-thumb that the best way to deal with an excess of emotion—whether it be tears or anger—is to allow it to "ventilate" for a while and then gently try to "close it off." But *never* meet anger with anger. And never attempt to minimize someone else's emotional pain by making light of it.

WHAT DO YOU DO ABOUT THE FRANTIC APPEAL?

The interviewer may be taken off guard by a strong, emotion-laden response. For example, personnel director Paul Adams is conducting an exit interview. The employee is unfortunately an unreliable person who has been given several chances to make good in the job, and failed. Adams agrees with the supervisor's decision to let the employee go, but the employee, aware of the fact that Adams is a person of some authority in the company, suddenly begins a tirade against what he describes as the bias of his supervisor, describes his home situation in dire terms, and pleads with the personnel director to either give him his job back or find him another one with the company.

Adams has a difficult and uncomfortable situation to cope with. Every big business organization feels a certain amount of concern for the welfare of its employees. Few businesses are ever "strictly business." But what does concern for the employee's situation permit Adams to do in this case?

One thing that Adams should *not* do is tax the employee again with the reasons he is being fired. Simply repeating the old charges invites the employee to offer excuses and to make extravagant promises about reforming. From now on, he'll be a changed man, he avers. . . .

The main pitfall to avoid is a weakening of resolve. If your initial decision was arrived at fairly and thoughtfully, it would be a mistake to back down under this kind of pressure. You must remain firm, although you can demonstrate your personal concern by pointing out the sources for help that are available, everything from unemployment insurance, if the money situation is the one that is stressed, or health, legal, or other community services that might alleviate the circumstances the employee has described.

HOW DO YOU HANDLE A TURNDOWN?

"Don't call us, we'll call you." That's the classic ploy used by interviewers who generally have already decided that, in the case of a job interview, the applicant isn't the person they want.

Is it fair to give the individual false hope? That's the implicit promise of the "We'll call you" approach.

As a matter of fact, the interviewer who really is not ruling out a job candidate would do well to avoid the old cliché, which has been so much abused that it's taken as a brush-off.

In other words, if the applicant is still in the running, it's advisable that you use some conclusion other than the "Don't call us" sentence. You can use it, of course, if you add something like "This isn't just a line, Miss Smith. Your qualifications are quite impressive, and we are considering you for the position. It's just that there are still other people to interview. . . ."

Of course, you can avoid the cliché altogether by simply stating the fact: "Thank you, Mr. Jones. As you can imagine, there are other candidates in the running with you. As soon as we've made all our interviews, we'll notify all those involved."

In some cases, particularly those in which an applicant has been seen several times or been given some other indication of particular interest, you may say, "We'll be in touch with you in the next few days, and we'll let you know the outcome one way or the other."

Should you tell the applicant "No dice" then and there? What is the advisability of telling a job applicant that he or she has been ruled out in the course of the interview, that the unfavorable decision has already been made? Most experienced interviewers agree that if the mismatch is clear to both parties, there is nothing to be gained by pretense. However, many personnel people find that a face-to-face turndown can often be unnecessarily hard on the applicant. That explains the popularity of the "We'll let you know within a few days" conclusion. However, don't promise to notify someone if you have no intention of following through. A simple form letter can inform. There is an implicit helpfulness, as well as a courtesy, in this kind of feedback. It keeps the applicant from nursing false hopes and yet turns him or her down with dignity.

SHOULD YOU USE THE STRESS INTERVIEW?

For a while, stress interviews—creating pressures on the interviewee—were a highly favored testing device. Interviewers practiced such gimmicks as:

arranging to be interrupted at frequent intervals;

providing an uncomfortable seat for the interviewee;

asking blunt, challenging questions;

having two or more interviewers firing questions at the interviewee.

The theory of the stress interview is that it unsettles the outward calm of an interviewee, breaks down defenses to the point where he or she will talk more freely, will blurt out things that might otherwise not get said, and so on.

In certain more extreme instances, the stress user might put on a show of anger over something the applicant has said, to see how the individual would stand up to such browbeating.

None of the approaches above is acceptable interview procedure for the normal business situation. While the stress tool may have some utility in the hands of a qualified psychologist, it can be extremely dangerous in the hands of a nonprofessional. The mental pain and discomfort imposed by stress techniques, aside from being the very opposite of courtesy and consideration, may even result in misleading evidence. Remember it's quite possible that the person who caves in under a stress-interview situation might eat up pressure on the job. And the one who comes through with flying colors may be able to do so because the interview situation is, in a way, "make-believe."

RULES FOR THE INTERVIEWEE

Most rulebooks are full of guidance for the interviewer and not much practical help to the person being interviewed. Yet of the two it's the interviewee who is likely to be under greater pressure. And often it's the interviewee who has most at stake. Here are some key matters you should have under control before you approach the interview in order to leave you free to do your best:

• *What should you wear?* Good starting consideration. The answer is: dress as unobtrusively as possible—*unless* there's a reason to do otherwise. Here's what we mean:

The best rapport between two people is established when there are no distractions, either outside or inside the meeting room. Just as a loud din in a neighboring room can disturb your conversation, an outlandish hat, a garish tie, a peculiarly matched pants and jacket, a nonworking type of hairdo can get the interviewer puzzled, diverted, and thinking about the disturbing element rather than focusing on you and what you're saying.

However, there are circumstances when you might want to call attention to some article of your attire, either to set a keynote or to have it act as a conversation piece; that is, a conversation that you feel would be to your advantage. For example:

Dan Codway is applying for the job of skipper of a yacht. He's being interviewed by the owner, Ari Bucks. The would-be skipper appears with an open shirt and a string of sharks' teeth. Bucks bites, and asks about the necklace. Codway is off and running, describing the cruises on which he boated some oversize man-eaters. No doubt about his saltiness, and, having the other requisites for the job, he gets it.

A job applicant might want to make a point by wearing a Phi Beta Kappa key—or not wearing it, but showing it on the résumé.

Don't neglect to consider the nature of the job you're applying for. You may not be able to anticipate the likes and dislikes of the interviewer. But if you're applying for a job as secretary to a bank president, for example, you'd dress more conservatively than you would to audition for a role in a Broadway play. Man or woman, this is the situation in which you want to dress as attractively as possible. Wear your favorite (let's hope that also means most becoming) shirt or suit or dress. While no one was ever hired simply because he or she was dressed attractively, it certainly adds to the total impression. This doesn't mean dress *up*. Many people would hesitate to hire as a secretary someone who looks like a fashion model. And don't dress down. Most people would hesitate to hire as a model someone who looks frumpy.

• *How should you behave?* The traditional answer to this is graven in stone: act natural. Of course. But that doesn't quite cover it. For one thing, the interview situation is not "natural." As interviewee, you're being observed, tested, evaluated. "Acting natural" would mean that if you're naturally talkative, why, just let 'er rip. And if you tend to be economical with words, be so with the interviewer.

Clearly, both these "natural" behaviors could be undesirable. They don't help you, and they don't necessarily show the interviewer the most relevant aspects of your manner, attitudes, and abilities.

Of course, unnatural behavior of the variety that might be called "putting on an act" is also undesirable. If the interview is for any purpose other than hiring—anything from a "Let's-get-acquainted meeting" with a colleague or higher-echelon manager to a progress review—your best approach is to be open, direct, and friendly.

Since in the world of reality it's possible that you may be closeted with a person you dislike, mistrust, or even feel hostile toward, proper business behavior suggests that you be neutral—certainly, hide your negative feelings. If, once the conversation starts, the discussion leads into areas where your negative feelings must be expressed, do so in a nonattacking way:

In a disciplinary meeting: "Mr. Lane, I want to make it clear that, as I see it, you're completely misjudging my motives. Yes, I did get involved in an argument with Tod Brown, but I didn't do it because of a grudge. The fact is, I really felt his treatment of me at that particular moment was biased and unfair. . . ."

A salary discussion: "Miss Bond, I must tell you that I am having great trouble understanding the long delay in giving me the raise that was promised. So far, none of the reasons I've heard is sufficient justification. . . ."

• *Should you "take over"?* Some people are afraid to depart from direct responses to the interviewer's questions or leads. But in some cases this could result in an unfair disadvantage. There's no reason for you not to:

- try to steer the conversation into directions that will help you achieve your interview objectives;
- represent the facts, opinions, views that you hold in the most impressive or persuasive way possible.

Not every interviewer is as skilled as he should be. But passivity in the interviewee is neither attractive nor useful in the average interview. If you are tactful in turning the conversation to constructive avenues, the interviewer will be most willing to follow your lead and is likely to admire your initiative.

• *Should one always tell the truth?* This is a moral and ethical question and should not be answered on that basis here. As far as etiquette is concerned, however, the answer is yes, one should be truthful because not to do so violates the faith and trust of the other person and lays the groundwork for possible difficulties if the untruth is exposed.

• *May one tell "white lies"?* The concept of the "white lie" suggests an untruth that is either harmless or may even be intended to help another person—to avoid upsetting him or her, and so on. In the interview context, the "white lie" is the small exaggeration or distortion of fact that is generally intended to help oneself.

Possibly the most-used deception of this kind in a hiring interview is the rolling back of one's age when it is felt that the actual fact might be a drawback. However, since antidiscrimination laws do not now permit an interviewer to ask questions having to do with age, the need for such mild prevarication no longer exists. In general, whether or not you use the "white lie" in response to a question or in making a point becomes entirely a matter of conscience, not etiquette.

WHEN AN ORGANIZATION REPRESENTATIVE IS INTERVIEWED BY THE PRESS

From time to time, key people in your organization become candidates for interviews by the press. The medium may be a trade publication covering a new product, a town paper doing a feature on a local resident who has just won a contest, or a major news weekly planning a "special" on "this year's climate in a changing economy" as seen by one of your firm's executives.

Some managers, articulate though they are, become a little anxious at the prospect of facing an interrogating reporter. After all, in the normal state of affairs *they* ask the questions. However, here are some guidelines that can minimize the difficulties and make the situation productive:

• *Check policy.* When you are going to face the press, it's a good idea to check on company policy. Does the top person like seeing his or her name in print, or prefer to remain in the background? Does your superior favor the publicity you'll be getting? Is there a rule about a public-relations representative being present? The more thorough your preparation, the fewer potential regrets.

• *Have a good grasp of what's expected.* When an interview is requested, find out what the reporter's objectives are as fully as possible. Are they details on a new marketing campaign, a new product, views on the business climate? The simplest way is to ask: "What are you most interested in talking about?"

By knowing the general subject matter as well as a couple of the key questions, you can prepare for the interview and avoid inaccuracies or uncertainties.

• *Be well prepared.* Have on hand any hard facts related to the subject of the interview. Ditto for any pertinent descriptive or statistical material. This helps ensure accuracy as well as provide usable material for the interviewer.

One way to avoid being caught by surprise is to work up a list of questions that might come up. Then rehearse the answers.

In addition, if you are unfamiliar with the reporter's publication, read some back issues. This should give you a feel for what's wanted.

• *Advance the organization's view.* Obviously, the interview provides an opportunity for making the interviewee—and the organization—look good. Clarify in your own mind the assertions you can make in the subject area that favor the organization's image and policy.

• *Allow enough time.* Ask the reporter how much time will be needed, and set aside a little more. Sometimes an interview may take longer than expected. Rushing to wind it up can leave you answering questions hurriedly and being misquoted—or thinking you were.

• *Try to come up with "news."* Reporters are always looking for information that hasn't been widely reported or is new. You improve the chances of having your interview prominently played up if you can give the interviewer a fresh insight or new facts. The news can come, for example, from future company plans or from an unconventional opinion backed up with new information.

• *Don't feel you must answer every question.* Particularly if you are asked to comment on a controversial matter, tell the interviewer you're "studying that matter" or need more information before answering. Then you can decide later on and phone your answer—if it's wanted—as to how the questions should be handled. Avoid loaded questions such as "Did the product fail because of poor design, or was it inadequate market know-how?"

Don't hesitate to say "I don't know" if that's the case. Offer to find out, if the matter deserves a follow-up. And feel free to fall back on the traditional "No comment" if a question is raised that, for one reason or another, you don't want to answer. If the interviewer presses, you might say, "I'm sorry, but there is nothing I can tell you on that point that would be useful."

• *Beware of "off-the-record" remarks.* Far better than telling the interviewer something is "off-the-record" or "confidential" is to never say anything you don't want reported. Furthermore, never assume that an invisible line divides your informal conversation from the start of the formal interview. No such dividing line may exist in the interviewer's mind. The reporter's job is to get a good story, not to act as your counsel or guide.

Should you ask for a chance to see the copy or approve it before publication? Some reporters will refuse or put you off. But with others, where time permits, they may go along. But only do so when there is a reason—a delicate subject has been touched on.

And if after all that work you never appear in print, don't be too surprised. Not many reporters can be sure what their editors will consider a useful story.

TELEPHONE USAGE

MAKING THE TELEPHONE HUMAN

The telephone has been billed as the world's greatest nuisance and disturber of the peace—and/or the greatest communications medium and timesaver ever invented.

Our interest here is not to strengthen the place of the telephone in organization communications but simply to make suggestions that prevent it from becoming an instrument of frustration and torture. The etiquette of good phone usage can help you reap all the benefits of Alexander Graham Bell's brainchild, and avoid its unpleasantnesses.

SIMPLE RULES THAT HELP IN TELEPHONE COMMUNICATION

There are a handful of simple practices that have come to be accepted business behavior in day-to-day telephone use that both speed up communication and make it more satisfactory:

YOUR OWN NAME. Whether it's Auren Uris, John or Jane Smith, or something else, stating your name when you answer a call, particularly if no secretary or other person has picked it up first, helps person-to-person contact. (Of course, if you are handling the company switchboard, you answer with the firm's name.)

"WHO'S CALLING PLEASE?" If the caller doesn't give his name at once, feel free to interject this question. It's obviously essential for good communications.

"TO WHOM AM I SPEAKING?" Same as above.

"CAN YOU HOLD ON FOR JUST A MOMENT, PLEASE?" Either when the call first comes in or later on, there may be reason for you to ask the other person to hold on while you either look for some reference material or go off momentarily for some other reason. Whatever the situation, assure the other person that the delay will be brief. And, of course, try to keep it so.

"MAY I PUT YOU ON HOLD?" This is merely the mechanical equivalent of the item above. If you have a phone that is equipped with a hold button, be sure to let the other person know that you are going to use it.

"IS THIS A CONVENIENT TIME FOR YOU?" When you initiate the call, checking the other person's situation is a special sign of your thoughtfulness. In most cases, a phone call is an interruption for the other person. By checking the situation, you make it possible for the person to tell you if it's inconvenient.

"MAY I CALL YOU BACK LATER?" If in the course of your conversation you get the idea that the other person is not as free as you would like in order to continue your conversation, give him or her the opportunity to suggest a time for you to call back.

"I AM CALLING BECAUSE. . . ." As soon as possible after being connected to your party, and if there's any doubt about your purpose, state it as briefly as possible.

"CAN YOU HEAR ME CLEARLY?" In some cases, either because of a faulty connection or because you or the other person are not using the phone properly, there may be an audibility problem. If the conversation isn't going as you expected and you feel that you're not being heard properly, check for voice level. If you've asked the question but the trouble is at your end, the other person can then respond: *"I can hear you well enough, do you hear me?"*

It occasionally happens that a faulty connection does not clear up. In that case the person who initiated the call should suggest that the other person hang up and wait for the call to be put through again. This usually solves the matter of the poor connection.

"UH-HUH." This is a crucial sound in a telephone conversation, basically intended to encourage. It's in the very nature of the medium that, not being able to see each other, the parties don't know if they're being heard or understood, particularly when one person speaks at some length. One way this doubt can be resolved is for the other party to let the speaker know that he is being properly heard. You may say, "Yes, I understand," or comment in some specific way on the content of what's being said: *"Yes, I agree."* Or: *"That's right."* Or: *"Yes, I would have done the same thing."*

But since the purpose of much response is to simply indicate that the message is being received, "Uh-huh" is perfectly adequate.

Particularly when the other person is holding forth on a difficult or complicated subject, it's important that he or she be kept informed of your understanding and attention. Failure to use encouraging sounds or responses as suggested above not only would create an obstacle but would increase the speaker's hesitation.

HOW MANY RINGS BEFORE YOU PICK UP?

Business efficiency would suggest that the phone be picked up as soon as possible after the first ring. And, generally, that's a sensible rule. However, many subtle messages can be communicated by the length of time it takes to answer the phone. You should be aware of them and use the possibilities to your advantage.

For example, after three or more rings an uncomfortable feeling of doubt—or sometimes impatience—begins to build up on the part of the caller. If the phone call is actually an intrusion—say, for example, you have a visitor—picking it up on the third ring and completing a sentence before you say "Hello" is a clear signal to the caller. It then becomes a simple matter to beg off with a promise to call back later.

Of course, if you can't get to the phone in two rings—our recommended number—answer it as soon as you can therafter, and if you feel it's appropriate, you may explain: "My secretary was away from her desk." Or: "I was out in the hall and didn't hear the ring until I came around the corner. . . ."

WHEN YOUR CALL ISN'T WELCOME

From time to time it's necessary to phone someone who may not be particularly pleased to hear from you. One example: The recipient of your call has promised to do something that remains undone. Your call, even before you've said a word, is in the nature of a reproof.

Another example, widely prevalent in the business world: You and the caller have a different evaluation of the importance of your call. If you're a salesman trying to get to see a company executive, *you* may feel that it's very much to the other person's interest to accept your call, even though this is not the recipient's view.

The etiquette aspect of this problem lies in the potential for discourtesy and exacerbated feelings at both ends of the phone connection. The key point is to proceed in such a way as to avoid being manipulative—for example, by misrepresenting the purpose of the call—and to avoid being insensitive by being aware of the attitude you face at the other end.

Here are the means that can make your phone call both acceptable in terms of etiquette and effective in achieveing your objective:

• *Getting secretarial cooperation.* Be sympathetic to the secretary's role. Every secretary's job is to screen the boss from unwanted visitors and callers. "If Mr. White calls, tell him I'm not in" is a common directive.

If you're Mr. White and it immediately becomes clear that you won't be put through to the person you're calling, you have three choices:

HANG UP AND SEND YOUR MESSAGE BY MAIL. At least you'll have a record and might very well get a written response that will move the matter along.

LEAVE A MESSAGE ASKING THE PERSON TO CALL BACK AT HIS OR HER CONVENIENCE. What often happens, if the person doesn't call back shortly, is that you call a second time, and then you do get a response.

PUT YOUR REQUEST TO TALK TO THE OTHER PERSON IN SUCH A WAY THAT THE SECRETARY WILL RELAY THE MESSAGE so that the target person will either pick up the phone ("Just a minute, Mr. Green just came into the office") or will call back soon. What can you say that will get such a response? Basically, you state that what you have is of sufficient importance to warrant Mr. Green's time: "I have some news for Mr. Green that I'm sure he'd want to hear."

• *Your tone of voice can make a difference.* When you do get the person you want to talk to on the line, keep your voice pleasant, direct, businesslike. The person who comes on too strong usually puts off his listener. And the ingratiating tone can be equally unacceptable.

• *Stress a benefit.* As soon as you can, tell the person at least one thing he'll gain from your call. Even a person who's trying to collect a debt can say: "Mr. Green, if I can have just a minute of your time, I'll explain how we can handle your bill in a way that will make it easier for you to take care of it." What you have in mind may be a part payment or some other procedure, but you've made your point.

• *Keep it low-pressure.* If the conversation lasts for one minute or ten, maintain the pleasant manner you used at the start. If you *are* a bill collector and the account is badly in arrears, you can talk of the consequences, if you like, in a matter-of-fact, nonthreatening tone.

WHEN YOU DON'T WANT TO TALK TO THE PERSON WHO'S CALLING

If your secretary says, "Mr. Henry Jones is calling," and you don't want to talk to Henry Jones, there are a number of ways of responding without any discourtesy:

ASK YOUR SECRETARY TO TAKE A MESSAGE. For example, "Mr. Butler is in a meeting just now. I'll be glad to give him your message when he's free. What would you like me to tell him?"

ASK YOUR SECRETARY TO PUT THE CALLER OFF EITHER TEMPORARILY OR PERMANENTLY. Examples (temporarily): "Mr. Butler will be completely tied up for the next week. Please call anytime after next Monday." Or (permanently): "Mr. Butler has asked me to tell you that he is definitely not interested in your proposal. . . ."

In this connection, there are a number of standard and perhaps frustrating responses: "Mr. White is out of town, and I'm not quite sure when he'll be coming back." Or: "He is in a meeting." Or: "He's out of the office, and I don't know when he'll be back."

IS STALLING PERMISSIBLE?

There are some business situations in which you want to put off talking to a caller. This is quite different from wanting the caller to understand that you aren't available, and probably never will be, to his or her call.

The question is: Is the stall ever an acceptable means of responding to a phone call? Although the stall—which is an evasion of the call without a definite turndown—is common practice, it is generally frustrating and demeaning to the caller and accordingly should be used only under the most unusual circumstances.

It should not be used if there is no positive reason for keeping the business of the call unresolved. For example, a candidate who's been interviewed for a job keeps calling to find out what his chances are. If the caller has been ruled out of the running or another candidate has finally been chosen, it's common courtesy to let the caller know that the opening is no longer available. Your own discomfort at explaining the reasons is not an adequate excuse for failing to impart the news.

HANDLING THE NUISANCE CALL

Sometimes you find yourself picking up the phone and you're stuck in a conversation with someone who is essentially wasting your time. Despite a few tentative efforts, the caller hangs on and continues to talk to you about a matter in which you're just not interested.

It's a misinterpretation of the canons of business courtesy to feel that you're obliged to listen while someone rattles on and wastes your time. There are several devices you have available to you. While they all require that you be blunt, in this case forthrightness is warranted. Here are some of the things you can do:

"I'M SORRY TO HAVE TO INTERRUPT YOU, BUT. . . ." Your explanation can be either real or fanciful. For example, you may say, "I have to rush off to catch a train [or plane, or see my boss]," or whatever. No recording angel is going to give you bad marks for a white lie that ends your discomfort, saves your time, and calls a halt to a rambling conversation or presentation or whatever that was going to be fruitless eventually anyhow.

SUM UP WHAT'S BEEN SAID. In some cases you want to make sure you understand what the other person is driving at. In this case you may say, "Mr. Butler, do I understand that you're calling about the X matter?"

This may not solve the situation because Mr. Butler may be canny and realize that if he simply assents, you may then be able to say, "I'm sorry but I'm not handling that," and hang up. So he may say, "No, not exactly," and then go on to another tack, but then this is the cue for saying, "Mr. Butler, I have very little time. Can you tell me in one or two sentences exactly what it is you're calling me about?"

If he responds to your satisfaction, you can then say that you are not interested, thank him, and hang up. But if he persists in being vague, you can then legitimately say, "I'm sorry, Mr. Butler, I've run out of time. I suggest that you write me a letter." Then hang up.

THE CALL-BACK YOU MAY NOT WANT TO MAKE

It's a common executive experience. You get back to your office and you're told that a Mr. Zilch phoned and asked that you call him back.

You ask your secretary what it is about, and she says, "I don't know, he didn't say." If your secretary means "he didn't say" because she didn't ask him, you might remind her that she should try to get unknown callers to state their business. You may drive this message home by asking him or her to phone and find out what the caller's business was.

However, if the caller refused to explain the purpose of the call, you'd be perfectly justified in not calling back. You're under no obligation to return a "mystery" phone call.

Generally there are two reasons for "never getting around to" returning a phone call:

EXCESSIVE PRESSURE. You almost literally don't have a moment to use for anything other than important matters at hand. Lack of time added to the fact that you know that the matter at the other end is not too important may mean that the person's request that you call back just doesn't get satisfied.

UNPLEASANTNESS OR DIFFICULTY. Another common reason for

failing to call back is that the message you have to convey will represent a blow to the caller or draw an argument that you'd rather avoid.

Both reasons can be understood sympathetically, but they are
unacceptable. Facing up to the situation—biting the bullet, as it
were—has the virtue of shortening the period of discomfort. The
problem here clearly does not stem from the medium itself. The
difficulty is one's hesitation about precipitating an abrasive situation
or, in the first instance, reluctance to take time out from a job of high
priority for a matter that's considered unimportant. You'd be helping
both yourself and the other person if, in the first case, you or your
secretary explained the reason for your nonavailability and either
suggested a later time when you would be free or possibly turned
the matter over to an assistant.

And where your indecision is due to reluctance to precipitate an
argument or other diverse reaction, it's far better to work out a plan
of action that will end the situation one way or the other rather than
prolong it and risk aggravating abraded nerves.

WHEN A SECRETARY MAKES A CALL FOR HIS OR HER BOSS

From time to time the telephone becomes the stage for a wres-
tling match. It may not be marked by grunts and groans, but the
conflict can nevertheless be quite intense. Here's the way it goes:

Executive A. asks his secretary to call executive B. and not put
him (executive A.) on the line until executive B. is already there. This
means that as far as executive B. is concerned, executive A.'s secretary has called and said, "Mr. B., Mr. A. is calling. Hold on, please."

At this point, a big status battle has been waged, won, and lost.
A key player not mentioned at this point is executive B.'s secretary.
Possibly because she is young and inexperienced, she has failed to
respond to protect Mr. B.'s status. Instead of putting Mr. B. on the
line, as she has, her proper play should have gone along these lines:

Executive A.'s secretary: "Hello, Mr. A. calling Mr. B. Would you
please put him on the line?"

Executive B.'s secretary: "Put Mr. A. on the line, and I'll have Mr.
B. pick up."

Now if A.'s secretary goes along with this counterattack, A. has
lost the battle. This war of the secretaries is a silly charade that
executives can avoid quite simply.

If you are executive A. calling executive B., it's all right to have
your secretary make the call, but then, as soon as B.'s secretary has
indicated that B. will accept the call, you get on and hold for the few

seconds that ordinarily are required. Similarly, if you are B. receiving the call and you're told that executive A. is on the line, respond as soon as possible to minimize the delay. Anything else is playacting and demeaning both to the person who initiates it and the person victimized by it.

IF YOU USE A TAPE MACHINE FOR RECEIVING CALLS

In certain situations people in business use a tape recorder that "answers" telephone callers. Professional people frequently do this—people in one-man or -woman businesses, and so on. If you use such a device, be kind to your caller. If you record the answering message yourself, use as pleasant a tone as possible. You may also want to add a word of apology or explanation for your absence. Also make it clear at the very outset that the caller is hearing a recording.

Here's a typical message that includes the elements that make for courtesy and a certain amount of friendliness: "This is John Smith with a recorded statement. Unfortunately I am out of the office at the moment, but I'll be glad to get back to you promptly. When you hear the beep, please give me your name and phone number and, if you like, a brief statement of why you're calling. Thank you."

Of course, your voice should be as pleasant as you can make it. Telephone experts suggest that you smile and gesture when making your recording so as to "humanize" the quality of the message.

WHEN YOU USE AN ANSWERING SERVICE

In addition to tape recording, another expedient for business people who must be away from their offices from time to time is to engage an answering service to handle their incoming calls.

A survey of this type of service shows there is a very wide range in quality, from excellent to atrocious. The well-run answering service uses courteous, intelligent people who answer promptly, give whatever message the subscriber wants them to deliver, and will then take messages to pass along.

But at the other end of the scale, the poorly run services employ poorly trained and apparently poorly motivated people. Undesirable results range all the way from discourtesy and general unpleasantness to garbled messages and, perhaps worst of all, failure to pass the message along to the subscriber at all.

The cost of the service doesn't always make the difference between good and bad. One suggestion: if you use a telephone answering service, call your own number once or twice and evaluate the way your inquiry is being taken care of. By using a fictitious name, you can also check to see whether messages are being relayed to you—failure to do this is a particularly common and serious weakness of some services.

HOW TO INTERRUPT

In general, interruptions are seldom welcome. By their very nature they tend to interfere with an ongoing activity or conversation. And yet they are often necessary, either because of the urgency of the interrupter's message or to spare him or her the embarrassment of waiting passively while an ongoing matter—sometimes of little import—continues.

Unlike the popular song that suggests it's not what you do but the way that you do it, in the case of interrupting, it's both *what* you say and *how* you say it that matter.

In many situations, interrupting gracefully is quite simple: Sylvia Jones walks to the doorway of a colleague who is carrying on a phone conversation. She conveys with gestures the fact that she wants to cut into the conversation.

The colleague says to the person at the other end of the phone, "Hold on a moment." Then: "What's up, Sylvia?"

"Sorry to cut in on you like this," Sylvia says, "but I have Hank on long distance from London, and he wants to know whether our report will be in the mail by the end of the week. . . ."

Sylvia Jones's interruption consists of three elements:

- getting the attention of the other party;
- an apology;
- a message made as brief as possible.

Interruptions that incorporate these three elements are generally acceptable. However, there are circumstances where even the most gracefully made interruption must be turned down. . . .

WHEN YOU REFUSE TO ACCEPT AN INTERRUPTION

In some cases the business at hand may be of greater priority or importance than the matter on the mind of the interrupter. Then the problem becomes: How do you interrupt the interrupter? Note this example:

Henry Larsen is speaking to a consultant who has been sent down by the front office. There's a knock at his door and it's opened by a colleague.

"Sorry, I didn't know you had company. May I ask you? . . ."

"That's all right," says Henry Larsen, "but I'm tied up. May I get back to you later in the afternoon?"

It's desirable for two reasons to put off the would-be interrupter courteously. Even if you're annoyed—and justifiably—hide your negative feelings as much as possible, not only to save the face of the interrupter but for the sake of your visitor as well, who may feel uncomfortable if a sharp rebuke is given for which he may feel partially responsible.

FROM APOLOGIES TO WELCOME: THE MEDIUM IS PART OF THE MESSAGE

In business, etiquette as well as good communications requires a whole range of exchanges that center on feelings. You want to apologize for an oversight or express gratitude for a favor done. Or sometimes a communication from a colleague, superior, or subordinate requires some kind of response—acknowledgment of a request, for example.

Messages of this type can be given either orally (face-to-face or by phone) or in writing.

When a message can be delivered either in writing or in person, most people have an automatic preference for the medium that is easiest for them to handle. Often, there is no "right" or "wrong" about the choice. However, there can be advantages in one method over the other, depending upon the circumstances. For example, you *can't* pat someone on the shoulder or shake his or her hand in a written memo, nor can you, face-to-face, put your message in a permanent form that makes it possible for the recipient to show it to others or keep it as a cherished memento or merely "for the record."

The following lists can help you make the choice between the spoken or written word:

Advantages

1. Spoken Word

- It's more immediate, more personal.
- The listener gets not only your meaning but your expression to reinforce it as you speak.

- You can be spontaneous and "speak from the heart."
- Your personal presence can be a factor. You can smile, shake the person's hand, register by the tone of voice the degree of your feelings.

2. Written Word

- The recipient has a permanent record.
- The message can be read and reread.
- The message can be retained "for the record."
- The writer can consider and reconsider the message carefully.

Disadvantages

1. Spoken Word

- Once delivered, the message disappears.
- It's sometimes difficult to find an appropriate time or, for that matter, the privacy that may be desired.
- Some people find themselves uncomfortable in this kind of face-to-face confrontation.
- The occasion may be important enough to warrant a somewhat lengthy and detailed statement that if spoken may be laborious and sound stilted.

2. Written Word

- For some people, it's more difficult to write than to speak.
- Writing skill may be required for anything other than a routine statement.
- If written poorly, even the most heartfelt sentiment may sound cold and impersonal.

As we've said, you have a choice of the spoken versus the written word. Since the content of this type of message, whether spoken or written, tends to be the same, it is felt that it can be more helpful to provide samples of written messages. For these samples and the range of such personal messages—acknowledgments, invitations, expressions of gratitude and so on—see Chapter 3, page 128, "Memos on Key Topics."

3

The Written Word

Business writing comprises a range as broad as the novel, with requirements as demanding as those of poetry. The variety of forms includes letters, memos, reports, special presentations. But whatever the form, the business setting creates special cautions that should be kept in mind whenever you put words on paper. The very quality that makes the written word effective—its permanence, its inflexibility—means that whatever is committed to writing must pass the test of time and, possibly, changed circumstances.

An ill-conceived interoffice memo to a colleague can rise to haunt you at a later date. An imprudent word or thought to a corporate "enemy" may forever stand in the way of an improved relationship. On the positive side are the countless occasions when writing can convey messages of grace and consideration that can help a person in distress or help a career.

The guidance in this section is aimed to improve effectiveness with the written word. For example, you'll be sensitized to avoidance of obsolete "courteous" forms—the "Your-obedient-servant" type of wording—and alerted to the many opportunities to help feelings and improve relationships.

TWO ASPECTS OF BUSINESS WRITING

In general, two aspects of writing are to be considered:

FORM. This takes in everything from the type of stationery you use to how you sign your name.

CONTENT. This has to do with the ideas and sentiments you express. Although openness and directness are important virtues when it comes to communication, the etiquette of business writing sometimes suggests a circumspection that can minimize the hurt of an unpleasant message or save the face of an individual who is on the verge of losing it. Here are specific considerations that take in both aspects of business writing.

BUSINESS STATIONERY

The mysterious word "paperwork" used in business suggests vague masses of documents, notes, and so on that ebb and flow over executive desks. A great deal of the paper consists of printed business letterheads or less formal sheets meant primarily for interoffice use.

To most companies, the design of their letterhead is an important part of the corporate image that is projected to the public. Accordingly, a good deal of care is devoted to the physical details involved in designing and printing the company name and related data. And sometimes a symbol or trademark—a logogram, or logo for short—is used for both stationery and business cards.

ELEMENTS TO BE INCLUDED IN A LETTERHEAD

The letterhead, not only to make the proper impression but to be most helpful to the recipient, should bear:

- the company name and logogram (if one exists);
- an identifying designation, such as "A subsidiary of the X Company";
- the department name, if desired—for example, "Public Affairs Department";
- the address, including town or city, state, and zip code;
- the telephone number;
- the cable address, if there is one.

The choice of a company letterhead is usually done by top management. As everyone knows who has been in on a discussion of letterhead design, eventually the choice is based on either one man's opinion or a consensus as to what "looks best."

ASSESSING THE CHARACTER OF AN ORGANIZATION'S LETTERHEAD

For the most part, a letterhead should be designed or selected on the basis of the "feel," the character that it projects. Such decisions as to whether it should be printed or engraved and the exact tone and color of the paper to be used fall into this category. It may be considered desirable that the letterhead conform to the style or quality of the respective industry or specific organization. For example:

Stationery selected by law firms or accounting firms has a dignified, regal, conservative look. A land-development firm might feel that something more showy and flamboyant would be more appropriate. (See sample letterheads, starting on page 108.)

In some cases, precisely because there is an industrywide style, an organization that wants to stand out will adopt a letterhead that is different and distinctive. This is a way of asserting individuality.

One of the factors that set a style is the tendency to repeat someone else's success. For example, a young firm, to establish its solidity and dependability, will emulate the letterhead style of an established industry leader. However, such "copying" may be seen as undesirable since it makes for a duller rather than a brighter corporate image.

Some letterheads are designed to fit the requirements established by typing practices; that is, margins are prescribed or desired to be of a specific width, and accordingly the name of the company must be within those margins so that the typewritten message does not project awkwardly outside the name of the company.

However, conforming to this visual prescription is a holdover from the past when letters were supposed to conform to a margin of one and a half inches on the left and one inch on the right. Nowadays, practices are more flexible. Such matters as margins and placement of elements of letters are altered to suit taste.

Another convention: letters were supposed to end two inches from the bottom of the sheet before the signature. All these practices are traditional, and at one time any deviation was considered not only ugly but also impolite. But letterhead design has changed greatly in recent years. Contemporary letterheads are quite different in appearance from those that represent the tastes of twenty or thirty years ago.

As some of the samples in the following pages show, the placement, type size, and design may be greatly varied, part of the type even being placed at the bottom of the sheet.

All the variables, from type size and design to color and sheet size of the paper, are likely to fare best with the guidance of experienced printers or designers. Since the organization name and its presentation to the public—by means of the letterhead, among other ways—is often considered crucial, original design or the updating of an antiquated one deserves special care. (See page 106 for further insight into the cost and thought that may go into the design of a company logogram.)

SHEET SIZE, COLOR, AND PAPER QUALITY

Almost all business stationery is white. Occasionally, organizations will permit themselves the latitude of an off-white, verging on the gray or beige. Color on a letterhead is usually confined to the printed name or logo.

The quality of paper is another consideration to be carefully made. Thin, flimsy paper with what printers call "show-through" (printing showing through the other side of the sheet) should be avoided. And many practical-minded companies avoid paper with surfaces that make erasure difficult. It can save considerable time and money if a typist can neatly erase a minor error. Letters with a single, barely perceptible erasure are generally acceptable in business. Anything more obvious should not be sent out, since it insults the recipient, in addition to suggesting the sender's low standards.

Two standard sizes of sheets are appropriate for business use. One is the 8½ x 11-inch sheet, which fits into the traditional file folder and neatly into a regular business envelope when folded into thirds. The other is the so-called monarch size, a sheet measuring 7½ x 10½ inches, for which suitably sized envelopes must be provided. All business envelopes should carry the company name and address.

THE EXECUTIVE'S PERSONAL OFFICE STATIONERY

Most executives have letterheads in either of the above sizes that, in addition to the company name, feature their name and related information:

> Special Services Department
> Graphics and Materials
> J. R. Henley, Manager

In some instances, the executive's name is prominently printed, while the company name, address, and so on are subordinated to it. (See sample, page 113.)

If the executive's position is not printed, the secretary may include it when he or she types the name below the signature. If the name and position are printed, there is no need for the name to be typed in connection with the signature.

WHEN TO USE THE INFORMAL NOTE

Generally you have a choice of sheets on which to do your communicating:

THE FORMAL BUSINESS LETTERHEAD. This is used for almost all outside correspondence—messages to customers, suppliers, business contacts of all kinds. In some cases, especially where the company letterhead also has your name and title, it may be used for informal messages within a company. For example, the branch manager of one plant may want to send a message to an executive in another part of the company. If these individuals have never met personally, the formal stationery would be proper.

INFORMAL PRINTED LETTERHEADS. Many executives have preprinted stationery, usually half-sheet size—5 x 8, for example, or 4 x 6—with some such message as "From the desk of . . ." or simply the individual's name. These sheets are acceptable for brief informal messages, either handwritten or typed. However, they should bear the date and either be hand-initialed or signed by the originator.

THE BLANK SHEET. Where the informal notepaper is not available, for informal messages it's sometimes necessary to use plain sheets of paper ranging anywhere in size from a 3 x 5 to a full 8 x 10 sheet. For brief messages and queries, these are acceptable. For example:

Andy,
     Is our meeting for Monday morning still O.K.? If so, see you at ten-thirty in the Conference Room. Please confirm.

                                                                          Bill

However, blank sheets have an impromptu quality that is generally undesirable. If you use them often, it's likely you need some informal stationery. Where the organization does not provide it, executives often procure their own, usually a simple preprinted pad carried by most stationers.

TIP-ONS. People who pass along printed material often use a small sheet—3 x 4 or 3 x 5—made even more helpful with their name printed at top or bottom. This is paper-clipped to the conveyed material, with the briefest of messages—"For your information" (FYI)—and signed with the sender's initials. Saves time, paper, and doesn't obscure the first page of the material—as would be the case with a large sheet.

PRINTED ANNOUNCEMENTS

Some formal and impersonal messages may be communicated by means of a completely preprinted card or letter. A firm that is changing the location of its offices or a well-known or key executive joining an organization may make the facts known by means of a brief printed card. There is generally no need to specify the recipient in any way. For example:

> *The XYZ Company*
> *Members: New York Stock Exchange*
> *announce*
> *The opening of additional offices at*
> *999 Main Street*
> *Los Angeles, California*
> *for the convenience of our California clientele*
> *to assist in closer contact with their representative*

USING A SELF-MAILER

Some executives use an efficient medium that although in a sense forces the recipient to reply in a specific way, still makes up for this rigidity by its effectivensss. This is the so-called self-mailer, in which the message is presented in such a form that the reply can be indicated with a checkmark, Yes/No, or whatever. Here's an example:

Frank Amster, Vice-President of Kayline Products, will be paying us a visit on Friday, January 21. He would like to meet key people in Engineering and Production. Please indicate below what time period would suit your schedule best.

/ / between 11 A.M. and 12 noon
/ / lunch
/ / between 1:30 and 2:30 P.M.
/ / between 2:30 and 3:30 P.M.
Other?_____
Soon as possible, please

Pat Masters

This self-mailer technique is particularly useful when:
• *You want to obtain fast replies from others within the depart-ment or within the company.*
• *You need 100 percent response.* Most people tend to complete a fast check-off form more easily than one that involves the time and thought that goes into an open-ended reply.
• *You are asking a number of people the same question.* It then becomes easier to tabulate the responses or plan a schedule, as shown in the example.
• *The answers you're looking for can be categorized* ("Yes" or "No," for example) or put into *numerical form* (0–25, 26–50, 51–75, and so on).

PITFALLS OF LOGO DESIGN: THROUGH A HUMORIST'S EYES

What's in a name? Shakespeare's line is taken with great serious-ness by business. To that question they would respond with an idea from Friedrich Nietzsche—that it is a name that gives a thing visibil-ity and substance. And business executives have found that a visual symbol is a useful way to give their organizations quick identification and memorability.

In the search for an appropriate logo, organizations have spent hundreds of thousands of dollars. In connection with one such hunt, columnist Art Buchwald did a piece that, while humorous, conveys the type of thinking that goes into such design. Buchwald's fan-tasy—excerpted here—is, of course, a distortion, but the intensity of the search is real enough:

NBC came up with a new logo a few weeks ago after hiring a research company for what is reported to have been $750,000. It turned out to be the letter "N." Much to their horror and surprise the NBC big shots discovered that the Nebraska Educational Television Network was using the same N which they had developed for less than $100. The only difference in the design was the NBC's N was red and blue while Nebras-ka's was all red. Everyone was laughing at NBC, but it's not very funny.

Selecting a new logo for anything is a very serious business, as I discovered when I decided to change the one on this column.

I went to Cratcher and Thumb, the industrial designers, and gave them the problem. "The logo on my column seems old-fashioned and not up to date. I would like you to design a new one which would look modern and catching to the eye."

Cratcher said, "We can do it, but it's not going to be cheap."

Four months later we had the big meeting in Cratcher and Thumb's private screening room.

The lights were dimmed and the first slide was flashed on the screen.

It was a large A superimposed over a large B.

"How do you like it?" Cratcher asked.

"It's not bad," I admitted, "but is this the image we want to give? It seems to me the B dominates the A. Don't you think both letters should be the same size?"

"Yes, we do," said Thumb. "That's why we threw that one out and came up with this one." He buzzed for the next slide.

I studied it closely. Finally I said, "The A and B are the same size, but they seem awfully small."

"You're very observant," said Cratcher. "Thumb and I caught that as soon as the artist showed it to us. So we came up with this radical idea which I'm sure will knock you dead."

The next slide just showed the letter B.

"Where's the A?" I asked.

"That's just it," Thumb said. "Everyone is going to say where's the A? It will call attention to the logo and you'll double your readership."

Cratcher said, "Look at NBC. They have only an N. One-letter logos are the wave of the future."

"Well, why can't it be an A then instead of a B? . . ."

"It's amazing how our thinking runs along the same lines. Here is a left-legged A. We tested it in 2000 supermarkets and everyone knew it was you right away."

"Gosh, you fellows did a great job. What do I owe you?"

Thumb said, "$635,000, including the cost of the art materials."

"Why," I said surprised, "that's $100,000 less than NBC paid for its logo."

"That's because your name started with an A," Cratcher said. "The further along in the alphabet you go, the harder it is to design a letter." *

Executives at NBC are prepared to defend the price they had to pay for the logo, even though the amount Buchwald quotes may not be quite on the mark.

* By permission of Art Buchwald.

SAMPLE LETTERHEADS

Practically the first thing a company does when it comes into existence is to have stationery printed. For small organizations, this usually means a trip to the local printer and a selection of paper, type style, size, and layout made on the basis of what the shop has available. But larger organizations put considerably more thought—and money—into the project.

Here are a number of letterheads, ranging from those of our giant corporations to some that are less well known, but which nevertheless put considerable effort into the project.

The executive who submitted this sample wrote: "This Du Pont letterhead has been in use as long as I can remember." The company name in the ellipse is a logo that is used wherever appropriate and, as shown below, is used advantageously with more modern type faces.

In some cases, a logo has been designed and used so effectively that it identifies the organization without the need for the company name—even though it may seldom be used that way. For example:

Car fanciers the world over recognize the Mercedes-Benz symbol.

This symbol is associated with the Bell System by consumers and business people alike.

This representation of the Rock of Gibraltar is the logo of the Prudential Insurance Company.

The sans-serif type used for the company name, in conjunction with the logo, is simple and dignified. The logo, of course, is known throughout the world because of the company's distribution in world markets. Another consideration: any elaborate typeface for the company name would have clashed with the logo.

Here is an interesting "before-and-after" pair of letterheads. The top one was replaced in 1972 when Exxon changed its name to unify

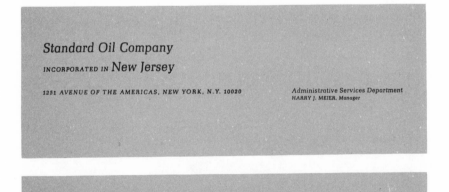

a broad range of locations and activities. No exact figure is available for the cost of the name change, but it can be put well into the millions, since everything from building signs to bill heads had to be redone. A company representative says, "There are several variations on the basic design for use by different divisions of the corporation, and certain of our affiliates have different designs to accommodate their specific objectives. However, this sample conveys the basic change in corporate identity that accompanied our name change."

McGraw-Hill, Inc.

1221 Avenue of the Americas
New York, New York 10020
Telephone 212/997-2825

Public Affairs Department

This large publishing firm uses a clean, unpretentious type for its name and related data, which gives increased impact to its unique logogram.

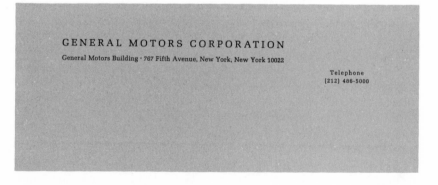

GENERAL MOTORS CORPORATION
General Motors Building · 767 Fifth Avenue, New York, New York 10022

Telephone
(212) 486-5000

This letterhead is an excellent example of a creative graphic idea; namely, when you're one of the largest corporations in the world, you can't easily represent this fact by any degree of size or type design, no matter how intricate. What to do? Be as simple as you can.

CUC

COMPUTER USAGE DEVELOPMENT CORPORATION

3121 Richmond Avenue, Houston, Texas 77006 | 713/526-3503

A striking logo and a simple layout of a modern typeface ties in with the technical nature of the firm's basic activity.

Fujita Design, Inc. 110 East 59th Street, New York, N.Y. 10022 (212) PL 2-5341

This is the letterhead Neil Fujita, a well-known designer, devised for his own use. Note the offbeat placement and the unusual manner in which the name of the enterprise is treated.

The following is a notable example of a letterhead that provides more material than the average one. In this case, the list of people helps fill an information gap and gives the publication substance that might otherwise require considerable explanation.

Public Relations News
The International Public Relations Weekly For Executives

Denny Griswold, Founder & Editor   127 East 80th Street, New York, N.Y. 10021 (212) 879-7090 Cable Address: PUBRELNEWS NEWYORK

PROUD TO SERVE PR

Barbara Whitmore

Directing Editor
The Research Institute of America, Inc.
589 Fifth Avenue, New York, N.Y. 10017

Here is an example of an executive's personal use of her company's insignia. The scriptlike type is a traditional one, here used by a well-known business publisher. Notable is the manner and degree to which the material at the right—including the corporate crest —has been subordinated to the executive's name.

LETTERS OF INTRODUCTION

Increased informality and greater use of the telephone have made letters of introduction less important than they once were. The occasion for which they are still used is for the job-hunter—or the traveler—who is attempting to penetrate circles in which he or she is not known, or to establish an identity in a new milieu. The purpose of this type of letter is to introduce one person or a group of people to others. An effective communication of this type should avoid excessive length and should be to the point. Preferably it should be typed on a company or organization letterhead. Here are some examples:

Jacob Foster & Sons

ANIMAL FOODS AND AGRICULTURAL PRODUCTS

Route 3, Loganburgh, Pennsylvania

Hedley and Smith
Leicester Square
London, England

Gentlemen:
    This is to introduce Mr. William Phipps, our European field representative, in the hope that you may be able to offer him some

assistance. Mr. Phipps is making a study of agricultural practices in Great Britain, and it would be greatly appreciated if you could furnish him with information that would get him started in this undertaking.

Sincerely,

The Forward Company

7000 CENTRAL AVENUE, CHICAGO, ILLINOIS

Mr. Edgar Worthy
Kuzmich Engineering Company
Laurel Drive, Oakland, California

Dear Mr. Worthy:

Ms. Gladys Lee has been with us for three years and is a highly qualified draftsperson. For personal reasons she has found it necessary to move to the West Coast in your general area. It occurs to me that there might be mutual advantages in your considering her background and capabilities as a basis for her employment by your company. Of course, if this is not possible at this time, perhaps you can offer some helpful suggestions that could help her resume her career.

I would personally appreciate any assistance you can offer Ms. Lee. Meanwhile, should you or any of your staff be coming east, I would enjoy the opportunity for another one of our business-and-dinner evening get-togethers.

Cordially,

Letters of introduction are not to be given too freely, should not make requests, or impose excessively on the good nature, the time, or the capabilities of the addressee. As in the above letter, you may want to make favorable comments about the capabilities, character, experience, and so on of the subject of the letter. However, remember that there is a difference between a letter of introduction and the kind of communication that is called a "reference," where the sole purpose is to help an individual get a job.

LETTERS OF REFERENCE

People are often called upon to write references for those who, for one reason or another, are leaving an organization. A preliminary decision you must make: whether or not to write such a letter and what its tone should be. Here are some rules for making these decisions. Never write a testimonial for an individual that hides or disguises a major fault. Under no circumstances, for example, should you write a favorable reference for someone who has been fired for dishonesty, destructiveness, and so on. It's desirable for the writer to have known the individual involved for some time, and to have adequate knowledge of his or her qualifications and abilities.

In some cases, letters of reference are requested from top people in an organization by an intermediary. In other words, a middle-management executive may ask his boss to write a reference for a subordinate. The obvious reason for such a request is that the president's signature on such a letter will carry more weight than the lower-echelon executive's.

If you're asked to write this kind of letter, remember that your name may indeed carry considerable weight and succeed in getting the individual a position. You may find that you are later held responsible for that person's performance. Accordingly, it is suggested that if you consent to having such a letter sent out over your name, you take the time and trouble involved to assure yourself of the worthiness of the individual.

Here are two letters of reference, one brief but adequate, the other with the obvious intention of "selling" an individual and the desirability of her employment. No need to use the outdated "to-whom-it-may-concern" form of address. Since the purpose of a testimonial letter is clear and aboveboard, you can get right down to business:

United Machine Tools

DETROIT, MICHIGAN

Mr. Paul (Andy) Anderson was a member of our field selling staff for five years. We found him to be a man of honesty, energy, imagination, and initiative. He is leaving our employment with mutual regrets. We would prefer to keep him in our employ, of course, but the health of his wife has made it necessary for him to move to what is for her a more benign climate. We believe that anyone employing Mr. Anderson will be very well satisfied with his performance. He is a natural salesman and built customer respect and sales volume each year he worked for us.

Sincerely,

Paul Stewart
Manufacturing Company

KINSEY LANE, ATLANTA, GA.

Ms. Mary Phelps has worked for me personally for the past six years as an executive secretary. Her abilities and experience fully qualify her for a top job in her field. Ms. Phelps is leaving our company because I myself am leaving to assume the presidency of an organization in another part of the country and she does not wish to relocate.

In the years she worked for me, Mary Phelps was able to perform with outstanding ability the most demanding aspects of the executive secretary's position. In addition to being a superb performer in the standard parts of the executive secretary's job, she also, functioning in fact as an assistant, took care with uniformly excellent results of many delegated responsibilities, helped me plan and organize my work schedules, and maintained an effective liaison with members of my staff and outside people.

I would like to offer my congratulations to the executive fortunate enough to acquire her services.

TURNING DOWN A REQUEST FOR A REFERENCE YOU'D RATHER NOT GIVE

In some cases you may be asked by an employee to write a letter of reference about which you have some reservations. You may not know the employee well enough or may simply feel you cannot register unqualified approval of his or her capabilities. In such a case, instead of a refusal, however courteous, possibly offering some such excuse as "I'm sorry, but I never write such letters," there is another alternative. This is to offer to reply personally to any inquiry made by a potential employer. In such a response, you can more easily stick to statements that reflect what you know of the person.

Also, if you as the employee's superior would rather not write a reference, you might suggest, "See Mr. Miller in Personnel. I'll ask him to give you a letter stating your history of employment here, which will probably serve your purpose." Such an "organization letter," as opposed to what is usually a personal letter written by the employee's superior, would read something like this:

Cresthaven Publishing
Company

42 PUBLISHERS ROW
GRAND ACRES, NEW JERSEY

Miss Helen Bailey has been employed by this company for the past two years as a typist. Her work has been quite satisfactory, and she is leaving as a personal choice.

LEGAL ASPECTS OF REFERENCE LETTERS

If you have any strong doubts as to the propriety or advisability of furnishing a letter of reference, you may feel free to refuse. There is no legal requirement that such letters be written.

Law aside, you should not refuse to provide a minimum statement along the lines that "So-and-so has been in our employ for such-and-such a time," usually giving the date of hire and the date of separation.

When what you say about an employee is favorable, as long as it conforms to your concept of accuracy and appropriateness, there's no problem. However, it's important that no statement be made that impugns the individual in any way that may be interpreted as malicious or libelous. For example, a statement like the following is to be avoided: "Mr. Smith has worked for us for five years and *apart from some occasional personal difficulties* his performance has been satisfactory. . . ."

Clearly, the italicized words represent a derogatory statement, or at least one that might be so viewed by a potential employer. Mr. Smith might take you to court. Even if the statement were true, it would have to be *proved,* and at the very least would involve you and your company in legal complications.

This does not mean that you cannot communicate to another potential employer a description of undesirable qualities or experiences with an employee.

Theoretically, if your statement were written and went only to a small, privileged group, you would be legally safe. This would mean, of course, that you were answering an inquiry and you took steps to see that the letter and envelope were marked "Private and

Confidential." But, of course, so labeling a message wouldn't make it so, and a far better course would be to make any adverse comments orally rather than in writing.

Another requirement is that your comments, verbal or written, be made in good faith. Any suggestion of malice, of "getting even" for any reason, might make you susceptible to a lawsuit.

SPECIAL PROBLEMS

From time to time, special problems arise in communication. Examples follow.

SHOULD YOU CIRCULATE OTHER PEOPLE'S LETTERS AND MEMOS?

Some messages sent to you personally could have an unintended impact if disclosed to others. When should you and shouldn't you treat such letters as "secret"?

One thing can be said definitely. If showing a letter to another person violates a confidence, it should not be shown. However, one of the business facts of life is that an individual who sends a written message is creating a matter of record. It would be naive for the individual not to anticipate that the message might get into hands other than those of the person to whom it is addressed. There are two considerations to be made in this connection:

• *Informing the writer.* You may let the individual know that you intend to show the message to other parties. There may be no objection. If there is, you have to deal with it on its merits.

• *Motives.* The reason for showing a message to others must also be taken into account. In some cases you may want to show the memo or letter to another person in secret, and yet have the most benign motives in doing so. For example, a manager shows an interoffice memo from another supervisor to her boss: "Dave, I'd like you to look at this note I got from John this morning. Apparently he plans to go ahead with the Smith and Company project. As you and I know, they're a very poor credit risk. Do you think maybe you ought to talk over the situation with him? . . ."

Where the intention behind the passing along of the message is going to be damaging to the writer, the recipient should at least be aware that a destructive tactic is being undertaken. Essentially what is involved here is a matter of conscience. It must be remembered that the writer has shown trust in expressing himself or herself in the message. It is certainly undesirable to violate this feeling even for the sake of tactical benefits.

Finally, there is a type of memo aimed at "covering" the writer. For example, manager Paul Lee wants to put his disapproval of a plan on the record, so he sends his written views to a colleague. If the plan fails, the writer can use the memo as evidence of his wisdom. (Of course, he's taking a risk. He won't look good if it succeeds.) Such a memo, intended to be a statement of record, may be shown to third parties.

THE TIMING OF A MESSAGE IS IMPORTANT

A message may be either premature or belated, and undesirable for either of these two reasons. An example of a *premature* communication: "Dear Boss," writes Alice Hicks, "just heard through the grapevine that you're due for a promotion to the job that Mr. Peters is retiring from next week. Congratulations."

Alice Hicks meets her boss in the corridor next morning, and he says, rather coolly, "Thanks for your good wishes, Alice, but the grapevine is wrong on this one. Joe Harris is getting that job. . . ."

Belated messages are just that. Thoughts communicated past the time when they were proper, whether birthday congratulations or a request for information that's satisfied a week after it was needed.

In some situations it's possible to make amends:

Dear Lois,

Just realized that last week was the eighth anniversary of your coming into the company. I'm terribly sorry to have let such an important event go by. Please forgive me, and I promise not to miss next year. Meanwhile, how about a lunch to celebrate? I'm sure the food and drinks at O'Malley's will be just as good this week as they would have been last. How about Friday?

A day ahead of time for most events—a retirement, promotion, transfer—is fine. However, birthdays and anniversaries are best marked by cards or congratulatory messages timed to arrive on the morning of the day itself.

HOW TO ANSWER A NASTY MEMO OR LETTER

Occasionally you receive a written message couched in unpleasant language. The natural temptation is to respond in kind. But oneupmanship in this kind of game can too easily boomerang.

Writing in the heat of anger is rarely recommended. It takes a cool head to respond to a verbal attack without losing one's sense of balance or propriety. Note the "nasty" memo following that takes a colleague to task for his behavior in a meeting.

Dear Bill:

I want to compliment you on your stupid behavior in the meeting today. Your uncivilized, boorish interruptions made it difficult for me to proceed, and thanks to your brilliant arguments, the group was given a distorted idea of my viewpoint.

My criticism was being directed not at any individuals then present, but at the failure of the division as a whole to make the hard decisions that are necessary for us to progress in the months ahead.

You added damned little light to the subject and, in my opinion, have created serious obstacles for us all.

Pete

The best answer to any such note may well be silence. But if the sender is of sufficient status in your organization that ignoring the message is impossible, or your considered judgment suggests a reply, base it on the following guidelines:

• *Show an understanding of the author's mood.* "I understand that you would feel very upset about the situation. . . ."

• *Express regret.* "I'm sorry to be the cause of such strong feelings." Then what follows depends on how you feel about the original situation. You may either:

• *Restate your original position.* "I must tell you now that I still feel exactly as I did before about. . . ." You may want to add additional arguments, describe evidence that you had that was not produced at the time that justifies your views, and so on.

Or, you may want to consider alternatives:

• *Apologize without a retraction.* "However, I want you to know that I have not changed my mind. I stand by what I said [or did]. . . ."

Or, you may want to consider a third course: you modify your statement. In some cases the feelings or ideas expressed by the sender of the message may cause you to reconsider or be willing to concede the validity of a counterargument. Here what you say may range from:

• *Modifying your stand.* "Although the basic situation is still as I described, I may have overstated. . . ."

• *Conceding.* Here, to one degree or another, you may want to admit the original statement or deed was ill-advised. You may still justify yourself, however: "At the time I made the statement, I thought I had all the facts in hand. I see now that I was partially misinformed." Or: "Although I believe my views made sense when and as I expressed them, subsequent developments do alter matters. . . ."

Here's how some of the guidelines described above would be used in a reply to the Pete–Bill exchange:

Dear Pete:

I'm truly sorry that you find so much to criticize in my behavior in yesterday's meeting. My hope is that the heat of the moment that may have affected my actions also distorted your perceptions of them.

I see nothing to be gained by rehashing our arguments at this time. Since we agree on the need to solve the problem, let's say that the second time around we'll try to do better—much better.

Sincerely,

Bill

WHEN TO AVOID PUTTING WORDS ON PAPER

The one quality about a written message that must always be kept in mind is its permanence. Spoken words exist for the moment. Even when they're recalled by memory, you're no longer dealing with the original message but a duplicate that comes out of someone's recollection.

The written message is impossible to "water down" later. Written words are there just as they were first put down. Accordingly, there are certain occasions when, to avoid regrets at a later date, you *don't* write:

• *During periods of extreme emotion.* When one is angry, upset, suffering from any of the negative emotions, writing should be postponed. It's inevitable that one's thinking and language will be influenced. It's most likely that when mental balance stabilizes, a more reasoned, moderate, and acceptable message can be phrased. Of course, there is a modified alternative. You may *write* the message but not send it until you've cooled off and can read what you've set down with a more objective eye.

Even so-called good emotions such as enthusiasm or excitement may have undesirable consequences in written messages. You may have just come up with an idea that seems to have tremendous implications and values. It's possible that if you set down your thoughts at that moment, you might produce an exaggerated message that would seem naive or unrealistic to others. Here again, it may be a good idea, if you must write, to hold off sending the message until you've had an opportunity to read it from a more objective viewpoint.

• *When the timing is wrong.* There may be nothing wrong with the message, but there may be something in the situation that makes for poor timing. For example, a small plant in a suburban area has just inaugurated new parking rules. A young manager, miffed because he has had trouble parking, gets off a blast to the personnel director about the "terrible new system." "Dear Bill, Still too early to tell," responds the personnel director. And sure enough, in a few days the kinks are out and the system works well.

• *When face-to-face is better.* At the end of Chapter 2, the advantages and disadvantages of the spoken and written words are compared. With respect to a specific piece of writing, such as a memo or report, it is possible to spell out a superiority of spoken versus written language that suggests occasions when not to write:

An employee is asked by her boss to read and send back reactions to a lengthy report. But the employee, not clear on a number of points, suggests a meeting instead. The boss agrees and is able to clarify key aspects of the report, whereupon the employee is able to make useful comments and suggestions. The constructive outcome would not have been possible without the advantage of give-and-take conversation.

SHOULD YOU EVER WRITE AN ANONYMOUS NOTE?

Everyone has been tempted at one time or another to get an important message across without revealing his or her identity. Anonymous notes have been written to accuse people and to defend them, to state a viewpoint that, however justified, finds the writer unwilling to put himself or herself on record.

Whatever the temptation or the seeming justification, it is wrong to send such messages anonymously, for several reasons:

• *Innocent people may be suspected.* If the message is so well disguised that the real sender cannot be identified, it's possible that one or more other people may be suspected.

• *Certain types of messages may be destructive and cowardly.* The classic prototype is the anonymous letter that sets out to reveal some devastating fact about an individual: "Mr. Smith is sleeping with his secretary." Or: "If you want to know what happened to the hundred dollars that's missing from petty cash, ask Mr. M. . . ."

Even if such accusations are true, having them appear in an anonymous letter is cowardly and unfair. Just consider the two cases mentioned:

If Mr. Smith is indeed sleeping with his secretary, that should be considered their personal business. If someone actually has proof that Mr. M. has had his hand in the till, then it's a message that an individual should be willing to convey and back up by identifying himself and his source of information.

In short, there are no circumstances that justify an anonymous message, no matter how horrendous the facts that a writer may want to reveal. If they should be communicated at all, it should be done in person and in as discreet a way as possible.

Occasionally, a writer is tempted to take the unsigned-letter route because of "do-gooder" motives—to warn a person against whom a scheme is brewing, to inform a person of a personal habit that is a serious social handicap. But even here, the potential for upset and complication may more than offset the benefit. The situation may not be as bad as the writer suggests. The social offender may be mortified by the message, exaggerate the "shame" that is suggested, and either grimly ignore the supposed good advice or quit. In short, if you're not willing to be identified with your message, that's a good clue that it should not be sent.

MISUSE OF AN ORGANIZATION'S LETTERHEAD

It's no secret that company letterheads are sometimes used by employees for personal letters. To write a letter at the office to Grandma back home or to a son in the military overseas, it is convenient to dip into the stationery drawer.

In some cases people use company letterheads to bring corporate prestige into play. Rightly or wrongly, it's felt that a letter of inquiry or complaint on a personal matter gets more favorable treatment when the writer is identified with an established organization.

Most companies tacitly permit the purloining of its stationery for such uses, since all that is usually involved is the small cost of the letterhead. And it is felt there is an offsetting advantage—a desirable identification of the employee with the organization.

But other uses may lead to trouble. For example:

Junior executive Henry Grey dashes off a nasty, scolding letter to the mayor of the town taking him to task for a decision concerning a local issue. He has used the company letterhead, which the mayor's secretary shows to her boss. The mayor gets on the phone and calls his good friend T. R. Peters: "Ted," says His Honor, "there's an employee of yours by the name of Henry Grey making bad noises about that local park situation. Are you in on this in any way? He used your company stationery." T. R. Peters assures the mayor that the message from Grey was written without his knowledge. Then he has Henry Grey on the carpet.

The moral here is that organization stationery should *not* be used for any partisan or controversial matter. The only exception: where the organization and its top policymakers wish to align themselves publicly on one side or another of an issue.

But there is a misuse of your organization's letterhead that may lead to legal complications. For example:

An executive of a large airline offered to assist in his wife's trip to a teachers' convention by making a motel reservation for her in Annapolis, Maryland, the scene of the convention. When his wife arrived at the motel, there was a mixup that ended up with her staying elsewhere.

When the husband heard about the episode, he shot off a letter on airline stationery to the Annapolis Chamber of Commerce, with copies to the motel and the college hosting the convention. One of the paragraphs read: "Judging from the description of the motel by my wife, the motel management may be more accustomed to booking rooms by the hour than by the night." He signed off: "Senior Manager, Public Relations."

The motel owner brought suit, even though the airline asserted that the letter was prepared without the company's knowledge, consent, approval, or authorization. After a considerable amount of legal hassling, the airline escaped legal judgment. But what it didn't escape was the loss in executive time, legal fees, and some damage to its public image.

As far as possible, then, management should make clear its prohibitions on unauthorized use of letterheads. Certainly, if any incident becomes a case in point, it should be publicized and used as illustration.

HANDWRITING VERSUS TYPEWRITING

More or less directly connected with the use of organization letterheads is the question of whether handwriting or typing is preferable. First of all, it's obvious that a message of intimacy should employ personal rather than business stationery. But there are some situations when top executives in an organization send out letters that are essentially personal but are also expressions in which the executive may be speaking both personally and as a representative of the organization. This may be the case in matters like these:

messages of condolence;
invitations and replies;
expressions of thanks or congratulations.

Messages like these are more acceptable when written by hand.

LANGUAGE TO AVOID

There are types of language and vocabulary that are undesirable. They're probably undesirable in any situation but certainly don't belong on the business scene. Avoidance of such language areas make communication easier on the recipient's nerves and mind:

• *Off-color language.* Few people would object to an occasional "damn it," "hell," or even "lousy" in a written business communication. But any excessive use of four-letter words, obscenities, expletives, and so on is likely to boomerang. Certainly English is sufficiently flexible so that you can communicate almost any message, even one expressing rage and outrage, without resorting to gutter vocabulary. And particularly in written messages there is a special reason: unlike the spoken word when you know who your audience is, you can never be sure who's going to get to see a written message.

• *High-flown language.* English is not a single, monolithic entity; it has many facets. Spoken language, for example, tends to differ from the written one. Idiomatic speech is different from the tongue one learns in the college and university. The newcomer on the business scene sometimes makes the mistake of clinging to language habits more appropriate to school. A formalistic and labored approach to phrasing or fuzzy wording can undermine communication. The twin lists below indicate the difference between unconscious pomposity and simple direct expression.

FUZZY	PREFERRED
"at the present time"	"at present" or "now"
"one and the same"	"the same"
"it's conceivable"	"perhaps" or "maybe"
"had intended to"	"meant"
"if and when"	"if"
"I deem it advisable"	"it's advisable"

"it is with regret that"	"I regret"
"an insufficiency of"	"not enough"
"it is with considerable pleasure that"	"I'm happy to"
"As I sat down at my desk today, I thought to myself . . ."	Skip it and get down to business.

Academic language tends to run to abstractions, generalities, and longer words. Business language tends to be brief, incisive, and specific. Here are some undesirable usages:

• *Garble.* One obstacle to a clear understanding of a written message is the failure of the writer to put a message into a series of brief, sequential, simple sentences. Note the two paragraphs below, both communicating essentially the same information. The difference is not just one of *writing style* but, more important, one of impact. The first is windy, overwritten. The second is both more temperate and more precise.

> There have been countless and exasperating instances where people from your department have interfered with work in my area, leading to serious disruptions and delays that have increased the operational course of running my unit, which, as you know, is under terrific pressure at all times, and any disruptions of the kind being caused by your people become costly losses for the company.

> From time to time, people from your department, probably unintentionally, have interfered with the work in my area. I am sure you agree this is an undesirable situation. Would you please take steps to prevent recurrences in the future.

• *Bureaucratese.* There is a type of language, commonly found in government circles, in which simple messages are built up into tremendous, tottering towers of words. Here's an example.

> On January 18 I issued a memorandum concerning reimbursement for round trips of less than 35 miles. In the memorandum, I indicated that we would allow reimbursement for round trips of 35 miles or less at the rate of $.08294 with no additional reimbursement for tolls or parking. It was our understanding that the $.08294 rate was established and required by the Department of Audit and Control.
>
> Thanks to the persistence of one of our bureau chiefs, we have found that the Department of Audit and Control officially does not require the rate to be carried to the fifth decimal place. They have indicated that we may use $.083 instead. Therefore, in the future please use the $.083 rate.

There are two possible cures for this kind of language abuse, either that bureau heads demand simplicity in writing or that writers be charged a certain amount per word for every message that is sent out—a charge, by the way, deductible from their paychecks.

EUPHEMISM: LANGUAGE THAT SOOTHES

There is a special kind of language that can be used in business to smooth over injured feelings, help individuals save face, and avoid upset. No one is fooled, but the good intentions behind the effort are appreciated.

From time to time, unfortunate, undesirable, or hurtful events take place on the workscene that must be reported for the record. As people who use language effectively are well aware, facts are not simply facts. A situation described in one way can be threatening; described another way, it can be accepted without anyone's turning a hair.

It's always desirable to write tactfully when dealing with certain sensitive situations. One can use language to soothe an individual or a group, protect a friend, or deal wisely with a foe.

Here's an example written by a language-wise secretary who's been getting along very poorly with her boss and has decided to take another job. She writes a memo that will give the executive no reason to blame himself for her departure.

Dear Mr. _____:

I have just been offered a position which includes special writing assignments, increased responsibility, and a chance to advance to a managerial job.

I hope you will understand my eagerness to accept this challenge. Accordingly, I will expect to be leaving in two weeks. Please be assured I'll do my part during this period to break in your new secretary to the best of my ability.

SITUATIONS THAT ARE BEST HANDLED EUPHEMISTICALLY

Ordinarily, openness and honesty are virtues in communication. But in some touchy and even explosive situations it can be the height of wisdom to use indirection and the euphemistic phrase. Here are some common examples:

"I have been asked by our president, Mr. Tom Cowley. . . ." (Tom Cowley *has ordered.*)

"You are invited to attend. . . ." (It's a *command* you'd better heed.)

"My assistant _____ has requested a two-month leave of absence to give him an opportunity to recoup his health. . . ." (An employee with a severe alcohol problem is being given a chance to resolve his difficulty.)

Additional situations that benefit from tactful wording:

A PERSON IS BEING FIRED. In either official announcements or in conversation, phrases like these can ease some of the sting: "Joe has resigned." Or: "Annette has left because of opportunities on the outside." Or: "Jack has left for personal reasons."

A PERSON WHO IS BEING FIRED FOR DISHONESTY. "Henrietta is being let go because her services are no longer required." Or: ". . . because the assignment that had been given to her was completed."

A PERSON WHO HAS BEEN LET GO FOR REASONS OF ALCOHOLISM, DRUG ABUSE, AND SO ON. "Hank has left for health reasons." Or: "A change was necessary in order to give Jane a chance to work out personal problems."

AN INDIVIDUAL HAS BEEN DEMOTED. "Greg has been asked to take on some of his former responsibilities where he proved his outstanding abilities."

There are many occasions when such language is highly desirable for legal as well as personal reasons. A public accusation of dishonesty, for example, can lead to a suit for libel and slander.

SAMPLE MEMOS ON SOME KEY TOPICS

Interoffice memos are a common medium of exchange. Any subject relevant to business communication—and sometimes the irrelevant—has been and will continue to be covered in the memo medium. The "paperwork burden" that marks the business scene is largely made up of this type of communication.

Memos on matter-of-fact subjects are usually written easily and with dispatch. Even long communications, if fact-oriented, trip lightly from the executive's tongue if he or she dictates, and then from a typist's machine.

But there are certain subjects—some because of their emotional overtones, others that we want to get "just right"—that may pose problems. Accordingly, the last part of this chapter consists of a number of subject categories for which samples can prove helpful.

You will find several examples in each category, and the attempt has been made to provide variety in both content and treatment.*

ACKNOWLEDGMENTS

Whether it's an item that has been received or an action that deserves comment, whenever acknowledgments *are* in order, they should be made promptly. Delay leads to a breach in communications or a puzzled person at the other end. Here are some examples:

IN SOME CASES THE ACKNOWLEDGMENT IS WRITTEN AND CAN BE STATED IN A SINGLE SENTENCE.

Thanks for the notes and sketches of the planning committee that arrived in this morning's mail.

SOMETIMES YOU HAVE TO ADD A QUALIFICATION: NOTE A MISSING ITEM AND SO ON.

This is to acknowledge receipt of the record of purchases made by my department for the first quarter. I've made a brief check and find that some purchases made in January are missing. After I've made a more thorough check, I'll let you have a complete report on any further discrepancies uncovered.

A WAREHOUSE MANAGER WRITES THE HEAD OF MAINTENANCE TO ACKNOWLEDGE AN OBLIGATION.

I know it's a week after the date I promised to have the twenty 50-gallon paint drums removed from the alley next to Building B. On Monday I expect an extra man to get us over the shorthandedness, and so the job should be done by Tuesday, latest.

ANNOUNCEMENTS

In the course of business, decisions are made, meetings arranged, jobs changed, people hired and retired. To clarify facts and avoid misunderstandings, accuracy of detail is essential. Such memos may be addressed to one person or to all employees.

This is one type of message in which errors can cause difficulties or embarrassment—for example, a meeting room occupied only by

* Some of this material has been adapted from Auren Uris, *Memos for Managers,* (New York: Thomas Y. Crowell, 1975).

the chairman because the incorrect time was stated in the memo. On the other hand, a well-phrased announcement can smooth the entrance of a new employee or make a newly promoted one feel particularly rewarded.

FROM A DIVISION HEAD TO HIS SUPERVISORS, ANNOUNCING A MEETING TO BE CHAIRED BY THE COMPANY PRESIDENT.

> Mr. Adams would like to meet with all supervisors on Monday, December 10, at 11:00 A.M. in the conference room. My understanding is that he would like to discuss the significance of the energy and other shortages for the company and their effect on the work we do.

A COMMON FORM OF THE "TO ALL EMPLOYEES" MESSAGE.

> The office will close at 3:00 P.M. on December 24, to help you beat the Christmas rush. Happy Holiday!

FROM A MANAGING EDITOR TO HIS STAFF, ABOUT WORK SCHEDULES. HUMOR IN DEAD-SERIOUS MATTERS CAN REPLACE GLOOMY ACQUIESCENCE BY SMILING ACCEPTANCE.

> The rush hour is upon us. Despite such things as energy shortages and wars, we still have a New Year's issue to put out. Accordingly, stories will be due for the New Year's issue by Friday the 14th. Monday the 17th will be the story meeting (2:30), and stories go to production on Thursday the 20th. For those too high on holiday spirits to remember these schedules, please hand in work earlier!
>
> About the New Year: don't panic. There was a time when people said, "Yes, things could get worse." That day is fast approaching.

A BEREAVEMENT—MOTHER OF AN EMPLOYEE.

> We deeply regret to announce the death of Carrie Nevins' mother, Grace Nevins, on Saturday, February 23.
> Funeral Parlor: George Weber Funeral Home
>   Glendale, Long Island
> Funeral Mass will be Wednesday, February 27, 10:15 A.M.
> at: Sacred Heart Church
>   Glendale, Long Island.

THE COMPANY PRESIDENT ANNOUNCES THE HIRING OF A PERSONNEL EXECUTIVE.

> It is my pleasant task to announce the addition to staff of William A. Langer as director of personnel. Bill will join us on Monday, November 3.
>
> Bill was chosen with particular care from among a number of well-qualified candidates. He is strongly people-oriented, a particular asset

in helping us meet certain governmental requirements. His career has been broad and varied, yielding experience at various levels of personnel work.

I believe you will be well pleased with the way Bill Langer will satisfy our personnel needs, and I ask you to welcome him warmly.

APOLOGY

Something has happened to make someone angry, upset, or disappointed. The writer wants to eliminate, or at least dissipate, these negative feelings. The apt apology can turn rage into good feeling and convert an upset individual into one who feels better about things.

AN EXECUTIVE WHO HAS LET THE CAT OUT OF THE BAG about a colleague's leaving the firm tries to right matters. Note the key points: explanation, statement of regret, request for forgiveness. This particular message also includes an offer of help.

> I didn't understand that you wanted news of your resignation kept confidential. There was certainly no intention on my part to go against your wishes. I hope you can forgive my thoughtlessness. Unfortunately, there is no remedy for the past. Perhaps the consequences will be less severe than you anticipate. Meanwhile, if I can help you in any way, please don't hesitate to call on me.

A PRODUCTION EXECUTIVE WRITES TO A SALESMAN ABOUT A MISSED DELIVERY. This is a model of constructive apologizing—no squirming, it's direct, and it makes a convincing promise for future improvement.

> I realize that missing the delivery date on the Morton order has put us in the hole with a very good customer. I'd like to give myself an easy way out and say that our best wasn't good enough, but that wouldn't be true. The reason for the missed deadline was my overoptimistic estimate on how quickly Fabricating could turn out that assembly. You can be sure I'll keep this failure in mind in future dealings. Meanwhile, you can assure Mr. Mackle at Morton that we'll go all out for him in the future.

A DIVISION MANAGER EXPLAINS TO A SUBORDINATE THAT AN APPARENT SLIGHT WAS CERTAINLY NOT INTENDED AS ONE.

> I'm awfully sorry I didn't get to introduce you to the people who came in from headquarters yesterday. Frankly, they were in a hurry and you

seemed to be so wrapped up in your work that it seemed better to just let things ride. Since I expect the same group back next week, it's an omission that I plan to correct.

AN EXECUTIVE DURING A MEETING HAS MADE A SEEMINGLY DEROGATORY COMMENT ABOUT A SUBORDINATE. Intended as humor, it backfired, with injured feelings as a consequence.

I have already been scolded by two of our colleagues about that unfortunate comment of mine during our meeting. Actually, I appreciate your forebearance in not adding your criticism to theirs.

There was no excuse for an intended bit of humor that fell flat. I hope you will find it possible to pardon what was essentially a stupid and ill-considered phrase.

CONDOLENCES

A misfortune, failure, or bereavement may call for an expression of sympathy. In this situation, even a brief message shows thoughtfulness. Silence is likely to be interpreted as indifference.

A MANAGER CHEERS UP A COLLEAGUE WHO HAS SUFFERED A SERIOUS CAREER SETBACK.

I understand that the decision has been made not to open a plant on the Coast. Since I know how much sweat you put into that project, I can realize how disappointed you must be.

But perhaps these can be two saving thoughts:

You've shown what you've got on the ball—and believe me, it's impressive.

Some worthwhile spinoff is sure to develop in the future. This company is too hot to let a guy like you fall back into a routine assignment.

You've lost a battle, but you'll sure as hell win the war.

THE PRESIDENT OF A COMPANY NOTES THE DEATH OF THE FATHER OF A MEMBER OF HIS STAFF.

Mr. Halley told me this morning of the death of your father. Unfortunately, I never met him, but in talking to people who knew him well, I get the picture of a richly endowed and warm human being who leaves the world poorer with his passing. Your own sense of personal loss, will, I trust, find solace with the passage of time and the many memories you must have of a loved and loving parent.

ONE EXECUTIVE SENDS ANOTHER A MOCK CONDOLENCE ON THE RETIREMENT OF THE LATTER'S SECRETARY. The copy to the secretary, of course, is the real reason for the message—a humorous but sincere tribute to her.

> Well, Agnes Warren is retiring, and after years of easy living, you're going to have to buckle down and go to work like the rest of us. Too bad! But then, be grateful for those lush years when Agnes did everything for you from watering your plants to helping you make your toughest decisions.
>
> You were a darned lucky fellow, and now you'll know why we always envied your having her to work with.
>
> P.S. I'm sending a copy of this note to Agnes, of course.

DISMISSAL

Generally an employee who is fired gets the news from his or her immediate superior. But this still leaves the need to put into writing a statement that notifies others in the company of this development. Here are some examples of how the firing situation has been handled:

A DEPARTMENT HEAD OF A TOY COMPANY ANNOUNCES TERMINATION OF AN EMPLOYEE. The use of "resignation" to explain a termination, even where the employee has been forced to leave by elimination of her job, is generally accepted as a graceful euphemism.

> I regret to have to announce the resignation of Linda Derringer. Linda's resignation flows from the fact that we have decided to discontinue production of special hobby materials.
>
> Linda has agreed to stay on for a period of four or five weeks in order to tie up loose ends, especially customer servicing. We shall miss her sorely and wish her the best for the future!

HERE'S AN EXCEPTION—A NOTE DIRECTLY TO THE DISMISSED EMPLOYEE. It's a somewhat impersonal announcement sent to an employee who has been with the company a short time. Note that the reason for the firing is not mentioned.

> It is with regret that I must tell you that your employment with the ABC Company will terminate on February 22. Please contact Mr. Chambers in Personnel to arrange for your separation check and related matters.

IN THIS DISMISSAL MEMO, THE TWO PRINCIPALS ARE OBVIOUSLY ON FRIENDLY TERMS. Note how the writer has said what had to be said and yet put the entire message in an acceptable framework. The reminder of a continuing relationship can be most helpful.

> This is one memo I never thought I'd have to write. And I want you to know that it is one of the most painful things I've ever had to do in my business career.
>
> But I've just had a long conversation with J.P., and although he's personally well disposed toward you, he says there's no alternative but to have you leave the company.
>
> I'm trying to avoid that old phrase "This is the best thing that can happen to you." I know that you'll be leaving many good friends and well-wishers behind. On the other hand, my own feeling now is that there has been something wrong about the chemistry of the situation. The future should be much brighter.
>
> J.P. has agreed that you be given any reasonable time to find a new affiliation or to develop your career plans. You know you can count on me for any assistance now or later on.

THE PERSONNEL OFFICE SENDS OUT AN ANNOUNCEMENT "TO ALL EMPLOYEES." The brevity of the message helps keep the statement as simple—and as unrevealing—as possible. This approach is used when, among other reasons, the separation has originated out of some controversy or facts that management wishes to shroud in secrecy.

> As of Friday, May 28, Irene London will be leaving the company. Her position as assistant manager of the parts division will be taken over by Jessie Lee.

GRATITUDE

Appreciation is one of the Holy Grails of organization life, more sought after than found. Yet the expression of gratitude is an extremely important element in the emotional life and rewards of any organization. There are many common situations that call for expressions of gratitude:

> assistance—someone has gone out of his or her way to help another person;
> appreciation of a generous or thoughtful act;
> efforts expended by one individual on behalf of another.

Here are some suggested models:
THANKS FOR HELP IN WINNING ADVANCEMENT.

We both know that promotions in this company are earned. And I'd have to agree that when the news came through today, my satisfaction included a certain amount of feeling that justice was being done. But I'd have to be both stupid and ungrateful if I failed to recognize the full extent of your contribution. Starting from that day three years ago when you sat me down and gave me a picture of what the possibilities were for me, and the countless times since when you helped with sound advice and encouragement, your efforts on my behalf made all the difference.

I'll never forget your kindness, your friendship, and your wisdom.

APPRECIATION TO A BOSS FOR PRAISE IN AN ESPECIALLY IMPOR-
TANT CIRCUMSTANCE.

That was certainly a great buildup you gave me in the board meeting this morning. I want you to know that my hat still fits—for two reasons:

Only a great boss can have great subordinates.

We both know that it has been your help and encouragement that moved me along every step of the way.

As the song goes, you made me what I am today, I hope you're satisfied. I am—and very grateful as well.

VICTIM OF A REORGANIZATION DUE TO A BUSINESS DOWN-
TURN—IN EFFECT, HE'S BEEN DEMOTED—EXPRESSES APPRECIATION
FOR KIND WORDS FROM A COLLEAGUE.

As you can imagine, these are pretty dismal days for me. At the moment, I'm not sure whether I'm going to continue to be an employee of this company—my decision. Mr. Davis has indicated that he hopes I'll stay on.

Your words of cheer and wisdom are a bright spot in an otherwise gloomy picture. Just knowing there's a guy like you around may prove a major factor in my decision. But whichever way the decision swings, thanks for your thoughtfulness.

A YOUNG JOB-HUNTER JUST STARTING HIS BUSINESS CAREER
THANKS AN EXECUTIVE FOR CONSENTING TO SEE HIM.

Thank you very much for the time you spent going over my résumé and for the advice you gave me. Your suggestions were most helpful, and I'm revising my résumé along the lines you suggested.

I'm also looking into the possibility of getting a starting job in the trade journal field. As you pointed out, there are a great number of these, and possibly my interest in business as well as my education in journalism will be helpful.

Again, thanks for your interest and your helpful guidance. I will keep you informed as to how I am progressing.

THE SAME YOUNG MAN WHO WROTE THE PREVIOUS LETTER SENDS A FOLLOW-UP MESSAGE THAT IS MOST APPROPRIATE.

Just wanted to tell you that I am now working as an editorial assistant for a trade journal in the plastics field. My getting this job was directly related to the excellent advice you gave me. I feel the success is shared, though you deserve major credit. If I can be of service to you in the future, please allow me that opportunity.

A WOMAN EXECUTIVE RESPONDS, BRIEFLY BUT WITH FEELING, TO AN ANNIVERSARY GIFT FROM A COLLEAGUE WHO HAPPENS TO BE AT A HIGHER ECHELON.

I should have thanked you before this for the absolutely beautiful flowers. They are still brightening my office and my day, and I thank you so much.

INVITATIONS

People are asked to attend all kinds of events, formal and informal, from a routine meeting to a grand affair. The list of invitees may be small and select or may include "all employees." The ideal message is made up of both cordiality and factuality.

A DEPARTMENT HEAD SENDS OUT INVITATIONS TO THE CO-WORKERS OF THE GUEST OF HONOR AND SOME PEOPLE FROM OTHER PARTS OF THE ORGANIZATION.

You are cordially invited to join us for a luncheon on Friday, April 16, to help us celebrate Ruth Bonhom's twentieth anniversary. The place is the fourteenth-floor Rec Room at 11:45 A.M.

THE PERSONNEL DEPARTMENT NOTIFIES ALL EMPLOYEES OF AN EVENT THAT IS OF SPECIAL IMPORTANCE BECAUSE THE GUEST OF HONOR IS A KEY EXECUTIVE. Notice the use of the "self-mailing" reply used to expedite responses and simplify the tally.

You are cordially invited to attend an anniversary party honoring Dave Grasso's thirty years with our company.

> Waldorf-Astoria
> "The Hilton Room"
> Monday, January 19, 19—
> 4:30–6:00 P.M.

- -

Please sign and return to the personnel department by Tuesday, 1/13.

/ /   Yes, I will attend.

/ /   No, I cannot attend.

Name _____

THIS FORMAL INVITATION WAS ENGRAVED ON OFF-WHITE HEAVY STOCK AND SENT TO ALL EMPLOYEES. Of course, such treatment emphasizes the special nature of the occasion.

On the occasion of its Twenty-Fifth Anniversary

The Chambers Manufacturing Company

has the honor to invite you

to the

Quarter Century Award Dinner

Grand Ballroom

Hotel Andrew

Dallas

Tuesday, April 27, 19–

at half past seven o'clock

Exclusively for

Employees and their Guests

R.S.V.P.   Black Tie

"JOIN OUR INFORMAL WORK-DISCUSSION GROUP."

A group of us are getting together, perhaps on a biweekly basis (to be decided later) for informal discussions of work problems or anything else that may develop. If you'd like to join us, we've reserved a table for lunch at Tony's for 12:30 next Tuesday.

A VICE-PRESIDENT INVITES HIS STAFF AND FRIENDS OF THE "AN-NIVERSARIAN" TO A CELEBRATION.

You are cordially invited to join me for a drink tomorrow afternoon, October 17, at four-thirty in my office to help celebrate Bert Feld's twentieth anniversary with the company.

I hope you can join us.

PROMOTION

Promotions of employees at all levels are big events in the business world. There are often strong feelings involved in even the most obscure promotion. A memo written in the subject area may want to take into account some of the feelings of pleasure, satisfaction, and so on. And employees can be reminded that the organization does encourage upward mobility. Colleagues can be informed of the promotee's new responsibility, title, and so on.

ENTER A NEW MARKETING DIRECTOR.

I am pleased to announce the appointment of Jane Smith as Marketing Director of Stone Products, Inc.

Ms. Smith's effectiveness in the sales area of this company has earned her this title. We applaud her past performance and wish her all the best in her new responsibility.

THE PERSONNEL DEPARTMENT ANNOUNCES SOME PROMOTIONS TO ALL EMPLOYEES.

It is always a pleasure to recognize superior performance. Finance Vice-President Peter Lewis has asked us to announce the following promotions:

Terry Caputo from Accounting Manager to Controller.

Henrietta Malnik from Accounting Supervisor to Accounting Manager.

Joy Parcells from Divisional Financial Adviser to Manager, Financial Planning.

We would like to take this opportunity to congratulate them and wish them well.

VICE-PRESIDENT OF MARKETING ANNOUNCES TWO PROMOTIONS
TO THE SALES FORCES.

I am delighted to announce a change, as of February 1, in our sales
management structure which will improve our operations as well as
recognize the talents of the two men involved.

Peter Groves will be Director of Marketing. Pete has been in charge
of most of our marketing in the past, but the new job envisages his
spending more time on planning, merchandising, and liaison with Production and the Business Office.

Ben Sanders will be National Sales Manager and report directly to
Peter Groves. The regional directors, service managers, and the field
sales force will report to Ben.

We are all fortunate to have these two men help us capitalize on a
very exciting future.

REGRETS

An event has taken place that is deplorable or unfortunate. It can
be anything from an appointment missed to a development that
creates a hardship for someone. This type of message should avoid
wordiness that drowns out sincerity. See how the models accomplish
this purpose:

ONE DEPARTMENT HEAD WRITES TO ANOTHER.

Awfully sorry that our get-together this morning didn't come off. As my
secretary explained, I got an unexpected call from the front office which
I couldn't defer. I hope you weren't too badly inconvenienced. Can we
reschedule our meeting? Let me know what would be convenient for
you.

AN EXECUTIVE TELLS A COLLEAGUE HE'LL BE UNABLE TO ACCEPT
AN INVITATION TO A DAUGHTER'S WEDDING.

Both Helen and I appreciate the invitation to Anne's wedding. As you
know, we've seen her grow up. I still remember her first visit to the
office here, a lively, bouncing young lady of ten or twelve.

But unhappily, Helen hasn't been well, and it's quite impossible for
her to make the trip. Please let me have Anne's address because we'd
like to wish her well and honor the great event in some tangible
way.

THE HEAD OF MAINTENANCE SENDS A NOTE TO THE OFFICE MANAGER.

> I very much regret that mess in your office when the hand truck one of my men was pushing cracked your water cooler. I hope the cleanup squad that I rushed over was able to minimize the damage.
>
> Of course we can't undo the mishap, but I have instructed my people to use another route in getting around the building with hand trucks.

SALUTATIONS: FORMALITY VERSUS INFORMALITY

Business letters, as a general rule, lean toward formality. Typical practice calls for the recipient's name, title, and company affiliation, followed by the company address, then: "Dear Mr. Smith [colon]."

But a salutation may vary, depending on the degree of friendliness with the recipient. With business friends of long standing, it is acceptable to do without the name, title, and so on—unless they are necessary for filing or the record. Commencing the letter with "Dear," followed by the recipient's first name—"Harry," "Tony," "Mary," "Elizabeth"—is acceptable informal practice.

Recently, some business correspondents have taken to using "Hello" in place of "Dear." They feel the latter form has a quaint suggestion of intimacy that is usually out of place. But to one observer, "Hello, Auren"—followed by a message however friendly—is the written form of a spoken greeting, frustrating because one cannot deliver the appropriate response—"Hello," "Hi," and so on.

First names ("Dear Bill") are proper in interoffice memos to a person with whom friendly relations are established. It is unacceptable, however, to use first names when addressing someone with whom you've never communicated. The one possible exception is one in which you may then follow a first-name salutation by some such explanation as "I'm taking the liberty of addressing you so familiarly because, thanks to our good mutual friend, Henry Blake, I feel as though we've already met."

With that somewhat gimmicky exception, the use of first names where one has not already established this usage by agreement ("Please call me Tom." "Gladly. And please call me Fred") is undesirable. Premature and "unauthorized" use of first names is sometimes practiced in advertising or related fields. Of course, where it's customary, a tendency to be more formal suggests stuffed-shirtism—so it's recommended that one go along with the accepted practice.

The formal salutation has two forms:

Mr. Emile Fields, President
Fields Enterprises
492 Chestnut Street
Philadelphia, Pennsylvania 19118

Dear Sir:

More personal is the form in which the "Dear Sir" or "Dear Madam" is replaced by the name of the recipient: "Dear Mr. Fields."

In business letters in which the content is formal, the name of the recipient, his company, and address are always used.

In recent years where the content of a business letter is informal, and particularly if the message is brief, it's acceptable to send out a letter on your regular business stationery like this:

Dear Alex:
Find at the last minute I won't be able to make our regular monthly lunch date next Monday. Really sorry. Won't miss the next one!

Resolutely,
Bob

There is another form sometimes used that effectively stands halfway between the familiarity of a first-name "Dear Fred" and the formal "Dear Mr. Clark." It reflects the fact that the writer feels friendly enough to the recipient to want to get away from the "Dear Mr." form but feels the familiar first-name salutation would be inappropriate:

Fred Clark
Zany Publications
645 Windsor Avenue
Toronto, Canada

Dear Fred Clark:
Here is the material I've described to you in the course of our past conversations. I look forward to your reaction with much eagerness.

Cordially,
Helen Brent

THE PASSING OF "ESQUIRE"

Practically never used these days is the designation "Harry Smith, Esq." The archaic form at one time meant a landed proprietor and was a common title of courtesy during the "your-obedient-servant" period of writing. It still may be used when writing to a lawyer or justice of the peace. If so, the correct form is to omit the "Mr." But try to avoid its use and help put an obsolete form to rest.

WRITING TO COMPANY OFFICIALS YOU DON'T KNOW

Every once in a while, you have reason to write to an individual whose rank or function you know—and that's about all. For example, you may be in selling and want to write to the purchasing agent of a company in another state. You've looked up a trade reference book and know that the purchasing agent is "E. G. Davies." But is it "Mr.," "Miss," "Mrs.," or "Ms."?

It's desirable to identify people as completely as you can. For this reason, it's usually worthwhile to make a phone call to the company to identify the individual more fully. Such a call—you can have your secretary make it—will not only establish the full name and correct form of address but will also verify another fact: whether or not the individual still holds the job as the reference book stated. There is sufficient job mobility for a reference book that has been in print for any length of time to have its information outdated.

In some cases inquiries may be impossible and the names are of uncertain gender; for example, Marion, Jean, Carol. Some names of foreign derivation may also leave the question unanswered. In such instances, you may use the person's full name. For example, "Dear Evelyn Waters," or "Dear Tiv Kaken."

WHEN WRITING TO A PERSON WHOSE SEX YOU DO NOT KNOW

Business letters are written every day where no particular recipient is designated. For example:

Service Department
Acme Hardware Company
Sarasota, Florida

Gentlemen:

The above salutation might also be "Dear Sir." Or, if one wanted to emphasize the fact that the message is intended for the operating head of the department, the address might be "Director of the Service Department," and the salutation, "Dear Sir."

Even in cases where the organization to which the letter is being sent is *likely* to be female rather than male, it is still preferred practice to use the male designation "Gentlemen" or "Dear Sir." However, there are certain organizations where you are fairly certain that a woman will be the recipient of your letter. This would be true, for example, of the women's auxiliary of a service organization, a women's league, or as recently came into existence, a women's bank. Here, if you have the name of the woman to whom your letter is to be addressed, the "Ms." form is perfectly acceptable if you don't know the recipient's preference as between "Miss" or "Mrs."

CLOSING A LETTER

The most effective closing to a letter is usually a simple one. The word "Sincerely" will suffice in the large majority of cases. Most businessmen prefer to avoid mucking up the simplicity of the closing by adding a "very" to "Sincerely," or even less, "Very sincerely yours." But there's nothing really wrong with either variation if it suits your taste.

"Yours truly" is still widely used, even though it already has the faded aura of the past.

The once common "Respectfully" is happily gone from the scene. Originally it was a term used to acknowledge superior status on the part of the recipient—as between a tradesman and a customer, for example.

"Faithfully" or "Faithfully yours" is another closing that has become obsolete. A rare exception might be made when the sender of the letter wants to stress loyalty or dedication.

The closing "Yours" for a long time flourished as an informal ending to informal business correspondence. But to modern ears this form suggests either a romantic attachment or else the acknowledgment of a condition of servitude that should eliminate it from common usage.

In some cases it may be desirable to make the closing other than just either adequate or perfunctory. In this case the writer has a range of adverbs from which to choose that will help him express his particular state of mind at the conclusion of the letter. Examples: "Hopefully" if you want to express the idea that you're encouraged by immediate prospects; "Optimistically" if the thrust of your message is to suggest hope for a given situation or course of action; "Gratefully" if you want to conclude a memo or letter in a way that reinforces the message.

Plumb your feelings, select the appropriate adverb.

SIGNING YOUR NAME

The proliferation of copies—particularly these days with the help of our fabulous copying technology—creates a question of signing. An original is usually signed or initialed. But when you're making numerous copies, there are several choices to consider. Even if it's a memo on a form that has a printed "From" line, it's generally advisable to initial or sign the message yourself. This signature accomplishes two things. First, it adds a personal quality to what otherwise might seem like a cold and mechanical message, and second, it suggests that you have read the message in its final form.

When there is to be a large distribution of a message, the writer may sign the original so that the copies will include the signature. But unless the number of copies is very large, it's desirable to emphasize the one-to-one aspect of a message by signing each copy individually:

• *Ordinarily, sign your full name,* "Paul Nichols," "Marion Harris," and so on, and make it legible. "Try-to-Read-the-Signature" is still a common office game that you don't want to propagate.

• *You may sign your first name only if the recipient is a friend or if in conversation you're on a first-name basis.*

• *Use initials only on routine communications when there is no question of your identity.*

• *"Dictated but not read"?* The traditional practice adopted by executives on the run may be used when warranted by time pressure. In this case an assistant or secretary may sign the sender's name adding his or her initials: "Per J.C." This usage is not flattering to the recipient but suggests that the writer has made the choice between delay and fast delivery. This procedure is recommended for noncrucial matters only.

WHO GETS THE ORIGINAL?

When you send a message, there's no problem about who gets the original typed page if there's only one recipient. But consider this situation:

Al Haines is sending a message to a colleague and wants Carrie Blake, their mutual boss, to get a copy. Should Blake get the original because of superior status? The answer is that the original always goes to the person who is the primary recipient. If a memo is to go to a group of people, the problem becomes somewhat different. Here, for example, a member of a committee wants to send a brief memo to others in the group who are of different status ranging from rank-and-file employees up to middle executives:

If there is a chairperson of the committee, the message should go to him or her and should be so indicated. For example:

TO: R. T. Jones, Chairman, and
     All Members of the Planning Committee

Here, R. T. Jones will get the original.

Even if R. T. Jones is not the person of highest rank, the fact that he's chairing the group entitles him to be the primary recipient. All others get copies with the indication (usually at the bottom following the message on the left-hand side):

cc: John Allen
     Jane Freeman

This indicates people other than the primary recipient who received carbon copies of the message. In these days of copying machines, the indication may be "xc," "x" for Xerox, or another letter indicating the nature of the copier.

PROPER USE OF BLIND COPIES

A writer may want to send a duplicate of the message to one or more people without the knowledge of the primary recipient. For example, an executive issues a directive to a subordinate and, wanting his boss to know the status of the matter, sends him a copy without indicating this fact on the original. There may be a variety of reasons—it might cause tension, for instance—for not wanting the subordinate to know that the Big Boss has been informed of the assignment. In that case the notation "cc: John Jones" does not appear on the original, and the copy is called "blind."

But in some cases the blind copy has political implications. A recipient of the memo might be unhappy to know others are being informed of the subject matter, for example. The blind-copy procedure can be a political weapon, and therefore subject to abuse. Accordingly, it should be used sparingly. It's desirable that the writer avoid sending blind copies to individuals where a confidence would be violated or the primary recipient might somehow be put in a bad light. This might properly be considered an underhanded tactic and undesirable from an ethical standpoint.

BUSINESS CARDS

The business card is a quick way of establishing the affiliation of an employee with an organization. Whether sales representative or president, an employee visiting another company sends his or her card into the person being called on if it's a first visit, or may leave it as a record. Cards are also given to people met in the course of business, to facilitate establishing contact.

Organizations clearly benefit by seeing to it that all their employees who may possibly require them are furnished with cards. Generally accepted usage suggests two basic forms:

An executive or company official has his or her name printed in the center of the card, with his or her position in similar letters immediately below. The name, address, and telephone number of the company are then put in either the lower left- or lower right-hand corner:

Harold Arlen

PRODUCTION MANAGER

ALLENTOWN ASSOCIATES
438 First Street
Allentown, New Mexico
Phone: 505–356–6778

The card of a salesman or employee not in an executive position generally has the name and address of the company at the center of the card with the employee's name and title either to the left or the right below:

RITEWAY PRODUCTS
CORPORATION

GREENDELL, NEW JERSEY

Harry Jones
Sales Representative
538–0987

It should be noted, however, that the practice of emphasizing an executive's name by its central placement on a card and the subordinating of a sales representative's name by placing it below the company name need not be slavishly followed. For example, some salesmen exceptionally well known in their fields deserve star billing.

In designing cards, be aware of the basic principle of emphasizing or subordinating company name versus individual name. Work out the balance that seems most desirable in individual cases.

Business cards are often set in the same type as the company letterhead, with type size and other proportions scaled down for the standard 2 x 3½-inch card.

THREE DON'T'S FOR BUSINESS CARDS

There are some practices used in connection with business cards that are undesirable:

• *Don't expect employees whose jobs require them to meet outsiders to function without cards.* Organizations mistakenly feel that employees at lower echelons—service personnel, for example—don't require cards. This is poor thinking indeed. It's often necessary for a contact to have the employee's name and company affiliation. What happens is that, lacking a card, the information is usually scrawled in longhand on a scrap of paper. This does little to enhance the company image.

• *Don't require employees who obviously have a need for a business card to use cards without their names.* The effect of such "blanks" is to give a feeling of "temporariness" to the individual.

What's sometimes done is to have the card printed with a line such as "Sales Representative" or "Sales Department." But this doesn't do anything to alleviate the impersonality and the virtual "nonexistence" of the employee.

Some companies go to the opposite extreme, are so eager to personalize the card that they print a representative's or salesperson's photo on the card itself. This is overdoing it, and is suggestive of identifying people to prevent vague criminal acts of one kind or another.

• *Avoid fancy titles.* This is particularly true in selling. A good deal of inventiveness has been devoted to avoiding a simple, factual designation such as "Sales Representative." Everything from "Service Consultant" to "Marketing Manager" has been used to disguise the individual's sales function.

This kind of benign misrepresentation is used in areas other than sales. It's generally undesirable not only because it misrepresents but because a fancy title may cause expectations that when violated may cause resentment.

• *Avoid the temptation of "fancy" stock for cards.* The representative of a precious-metals company has his business card printed on thin silver stock at a cost of about five dollars per card. Although such a display may be justified—presumably these cards go only to select customers—they are generally undesirable for purely functional purposes. The same thing is true of cards on fancy plastic. As striking to the eye as they may be, they defeat a basic functional use; that is, they can't be written on, a common practice to note down some important data, a price, a good time to call the individual, and so on.

• *Men's names are rarely preceded by "Mr."* Women may, if they like, include "Miss," "Mrs.," or "Ms." However, no such designation is required and should be used only if the individual has a preference.

4

Special Problems
in Dealing with People

We're all human, we're all fallible, and we all have problems and hangups that often show up on the job.

Sometimes the problems arise because the work milieu has values and requirements that conflict with the individual's social and personal values. In other cases problems arise because an individual's habits or character causes trouble with colleagues or others.

In this chapter you will find some of the most difficult and most demanding situations that can arise among people who work together. The wisdom of company policy as well as skill of individual executives and supervisors get their severest tests in these areas—tests of fairness to others that are essential to etiquette.

GENERAL RULES AND CLARIFICATIONS ABOUT FRIENDSHIP

The problem of friendships on the workscene has troubled many people. If you are a person with authority, you can avoid the hazards of improper conduct and unfairness by a better understanding of exactly what is involved.

First, realize the difference between two different ideas:

Friendliness implies a warm and sympathetic attitude that may be shown to all.

Friendship involves intimacy and special consideration.

If you develop friendships on the job:

• *Compensate for it by efforts at friendliness with others.*

• *Make it clear to your friend that he or she, like yourself, must be prepared to pay a price for the friendship.* In some cases you may have to lean over backward since you cannot seem to allow friendship to interfere with your judgment.

To protect your friendships, these guides can help:

• *Show no favoritism for one employee over another.* Realistically, this is an ideal that requires continuing effort.

• *Don't accept friendly overtures from cliques.* While it may be pleasant to be "in" with one group, it's likely to lead to your being "out" with everybody else. Try to avoid showing recognition and, hence, approval of cliques. A barrier between you and the nonclique people would become unavoidable.

• *Show friendliness to newcomers and to those who have less standing in the group.* This move boosts their morale and emphasizes that you play no favorites on the job.

Finally, to maintain friendships with colleagues or others on the business scene:

• *Don't be overly selective.* It's not simply a matter of avoiding the accusation of snobbishness. More important, it is the need to make your friendships across the board for the fullest rewards and enrichments.

• *Act with a sense of the appropriate.* This isn't a matter of a snobbish concern with "what people think." For your own sake, good judgment must temper the contacts you foster.

• *Be aboveboard with the other person.* Your motives, your real feelings toward a superior, a customer, or a subordinate may be neither simple nor clear. If you have doubts about the motives of your friendly interest or feeling toward an individual, think twice before undertaking any social gambit. Nothing is as cold as a chilled friendship.

And it's possible that overtures to individuals of authority may be intended to secure special consideration or influence. It may require special perceptiveness to distinguish between friendly moves in your direction that arise from sincere feelings and those made with exploitive motives. Feel free to respond reasonably to the former, and tactfully evade the latter.

In addition to the above general recommendations, there are unique situations that require special consideration:

WHEN YOU HAVE TO FIRE A FRIEND

Every once in a while a situation develops that becomes a personal nightmare for an executive; it becomes necessary to fire someone with whom a strong bond of friendship has been developed. What are the rights and wrongs of this situation? What can and should be done?

Typically in the higher echelons, executives may socialize outside the job. This may include everything from an occasional round of golf or tennis to intimate double-dating with spouses, weekending away together with families, and so on. The bonds, then, can become very close.

Into this relationship comes the serpent of exigency. A decision, perhaps made at a higher echelon, decrees that one's friend must be fired. Almost regardless of the reason—it may be for poor performance or simply that the friend's job is to be eliminated—steps like these can ease what is admittedly a traumatic situation:

• *Square the act with your own conscience.* The largest part of the trauma has to do with one's own feelings of guilt and regret. The very words "firing a friend" carry the message of strain.

Nevertheless, the firing executive must face up to the realities of the situation. Presumably if the move were unfair or unjustified, the executive would argue in favor of the friend or make other efforts to prevent the decision.

• *Temporize.* If possible, look for some method to modify the decision: "Let's keep Jim on for another six months and then reconsider the situation." That type of suggestion may be in the cards. Another helpful—and friendly—move may be to modify the circumstances of the firing: "I'll suggest that he start looking for another affiliation, but meanwhile let's give him a reasonable time . . ."

Generous separation arrangements—for example, continuing salary payments for an extended period, continuing insurance and health-care benefits— further temper possible hardships. But when all moves and mitigations have been contemplated:

• *Tell the person face-to-face.* There's a famous case in which a vice-president had to separate a division manager who was a good friend of his. Not having the heart to face the man directly, he typed out a memo informing the manager of the separation. The manager found the note, tore it up, and continued on in his job as he always had. The vice-president waited for some kind of reaction, which was not forthcoming. The actual denouement, as the story is told, is that the political climate changed, the vice-president himself was fired, and the manager was given the vice-president's job.

The firing executive would want to confront the person being fired in any event. First, some explanation is owed the individual, and presumably the person doing the firing, as a friend, would be in a better position to do the sensitive job of conducting the firing interview.

GUIDELINES FOR A FIRING INTERVIEW

The points below are specifically suggested for the executive who must fire a subordinate with whom a strong friendliness or friendship has been established. They can also serve in any firing interview:

• *Make it a formal situation.* The executive who in the course of a casual meeting in the corridor says, "By the way, if you have a moment, step into my office," and then launches into a firing interview would justifiably have an irate and badly upset employee on his or her hands. By formalizing the situation, you show the importance you attribute to it and the regard in which you hold the employee. Set a specific time and place for the meeting.

• *Use a signal phrase.* It's recommended that this be one interview that is not started on a friendly and jolly note. Avoid such openings as "How are things going?" or other pleasant small talk. You set an appropriate tone and give the employee forewarning by something like "I'm afraid I have some bad news. . . ." Or, somewhat less ominous (after all, the firee may not be that upset): "I have something to say about your situation here. . . ."

Quickly state your feelings of regret: "I want you to know that this is extremely difficult for me. . . ." Or: "This is one of the most difficult things I've ever had to do. . . ."

The third element of your statement should not be "You're fired" or the equivalent, but should address itself to the reasons for the decision: "As you probably know, we've had to cut down drastically on personnel. Now even these cuts haven't been enough. . . ."

Now state the firing decision and, to avoid argument, last-minute appeals, and so on, make it absolutely unequivocal: "As painful as it is to me personally, and as difficult as it is for the organization, the decision has been made to end your employment here. . . ."

Spell out the ameliorating circumstances: "However, Frank, in recognition of your past contributions and performance, there are some positive elements. . . ."

Typically, executives are asked to resign rather than be fired. In addition, they are usually permitted to supply their own explanation for leaving: "Frank Billings will be leaving the company as of January 1, 19—. He intends to go into general consulting in the management field. Needless to say, we regret this move," and so on. (For more on this type of communication, see the heading "Dismissal," in Chapter 3, page 133.)

• *Give the person who is being fired a chance to speak up.* No matter what the circumstances, the firee will want to respond in some way to the news. This statement should be listened to in a friendly and compassionate way. The bright side of the situation should be stressed: "You've had abilities your position here was never able to utilize. . . ." Then assistance in finding other positions should be offered, if possible, and assurances of continuing friendship.

DESTRUCTIVE ACTS AND ATTITUDES

For the most part, the atmosphere of places of business are businesslike. This means that there is a kind of purposeful air, the result of people going about their jobs in a direct and matter-of-fact way. This businesslike climate is from time to time interlarded with humor, friendliness, personal exchanges from which everybody generally benefits. The world of work can be a happy, productive place. But individuals may bring undesirable elements into the work atmosphere. . . .

PROFANITY

"Profanity? You must be kidding!" an employee responds to his boss, who has called him on overly purple vocabulary. "No one complains about that any more."

You might well think so. In many departments, employees—men and women alike—use colorful language and no one notices. Words once considered "not for mixed company" can be heard in any movie theater and on many TV channels. Why should they be out of place at work?

But the fact is, some employees *do* find profanity offensive. And when managers get a complaint, they must act. Basically, one should try to keep both the cursers and complainers happy. Here is a recommended middle-of-the-road course:

1. *Keep it light.* Language that offends some employees *is* a problem but not a crisis. In talking to the offender, make it clear that you've kept your sense of proportion: "I don't expect you to sound like a member of a garden society, but I'd appreciate it if you keep the language a bit cleaner. It bothers some people." If the case warrants, you might add, ". . . and it's distracting them from their work."

2. *Avoid being judgmental.* It is undesirable—and also unwarranted—to seem to be finding fault, or to say anything aimed at creating a sense of guilt. Sole interest here is to persuade the individual to modify his or her speech because it is interfering with the harmony of the workscene. It will be helpful if argument that seeks to establish a line between acceptable and unacceptable language can be prevented. Of course it exists—in some vague and intricate way—but

attempts have been made for years by legislators and censors to resolve that problem in vain. You are on firmer ground if you make it clear that what is involved is a minor matter, one that can be eased if both parties adjust.

3. *Treat both sides.* Ask the offenders to cooperate: "Men, this is no big deal. I'd appreciate it, and you'll be making life a bit easier for others, if you cut down on the hot language . . ." And try to get the complainer to bend: "I spoke to the men, and I expect improvement." One manager told a complainer, "I know that it's language you wouldn't use, but it is a natural form of expression for these men. I suspect that after a while, you'll get used to it and won't even hear it."

(For additional discussion on this subject, see "Obscenity," page 265.)

BIGOTRY

The bigot, whether racial, religious, or otherwise, represents a somewhat more delicate problem than the user of profanity. The person who uses obscene language is guilty of conduct that is fairly well defined. The bigot can be more subtle. For example:

Office Manager Grace Walter has been successful in borrowing a typist from another department to fill in for an absent employee. She leads the typist—an attractive black girl—to the desk and proceeds to give her her first assignment. As Ms. Walter goes back to her desk, Susan Smith says, "I see it's getting cloudy."

"What's that?" Grace Walter asks.

"I see there's a black cloud," the clerk says. "I guess we've been lucky up to now. I'm glad it's only temporary."

Grace Walter is now faced by the basic dilemma that usually arises in connection with bigotry: Should she ignore Susan's clearly racist remarks or should she make an issue of them?

The answer is that a person in authority should always make clear his or her disapproval of bigotry in any of its aspects. If the incident or the affront is mild and offhand or not likely to precipitate any working crisis, the disapproval may be mild but unequivocal. For example, Grace Walter might say: "I disapprove of that kind of thinking, Susan. In this day and age, I thought most of us were more enlightened than to have such negative feelings."

But let's modify the situation somewhat. Let's say that Susan Smith's reactions were more pointed, more hostile. In that case, the manager might increase the weight of disapproval: "Susan, you're being insulting. Unfortunately, I can't change your feelings, but your behavior is completely unacceptable. I insist on your refraining from any such remarks in the future."

One of the strengths of Grace Walter's situation is that she herself heard the racial slur and is able to deal with it on the spot. When the comments are hearsay, the supervisor or executive may not be able to proceed forthrightly. In this case, a recommended course of action might follow these lines:

• *To act or not to act?* If it's felt that the incident was trivial or isolated, the decision might well be to do nothing. But if there has been a repetition and the target is suffering, then action should be taken.

• *Investigate.* Since your information is hearsay, you can't accept it automatically. Give the person who was the target opportunity to describe what happened. If you hesitate to make a direct approach, you might seek the facts in the course of a discussion about how the employee is doing.

For the inquiry to be more pointed, the executive might say: "How are you getting along with? . . ." and mention the name of the alleged bigot. The question so worded puts it squarely to the injured party. If he or she is willing to let matters go and responds in some noncommital way, the supervisor might simply show his knowledge of what is going on and support by saying: "If you ever have any problems at all with anyone, don't hesitate to discuss them with me."

If the individual is willing to have the supervisor intercede and describes the affront, an effective series of steps would be to:

Have a private talk with the alleged wrongdoer. It's a good idea *not* to bring the two parties together at the beginning. It's more important to get a clear idea of just what the purported bigot feels and to get that side of the picture directly.

If the employee volunteers no statement or act or indicates no feeling of bias, the supervisor may say: "That's fine, I guess there's been a misunderstanding." Even if this isn't quite the case, the signal has been made very clear that the alleged bigot is on notice. Any repetition will be dealt with.

The supervisor should then go back to the individual who has brought word of the affront, and give an explanation of just what has taken place. This should give the alleged victim the reassurance that he or she will be protected in the future.

PERSONAL INSULT

Tempers flair and one employee assaults another verbally, whether it's name-calling or some other kind of designation. Harmony on the workscene has been given a jarring blow. Again it's up to the supervisor to take measures both to prevent the insult from escalating into a physical battle and also to take the steps that will prevent a recurrence. For example:

If the supervisor has been present during the altercation or can get to the scene before it's over, the first step is to insist that both parties cool off. The second step is to get the two people into a place where quiet and privacy will make a three-way conversation possible.

The situation now is one that can be handled by an experienced supervisor but is still somewhat explosive. The next step is to try to find out just who said what without getting tempers to flair all over again.

The supervisor must make clear at the outset that he or she is being completely neutral. And actually that's an important requirement. No appearance should be given of taking sides or making any prejudgments.

Each employee must be given a chance to speak his or her piece to describe what happened. As likely as not, there will be contradictions. Nevertheless, the supervisor should try to get each employee to give more or less completely his or her version of what happened.

It may be desirable to suspend the probing both to provide more of a cooling-off period and also to give the supervisor a chance to check with onlookers or witnesses to get other descriptions of what took place.

But if the hearing is to be suspended, the supervisor should make it clear that there will be another meeting—as soon as possible. This may be that same afternoon or next day. Clearly, any undue delay will be unwise since the feelings involved may fester and show up again.

HAS THERE BEEN A MISUNDERSTANDING? If the actual problem is due to an overreaction on the part of one employee or an actual misrepresentation of something that has been said, the supervisor may clarify this with both parties and end up with: "It's too bad there's been this misunderstanding. Now that we've clarified the situation and we all understand that no harm was intended, I hope we could go back to work without any hard feelings. . . ."

HOW MUCH BLAME? If the supervisor feels that a personal insult was actually intended, he should place the blame, but scale it in degree to fit the situation. If the insult has been minor, a mild reproof may be in order. If the insult was of a particularly biting kind, a sterner tone should be taken and a final admonition should be added: "I trust this will be the end of any such remarks. Needless to say, if there's a repetition, I'll deal with it in the strongest possible way."

IS THERE SURE TO BE A REPETITION? If the hostile feelings involved run deep, the supervisor may feel that giving the employee "another chance" is unwise. In this case an attempt should be made to get the insulter to promise an acceptable course of future conduct: "I want you to tell me here and now, Chad, that there won't be any repeat of this situation. . . ."

SHAKE HANDS? The traditional ending of such a confrontation has been to ask the principals to shake hands. It's a wise move because it constitutes a test of present feelings and future intentions. If people will shake hands, it generally means that they accept the peacemaking that has taken place. If they don't, chances are the problem is not over.

SHOULD THE INSULTER BE FIRED? Perhaps firing is too extreme a punishment, except in a particularly heinous assault. However, other degrees of discipline are possible—transfer, furlough, and so on. (For more on this aspect, see the section on "Discipline," page 178.)

THE MINORITY PROBLEM: HOW TO KEEP IT FROM BECOMING MAJOR

In the last decade or so, the entire problem of minorities—racial, religious, and so on—has come very much to the fore. While this has been a general social problem, important aspects have turned up on the business scene. Certainly the federal legislation involving antidiscrimination and equality-of-treatment laws has become a major preoccupation for most business organizations.

LEGAL ASPECTS

The federal laws have clarified the situations of specific minority groups—racial, religious, ethnic. Also, older people and women have been made the particular beneficiaries of protective legislation. The laws provide not only guidelines but punishment for organizations and their representatives who discriminate against minority groups in such basic matters as hiring, firing, promotions, training, on-the-job privileges, and so on.

INTERPERSONAL SITUATIONS INVOLVING MINORITY EMPLOYEES

Actually, the legal considerations are as much a help as they are a restriction. Employers who are perfectly willing to be fair and evenhanded in their treatment of minorities now have the backing of the government in their efforts. Hostile attitudes or behavior from individuals or opposed groups can, in the last resort, be dealt with by law.

But there are crucial considerations of etiquette; that is, problems of personal conflict and feeling that must be considered by organizations, managers, and employees. Being aware of the abrasive areas goes a long way toward minimizing potential trouble.

THE HATER

There are some individuals who assume the role of "professional hater." A hostile streak in their nature accounts for the negative feelings they have toward minorities.

But since human nature isn't simple, don't count on these individuals being total villains. On the contrary, it's astonishing how often individuals who seem to fit the proverbial "salt-of-the-earth" category—they love children, show all the signs of general friendliness and outgoing warmth—nevertheless speak with almost malevolent intensity about a particular minority group that for one reason or another threatens or incites them. This type of individual becomes a problem on the workscene when he or she is somehow exposed to the "hated" minority. This is the kind of individual who protested violently in the early days of equal-employment legislation when blacks, for example, were first introduced into organizations and departments from which they had been notably absent.

Some people in the "hater" category will continue to resent "aliens" and their resentment generally appears in three phases:

PROTEST. "I'm not going to work alongside a. . . ."

ONE-TO-ONE HOSTILITY. Here the individual makes a more or less direct attack on the person he thinks of as an intruder.

BACKBITING. The final phase is one where resentment goes underground and surfaces only in specific situations. The following shows what can be done to protect minority individuals and, it is hoped, eventually wear down the animosity of the intolerant person. . . .

MANAGEMENT'S ROLE

Experience shows that if management makes the proper moves, the appearance on the workscene of minority people for the first time can be accomplished more or less painlessly:

• *Select the new people with care.* Obviously any group has in-dividuals with a range of social acceptability in terms of appearance, manner, attitude, and so on. In a case where women are to take on jobs for the first time, for example, it will be helpful for the first individuals in these positions to be capable of doing the work and have other attributes that will make their acceptance easier for their incumbent colleagues.

• *Make clear management's resolve.* In some cases where women were given jobs previously held by men, management vacillated. It was suggested, for example, that the women were "on trial," which gave the new situation a feeling of shakiness and uncertainty. When this was done, the resistance increased notably. But in organizations where it was made clear to all employees that having the minorities on new jobs was an established fact and a permanent situation that people would have to learn to accept and work with, this show of complete management backing tended to damp down re-sistance.

• *Deal with conflict.* In departments where blacks work with whites, men with women, and so on—as in any other work situa-tion—feuds and quarrels may flare. Where the conflict has minority overtones, the supervisor has an immediate problem. Such confron-tations tend to develop considerable heat, may even become explo-sive. The best chance for limiting the flare-up suggests that the super-visor try to confine the conflict. A good first move is to get the two antagonists away from the rest of the group. The supervisor's office is a good place in which to put out the sparks. The supervisor should move in these directions:

Try to get to the bottom of the argument. Who said what to whom and why? Of course, this is standard operating procedure for any quarrel. In pursuing these traditional tactics, the supervisor in the case of minority-versus-majority individuals must go through the same steps with the reminder that he or she is dealing with a situation in the same way as in other squabbles: "I don't care what your personal differences are. In my eyes, every individual has equal rights. Just do your job—that's what we're all paid for and why we're here."

If in the course of the discussion there is any hint of hostility, it's up to the supervisor to come down on it hard. "Pete, I don't want any talk or reference of that kind. It doesn't belong on the work-scene. You can feel whatever you want and behave any way you like on the outside, but in my department everybody is entitled to a fair shake, regardless of race, sex, and so on."

MINORITY ATTITUDES

It's unrealistic to believe that minority individuals tend to be passive victims of the majority. Out of resentment for past injustices, blacks, women, ethnic groups may display a militancy that, however justified, becomes a potential source of conflict. The person in authority must keep this possibility in mind in dealing with minority problems. The practical stance for managers is to tie behavior down to the here-and-now: "I can't do anything about the inequities of the past, Susan. Let's stick to the present situation. Why do you feel you're not being treated fairly? . . ."

In addition to resentments of the past, minorities may dislike, or have difficulty dealing with, the majority in authority. For example, blacks may not like dealing with whites. Again, the practicalities of the here-and-now must be stressed: "It's part of my job to give orders. As long as I do so fairly, there should be no reason for resentment." The creation of more favorable feelings is a long-range goal toward which managers and others of goodwill must work.

FAVORS: THEIR PLACE ON THE BUSINESS SCENE

In a world that's "strictly business," favors theoretically should have no place. The very act of "doing a favor" for someone suggests that a rule is being bent or broken, that possibly an advantage is being given to a person who doesn't deserve it, and so on.

But in actual fact, the asking for, and giving of, favors is widespread. The whole fabric of the workscene is marked by favors of one kind or another:

A person is put on the payroll—presumably in preference to other applicants—because the hiring executive is doing a favor for a friend, a colleague, a relative.

Many a minor decision is made—for example, having to do with assignments or privileges—on the basis of a "favor."

And at the end of the cycle—when a person is fired—he or she is sometimes given special favors in the form of a slightly inflated reference, an overly generous separation arrangement, and so on.

"GOOD" FAVORS AND "BAD" FAVORS

There is basically nothing unethical about favors. And doing a good turn is often a thoughtful and gracious act, highly desirable in terms of etiquette.

But the word "favor" may take on a special connotation that makes it decidedly less attractive. For example, when an executive "shows favoritism," the act is no longer harmless and desirable, but hurtful and discriminatory.

FAVORS THAT SHOULDN'T BE ASKED

Some circumstances make it inadvisable to ask a favor of someone who theoretically is in a position to grant it. For example:

Helen Little asks her boss, Roy Wayne, for permission to take half a day off for Christmas shopping.

"But, Helen, you know it's against company policy."

"I thought you could do me a special favor"—and Helen throws her most devastating smile.

Wayne shakes his head. "I just turned down a similar request. Couldn't you do the shopping on Saturday?"

A request for special privilege under the heading of a "favor" should not be made:

• *If it requires breaking rules,* as in the case above.

• *If satisfying the request puts a person on the spot*—risks his or her standing, may lead to complications: "If I permit you to park in the executive area, it's bound to bring flak from a number of people. . . ."

• *If acceding leads to an action against his or her principles.* For example, a colleague asks an executive to appoint his protégé to head up a committee. The executive says, "I'm sorry, but I've always believed that this selection should be made by vote of the committee itself. Even though I have the authority, I must refuse."

• *If granting the favor may lead to a dishonest or unethical act.* For example, don't ask, as a favor, to be given information or news that is secret or confidential.

• *If it is against the individual's self-interest.* "I'd appreciate it very much," Terry Tyler tells his friend Ed Grimes, "if you'd make Pete your assistant. You know, he's my nephew. . . ." Blood may be thicker than water, but the fact is that Pete is a poor performer and Tyler shouldn't expect Grimes to make a move that will saddle him with a second-rater in a key position.

WHEN A "FAVOR" IS REALLY AN EMERGENCY

Under exceptional circumstances a rule may be overlooked or regular procedures set aside. For example, an employee asks her boss: "Could I please bring my twelve-year-old to work with me tomorrow? There's been some trouble at school, and I'd like to keep her out for the day."

Ordinarily, children are not welcome during regular work periods, but if the circumstances are indeed extreme enough to warrant an exception, what is being sought is no longer a favor but recognition of a special circumstance that justifies the exception.

ASKING FAVORS OF SUBORDINATES

Executive Gary Palmer says to his secretary, "Do me a favor, Liz. On your lunch hour would you mind stopping off at a hosiery shop and picking up some pantyhose for my wife?"

The Women's Liberation Movement has made women in general, and secretaries in particular, sensitive to the tendency to expect services based on obsolete attitudes. In the "bad old days'" secretaries, because they were women, were expected to do everything from their male boss's Christmas shopping to cleaning up after his deskside lunch. Unless Gary Palmer knows for a fact that his secretary really doesn't mind doing these little personal chores, such requests should be avoided. Even practices that were acceptable in previous years are now frowned upon as reminiscent of the days when unequal treatment of minorities was accepted as a matter of course.

Circumstances like these may, however, offset the implication of a "forced" favor:

• *If the superior is willing to perform similar services for the subordinate.*

• *If there is an established relationship in which the subordinate's little favors or services have become ingrained* and, as a matter of fact, a cessation *might* somewhat disturb things.

• *If the subordinate elects to act out of choice.* To make this point clear, the superior should put the request in such a way that refusal is made easy: "I know it's asking a great deal to have you stay overtime to type those personal letters. Are you sure you won't miss your train [or foul up an after-hours date, or whatever]? . . ." If the subordinate is disinclined to do the favor, the ready-made excuse should be used: "As a matter of fact, I'm supposed to meet my husband in a few minutes. . . ."

MUST A FAVOR BE RETURNED?

Favors are usually done out of generosity or goodwill, without thought of return. Nevertheless, a moral obligation *is* incurred. A person who has done a favor for you is justified in expecting you to reciprocate. And a favor asked under this circumstance is not easy to turn down. And this is true even if what is asked represents a considerable escalation. To put the case in numerical terms:

Al Byas has from time to time borrowed small sums—five or ten dollars—from Joe Nelson. One day Nelson asks Byas to lend him a hundred dollars—for just a few days. It's possible that Nelson would not have made the request if the borrowing pattern hadn't been started by Byas. But now that he's been asked, it is difficult for Byas to say no. If he does want to refuse, he must come up with a strong excuse.

WHEN A FAVOR IS RESENTED—IN RETROSPECT

James A. Farley, well-known Democratic bigwig, once stopped off at a small town to do some politicking. An aide told him, "Stay away from O'Keefe. He's angry at you."

Said Farley, "I can't imagine why he would be. I never did anything for him."

Farley's implication cuts below the surface of human nature. Instead of gratitude, a favor may leave ill will in its wake. An example explains:

The author of a book on how to find a job reports that after his book was published he got calls from many people, mostly total strangers, asking for personal assistance. The author gave as much assistance as he could—free of charge. And yet, of the scores of people he helped—in some cases to the point of securing employment—only two or three ever expressed thanks. "I understand why," he says. "The whole experience of job-hunting was something they wanted to forget."

After a request has been granted, the person regrets having had to ask. Looking back, he or she is uncomfortable at the thought of "having to beg" or the thought that a weakness or feeling of ineffectuality was revealed. Or it may be the feeling of obligation that is resented, the possibility that the favor-doer now is owed something that may be difficult to repay.

The remedy for this situation lies in knowing . . .

HOW TO GRANT A FAVOR

Of course, one knows that in doing someone a favor one should be "gracious." But aside from using a pleasant manner during the conversation in which the favor is being asked, exactly what does "being gracious" mean under the circumstances? Here are the ingredients:

• *Make it easy for the person to ask.* In some cases just getting the words out may be difficult for the petitioner. Help if you can. Encourage the person to speak up: "It seems to be troublesome for you to broach the subject. It shouldn't be. I'm interested in whatever you have to say."

• *Clarify what's being asked.* The individual may have trouble coming to the point or in making a clear statement of what he or she wants. If after the individual has made the attempt and perhaps hasn't succeeded in clarifying the point, you should restate or possibly summarize what's been said: "If I understand correctly, you're asking me to ask Payroll to advance you some money against next month's wages. Is that it?"

• *Avoid making promises.* Unless the favor is of such a nature that doing it is no problem at all, don't give the impression that the deed is as good as done. For one thing, there may be delays. For another, and especially if other people are involved, you may discover obstacles that will prevent your delivering. Or what you actually can do may be somewhat less than is expected. "I'll see what I can do" or "I'll talk to Mr. Smith" are safe statements that avoid the hazard of creating expectations that later on may have to be disappointed.

• *If the news is good, break it happily.* If you are able to deliver, say so in happy terms: "You'll be glad to hear that I was able to get that transfer for you."

Occasionally one finds the announcement of a favor delivered couched in a grudging, almost resentful way. This attitude may reflect the doer's difficulties in accomplishing the favor or some bitterness about having been asked in the first place. Where this is the case—and it's obviously unfortunate—the favor-granter should make every effort to mask these negative feelings. They will at least partly destroy the good that's being done and will obviously add to the guilt and discomfort of the other person.

• *Follow-up.* The same interest the individual showed in doing the favor would suggest that he or she be concerned about the consequences: "How is Tim doing in his job?" asks an executive of an employee whose son he has been able to place on the payroll.

Any signs of continuing interest assure the person that the relationship has not suffered—indeed, it may have been strengthened—by the granting of the favor.

HOW TO ASK FOR A FAVOR

As has been made clear by the examples above, favors may be asked of superiors by subordinates and also of subordinates by superiors. Regardless of which direction up or down the echelons the favor is asked, here are some guidelines to keep favors within practical limits:

• *Make sure the request is reasonable.* Avoid asking people to do things that exceed their authority, require extreme effort, or pose some kind of hazard. For example, your friend may be in charge of the petty-cash box. If lending you a small sum of money until payday represents a favor that can be accomplished only by borrowing from company funds, you're clearly creating a risk for the person. Similarly, a request to an executive to do something that exceeds his or her authority or might violate his or her own sense of ethics is a favor that is off limits.

• *Make the request tentative.* The person asking the favor should phrase the request in such a way that the other person has the option of refusing. Such phrases as "Would you mind? . . ." or "I hope it's not an imposition, but would you? . . ." set the proper tone.

• *Make the favor as easy to do as possible.* Occasionally the person asking a favor seems to regard it as a test of the other person's willingness to help or even to make some personal sacrifice. This approach tacks an extra burden onto the entire process and even takes it out of the category of "doing a favor." The person asking the favor should go in the opposite direction—help minimize the time, effort, and so on involved in getting the favor done.

• *Realize that frequent requests may represent dependency.* If you're the asker or the doer of the favor, it should be realized that requests for favors may become habitual. A favor once granted sometimes seems to represent an attractive precedent. The small loan until payday becomes an expected procedure. The request for a specific privilege may be repeated until it becomes a ritual.

The repeated request may represent a habit or be a sign that the asker has become dependent on the doer of the favor. It's up to the dispenser of the favor to eventually refuse, preferably with tact, at the point where the repetition becomes clearly undesirable.

• *Don't forget gratitude.* You might think that an expression of thanks for a favor would result almost automatically. Unfortunately, this isn't the case. Gratitude is an expression marked by neglect as much as by observance. Even in instances where someone has attempted to perform a service and has succeeded only partially or even failed, the effort is worth thanks. And, of course, where the favor has been delivered in full, gratitude is certainly the order of the day. The expression of thanks may be oral, written, or in the form of an appropriate gift. (See pages 348–359 for gift-giving ideas.)

HOW TO REFUSE A FAVOR

Of course, there are small favors and large ones, and the relationship between asker and doer may vary widely. But regardless of these factors, at some point you may be asked to do a favor that you can't or don't want to do. A major point to keep in mind is the position of the suppliant. He or she has exposed circumstances and vulnerabilities. Like a boil, the slightest pressure or blow may be extremely painful. To let the person down gently, action is suggested along these lines:

• *Use a friendly tone.* Even if you're irritated or annoyed by the request, try to cover up your negative reaction.

• *Assert your willingness.* Usually it will be true that you're not averse to doing a favor for the person who has asked it. Even if you are, as a form of courtesy it's advisable to say, "I'm awfully sorry, and I certainly would do what you ask if I possibly could. . . ."

• *Give a reason or excuse.* Something should be said that will make your refusal acceptable. There may be a perfectly sound reason: "I'm awfully sorry, but I can't give you that assignment. It's up to Mr. Jones to do that. . . ." In some cases you may turn down the favor on a matter of principle: "That promotion is going to be awarded strictly on the basis of merit. A rating scale has been set up, and the eventual choice will be based on the record. Therefore, you see, it's out of my hands. . . ."

• *Make it clear there are no hard feelings.* In the average case there is no problem. Your friendly tone and your positive statements about the favor show that you have not been upset or offended. However, if the favor asked has really been an imposition—it may even have been offensive—you may want to clarify your feelings; "Even though I resent your making what I consider an entirely unreasonable request, I don't want you to think it's made any difference in our relationship. . . ."

In some rarer instances, if the request is of such an extreme nature that it impugns your ethics or honesty, you may want to show your displeasure. In such a case it's best to make a simple statement without moralizing or creating guilt: "I'm very disappointed, Harry, that you think I would possibly do such a thing. Your request suggests a rather low opinion of my standards, which I find unaccountable in a friend. I guess maybe our friendship hasn't been as strong as I thought it was."

LEGAL CONSEQUENCES OF DOING FAVORS

A lawsuit demonstrates that favors may have legal consequences. Here's an example:

Hank Correll, a company truck driver, was asked by an executive to do him a favor and truck a load of gravel to the executive's summer cabin. Correll agreed, but in the course of dumping the gravel the executive's watchdog broke loose and Correll was badly bitten. The truck driver was granted workmen's compensation for his injuries because it was felt they occurred in the course of his employment. After all, he was working on a job requested by a company official. However, Correll also sued the executive personally for damages. A court of appeals eventually ruled that the truck driver had the right to sue the executive as an individual who owned the property on which he had been injured by the executive's watchdog.

The moral of this story is plain: for the executive who is tempted to ask an employee to work around his house, remember that a personal suit for damages may be instituted if the worker is injured while on the executive's property.

WHAT TO DO WHEN AN EMPLOYEE BRINGS PERSONAL PROBLEMS TO WORK

It's an old saying in management: "You can't divide a person in half. Few people can check their personal problems at the office door."

The fact is, personal problems of almost every kind can haunt an employee while he or she is on the job—marital discord, financial difficulties, ill health, and so on.

These personal problems can come to the attention of a supervisor or executive in two ways. The employee is troubled to the extent that his or her work suffers. Or the employee may come to the boss seeking help. Each of these requires different treatment:

WHEN PERFORMANCE SAGS

Consider this situation: Ted Halper, head of the company mail room, begins coming in late. Several times his boss has gone to the mail room in the morning and found the three mail clerks sitting around waiting for Ted to put in an appearance. With this discovery the boss has noted other lapses, all adding up to a falling-off of mail service. A little investigation turns up the fact that Ted Halper is having a major problem with an older child who has developed mental problems.

Ted's boss is inclined to try to help Ted and has a conversation with him. However, a few tentative efforts to get Halper to talk about his home problem get no response. His boss then takes the most constructive tack. He says, "O.K., Ted, I don't want to pry into your personal affairs. But I am concerned about your work. . . ." And then the executive begins a discussion dealing with the work problems that have arisen.

A guiding rule: keep focused on job performance. If a personal problem of any kind is involved and the employee is disinclined to discuss it, then the supervisor should consider only the job facts—the instances of work failure, sagging performance, and so on. In other words, the whole situation should be treated as a work problem rather than as a personal problem.

WHEN THE EMPLOYEE BRINGS THE PROBLEM TO THE BOSS'S ATTENTION

It is obvious to Hank Clay that his assistant, Paul Reiner, is having some kind of trouble. The work seems to be going along all right, but Paul walks around with a preoccupied air and a slight frown. Finally Paul steps into his boss's office:

"See you a minute, Hank?"

"Sure. What's up?"

And the answer finally comes out slowly and with frequent pauses. It seems that Paul is having serious problems with his wife. The quarreling at home has become incessant. The kids are upset. ". . . and if I don't get some kind of help, I'll be ready for the nuthouse," Paul concludes.

Hank Clay is being asked to help his assistant in a time of need. Clay would want to help in any event because he and his assistant have a friendly relationship. But despite his good intentions Hank Clay and other supervisors must keep certain guidelines in mind in this situation:

LISTEN WITH SYMPATHY? Yes, of course. In some cases the chance to ventilate, to discuss one's personal problems with someone with understanding can of itself be helpful.

ASK QUESTIONS, PROBE? Of course, you may have to ask some

questions to clarify the situation that's being discussed. But these should be of a limited nature. You don't want to be accused of probing. To make sure that this hazard is avoided, if you do have a question that seems to be on the borderline between the permissible and the doubtful, say, "Paul, what we're talking about is extremely personal and I don't want to get out of line, so don't answer this question if you'd rather not, but. . . ."

MAKE JUDGMENTS OR EVALUATIONS? Preferably not at all. Even if the situation that's being described to you seems clear-cut, don't take sides. Don't make judgments. For one thing, you're hearing only one side of a story, and the account you're getting may be highly colored. The important thing is to be sympathetic and understanding without making judgments that in the end may serve only to intensify or complicate the situation. Such expressions as "Yes, I can understand how you feel" or "That must be very difficult to take" can properly register your sympathetic concern and still stay away from offering gratuitous opinions.

GIVE ADVICE? If you can possibly avoid it, don't—even on minor points. In some cases the temptation may be very strong. After all, the situation is based on the assumption that you are being appealed to as a person of wisdom and helpfulness. But anything you may say that puts you in the position of counselor and guide is likely to lead to undesirable complications. The next point explains why. . . .

SHOULD YOU GET INVOLVED?

An employee who brings a personal problem to you may be looking for a parental or authority figure on whom to place a personal burden. But chances are that more harm than good will come from your direct involvement. After all, the problem is not yours. If you assume the burden, it removes it from the shoulders of the other person. This makes for dependency on his or her part, and for the boss, the possibility of getting in too deep.

HOW CAN YOU HELP? There *is* assistance that you can offer. For example, an employee comes to you with a financial problem. As has already been said, it's inadvisable for you to make other than the most superficial or innocuous suggestions. But there are sources of help that you can suggest to the employee. For example, there are probably people in your own organization who may be able to offer useful assistance—someone in Personnel, for example, or even your business office if there's a money matter about which they can supply some information.

And then there are other possible sources of help outside your organization. But before these are recommended, you have to make a preliminary decision. . . .

SHOULD YOU SUGGEST PROFESSIONAL HELP? Remember, we're talking about the touchy area of personal problems. For example, an employee may be an alcoholic, and to you the solution seems clear: professional help is needed. But in such cases simply saying, "You ought to see a psychiatrist"—or in other cases it may be a doctor, lawyer, marital counselor, and so on—may bring a negative, and in some cases a strongly resentful, reaction.

So if you do feel that professional help is in order, make the first move in this direction a tentative question: "Do you think possibly some kind of professional assistance might take some of the load off your shoulders?" The employee will probably ask you what you mean, and then you can suggest the particular help you had in mind. Remember that some types of professionals represent more of a threat than others. A person with an emotional problem might be perfectly willing to see a doctor—who can then make the referral to a psychotherapist. But for you to suggest a psychotherapist yourself might bring to the employee's mind all the pejorative aspects— "shrink," "nut doctor," and so on.

In the case of emotional problems, if your organization has a medical office or physician on the staff, this is the most logical direction in which to guide the employee. Any further reference will originate there.

SHOULD YOU RECOMMEND A SPECIFIC SOURCE? You may think the world of your own doctor, lawyer, dentist, and if an employee comes to you with a situation where the professional you yourself use seems to be a good prospect, it may seem perfectly natural to make this recommendation. DON'T DO IT! The danger is that on your advice the employee may go to see the professional whom you have recommended and something may go wrong. The lawyer loses the case, the doctor's bill seems to be inordinately high, and so on. Any such complication immediately involves you. It was "your lawyer" who lost the case or whatever.

There is a simple and much safer alternative: give the employee a choice from among two or more professionals. If what's involved is dental work, for example, get the names—from colleagues, friends, or possibly Personnel—of two or more dentists in the area. Let the employee be the one to make the choice. You may even suggest: "Why don't you get a preliminary examination from both these people, get some idea of their charges, and then you can make your choice more intelligently."

HOW TO BE OBJECTIVE—WITH HEART

None of what's said above is intended to suggest that your dealings with an employee who's in trouble should be cool, aloof, and simply "correct." The employee has approached you as a sign of trust. You certainly want to make clear your concern and friendliness. But in the long run you'll be most helpful if you avoid "taking over" the employee's problem and trying to solve it. By regarding the problem as entirely his or hers, you're avoiding complications and staying out of an area in which you don't properly belong.

However, in matters having to do with the employee's work, you may be able to make a very helpful contribution. A disturbed employee or one whose energies have been sapped by off-the-job concerns may benefit from work relief in the form of a temporarily modified schedule and separation from the more demanding parts of the job. This should not be taken to mean that you relieve the employee of all responsibilities. A person with nothing to do can be worse off than one who can somewhat alleviate personal problems by preoccupation with immediate tasks.

EMOTIONS ON THE WORKSCENE

It's seldom that the world of business remains completely "businesslike." Not only do outside problems tend to intrude—in terms of people's moods and preoccupations, for example—but the work scene itself produces the same range of emotions to which we are susceptible off the job.

And yet emotions may cause special problems on the workscene. For example, a good deal has been said and written about the shedding of tears by a person on the job. A man who wept was considered less than manly. A woman's tears were usually something to be accepted with a shrug and passed over as quickly as possible.

And the evaluation of the weeping man changed at different echelons. A lower-echelon male who wept was either considered emotionally unstable or was automatically tagged as belonging to some undesirable culture where male tears were considered signs of unbridled emotions. But tears from an executive were only taken as a sign of instability and usually became a permanent barrier to future advancement.

This statement may seem farfetched. If so, just think back to the presidential campaign of 1972 when a leading political contender was put out of contention overnight because he burst into tears during a speech in which he sought to contradict some personal aspersions.

Here are some of the kinds of emotional upsets that may require intercession. . . .

THE CASE OF THE CRYING SECRETARY

Strong men have been known to quail and retreat in the face of a woman's tears. They seem to feel a special anxiety when a woman starts to cry. But whether tears come from a woman's eyes or a man's, there are things that can be done to ease the situation for the benefit of all concerned. Consider:

Manager Al Bertrand is trying to straighten out a misunderstanding between his secretary, Rita Maffey, and one of his programmers. Bertrand has scarcely started to get into his questioning of Rita to get to the bottom of the situation when she puts her head on her desk and starts to sob. If Bertrand followed his impulses, he would flee from the room. His immediate discomfort is added to by the fact that three other people in the room have looked up and are watching.

Here's a recommended course of action for people in Bertrand's position:

• *Keep your equilibrium.* Try not to show any upset (which is different from concern, which should be shown). Also, avoid apologies or any suggestion that the reaction is the result of excesses on your part. Even if you're criticizing an employee, this isn't the point at which to apologize. If a person feels bad about being criticized, he or she might feel even worse if now told that the criticism was ill founded or unintentional.

• *Recognize the feelings.* There's a tendency for people in this situation to try to disguise it, even make believe it's not happening. It's better to recognize what's going on: "Rita, I'm sorry you feel so bad about this. However, I do think there's a problem that we should try to understand, and that's what I was doing. It's part of my job."

• *Take the pressure off.* Treat the situation matter-of-factly. It would be helpful, for example, for Bertrand to tell Rita Maffey, "Take a few minutes to get hold of yourself, then come back into my office."

• *Don't postpone.* It might seem easier for Al to say, "Would you rather talk about it later?" But doing this might only increase the anxiety for both the supervisor and his secretary, and it might make a second encounter more embarrassing for both.

• *Resume on a sympathetic note.* When Al and Rita have gotten together again in his office, a good opening for Al would be one that makes it clear he has not been shaken up or made resentful by what's happened: "You seem to be O.K. now. Why not tell me why you were so upset? Let's talk about it."

• *Provide the opportunity for emotional unloading.* A person who has burst into tears is obviously under some internal stress. You can provide relief by giving the other person the chance to express some of the feelings represented by the outburst. In other words, try to hold back on your questioning. Do what you can to get the person to touch on the causes of the upset.

• *Be supportive.* Be encouraging. Show your understanding. A few words and phrases from time to time will make it easier: "Yes, I understand. . . ." Or: "Yes, that must have been hard to take. . . ."

• *Offer reassurance about the future of your relationship.* It's likely that Rita Maffey now feels guilty about the "trouble she's caused." It's up to Bertrand to make it clear that their relationship is as good—or even better—than it's ever been: "Now I think we both have a better idea of the situation. . . ." And: "I'm sure this will improve matters for all of us from now on."

WHEN AN EMPLOYEE SUFFERS FROM TEMPORARY DEPRESSION

We're all depressed at one time or another. A temporary setback, a failure, a disappointment can put any of us in a down mood. Fortunately these tend to come and go. But occasionally an employee, because of difficulties in his or her personal life, may slip into a depressed mood that lingers on.

Depression may not be as visible as some of our other moods. An individual may simply become more quiet and his or her responses may be more downbeat than usual. A remark that ordinarily might draw a laugh or a smile receives merely a nod in passing.

One of the unfortunate aspects of depression is that sometimes the sufferer is unaware of it. Again it must be stated that the supervisor or executive should avoid playing doctor, psychiatrist, or any other type of professional. While you do have some responsibility toward the individual and would want to be helpful just out of the warmth of your personal relationship, assistance must in this case be given with circumspection. Here are some helpful moves:

• *Probe gently.* You're in a better position to help if you have some idea of the trouble. Depending on the nature of your relationship with the individual, broach the subject with a question that may range from the tentative to the direct. Examples: "You seem just a bit down today, Gale. Anything wrong?" Or: "Something seems to be bothering you. Can I help?"

• *Permit the person to ventilate.* Getting a load off one's chest is a traditional relief from emotional stress. As a starter, try to get the individual to talk, if only in general terms. He or she may begin by mentioning some work problem or situation—"The pressure's really been on"—and eventually get to deeper concerns. Ask enough questions just to keep the talk flowing.

• *Do what you can.* If the cause of the low mood is something for which you can offer some help—a financial difficulty may be eased if you can arrange for the person to see the organization treasurer, for example—do so. But remember to place limits on your assistance. You can't—and shouldn't—take over other people's troubles.

• *Be encouraging and supportive.* In some cases you can ease the gloom just by sounding a cheerful note. Don't scorn the old clichés: "I'm sure things will work out" or "I can understand your feeling down, but you know, it could be a lot worse." If there is a bright side, point it out: "My wife had a similar operation, and she recovered fully. . . ."

• *Suggest getting help.* Feelings of depression are a deep misery. If the mood continues for more than a day or so, consider suggesting medical help. A doctor might help directly with drug therapy or by guiding the individual to a psychotherapist.

• *Can a new assignment improve matters?* If you are the sufferer's supervisor or have access to him or her, keep in mind the alleviating potential of work. For example, for a person burdened by a recent bereavement, the passage of time is the most dependable cure. But immediate pain can be eased by a new and stimulating assignment, one that will, in the traditional phrase, take the person's mind off his or her troubles. A task in areas where the individual has a special interest or a personal stake will be most helpful.

HOW TO DEAL WITH AN ANGRY PERSON

Anger on the workscene is very upsetting, not only to the person who feels the emotion but to those who are exposed to it. Anger, like a fire, calls for immediate action, since the longer it continues, the more damaging it becomes.

Generally it is the boss of the angered person who should take action. But it needn't be. Almost anyone with a certain amount of self-assurance may step forward and assume the role of informal leader. Here are some guidelines for ameliorating action:

• *Face the individual firmly and assert your authority.* "Al, I'm asking you to stop this behavior. You're getting everyone upset, and there's no need for it."

• *Show a strong mien.* But be firm without showing anger. Your immediate aim is to cool things down. The strongly asserted phrase "Cool it" can do just that.

• *Isolate the person.* Take him or her off to a corner or a separate room. However, if you meet resistance, be prepared to proceed on the spot.

• *Ask the reason for the upset—even if you think you know it.* You want to shift the feeling from inarticulate rage to verbal expression. Even the hottest words are better than muscular destruction seeking a target.

• *Listen to the statement.* Don't judge hastily. If you feel there is reason for the upset, simply say, "I can understand that that would be hard to take," or make some similar nonjudgmental statement. If you feel the anger is unjustified, don't say so, but try to get the person to restate the reason: "You think Josh spilled that coffee on your desk on purpose, is that it? But isn't it also possible that it was accidental?"

• *Be prepared to deal with embarrassment.* Often there is a revulsion of feeling in which the individual regrets what has happened. Alleviate this by assurances that "it was just one of those things" or that "we all fly off the handle one time or another."

If the anger is the result of a disagreement between two people, it usually requires a person in authority to take on the arbiter's role. Here it's important for the executive to be neutral, give both parties the opportunity to present their viewpoints. If the case is clear-cut and there has been an aggressor and a victim, you should use your authority in making a judgment and either warn the aggressor or mete out the punishment the nature of the act warrants. (For more on this point, see the section on "Discipline," page 178.)

If basically the situation is the result of a misunderstanding, emphasize this point and permit the two people to return to work with the feeling that no stigma or blame will persist.

WHEN LOVE REARS ITS LOVELY, PUZZLING HEAD

Among the emotions on the workscene that may upset the orderly state of things, love must be included. Love supposedly makes the world go round. Perhaps it does, but there is less doubt about its capacity for stopping the wheels of industry. Amour, a wonderful thing, when rampant on the workscene can get things and people tossed about. There is so much to be said on this subject—including the fact that what is and isn't acceptable on the workscene has vastly changed over the last few years—that it will be covered at considerable length later. (See Chapter 11, "Sex on the Workscene: The New Look.")

EMOTIONAL FIRST AID

None of the emotions natural to man and woman is interdicted on the workscene. Since a broad range of unusual behavior may turn up, it can be helpful for executives and supervisors to have in mind an overall approach to rampant emotions.

Your objective, of course, is not just to "quiet things down" and keep the wheels of industry turning. The emotional problems represent human and personal values that must be confronted and dealt with. In general, then, in cases where emotions have destroyed the ordinary routines and put an individual in direct need of assistance, consider these steps:

• *Someone must take command.* Unfortunately, the sight of an individual in the grip of high emotions may panic or terrorize people. It's up to the person in authority—the department head, supervisor, or executive—to step forward and make clear his or her takeover role. However, if a supervisor is not present, it is desirable that someone take on the role of leader.

• *First moves should address themselves to the hazards.* When a person erupts in anger, a general situation may be created involving several other people. But the first moves in some situations may have to be directed at related elements rather than the personal crisis. For example, a machine being operated by an upset individual may have to be turned off. An onlooker physically threatened by the situation may have to be safely removed. The person in charge doesn't have to make these moves himself or herself. Orders given should be precise and delivered in a loud, clear tone: "Jim, pull the switch on Bill's machine." Or: "Susan, push the off button on the mixer." Once these physical and related dangers have been taken care of, the focus can shift to the individual.

• *Attend to the upset individual.* A person in anger must be cooled down. An individual suffering from hysteria has to be quieted. The best move is to take the individual to a place where he or she can be seated and talked to quietly. It may be that the presence of a third person would be helpful. If so, specifically select the individual you feel can be most effective: "Barbara, give me a hand in getting Alberta into my office."

If the problem has to do with anger or rage, address the individual in a calm and direct way: "Phil, I want you to come into the office with me right now." It's inadvisable to touch a person, even in a friendly way, who's suffering from rage. This might represent a physical limitation that will be reacted to by pushing or shoving. Let the angry one move under his or her own steam.

• *Make the person comfortable.* In some cases you may want to have the person lie down, but, sitting or otherwise, you want to get the individual as relaxed as possible. You may offer a glass of water, for example.

• *Give the individual a chance to ventilate.* Usually the best way to ease tensions is to give the person a chance to express or explain what it is that is causing the problem. An individual who has burst into sudden hysterical tears may explain the cause: "I had a terrible fight with my mother before coming to work this morning. I got to thinking about it, and suddenly—I guess I just broke down."

• *Gauge your action to the nature of the problem* Many emotional upsets are temporary. Where this is the case, do your best to help the individual regain his or her calm. If advisable, permit a respite: "Why don't you take your lunch early, Connie? Go out now. I'm sure when you get back, you'll be feeling better."

Where the problem is more severe and follow-up action seems to be indicated, you may want to consider one of these alternatives:

- permitting the employee to go home for the rest of the day;
- sending the employee home with a friend so that he or she won't be alone;
- suggesting that the employee see the doctor or nurse if your organization has one (otherwise, have the employee see his or her own physician).

• *What do you do about the others in the department?* Usually other people have witnessed the flare-up, breakdown, or whatever the particular nature of the upset has been. Should anything be done about the incident with respect to them? The answer is "Yes." What is done or not done can play an important part in how quickly and how well matters return to normal.

The best course of conduct is to be matter-of-fact about the situation. No criticism or blame should be directed at any of the individuals. Tolerate brief comment, but not extended discussions.

DISCIPLINE

Discipline is the outer limit of etiquette. It represents the arm of authority that in the last analysis protects the weak and the innocent from aggression or nefarious design and maintains levels of order essential to good conduct and work satisfaction.

The subject of discipline belongs on the agenda of business manners because minimizing hurt and maximizing fairness are basic aims. An undisciplined environment would feature discourtesy, tumult, and insult. In short, the regulation that discipline brings is essential for a work climate conducive to the forms and spirit of etiquette.

Since organizations are usually hierarchical, some people must inevitably have authority over others. When this authority—in the form of organization rules—is flouted, then discipline as a countervailing force is called for to restore order and balance.

WHERE THE PROBLEMS ARISE

One common source of disciplinary problems is the young, inexperienced, or rebellious person who enters the organization with negative attitudes toward established policies, practices, and traditions. Superiors may not get the respect or obedience that they desire. And for the organization's work to get done, such recalcitrance must be dealt with if the employee is to be returned to productive effort or is to be prevented from infecting others with antiorganization feeling.

Nor are disciplinary problems completely absent from the executive suite. An executive in the upper echelons is as capable of flouting authority as is a rank-and-file employee. But usually the thrust of a higher-level employee's recalcitrance is different in nature from that at lower levels. An executive who refutes the boss's authority may be making a power play. And frequently when an executive violates a company policy, he or she honestly believes the rule is merely being "bent," not broken.

The question of discipline, then, often becomes a matter of agreeing where to draw the line. The ultimate disciplinary act in organization life is to fire, and as the world of business knows from occasional startling headlines, even company presidents have been "disciplined"—that is, fired—by a board of directors because of some unacceptable act of resistance to, or failure to comply with, a "rule" that has been set forth by the higher authority.

THE BEST FORM DISCIPLINE CAN TAKE

The most effective discipline at any echelon is that which is accomplished without visible action. It is integrated into the climate of the organization and is enforced by the "law of the situation."

The law of the situation was set forth by Mary Follett, an early management expert and philosopher. She pointed out that there are usually situational factors that of themselves promote or induce certain modes of behavior. For example, a conscientious secretary remains at her desk and completes an important letter not because her boss demands it, and not because she fears that she will be punished if she doesn't do it, but because she has accepted the responsibility for doing certain acts of work by taking on the job initially. No one has to remind her: "That's what you're being paid for." The guidelines for right and wrong are clear to her from the situation itself.

Of course, the law of the situation operates most effectively where familiarity with the circumstances makes the response almost automatic. The farmhand rushes out to bring in the hay at the first hint of rain. The salesman smiles patiently while the customer examines the merchandise. The reporter dashes to the phone to make the deadline.

Unfortunately, not all on-the-job "situations" are so clear-cut as to have well-established "laws." And not all employees are so conscientious—or so selfless—as to be constantly bound by them.

Where you must take action to bring a subordinate's behavior into line, it's desirable that you proceed with minimum damage to the employee and, equally important, to the image and reputation of the organization.

THE HIGHLY DESIRABLE AIMS OF DISCIPLINE

The purpose of discipline on the workscene is to maintain a constructive and stable environment. It is the business equivalent of civic law and order. Just as law and order means safety in the streets, freedom for citizens to go about their business without personal fear or the risk of material loss, discipline on the workscene is the ultimate means by which safety, stability, and individual liberty are maintained.

Some managers abhor the whole subject of discipline and shy away from the use of the authority that is its ultimate tool. Yet there are times when you have no choice. If you are in authority, you must enforce discipline when recalcitrance gets out of hand or you will be abdicating your leadership role. For example, you must discipline when:

there's willful interference with the work;
there's waste or damage;
the morale or the safety of others is threatened.

Actually, employees themselves want the benefits of a well-disciplined work group. The absence of consistent discipline can be a major source of frustration and anxiety.

A major reason for discipline's generally having the negative aura it sometimes carries is that its real nature is not clearly understood. Unfortunately, people too often equate discipline with punishment. That *may* be a part of it, but there are two other aspects that are at least equally important. To understand when and how to use discipline and when not to, one must understand the three aspects that discipline can take:

1. *Discipline That Prevents*

There's a lot more to discipline than just enforcement and punishment. The most constructive sort of discipline adds to a pleasant work climate by preventing problems.

Preventive discipline is a part of training. It starts the minute a new person walks on the job. He or she can then be taught that regulations—the rules that people observe and work by—are a natural and established part of the work situation. They're not rules that have been made as an arbitrary set of restrictions and imposed erratically, but rather an ongoing set of guidelines for the benefit of the individual and the group.

In order to get the benefits of preventive discipline, here are the things that a representative of the organization must do:

• *Be prepared to explain.* Your newcomers should be told the rationale behind specific rules. Old-timers should be reminded occasionally.

• *Let subordinates help make the rules.* People are much more likely to follow a rule they have helped formulate. Take advantage of this fact by calling your group together whenever a new disciplinary problem comes up. Once you've outlined the problem, toss the ball to the group. But use these guidelines to make discussion effective: bring out the essential differences among various views of the problem; help group members come to an agreement on just what the basic problem is; have them suggest preventive and disciplinary measures that fit needs; try to get general agreement on the rules that are to be finally adopted.

• *Appeal to self-discipline.* Generally, if you give people a chance to use their own judgment, they'll make mature choices. Here's an example of this approach as used by a large pharmaceutical company. As stated in its employee handbook: "We don't have a long list of Don't's because such things as rules about parking, smoking, horseplay, language, good housekeeping, use of the phone are matters in which our employees are adequately governed by natural courtesy and good taste."

Note that a strong appeal is made to the employees' sense of personal dignity by praising their courtesy and taste, putting them on their own, and by stating that no rules would be established with respect to the behavior mentioned. Notice the clarity and specificity of the wording. The handbook did not say that "Everyone is expected to be on their best behavior at all times." There was no guesswork necessary. Just stating terms like "horseplay," "language," and so on is the same as saying, "No horseplay, language [and so on]."

Of course, the rule of reason doesn't always work. Some people may not be up to the self-discipline required. Still, most people are, and the result is that the problem then narrows down to a few malcontents.

• *Be consistent.* In order to get discipline to work as a preventive, it's essential that it be applied to everyone on a fair and uniform basis. Therefore it's necessary that the company representatives—that is, supervisors, managers, and so on—who are in charge must play by the rules or observe the standards of behavior with unwavering fairness and consistency.

2. Discipline That Controls

The focus of discipline that controls is on correcting infractions when action short of punishment is required.

In order to apply this phase of discipline, you must know what led this individual or group to break this particular rule at this particular time. The answer is your guide in selecting the proper disciplinary measures. Here are the specific questions that help you get to the heart of the matter:

Is there any misunderstanding about the rule or policy because . . .

- the rule itself is poorly stated?
- the person who broke it never heard it or heard only a distorted version?
- situations in which the rule does and doesn't apply were never spelled out?

WAS THE INDIVIDUAL OR GROUP UNDER ANY SPECIAL PRESSURES? For example, could it have been an oversight or attempted shortcut induced by:

- unusual workloads resulting from unexpected orders or moved-up deadlines?
- procedural changes that invited the use of undesirable or slipshod work methods?
- personal tensions that took an individual's attention off the work or made him or her feel reckless?

WHAT COULD THE RULE-BREAKER HAVE HOPED TO ACHIEVE BY HIS ACTION? Might it have been:

- some specific but unwarranted benefit or advantage?
- a desire to save effort?
- a need for more attention from the others or from you?
- an outlet for hostility that is harbored against other employees, the company, you?

Note that each of the questions uncovers very different reasons for the broken rule, requiring different treatment.

LOOK AT THE INDIVIDUAL. But before wading in with corrective action, there are two more factors that deserve close attention: the rule-breaker's *history of conduct* in your department and his or her *personal sensitivity* to criticism and reprimands.

Make sure you have an accurate and detailed picture of the rule-breaker in these two respects. For example, an employee with a clean slate usually doesn't deserve the kind of worrying you'd give a repeater. The same thing holds for the sensitive type of employee as compared with a thick-skinned individual.

THE ART OF WARNING. Since discipline that controls does not

include outright punishment, the corrective measures used here are all *warnings* of some kind.

This doesn't limit you. On the contrary, issuing a "warning" can mean anything from a casual "Come on, Frances, let's watch that" to a clear-cut "If that happens once more, you're through!" The important point is to match the seriousness of the infraction.

Overwarning takes two forms: warning too many times or putting an exaggerated threat into your warnings. People will quickly see through either approach. As a result, your warnings soon lose corrective force.

Underwarning also takes two forms: not giving enough warnings before taking more extreme measures, or warning too lightly, so that the rule-breaker doesn't realize how serious you consider the offense. Either form of underwarning is likely to bring deep resentment from the objects of your discipline. They don't mind the light warnings, but when further misbehavior forces you to take serious steps, they feel that they've been led into a trap. "Why didn't you tell me it was so serious?" is the complaint you'll get.

3. *Discipline That Punishes*

This is the final, extreme stage of discipline—the step you take when prevention or warning has failed. According to Webster, punishment is "a penalty inflicted on an offender as a retribution, and incidentally for reformation and prevention." The dictionary emphasizes retribution—the "getting-even" element in punishment —and only incidentally brings in "reformation and prevention." This is the way most people think of punishment, but it is *not* the most helpful approach.

On the contrary, punishment that aims first at getting even is the most dangerous kind of discipline. It's the type most likely to arouse deep and long-lived resentment in the offender, his or her friends, even those who had disapproved of the behavior.

Reformation and prevention should be the primary objective of any disciplinary penalty. That's the whole point of using this third type of discipline: it's an all-out attempt to bring rule-breakers back into line.

TESTING THE PENALTY. To make your discipline most effective and most acceptable, the focus should be on points like these:

- Does the proposed punishment tie in directly with the nature of the offense?

- Will it make the offender realize the seriousness of the misconduct?
- Does the punishment take the individual's previous record into consideration?
- Will the disciplinary action leave the person open to future cooperation?
- Will others understand clearly why this form of punishment has been chosen?
- Will this keep the culprit from doing the same thing in the future?
- Is this punishment consistent with past measures for similar offenses?
- Does the punishment set a precedent that will be acceptable six months or a year from now?
- Is there anyone else whose opinion should be sought—a colleague, one's superior, the personnel manager—before going ahead with the discipline?
- Does personnel policy or a contract limit the measures that may be taken?

Occasionally, problems of discipline are created by a group. When this is the case, you may have a broad-gauge organization matter that involves not merely a single executive but may require consideration at the very top. When a group of people breaks the rules or takes issue with them, management must consider the weight of the numbers and go about assisting and dealing with the problem as a major matter.

But by far the usual disciplinary situation involves the individual. And here the manager is on a one-to-one basis that may require that considerable interpersonal skill be brought to bear.

PRIVACY SAVES FACE. The setting of an interview on discipline may be a decisive factor in its effectiveness. A discussion about rule-breaking tends to be intensive and becomes more critical when there are onlookers. Accordingly, even if the rule-breaking incident has taken place in the presence of others, it is advisable to arrange for the discussion to take place in privacy—an office or other isolated spot.

In this neutral surrounding, you can more freely ask the questions that will help get to the bottom of the behavior. And your subordinate is less likely to feel the need to resort to bravado or, for that matter, to intensify any bitterness of feeling he or she may have. In the role of questioner, you want to emphasize that you're trying to understand the rule-breaker's behavior—what was done, when and how it was done, and also the *feeling* behind the act. Was it done in anger? Out of fear? Frustration? Motivation may be difficult to pin down, but it often holds the key both to the true cause of the misdeed and to its penalty. Try to understand what's involved by questions and evaluation of the answers. Out of this conversation will come your decision. Generally it can have two outcomes:

A warning, in which the unacceptable conduct is specified and the serious consequences of repetition are stressed.

A penalty or punishment that in your opinion is appropriate to the misconduct.

5

Status, Status Symbols, and Politics

Status is a major consideration in every culture. In business, where status has money and power implications, rank tells you not only where a person stands on the organization chart but also suggests the degree of clout with which he or she may operate.

Even in organizations that think of themselves as democratic, there are superiors and subordinates. And, as Dick Deadeye says in Gilbert and Sullivan's *H.M.S. Pinafore,* when one person has to obey another's commands, equality is out of the question. It is *inequality,* the authority that higher echelons have over lower ones, that creates status problems and questions of protocol between boss and subordinate. In fact, it is status that *makes* a boss a boss and a subordinate a subordinate. Ignorance of the etiquette considerations imposed by status can cause insult and upset of major proportions.

HOW STATUS AFFECTS EVEN CASUAL CONVERSATION

You are standing at the elevators a few minutes before quitting time and a colleague comes along and says, "Working only half a day?" You laugh at the remark and say goodnight. A few seconds later, the Big Boss comes along. "Working half a day?" he says. You laugh this time, too, but it has a hollow ring, and you go down the elevator thinking, "Was that a reprimand?"

Both superiors and subordinates should be aware of the effect that status may have on conversation . . .

HOW TO TALK TO A SUBORDINATE AND MINIMIZE OVERREACTION

A boss may be able to joke with subordinates with whom he or she works closely. But with most people, the lightest pronouncements from someone up the line take on weight that may lead to shock or injured feelings.

In dealing with individuals down the line, a boss should:

• *Be aware of the "exaggeration effect" of status.* For instance, kidding, generally undertaken for purposes of humor, may seem less than funny if it can be interpreted as containing a hidden barb. And "reading in" unintended meanings is not the only hazard. Subordinates may be overeager to respond. This requires that a boss:

• *Be as simple and unambiguous as possible.* "I'd like to have that report as soon as you can get to it," a department head tells a clerk. The desired document is on the boss's desk next morning, and the supervisor is chagrined to learn that the clerk put in four hours of overtime to accomplish the feat. "How dumb," the boss thinks, knowing it would have been all right to get the report by the afternoon. That being the case, he should have said so: "I'd like to have the report no later than five o'clock tomorrow."

HOW TO LISTEN TO A BOSS AND MINIMIZE OVERREACTION

Subordinates should be on guard against reading meaning into the words of upper-echelon people. A superior may be blunt, curt, or simply vague; but the message may come through as being *very* blunt, *disturbingly* curt, or *mysteriously* vague if one is overly conscious of the status difference. To avoid overreacting, a subordinate should:

• *Listen for meaning.* Don't be too literal in interpreting the words a superior uses. You may hear: "That's the last time I'm going to ask Janet to do the totals." That doesn't call for you to look up your colleague Janet and tell her the boss is through giving her a particular type of assignment. It *may* mean that. It might also mean a piqued and harried boss is merely reacting to the frustration of the moment and will forget all about the annoyance tomorrow. Careful listening can clarify the subtle nuances of meaning and intention behind the words.

• *Avoid taking matters personally.* Some bosses are prone to fly off the handle. They'll scold or blame a subordinate for an error or oversight. Seldom are such tirades intended in a personal away—even when they seem to be. Most working people—at all levels—

realistically accept the work objectives of the department and organization. It's understood that a person may make a mistake without being lazy, careless, or irresponsible.

• *Put what a superior says in the context of the past relationship.* If the subordinate and superior have a friendly feeling between them, the former should realize that one falling-out is likely to be temporary. The long-range factors that made for good relations are likely to outweigh short-range difficulties.

INFORMALITY AS A STATUS EQUALIZER

The informal manner used between people of different status tends to minimize discrepancies of rank, such elements of informality as

- the use of first names
- a breezy, friendly manner
- willingness of the superior to unbend and avoid any suggestion of superior status—tend to lower status barriers.

It is usually the superior's choice and initiative that determine the degree of formality or informality that permeates relationships. Reasons for minimizing status barriers, such as increased openness and a freer flow of communication, are the benefits that might induce a person of higher status to prefer more informal relations with people on lower rungs of the status ladder.

A person of lower status who may feel that informality will make for a better working atmosphere and relationship may initiate less formal relations by *being* friendly, *being* open, and probably influencing the higher-status individual to do likewise.

HOW TO IDENTIFY THE "BOSS"

A visitor to a company is introduced to two executives, Mr. Jones and Miss Smith. Somehow the visitor doesn't catch the titles. His perception of status is shaped by the fact that Mr. Jones is talkative and assertive, while Miss Smith is somewhat reticent. The visitor, wanting to work with the "power" in the organization, inivites Mr. Jones to lunch, and subsequently learns to his embarrassment that Miss Smith is Mr. Jones's boss.

It's unwise to make assumptions about people's rank on the basis of behavior. You can expect to meet shy presidents and big-mouth file clerks. Also, when an action you plan to take depends on the relative rank and status of people, make sure to pin down the information you need to move properly: "Am I right in thinking that it's Mr. Miller who makes the buying decisions in the personnel services area?"

RANK AND STATUS CONFER SPECIAL PRIVILEGES

While we may all have been created equal, we surely don't end up that way, particularly as we find our niches in organizational echelons. And most organizations, in many ways ranging from facilities to daily custom, give preferred treatment to those of higher rank.

It's important that every organization citizen—or visitor, too, for that matter—become acquainted with the privileges of rank extended within a given organization. In one case it may be an executive dining room, special recreation privileges, special services—everything from a company car to exclusive parking space. The considerate manager will go out of his or her way to keep from focusing on these special privileges in the presence of people who don't have them.

By and large, it's advisable for people at all echelons to go along with the organization's tradition. In other words, not only should the nonqualified individual not try to crash the barriers of rank but, similarly, the higher executive is ill-advised to flout the system. Yes, of course, the executive may from time to time eat in the employees' cafeteria rather than the executive dining quarters. But unless boat-rocking and rebellion is intentional and purposeful, it's an affront to all those who abide by the "rules"—executive as well as employee—to reject offered privileges.

NEWCOMERS SHOULD LEARN THE ROPES

From time to time, an individual appears on the workscene who finds the milieu unfamiliar for a number of reasons:

- It's a new job with a new company.
- It's a new situation as the result of a job transfer.
- One is a "semipermanent" visitor—a consultant, for example.

Whatever the reason, the customs and observances of rank and status are not known. The height of wisdom in this situation, both for reasons of etiquette and for the future relationship with those present, is not to make assumptions as to what is and isn't acceptable behavior. The Easterner who rejects the more relaxed style—everything from clothes to conversation—of new Western colleagues, is causing unnecessary problems for himself or herself. The individual who is used to socializing after hours in a work locale where this is seldom done will only be making everyone uncomfortable by trying to force fraternization.

Of course, one needn't depend on the slow passage of time and exposure to learn the score. Best move is to talk to a colleague, neighbor, one's superior, or assigned contact person and ask about what goes and doesn't go in the areas of activity of which you're a part. You may want to cover anything from the location of the key to the bathroom you're entitled to use to getting the lowdown on the restaurants frequented by people at your level. Again, how closely you want to adhere to custom and how much flexibility you want to allow yourself depend on your personal set of values. In general, one must say that the person who doesn't like the game shouldn't be playing.

WHAT ABOUT RANK OFF THE JOB?

For some people, a difficulty occurs when they encounter a person of different status "on the outside." For example:

Executive Gil Hadley has been invited to join some members of his staff for a couple of beers in the local pub, to be followed by an evening of bowling. He feels it would be both stuffy and undesirable—he likes the people, beer, and bowling—to refuse. But how should he behave? Is he still "boss" off the job, or is hail-fellow-well-met the keynote for his behavior?

Gil Hadley would probably be wise to avoid acting out his usual leadership role. True enough, if a boss tries to be the life of the party over a beer or two, his subordinates will probably go along. But their laughter will be a little more raucous than the boss's jokes justify, and in retrospect the evening will probably be thought of as one where the boss threw his weight around socially and perverted the true nature of the event. After all, the boss was invited along as a guest. This requires *not* usurping the position or role of the host.

In one's attempt to be "one of the boys" or "one of the girls," some people are tempted to play the clown. Accordingly, they display exaggerated discomfort or "comical" reactions. For example, a boss behaves as though he never drank a glass of beer and acts drunk, or suggests he's never been bowling and goes down the alley with his fingers locked in the ball. Acting in a normal, relaxed way and letting the others set the pace and mode of conduct is likely to be the best bet for optimum enjoyment and minimum embarrassment to anyone.

THE IMPORTANCE OF "CHANNELS"

Organizations tend to institutionalize status levels by creating channels of communication; that is, designated paths by which messages move between the echelons. If, for example, a supervisor wants to suggest an idea to a level of management with which he or she is not usually in contact, proper channels dictate that the message go to the boss, who will pass along the item if it's deemed appropriate.

Channels can become an *obstacle* to communication or can *facilitate* it by providing an orderly flow up and down the organization. Whether the former or the latter is the case depends on the degree of flexibility executives permit. A policy of medium permissiveness makes the most sense. When executives are too permissive ("My door is open to anyone at any time") or bypassing is encouraged, channels disintegrate and chaos takes over. But absolute adherence to channels chokes off communication from below, largely because there's a tendency for intermediary people—secretaries, lower-level managers—to block would-be communicators from the lower ranks.

HOW TO MAKE BYPASSING ACCEPTABLE

Some people fret at the need to "go through channels" in communications. "Just a lot of red tape," they say. And they resent the individual who must be used as a go-between or routing station for a communication aimed elsewhere. For example:

Ken Black wants to suggest an idea for a new sales approach that he feels will help sell one of the company's products that is not doing well. He feels, and correctly, that the right person to judge the idea is the V.P. Marketing. And he knows that he shouldn't try to contact the V.P. directly, but to explain the idea to his boss and hope that it will be passed along.

To try to get to the V.P. *without* getting his boss into the act would be bypassing, Black knows, and bypassing, he also knows, is often considered a punishable "crime" in management circles. No one likes to have his position or status flouted.

The fact is that bypassing can be done to expedite communication, to make sure that a message gets through to an eventual destination undistorted by intermediaries—and without upsetting people's feelings about their own role or status:

• *First, be sure you know what the "proper channel" is.* You spell this out in your own mind to pinpoint the individuals—or even the procedures—that you will be shortcutting. For example, in Ken Black's case, he knew it was just his boss involved in the bypass. In other situations, two or more people might properly make up the "channel" you are trying to circumvent.

• *Get permission to bypass.* If you can get the intermediaries to O.K. your move, you're in the clear. But you must go high enough up in the chain, *to the person in position to take the last step.* What this means: Say Ken Black's boss would have to pass an idea to *his* boss before it could go to the V.P. Marketing. Then Black's boss's boss would have to approve the contact between Black and the V.P.

• *Report back on the outcome.* It's a simple courtesy to let the people who have given their permission in on the result. This may be given in a general way: "I talked to Mr. Walker about the idea. He seemed interested and said he'd let me know in a few days whether it could be used."

HOW TO HANDLE THE UNPLANNED BYPASS

Let's stick with Ken Black for another moment. He's going down in the elevator one evening and who should be standing next to him but the V.P. Marketing. They know each other from a few previous contacts.

"Hi, Ken. How are things going?"

"Fine, Mr. Walker. We're really moving ahead with those plans on the new line."

"Glad to hear it. Customer interest in the standard line is falling off. . . ."

Now Ken has a ready-made opening for his idea about a new presentation. He mentions it to Mr. Walker, who seems to respond favorably and says he'll get back to him in a couple of days.

Now what Ken must do to prevent his boss's upset is to mention the conversation as soon as possible: "Mr. Walker and I met by chance in the elevator last night, and we got to talking about the X line. I mentioned an idea I had for changing the sales presentation, and he seemed interested enough to say he'd think it over. . . ."

One additional point: if and when Walker does want to get back to Ken, he should include Ken's boss in the meeting—or copy him in if it's a written communication. This is to avoid *downward* bypassing, which can be as objectionable as the more common variety.

ABUSES OF STATUS

Status suggests superiority and inferiority. A person of superior status wields a kind of power over a subordinate. Power misapplied may take unacceptable forms. Examples of these abuses will shortly be given. But first, some preliminary guidelines to correct the misuse of status:

First, it should be clearly recognized that each of the examples given below are *abuses* of authority and, as such, are to be avoided by holders of rank as far as possible.

Second, victims or witnesses of the status-abusers, when catching the latter in the act, should tactfully let their erring colleague know that he or she is not playing the game properly, that bullying subordinates or otherwise taking advantage of one's status to browbeat or manipulate is distasteful behavior.

Here are some incidents that show the status-abuser in action:

PULLING RANK

A higher-status person can use his or her position as a direct means of achieving some desired objective. For example:

Grace Falcon is about to pull into the lone unoccupied space left in the company parking lot. It's raining, and she is relieved that she won't have to park either in the street or in a commercial parking lot two blocks away. Suddenly, with a considerable amount of horn-blowing, her boss's car bears down on hers, and the boss waves her away. "Got a meeting I'm late for," he shouts out the window and takes the spot.

The person against whom rank is pulled has two possible courses of action:

• *Immediate.* An individual intimidated by a superior pulling rank *may* take issue with the rank-puller if it is perceived as it happens. One can speak up in the midst of the process, for example, and ask a blunt question: "Sir, are you pulling rank on me?" In some cases the offender may back off, since the out-of-line behavior has been brought into the spotlight—where it doesn't look attractive.

If the person is stiff-necked, however, he or she may persist: "Yes, I am. And I intend to. . . ." If the individual does have authority in the situation involved, then the victim may have no further recourse and must for the moment be content with having voiced a protest. A counterstatement may be made: "I'm sorry you're adopting this tactic in order to have your way."

• *After the fact.* Again using the Grace Falcon situation, if the rank-pulling rankles or the victim is sufficiently angry to want to speak up, not only to prevent a repetition in the future but also as a definition of his or her own sense of justice and integrity, it should be done in the following way:

FORMALIZE THE SITUATION. To give what's being said sufficient impact, don't make the exchange on the fly. Either make an appointment or somehow arrange to be closeted with the executive in privacy. At the very outset make clear the purpose of the meeting: "I'm here because I want to discuss the incident that happened this morning. . . ."

DON'T BE ACCUSATORY. You don't want a hassle. So that your comments will be taken to heart, avoid immediate criticism. As a matter of fact, begin by mitigating the circumstance: "Perhaps you weren't aware of just how your behavior looked to an observer. But as the person involved, I can tell you that what you said and the way you said it made a very unpleasant impression. It's the closest I've come to being bullied since I was a child. . . ."

What you say should be the result of the nature of the rank-pulling. But whatever is said should be couched as far as possible in nonaccusatory and matter-of-fact language. If the words and their tone are properly selected, the executive, much as he might dislike having his hand called, should have little reason for resentment.

USING "CLOUT"

"Jerry is throwing his weight around." That's the way a colleague described a middle-level executive with an overinflated sense of his own importance and a distorted idea of how his authority should be used. One example of Jerry's use of what he thinks of as "clout" (he's on the phone with a clerk in Maintenance: "Listen, Ellie," he says, "that water cooler has been out of order since yesterday. I want you to get an electrician down here no later than noon today, and that's final."

He hangs up with the self-satisfied feeling that he certainly knows how to get action. Less obvious to him is the fact that he's being *unreasonable.* It's not Ellie's fault that the outside service firm is holding up the works. He's well on his way to being the most unpopular manager on the block not only because of his demand for instant service but because he's treating a minor matter like a major crisis.

The "I'm-the-boss" syndrome crops up in a broad range of situations, from one like the browbeating of the maintenance clerk to matters of greater moment in company operations. For example, a top executive may insist that his decision or solution be accepted by subordinates simply because it *is* his. Regardless of the justification for this type of behavior from an efficiency standpoint—after all, the boss actually *may* know better than his subordinates—it's highly undesirable that such moves be crammed down subordinates' throats. A boss may decide his way is best and try to persuade subordinates to see things his way. If not, a conclusion such as "You may be right, but I'm going to risk doing it my way. . . ." takes some of the sting out of the move.

In instances of browbeating or bullying, the idea seems to be that the subordinate "must take it" because of lower rank. In the business situation, unlike the military, a subordinate does have some recourse:

QUIT. If the provocation is sufficiently severe, the subordinate may threaten to quit or actually give up the job.

FIGHT BACK. "I don't have to stand for that kind of talk," an employee says to a raging and insulting superior. "If I've done something wrong, let's discuss it. But nothing I may have done gives you the right to use abusive language."

APPEAL TO A HIGHER AUTHORITY. Either as a threat or as a means of seeking justice, one may advise the browbeater that counsel and judgment will be sought at a higher echelon: "I'm going to talk to Mr. Todd about this matter, to get the benefits of his objectivity."

Of course, this move may sour a subordinate's position with the boss. But where the affront has been unforgivable or it has happened more than once, one owes it to one's own self-respect to seek remedial action.

LEAVE THE SCENE. In some cases, a subordinate may simply turn and leave the room. He or she may be putting the job on the line. But the move is a nonverbal way of getting across the message: "I refuse to take this kind of treatment from anyone. If you want to talk about the problem at a later date, O.K. But right now, I'm getting out of the line of fire."

UNDERCUTTING OTHERS

"Pauline sure likes to chop people down." Pauline Tracy may not even be aware of it herself, but too often she uses her authority to undercut people. One example: She's talking to an assistant purchasing agent and isn't satisfied with the answers she gets to her questions. "Switch me to your boss," she says angrily, "I'm just wasting my time talking to you."

What should the assistant do in this situation? Here is a recommended course of action:

• *Switch her.* No point in continuing the conversation or refusing to accede. The assistant should turn Pauline over to the boss.

• *Check with the boss.* As soon as possible, the assistant should go to the boss to clarify what it was that Pauline Tracy wanted and try to ascertain why it was that she wasn't getting the information she wanted.

• *Check with Pauline.* As soon as convenient, the assistant should talk to Pauline Tracy. The reason for the difficulty should be explained: "I'm sorry, but it wasn't clear to me that you were talking about material we had already received." Willingness to help should be made clear: "If you have any similar requests in the future, please don't hesitate to call me. I'm sure we can get matters like that straightened out without any trouble."

If these steps are executed properly, working relations will improve.

A "PROPER USE OF AUTHORITY" REVIEW

The three cases described and any other instances where authority is misused are clearly to be avoided. The point made in the Pauline Tracy case is especially worth emphasizing: people may abuse their status *without being aware of it.*

It may not be enough to counsel, "Don't abuse your authority." But it may help to suggest, "Review your use of authority," by questions like these:

Do I avoid using authority as a weapon to manipulate people or to put them down?

When appropriate, do I use authority to protect others, use it defensively rather than offensively?

Do I respect it in others without going overboard?

And finally, an important clincher:

Do I use authority only as a last resort? (This suggests avoiding "being bossy"—using your clout only when other moves have failed in order to fulfill your job responsibilities).

PRACTICAL LIMITS OF EXECUTIVE AUTHORITY

Executives can hire, fire, discipline, promote, and sometimes move people from Maine to California or, indeed, from New York to Timbuktu. That the executive has power is clear. And, noting the many manifestations of executive power, there's sometimes a tendency to think of the executive as omnipotent. Well, at one time, perhaps, employers could be harsh and arbitrary with employees. But in contemporary times executive authority is limited, sometimes severely so.

Managers at every level will avoid embarrassing themselves and causing unnecessary complications in their relations with subordinates by being aware of the restrictions on their use of authority. Here are some of the areas in which executive authority is off limits:

SUBORDINATE'S PERSONAL INTEGRITY IN SELF-RELATED ACTIVITIES

The president of a Philadelphia bank tells a friend, "My staff people are badly in need of management training. Although they're good in their jobs, each one is severely limited by ignorance of the concepts and techniques of professional management."

Replies the other, "Why don't you send them to seminars or have them enroll in management-training courses at some of the local universities?"

The president shakes his head. "I can't order men with their status to take actions of that kind. They have to want to do it on their own. . . ."

POLICY AND UPPER ECHELONS CAP ONE'S AUTHORITY

An executive would be running into trouble if he or she contradicted an action or privilege that was condoned by company policy. If, for example, management has agreed that employees may have a particular day off as a paid holiday, no executive is in a position to rescind this permission.

In some cases a manager's superior may be the higher authority that restricts one's ability to act.

ORDER MUST GO THROUGH CHANNELS—DOWNWARD AS WELL AS UPWARD

"Please don't give my subordinates instructions," a supervisor tells his boss. "If there's anything you want done, let me know and I'll see that the appropriate action is taken." The supervisor is making a perfectly valid point. No matter at what echelon an executive may be, it's unacceptable practice to give orders to an employee who reports to another manager. The fact that this is sometimes done doesn't make it right or acceptable. This particular infringement, sometimes called "double-bossing," is not only improper from an etiquette standpoint, it can also be demoralizing in terms of individual roles and responsibilities.

AN EXECUTIVE'S EMPIRE USUALLY STOPS AT THE COMPANY'S FRONT DOOR

Another restriction that can be both geographic and social: executives may not dictate behavior off the organization's premises or in an individual's personal affairs. And this may be true even though the executive has good intentions. For example:

Hal Deems notices that a young newcomer in his department has become friendly with one of the old-timers. He's aware that they're socializing on the outside, and Deems, partly out of a parental interest, feels that the young man is going to be traduced by his contacts with the older colleague—who has a reputation as a heavy drinker, a frequenter of questionable places of entertainment, and so on. With this in mind, Deems tries to play Dutch uncle to the young employee and counsels him against spending time with the other man.

"How I spend my time and with whom is my own business," the youngster says and walks off.

Ruefully, Deems realizes the rebuff is perfectly justified and somewhat reluctantly makes the right decision—which is to butt out.

THE SUBTLE LINE BETWEEN PROPER AND IMPROPER USE OF AUTHORITY

The instances we've been talking about above are fairly clear-cut. There's no question that an executive, however good his intentions, may not intrude on a subordinate's private affairs. But even within the limits of a subordinate's job there are restrictions on what a boss may do because of the consequences. For example, there can be adverse results from a boss offering too much help, trying to win acceptance for his own personal values. The problem with such use of influence is that it can be destructive of the subordinate's individuality, initiative, and creativity. A superior who is too dominant tends to create either dependence or rebellion. Either of these represents limiting constrictions on what a superior may or may not do with authority.

MEETING THE BOSS IN SOCIAL SITUATIONS

An organization affair, a trade convention, a promotional or departmental cocktail party may bring you into contact with people up the line. This may be your boss, your boss's boss, or other higher-echelon executives. For some people the prospect of meeting top brass in such situations suggests problems:

The very first one may be: "Should I go up and talk to the boss [or other top executive] or stay away?" Usually this consideration arises out of the individual's shyness or doubts as to what to say. Second question: "Should I be formal, or act naturally?" It's most likely that if these matters can be handled comfortably, even a strong tendency toward shyness can be minimized. Here are some suggestions that can help convert this edgy situation into a pleasant and worthwhile occasion:

• *Step right up.* To the question: "Should I or shouldn't I?" the answer is: "By all means, yes." Opportunities for meeting people in the higher echelons outside routine work situations can yield opportunities for improving relations and better understanding.

• *Relax—there are no rules.* Don't feel that you have to live up to any specific expectation or any special mode of conduct. Yes, of course you'll be pleasant, courteous, and so on. But chances are that informality will be more welcome than a high level of decorum. Men and women at the top are as varied in individual taste and manner as are other people, and to some extent you can be guided by cues offered by the people themselves. If you are met by a jovial, shoulder-patting approach, you can increase the degree of your informality. If the other person is quiet and somewhat withdrawn, your approach can be toned down.

• *If you can, avoid weather talk.* Of course, as a last resort and if other subjects don't come to mind, any small-talk subject from the weather to an item in the day's newspaper will serve. But, fortunately, there are steps you can take and approaches you can make that will make it possible to avoid the inanity of meaningless chitchat. (To make small talk meaningful communication, see "Making Small Talk Sound Big," page 201.)

• *Do some homework.* If you expect a particular member of the top brass to be present, try to learn a little about him or her personally. Certainly get the name right. But a few bits of information can remove some of the question marks. It will be helpful, for example, to learn his or her:

rank and title;
length of time with the firm;
nature of the job (head of Sales, and so on);
mutual friends you may have in or out of the organization;
special interest or hobby;

sports interest;
charitable or philanthropic interests;
university;
club or other professional affiliation.

Somewhere in your organization there should be a biographical sketch that will provide the helpful information—a company handbook, a press release at the time of a promotion, the recollections of other people you know who have the information, or possibly a reference book such as *Who's Who in America.*

Covering this type of information helps you figure out in advance some of the topics that might be appropriate. At the very least, you will see the outlines of a human being, not just a high-sounding title.

• *If you're nervous, try to forget yourself.* Chances are, the top executive is aware that you might be ill at ease in his company. He may, in fact, be shy himself. But he'll undoubtedly try to make the situation more comfortable for both of you. You help this entente by keeping your mind off your timidity, your possible awe at the difference between your stations, your hopes of impressing him favorably, and so on.

• *Avoid the hazards.* Some subjects are even worse than the small-talk items. For example, here's a list of things to *stay away* from:

what's wrong with the organization;
what's wrong with your department;
what's wrong with a colleague;
what's wrong with your boss;
what you would do if you were head of the company;
religion (unless he or she brings it up);
politics (ditto);
his or her job and how he or she is doing it;
"inside information" about the organization;
anything controversial that may lead to disagreement or argument.

• *Prethink a list of worthwhile subjects.* Just as there are some subjects that create conversational hazards, there are others that make for relevant and pleasant talk. Consider these possibilities:

something good that's happened in the company;
an outstanding performance by a colleague or subordinate;

your interest in a new development in the organization or related
   area;
a positive comment on some area of his interest ("As a tennis
   player you must have found yesterday's championship matches
   pretty interesting");
subjects in which you may have a common interest—you both
   may be sailors, collect stamps, or whatever;
favorable things about the present surroundings—anything from
   "The canapés are unusually good" to the bright decor of the
   room.

• *Ask questions.* An approved way to get someone—anyone—
talking is to ask a question on a subject in which the person is expert
or interested. Naturally you'll want to avoid the taboo subjects mentioned above. But, knowing something of his or her background, a
single question can start the conversation going.

• *Remember that a good listener makes a good impression.* And
you're not expected to put on a performance. As the conversation
moves along, relax. One subject often suggests another, and you'll
be on your way.

One of the happier things that may result—some matter will
come up that warrants some later contact: "Why, yes, Mr. Jones, I
do happen to have the photograph of the cornerstone ceremony of
the main building in my study at home. I'll be glad to bring it
in. . . ."

You won't be surprised to learn that your boss, or whoever the
other top-echelon person may be, will be as pleased at a friendly
exchange as you are.

MAKING SMALL TALK SOUND BIG

Small talk—conversation about seemingly innocuous subjects—is
usually considered an escape hatch. One resorts to it when there
seems to be no relevant matter of substance to talk about. It is dealt
with in the context of status because it is so often used when two
people from an upper and a lower echelon meet in a non-task-ori-
ented situation.

Most people use small talk defensively. They use it "to relax tension," to "fill the silence." Most people advocate small talk as a line
of chatter to fall back on when nothing better offers.

But listen to a real master of small talk and you become aware
that, used properly, it can:

- create a positive and pleasant atmosphere;
- be a personal asset, project you as a fluent and attractive individual.

Some people have developed the knack of making small talk seem relevant, even vital. An analysis of those who use small talk effectively shows that they do the following:

- *Make it specific.* They select subject matter that often grows out of the situation—what is visible on the scene, something that has just happened.

- *Speak up, assert.* Unlike the defensive small-talker, who kind of tentatively suggests that it's a nice day, or what a good game the local ball team played, the effective small-talker speaks affirmatively, even with zest: "What a beautiful day! You know, it's weather like this that makes one glad to be alive. As I walked across the yard, I looked up at that pure blue sky and all the world's troubles seemed to shrink away. . . ."

O.K. Some people reading the above might utter a loud horse-laugh and say, "Who are you kidding? I can just see the look on my boss's face if I were to go off on some kind of lyrical trip. . . ."

No one suggests that small talk be injected inappropriately, so that it becomes obtrusive. What is recommended is that, at the times when you use small talk, it be delivered in a warm and positive tone. Essentially, what you're after is:

- *A communication of feeling.* There is certainly nothing newsworthy in a conversation about the weather or your comment on a recent news item. What you are communicating is not *meaning* but *feeling.* It is your *emotion* that should be the content of your words —your *pleasure* at seeing a gem-blue sky, your *excitement* over an impending sports event, your impulse to *share* an experience you've just had. It is this kind of small talk that stimulates a positive frame of mind in the listener.

- *Injection and transition.* Finally, the thing that makes the expert small-talker effective is that he or she is able to *introduce* remarks into the conversation, then switch back to any business at hand with naturalness. For example:

Secretary Joan Beck is in the office of the company's purchasing agent, explaining what her boss's equipment needs will be when the new MT/ST system is installed. A call comes in and the P.A. excuses himself and has a three-minute conversation with someone about a delayed order.

Joan Beck stands and goes over to the window. The P.A. hangs up, and Beck, standing at the window, says, "I just love looking at this view. How the city has changed. I grew up in this town, and when I was a youngster there wasn't a single building over five stories high."

"You're right. Those three tall buildings have gone up in the last few years."

Joan Beck sits down. "I guess growth and change is the natural order of things. Well"—a slight pause—"to get back to what we were saying . . . "And she's back on track again.

Notice two things about Joan Beck's small talk. First, she hasn't reached out for some irrelevant topic. At the window it becomes perfectly natural for her to comment about the view. And second, she avoids an attempt at a strained switch back. She lets a pause signal the return to the business at hand.

One hazard of small talk is that it may become too interesting in its own right, and therefore difficult to break away from. But if the transition is made well, the time span can be controlled.

Be assured that the seeming irrelevancy is building a stronger relationship between you and your listener. You have broken—to good advantage—the "strictly business" mold. For example, you can be sure that Joan Beck's image as a person has improved in the purchasing agent's mind.

WHEN THE BOSS VISITS YOU AT HOME

It's a situation celebrated in cartoon and story. The employee brings his boss home for dinner. And everything that can go wrong does! But it need not go that way. Remember, it's only the first visit that creates unknowns—and the shakes. Subsequent visits come easily.

There are times when inviting the boss to your home is natural and appropriate—without having your motives be suspect. For example:

The boss frets over a crucial meeting: "I wish there were some-place the four of us could meet out of the office. . . ."

"Let's use my apartment. The family is going to be away, and it's just a few minutes' drive," you may suggest.

Assuming there's a first-time visit coming up, here are the kinds of questions to resolve:

HOW ABOUT AN IMPROMPTU INVITATION? Some people might turn thumbs down on this one. They have in mind the burden this may create for one's spouse, children, and so on. But there's a difference between an *impromptu invitation* and an *unexpected visit.*

There are occasions—perhaps you're at a local trade fair with your boss, and your home is just a few blocks away—when an invitation to accompany you home for a drink may be a highly desirable way of improving a relationship. If there are others at home, the invitation should be made provisionally:

"Bill, I'd love you to stop in for a few minutes and meet my wife and family. Let me just telephone to make sure that there won't be any problem. . . ."

When you call, if it's your spouse you're talking to, *ask* her if it will be all right. Of course, if there are any strong objections, it isn't. And you can turn to your boss and back off with some general explanation of why you'll have to make it another time. At any rate, your move to alert your spouse or others should be appreciated by your boss as a thoughtful gesture.

But if your wife is agreeable, it will be helpful to her to explain what you have in mind—is the boss coming for a drink, or do you think he'll expect a dinner invitation? Whatever it is, tell her whatever she needs to know to make at least minimum preparations.

MAKING THE BOSS FEEL AT HOME IN YOUR HOME

The more smoothly and pleasantly things go, the better for all concerned, of course. You'll be helped toward this end by adopting these guidelines:

• *First names?* One question, a minor one but important because it sets a tone: Should you use first names? If you introduce your spouse, for example, by saying, "Louise, I'd like you to meet Mr. Jones," then you're creating a superior-subordinate situation. This is not necessarily wrong. The point is to realize that the way the introductions are made will set a level at which people will be interacting.

Part of the answer depends on how you and your boss address each other at the office. If you're on a first-name basis there, there's no reason not to make the introductions:

"This is my wife, Jane. Pete Jones . . ."

Juniors in the family should be introduced only by their first names unless for some reason their second name is different from yours, in which case a word of explanation is required:

"This is my nephew, Al Lucas. He's staying with us for a few days. . . ."

• *Relaxed atmosphere.* To a large extent, the climate will be a reflection of your own attitude. If you feel any tensions or anxiety about the situation, try to keep them from infecting others. As far as you can, *act* in an easygoing, nothing-to-get-excited-about manner.

One of the things that may detract from an appearance of ease, and accordingly is to be avoided, is an elaborate briefing of other family members:

Don't warn of terrible punishments if "anything goes wrong."

Don't demand artificial behavior, such as rigid politeness and stiff courtesy.

Don't try to "reset the stage."

One overanxious person borrowed a portable bar from a kind-hearted neighbor in order to make a favorable impression, and then discovered that his boss frowned on the use of liquor.

• *Minimum fuss.* Of course, you want your domicile to look as pleasant and attractive as possible. But if last-minute changes are needed, keep them at a minimum. Actually it's better for a house to have a reasonably "lived-in" look than to have your spouse come up to the wire with a spotless and gleaming living room, kitchen, and bath, but also breathless and too tired to be gracious.

• *Briefing.* Don't overload family members with all kinds of information and instructions about what to say, how to behave, and so on. A few positive words will be helpful:

"Kids, my boss, Mr. Jones, is coming to dinner tonight. He has children about your age, and I think you'll like him."

You may want to make suggestions of a generally low-pressure nature that can be helpful. Say to younger family members:

"Mary, I'd like you to come down and meet my boss, Mr. Jones, but if you'd like to leave after a few minutes, just excuse yourself and go."

However, with your spouse or other family members who will be spending some time with your boss, you may want to provide other cues for conversation:

"Mr. Smith just came back from a month's visit to Australia. He probably has some interesting stories to tell."

Or: "Mr. White is a great vegetable gardener, Helen. He might be able to give you some tips on how to get better results with your tomatoes this summer."

• *His or her good standing in your household.* A boss's reputation with an employee's family is entirely a reflection of what the employee makes it. Where the boss has been painted as an irascible tyrant, a special mitigating message is probably called for before he arrives:

"Although Mr. Green is a pretty tough-minded person at work, he's really quite nice in a social situation."

But if your boss's reputation is a good one, the whole evening is off to a good start. The atmosphere, for example, will move several notches toward the desirable end of the scale if your spouse can honestly say, "Tom has been telling us for years how lucky he is to have you for a boss."

In some cases the comment may address itself to a recent success:

"Tom has told me about the great job you did putting the X Division back on its feet. . . ."

Or, from an older child: "Dad has told us that he really enjoys working with you."

If none of these happy statements can be made honestly, the next best thing is to make clear your hospitable feelings:

"It's really a great pleasure to meet you. . . ."

"After all these months that you and my husband have been working together, it's about time you paid us a visit."

• *Show the boss around?* Everyone has things at home that he's proud of. On the other hand, if the visit is somewhat unexpected and there's been insufficient time to straighten out anything but the living room and bathroom, you can skip the tour. But if there's no reason not to, then take the boss around, show him your den, the garden, your prize roses, and so on.

• *Conversational gambits.* Of course, what to talk about and what to avoid is always a prime consideration. Stick to the good subjects. This means essentially things you can be positive about. You can even talk shop as long as the tone of the conversation is pleasant and positive. The boss may have ideas about which way the conversation should go. If this is the case, let him or her set the tone. There's just one situation to be wary of:

"Henry," the boss says to you, "I'd like your honest opinion on something. What do you really think of Harriet Miller for the assistant buyer's spot?"

If you think Harriet Miller is a good choice, then say so, particularly if it's your hunch that this is in line with what the boss would like to hear. But if you think Miller is a terrible choice, be less explicit in your comments. You don't want your home to be the setting for a character assassination, no matter how deserved. You can make clear your reservations and doubts about Miller, making your judgment in a temperate way without being trapped in either hypocrisy or vilification.

• *"Please stay for dinner."* A common situation is one where the boss has been invited in for a before-dinner drink and gradually dinnertime has been approaching. Are you obliged to offer a dinner invitation?

If you don't want to tender such an invitation, don't. You may let yourself off the hook by such statements as:

"I'm sorry we can't ask you to stay for dinner, but we're eating out tonight" (or whatever explanation you can muster that is appropriate to the situation.)

If you do want to extend the invitation, of course go ahead. The "chef" may want to make clear what the menu is, particularly if it's a modest one and the boss's expectations are to be kept at a low level. Always better to play down to avoid disappointments.

But there's an in-between situation where you're not too eager to have the boss stay, but neither do you want to fail to make the invitation. In this case the message can be put in tentative terms in such a way that the initiative is left with the boss. For example:

"I'd love to have you stay for dinner, but of course you may have a previous engagement, and in that case. . . ."

Or: "If you don't mind taking pot luck—you know we're vegetarians here—we'd very much like to have you join us. . . ."

• *End the visit on a positive note.* Hosts have a final opportunity to tie a neat ribbon on a visit. This is the farewell that's said as the boss is leaving. You send him on his journey in the best possible way if your good-byes or goodnights sound a strong, positive note:

"We've enjoyed the evening tremendously and hope you have, too. . . ."

INVITATION TO THE BOSS'S HOME: TREAT OR THREAT?

It may be your fond wish to get an invitation from your boss— perhaps to dinner, an "election watch" and late supper, a Sunday brunch, or whatever. Here are some of the considerations to make:

• *Should you ever refuse?* This may seem like an unlikely possibility. After all, such an invitation is usually a much-sought-after opportunity by most people. Still, there are occasions when you may have to turn down an offer and express your regrets:

When a prior engagement or a commitment elsewhere causes a time conflict. One instance when a person refused her boss's invitation involved not the boss but the boss's wife: "My relations with Mr. Miller are perfectly pleasant," says one executive secretary, "but I've had enough contact with Mrs. Miller to know she's a difficult woman. I think I'd feel very uncomfortable as her guest. . . ."

Of course, the argument might be made that perhaps Mrs. Miller should be given a chance to overcome her bad image at least once.

If the secretary's first visit has confirmed her feelings, then she may probably wisely turn down the second.

In some cases an invitation may be a kind of "reward" given to subordinates as a sop for the boss's malpractices at the office. This may make an invitation uninviting and refusable. A polite excuse—young kids at home, an ailing spouse, and so on—will solve the problem.

And one manager says, "I don't intend ever to set foot inside that man's door again. I'm sick and tired of being used as a captive audience to hear about his high-power lawn mower, how much it cost to build his patio, and the amount of time he spends cleaning his pool."

But with these rare exceptions, an invitation to the boss's home should be an occasion for both pleasure and relationship-building. Here are some of the points that can maximize the situation:

• *What's it for?* Be sure you understand the nature of the occasion to which you're being asked. Is it dinner? Is it a large, formal dinner? Is it an informal brunch? Is it a breakfast meeting with just you and a few of your colleagues? Whatever the occasion, be clear on it in advance.

• *Who's invited?* Sometimes the invitation may be for you alone. In other cases it's for you and your spouse or possibly even the entire family. Just make sure that you're clear on who's included.

There are some special questions that arise here. Perhaps you're not married but have a fiancée or dear friend with whom you have a close relationship. In these days of more relaxed social codes, you may feel that the invitation should include your friend just as it might your colleagues' spouses. If this is a matter of principle with you, you should tactfully inform your boss of the situation. If the response is other than the one you hoped for, you may then turn down the invitation simply by saying, "I'm awfully sorry, but Jane and I had planned to spend that evening together. . . ."

• *Appropriate dress.* You don't want to show up at a formal dinner wearing slacks, a sport shirt, and sneakers. Nor do you want to appear at a picnic in a business suit. Don't hesitate to ask a direct question: "Would blue jeans and a T-shirt be O.K.?"

• *Let the boss set the tone.* It's the boss's party, and he or she has the privilege of determining everything from the noise level to the degree of informality to be observed. And, of course, the "program" of the occasion is also the host's decision.

However, don't be surprised if your host and hostess simply set the stage and leave it up to you and the other guests to create the atmosphere for the occasion. If it's an outdoor picnic in the boss's backyard, you can sit around and sip cool drinks. Or if you're sports-minded, you may suggest anything from throwing a ball around to practice putting on a smooth part of the lawn.

• *Get set for the tour.* If this is your first visit—and sometimes even if it isn't—the boss may offer to "show you around." Usually such an offer is made when the homeowner has things of which he or she is particularly proud. Certainly, praise whatever you feel is praiseworthy—kitchen, workshop, art collection, greenhouse, and so on. If by chance there's very little you see that deserves commendation—some bosses, like other people, have abominable taste in home decoration—you should nevertheless look for something to praise. But make sure it is something you really find worthwhile—even if it's the kids, a stained-glass window, or a Picasso print.

• *Don't slight your farewell.* Of course, if the visit has been a disaster or everyone has been bored to death, you don't want to overstate. In this case—happily a rare one—you simply express your gratitude for the invitation. Certainly the intention was exemplary.

But, generally speaking, don't play down your farewell. The moment of leavetaking provides an opportunity for you to register several things: thanks for the invitation, the pleasures of the visit, and so on. Whatever your message is, say your good-byes in the warmest possible tone. And, next day, mention what a good time you had if the opportunity arises. If it doesn't, help it along a bit.

STATUS SYMBOLS IN BUSINESS

Status and the power on which it rests are both intangible. To make status visible, symbols are used: the tribal leader wields the ceremonial spear, the king displays his crown, and the company president has the largest office.

Status symbols are taken seriously, especially at the higher echelons. As a sign of prestige, a difference of inches in desk size has been contested to make sure that the president of a firm is not upstaged by a vice-president. The fact is, symbols of status abound on the business scene:

Judith Hull really knows she has arrived when the plastic nameplate on her door is replaced by a gold-leaf, hand-lettered job. Everything from the type and size of a potted plant to the texture of draperies in an office measures an executive's status and thereby her importance to the organization. From decoration to privilege, Hull quickly gets to understand what is appropriate to her rank.

TITLES

Titles in business are a key to status. Just as the president is usually the top man in the organization, a supervisor, while the lowest echelon of management, is nevertheless higher than a member of the rank-and-file.

In business tradition, the status conveyed by a title may be much sought even if there is no corresponding increase in salary. Management, aware of the value attributed to titles, will think up a special designation for an employee in lieu of, or in addition to, a promotion or raise. Accordingly:

- A "salesman" may become a "sales engineer" or "service consultant."
- A foreman of a factory unit may become a "production manager."
- One publishing organization gives its secretaries the title of "editorial assistant."

The point is that a title can be an effective means of delineating status. In the case of the "editorial assistant" mentioned above, the people bearing the title much prefer it to that of "secretary," and it is likely that there is a benefit in terms of the way these people see themselves and their work.

A virtue of the title "editorial assistant" is that it is appropriate to the work being done. Titles that on their face are farfetched—for example, calling a porter and handyman a "maintenance engineer" —are usually laughable, more a cause of discomfort than satisfaction.

TOO MANY VICE-PRESIDENTS?

Of vice-presidents there may be no end. Some companies—typically those in service industries, where managers are often in contact with the public or customers—may have an inordinate number of vice-presidents. The title in such cases doesn't signify an individual who is head of a function—such as V.P. Marketing, V.P. Finance— but an operating executive for whom the largely honorary title is intended to win prestige and regard. Interestingly enough, it often does.

Organizations that have reason to be concerned about the status feelings or possibly dissatisfactions of employees may wisely spend some time reviewing the job titles assigned to employees. One benefit: changing a title may very well bring about an improved idea of the potential of the job responsibility to which it refers.

A HIERARCHY OF TITLES

Traditional business practice has clearly delineated titles to indicate rank. Typical examples:

member of the board;
president;
executive vice-president;
vice-president;
division manager;
manager;
superintendent;
foreman.

However, there are some titles that fall outside the traditional designations above. These tend to be used for several different and important purposes:

• *A title is created to avoid conflict or resentment.* Or, a title is created to award special recognition—"coordinator" is sometimes so used.

• *A title is given to indicate special responsibility or authority.* For example, a Chief Executive Officer (CEO) outranks the president.

• *A title is created to save face.* This seems to imply status or authority that actually does not exist—such as the "vice-president" usage mentioned earlier.

• *The title without the authority.* In some cases an individual may be given a title—he may be the son of the founder—that conveys status without real power. For example, from time to time you will find an organization "president" whose duties may be purely ceremonial. The real clout in the organization may be wielded by a person with an entirely different title.

WHEN TO USE TITLES

There are several occasions on which titles should be used:

IN FORMAL MESSAGES. For example, a letter to someone in another company or even in one's own organization:

Ernest Lear, President;
Jack Flynn, Chief Engineer;
Mary Traynor, Color Room Manager.

IN INTRODUCTIONS. When you introduce a visitor to a member of your organization: "Jack, I'd like you to meet the man in charge of our technical operations, Chief Engineer Wilbur Hunt. Wilbur, this is Jack Smith, Vice-President of Sales at Hanlon Mills." Now both people have a clear idea of the position and function of the other.

Unlike the government, where people may be addressed by their titles—the President of the United States is "Mr. President," a governor may be addressed as "Governor"—the business world seldom uses a person's title orally. The exception is when a person has achieved the academic status of doctor, in which case a Ph.D. in science would, on the job, be addressed as "Dr. Jones."

WHEN AND HOW TO USE "MS."

Out of the Women's Liberation Movement came an awareness that bothered some people: men are not earmarked as to their marital situation. A man is "Mr." whether or not he's married, whereas "Miss" and "Mrs." make the distinction for women.

The resentment of women toward this sexist practice took two directions. One was that *married* women in business felt it was both unnecessary and irrelevant to indicate their marital status—and, in the minds of some, thereby a dependency.

Some *unmarried* women—the few who considered themselves social failures because they weren't married—disliked the title "Miss," especially when—as in a school roster, for example—a "Miss" tended to stand out alongside the women listed as "Mrs."

At any rate, the title "Ms." has come into use for both married and single women and seems to be taking hold. There are some aspects of usage worth noting:

A woman who signs a letter these days need not append any sex-designating title, particularly if the name is obviously female.

Occasionally there are names whose sex-relatedness is unclear. For example, since there are male Evelyns, Leslies, and even Junes, women who have names that are not clearly female and want to indicate that they are have the choice of "Miss," "Mrs.," or "Ms." Of course, they will use the "Ms." when they feel it's no one's business as to whether they are or aren't married. If you receive a letter signed Ms., use that designation in your reply.

USE OF FIRST NAMES

When Peter Kemp was a mailboy, he was called "Pete." Now that he's head of a department, it's "Mr. Kemp"—except to his old friends.

A person generally should be called by the name he or she prefers. "Pete" was all right when Peter Kemp was a young beginner. "Mr. Kemp," he feels, is more suited to his higher status.

But the use of names—first name, surname, nickname—varies widely in business. One can't generalize, still less prescribe, because organizations often have a policy that overrides personal preference. For example:

There is a three-hundred-employee chemical firm in Boston that uses employees' first names all the way up and down the line. Most people like the practice. It emphasizes the informality and friendliness of the place. The custom has a simple explanation: it started when the firm was small, and the president decided to continue despite the increase in size.

In organizations that use first names at all levels, even a handyman may call the president "Jim." However, it's interesting to see the problem that some newcomers unused to it have with this practice. In time, of course, the strangeness disappears and a young girl secretary may call her mature male boss by his first name—eventually without a twinge, and still later as a matter of course.

But there are exceptions. For example:

When outside people are involved, more formal procedures must be used. A secretary answering an outside call will say to her boss, who just a moment ago she was addressing as "Larry": "Mr. Miller, Mr. Lee is calling. . . ."

Secretaries and other subordinates who work for executives who frequently have contact with outside people should retain the formal "Mr.," "Mrs.," "Miss," or "Ms." to prevent slipups. To the uninitiated, first names of higher-echelon people used by subordinates is startling and suggests flippancy at best, looseness at worst. If first-name exchanges exist elsewhere in the organization, they may be used, but only when there are no outsiders present.

OBJECTIONABLE FIRST-NAME PRACTICE

It's wrong to assume that people prefer to be called by their first names. Yet many people make this assumption. And as a result, without intending to, they raise the hackles of strangers:

Eric Hardy has an appointment to call on an executive in the television broadcasting field. There has been an exchange of letters, and one phone conversation. But as Eric Hardy enters the executive's office, he's greeted with: "Hi, Eric." Eric Hardy—and many others—are more taken aback by the unwarranted breeziness of the greeting than they are taken with the intended friendliness of it.

It's a good rule that the surname of an individual be used until, by subtle cues, one gets the idea that a rapport has been established that makes the request "May I call you by your first name?" appropriate. Or one may take the initiative and say: "Please call me Eric." It is then proper for the other person to respond with: "Gladly. And please call me John" (or Jane, or whatever).

One more step in the direction of informality on which it is wise to get the individual's consent: the use of shortened names, such as "Don" for Donald, "Marge" for Margaret, "Larry" for Lawrence. There are some Charleses for whom "Charlie" is an abomination. Others think "Charles" sounds strange.

(What is involved here essentially is degrees of formality. For more on this, check back to "Formality and Informality," Chapter 1, page 9.)

NICKNAMES

Some individuals come into organizations equipped with a nickname. Others have them made up on the spot. For example, a sales manager hired a salesman whose name was Oscar Anderson. The first day on the job, the manager said, "I hope you don't mind, but I have trouble with the name Oscar. Would you mind if I called you 'Andy'?"

The use of derogatory nicknames, of course, is highly undesirable. There is always a certain amount of humiliation for the individual who against his or her wishes is referred to as "Slim," "Chubby," "Shorty," and so on. The rule is that if a person has a nickname that he or she is fond of and would like to have used, fine—up to a point. For example:

Len Peters has been calling his secretary "Blondie" with her consent, but when a customer or other outside business contact comes into the office, use of such an informal name suggests a kind of raffishness that is usually out of keeping with a desirable business atmosphere.

AGE AND STATUS INFLUENCE NAME USAGE

It's no surprise to people who are experienced in business that a superior may call a subordinate by his first name, but not vice versa. This is a common practice and reflects the difference in status between boss and subordinate. The superior, of course, is always free to say to the subordinate: "Please call me Helen" (or John, or whatever the first name may be).

Age sometimes makes a difference. The head of a department may address everyone else by his or her first name, but a senior employee might be called "Mr.," "Miss," or "Mrs." As a matter of fact, this can be a subtle way in which the manager can convey superior status to an old-time and esteemed member of the staff.

STATUS SYMBOLS AS TOOLS OF COMPETITION

Two vice-presidential rivals measure their offices to the inch to ascertain whether or not the other has an advantage. The one who finds his room is a couple of square feet smaller makes a serious complaint to the president.

Office size is only one of the qualities that are seen as having status implications. Every piece of furniture, every item that adorns wall or floor, the number of windows, the number of phones on the desk—and the type of desk—are taken as status indicators. As a matter of fact, the executive office is one of the greatest concentrations of status symbols anywhere on earth.

And the importance given these symbols is often ludicrous, demeaning, and unworthy of the individuals so preoccupied. Executives are not the only culprits. People at every level get upset about symbols that they feel suggest their status inadequately: An executive secretary demands that the nameplate on her desk, set in a plastic holder, be replaced by one of metal set in polished walnut.

Since my views are unorthodox on the matter of status symbols and how they are dealt with in business, the coverage of this subject will reflect:

- the view that the traditional weight given status symbols is excessive and should be moderated—there are meaningless and meaningful status considerations;
- the distinction between traditional status values and good taste;
- the difference between traditional values and convenience and efficiency.

SOME TRADITIONAL STATUS SYMBOLS AND THEIR ABUSE

Some of the status elements have been mentioned above. Here's an extended list, offered to fill out the status picture:

office—size and location;
furniture—quality and amount;
carpets, curtains, and drapes;
windows—size and number;
art—pictures and sculpture;
plants—size, type and number;
special equipment—facsimile machine (for sending and receiving printed material), computer terminal, and so on;
special facilities—bar, kitchen equipment, shower;
automobile—style and make;
company phone;
services—anything from car and chauffeur to serving of meals;
company-sponsored country club or shooting lodge membership.

The point with regard to the above list is that organizations themselves too often foster the status-symbol game. For example:

The Harrington Company headquarters is in a suburban area. Car ownership is universal, and almost every employee starts the day by pulling into the firm's parking lot—where locations are assigned according to status. (This practice at least makes sense. The time and convenience of the president—who parks right at the front door—should be regarded as more important than that of an assistant color matcher.)

C. D. Harrington, company president, drives a Buick. A newly hired junior executive, reporting the first day on the job, shows up with a Mercedes. His boss discreetly but firmly calls the inequity to his attention and suggests something less elegant.

This type of "measuring" is old-fashioned and undesirable. And, indeed, the rigidity of this system has happily been easing in the last fifteen years or so. The holdout areas, as you might expect, are those where the old traditions in general tend to hold on. Perhaps our increased sophistication and an appreciation of the realities of working life—people should be judged not by the symbols of authority but by the degree of their authority and the expertness with which it is used—will finally end the status-symbol war.

The point deserves repeating: it is the hairsplitting, exaggerated feelings that center around the factors that represent status that are undesirable. However, the practical and functional aspects of status-projecting elements deserve consideration:

• *An executive* whose job requires meeting customers, suppliers, the public, and so on in his or her office should have a roomy, attractive office so that visitors don't feel cramped and the company image benefits from their favorable reaction.

• *An organization* that prescribes a standard decor for people of a particular echelon understandably would prefer a certain amount of uniformity. The problem of designing and furnishing ten different work areas is avoided, costs are standardized and kept down by quantity purchases.

But within practical—and, it is hoped, loose—limits, it is desirable for individuals to have the privilege of exercising personal taste and preference.

PERSONAL TASTE IN OFFICE DECOR

To start on the right foot: if you're moving into a new office or redecorating, you want to make sure you're playing inside the ballpark. Talk to your superior, get his or her ideas about costs, style, number of pieces and types of furniture your office should have. This is the point at which you get an idea of how much of a free hand you have, or discuss the preferences you have.

Some people have a strong sense of style, know what they like, and are uncomfortable in quarters designed by others whose taste, professional though it may be, is decidedly different from their own.

If your organization has available the services of a decorator, give him or her some idea of the kinds of things you like and don't like. If you spark to Scandinavian austerity, you won't be happy with a Mediterranean credenza. If your reflexes tell you that a rectangular desk of a particular size and shape is what you want, make sure that a free-form or kidney-shape isn't what gets ordered.

If you want to take a somewhat active hand in the decoration, perhaps you can work with your company's purchasing agent and furniture catalogs. If pictures don't give you a good enough sense of what you're looking at, the purchasing agent can arrange a visit to the showrooms of the furniture suppliers—if they're local. Here you can see exactly how large a 6 x 3 desk is. You can see and feel the difference between a wooden desk and a metal one. You can see how dark a mahogany stain is as compared to oak or walnut.

GOOD TASTE IN DECORATING AN OFFICE

A key element in the impression an office makes is the pictures on view. In the "olden days," a picture in an office was what a wife or secretary could go out and buy at the local department store. Nowadays, art on an organization's premises is an important way of reflecting individual tastes as well as revealing of the corporate image.

One expert who is an art consultant to corporations sees his job as not merely providing pictures and sculpture for corporate space but also as that of educating the executive. In a recent instance, a company president was dissuaded from buying a pop-art canvas at enormous expense:

"It was an interesting canvas but not for that man and not in that company," explained the consultant. Eventually the executive selected an Edward Hopper, which he subsequently agreed was better suited to his office.

We work better and feel better in surroundings in which we feel at ease. An executive who likes books—in addition to those used in his or her work—may understandably want a floor-to-ceiling bookcase. The yachtsman increases the psychological comfort of his office by a picture of his sloop, spinnaker aloft, running before the wind.

Elements that reflect a personal interest and preference have a double purpose. They make you feel at home in your quarters, and they tell others the kind of person you are.

Because of this latter consideration, there are limits to the kind of pictures, trophies, desk objects, or other personal items one should consider for office use. Some of the excesses are obvious and easy to rule out. You might have a splendid picture of your wife in a bikini, great in your home bedroom but out of place as a desk decoration. And a woman with a husband or friend caught by the camera in a romantic pose will do better using the shot for home rather than office display.

A common practice is to have pictures of the family—a group picture, graduation shots of a son or daughter, or perhaps your children's wedding photos. These are fine. But one's own wedding pictures are too personal and should be considered off limits in the office.

Diplomas, certificates, awards of merit, sports trophies are usually appropriate. An award or certificate of achievement may, in addition to its use as decoration, offer a good conversation piece.

TV AND HI-FI

A television set and/or hi-fidelity sound equipment add a communications dimension, a "today" quality to an office. Both television and radio are prime conveyors of spot news and special news features. Accordingly, executives for reasons of professionalism would want to view or listen to important current events—a top government figure making a key policy statement, for example. And as already mentioned, the presence of this equipment in an office suggests that the executive is in touch with the here-and-now world. Furthermore, it is not uncommon for executives to invite employees, staff people, in to witness or listen to special news broadcasts. These special events taking place during working hours when employees would not otherwise be able to see or hear them become a means of stimulating group unity initiated by the executive leader.

Abuses are possible. The office from which music, however pleasant, continually emerges, and at high volume, won't be seen as the workplace of a serious worker. The individual who is too often found watching the races, ball games, and other entertainments on the tube will also create doubts of his or her interest in the work.

The location of the equipment is another consideration. Even if not in use, the glaring eye of the TV tube may set some nerves on edge. And hi-fi equipment that dominates the key spot in an office may create some question in the minds of visitors as to just what the executive's job really is. In other words, the placement of the equipment is least distracting when it is discreet and doesn't dominate. Many executives solve the glaring-eye effect of the TV set by having it inside a cabinet with doors.

PLANTS FOR THE OFFICE

In recent years, plant life has triumphantly invaded the executive suite. Whether it is because of psychic forces or the subtle promotion of nursery interests, plants are increasingly adding distinction and airy pleasantness to the business scene.

The size, shape, type, and quantity of flora have unfortunately acquired status ratings, just as automobiles have. Just for your information—and please don't be guided by them but by your own taste—here are some of the cues:

The traditional (and relatively inexpensive) rubber plant is the Volkswagen of the plant world. Philodendron, dieffenbachia, ficus, schifflera are solid middle-management decor. For the top brass, you simply veer to the more exotic, more expensive, and perhaps larger. Large cacti are especially popular because of their unique shapes. For the really top man, the Rolls-Royce of the business world is a five-hundred-year old bonsai, at two or three thousand dollars and up.

Artificial plants, flowers, foliage? Not·if you can possibly help it. Admittedly, some of the artificial flora is done with great expertness. Their best use seems to be in reception areas, which often have no windows, and in which live plants would fare poorly.

DECOR AND THE ORGANIZATION'S IMAGE

Topflight office designers use the phrase "institutional face" to suggest one of the limits in decoration of business premises. A company that professes to be a progressive, up-to-the-minute outfit is more suitably done in contemporary style than in a pleasing but old-fashioned look (which might be just perfect for a company in the spice trade).

There was good reason for bankers to go in for the heavy and staid. The slickness and high fashion that would be right for an advertising agency would suggest that the bank was flighty, even unreliable. But have you noticed the change in banking decoration? New times, new standards. Banks are now at the forefront in bright, contemporary styles.

At one time an intriguing idea was held in some sales quarters that the "right" style of decoration could change a customer's firm "No" to an unsteady "Yes." Bizarre decoration, known in the trade as "gas-station modern," was said to be effective in high-pressure selling operations. Screaming reds next to clashing blues, chopped-up zigzag color areas created an unusual environment that could throw an individual off guard by creating a minor mental crisis, a disorientation that could render a person more suggestible.

The cagey experts may have a point. To date, however, they have failed to describe the effect of this type of surroundings on the unfortunate people who perforce must stand up to it eight hours a day.

THE PLACEMENT OF SUBORDINATES' WORK STATIONS

There are considerations of both status and practicality involved in planning the location of a subordinate's workplace in relation to his or her boss and to peers. If everyone is content with the status quo, there's no point in changing. But if you're moving into new quarters, or for some reason there is to be a reshuffling of offices or desks, here are guidelines that can prevent inequities and minimize inconvenience:

PROXIMITY. Closeness to a superior usually implies a close working relationship. For example:

Lillian Grover is secretary to two executives. Her desk is closer to Paul Fay's office door. Accordingly, she is thought of as "Fay's secretary"—who also does some work for the other executive. This is also the way she perceives the situation as a result of the desk positioning.

"SATELLITE CONFIGURATION." The location of any one work-place should be viewed in relation to others. Space analysts use the phrase "satellite configuration" to describe the need for arranging the work areas of subordinates in efficient relationship to the executive to whom they report.

Simply put, the question comes down to who should be near whom. The president may want the treasurer close by. The treasurer may want to be near the accounting office. Working interrelationships are, accordingly, a major factor in workplace location. Other things being equal, the subordinate closest to the boss is thought of as "top subordinate," since he or she is closest to the seat of power.

CONSTRUCTION FEATURES. Some locations suggest higher status than others. A *New Yorker* cartoon shows a desk jammed up alongside a furnace at which sits an executive, head down, to keep from banging into a heating duct. He's talking into the phone, and the caption records his words: "Marjorie, I wasn't kicked upstairs after all!"

Just as a spot in the furnace room conveys low status, building elements may suggest desirable or undesirable locations. For example:

Three clerks have desks at right angles to the same wall. But one desk is near a window, and that desk-user accordingly feels he has an edge. Similarly, a jog in a wall that half hides a desk suggests low status.

These factors, unlike others, are not artificial but specific and material. Presumably, an aware executive would take them into account when positioning people, to avoid the upset of those who because of length of service, degree of responsibility, or rank deserve special consideration.

"DOG" LOCATIONS. Any out-of-the-mainstream location, such as a "dead" corner or off a side corridor, is usually taken as a less desirable location, along with those near coffee- or cigarette-dispensing machines. Another low-rated spot is one near a center of noise or *incidental,* as opposed to *work-related,* bustle. Accordingly, a desk or office near elevators, busy meeting rooms, or corridors with high pedestrian density are less desirable.

COMPENSATIONS FOR A POOR LOCATION. In deciding where to place subordinates, you are obviously limited by the amount and quality of space. Someone will undoubtedly have to be placed in an undesirable location. But you can take steps to offset a negative spot. For example, an assistant assigned to an office next to a utility workroom may have his or her spirits and sense of position improved by carpeting, new drapes, or similar status items.

HOW TO CHOOSE A SECRETARY

The executive who is hiring a new secretary or is selecting one from among applications generated in his or her own organization may be interested in the status aspects of such a choice. As will soon become evident, the good-management aspects coincide to a large degree with the qualities that suggest status to the executive making this choice. For purposes of this discussion, the more usual situation of male boss and female secretary will be assumed. . . .

Having a secretary of one's own is in itself a sign of status. As a matter of fact, the ladder-climber newly arrived at the executive echelon really knows he has made it when a secretary is assigned.

But it's not enough to have a secretary. The kind of person who sits outside the executive door suggests the level of status the executive has achieved.

It's not a clear-cut picture, and, as a matter of fact, preferences change. In the early sixties, young women with English accents became much sought after by New York City executives. If Eliza Doolittle had been able to type, her career troubles would have been over. And this would have been *before* she'd been Higgins-ized. The reason: to the average executive, it didn't matter whether the accent was cockney or Oxford, as long as it seemed to be British.

Later, in the flush of civil liberties and racial equality, executives whose secretaries were black scored prestige points for being "with it." Nowadays, one sees black secretaries along with white and Oriental, but the racial quality has ceased to be a status factor. However, other qualities persist as meaningful indicators of status:

SKILL. The skill of your secretary is not only a matter of convenience and efficient operation. The executive who has a brisk, adept, intelligent, clear-thinking teammate is making out well, statuswise. The higher-echelon executive is usually the one who gets the more capable secretary because he or she has the clout to request and acquire such a person. Conversely, then, the executive who *has* such an assistant is seen as one of higher status.

AGE. In the typical case, the more mature person is seen as embodying higher status than the flossy young thing. Top executives almost invariably look for the benefits of greater experience and maturity—no matter what popular films may suggest.

APPEARANCE. How the secretary looks is another status consideration, but it's not as simple a matter as one might think. Aside from the general considerations of dress (see Chapter 6, page 247, for this discussion), one cannot say, for example, that the "better dressed" a secretary is, the higher the status indication. For one thing, what does "better dressed" mean? More in fashion? But what fashion? Certainly, *Vogue*-type high fashion might be incongruous behind a secretary's desk.

The rule seems to lean more toward "appropriate" dress and appearance. But let it be said that at the very highest levels, where secretaries often wield substantial power, their appearance follows the same rules as for the executive; which is to say, no rules whatsoever. A female secretary to the head of a large banking organization looks as though her clothes come from the local thrift shop, and Helena Rubinstein would have to close up shop if it depended on women like her for its customers.

But below that level, clothing in modest good taste and careful grooming are the marks of the high-status executive secretary.

The secretary is a key to the boss's status because she is his representative. Often, for example, the first impression a visitor to the executive suite gets is formed by the manner and appearance of a secretary.

And then, on another level, a secretary's capability in terms of both *what* is done and *how* it is done reflect on the boss. Peter Drucker, among other management authorities, has always maintained that an executive is as good as the secretary can help him to be.

AGE AS A STATUS FACTOR

Every culture, every ethnic group has its own attitudes—negative or positive—about age. In some societies, youth is equated with inexperience, and old age with wisdom. In our own culture, older people may be given high status up to a certain point, but then, passing over an invisible dateline, they lose status as they are thought of as being "over the hill" or "has-beens." A person who is considered "too young" may automatically be seen as an upstart.

ORGANIZATIONAL ASPECTS OF AGE

Age is a subtle but ever-present element in organization life:
• *Age affects physical behavior, attitudes, and capabilities.* For

example, the middle-aged person tends to chafe at unaccustomed limits on his or her energy. Past middle age, skills and experience may be downgraded. In organizations that see themselves as young and swinging, the young virtuoso executive has special status, and the elderly tend to lose out in executive standing.

• *Feelings about age* tend to create sensitivities and expectations that must be taken into account:

A young person surrounded by older colleagues may feel either "out of it" or resentful of being "in an old persons' home."

An older person in a younger age group may feel isolated or resent the feeling that his or her experience and mature values are being trivialized.

Both the individual and the organization must develop attitudes and policies to minimize the status aspects of age. Since age is a quality the individual can do nothing about, it is repressive to downgrade or limit the opportunities of a person because he or she is "too young" or "too old." And since advancing age, as a matter of fact, may bring with it decreasing capabilities, organizations and managers, for humane as well as efficiency reasons, may want to give special attention to ways and means of making assignment and responsibility modifications that make optimum use of an aging person's capabilities, and minimize activities in areas where ability is waning.

THE SITUATION OF THE YOUNG EMPLOYEE

Contemporary experience of dealing with young employees has made the average management aware of both the potential and the hazards. Thoughtful management seeks to strike a balance among several factors:

- the need to provide a career path that will make it possible for the youngster with something on the ball to progress (in some cases, where this opportunity is lacking, the employee becomes disillusioned, frustrated, and quits);
- the need to make it possible for the young person to learn and grow by on-the-job and other training exposure;
- the control of promotions and succession so that the older people are not trampled by the overheated ambitions of young people;
- the need to influence the appreciation of the old by the young so that the former are viewed with respect (perhaps even deference) rather than being seen as potential victims.

Both "real" and "perceived" problems influence the relationships between generations. The dealings with older or younger people by the person in authority is a cue and example of what the organization expects. Accordingly, it's up to the influential executive to take the initiative, to set the tone and the "rules" of intergenerational relationships.

AGE AND "SENIORITY"

Our business culture is age-oriented. That's why one hears judgmental phrases such as "too old," "too young," and so on used in describing individuals. (And that's why the government has passed legislation to enforce fair treatment of older employees.) A person whose chronological age puts him or her in the upper brackets may no longer be automatically ruled out of a job opportunity or even an advancement opportunity because of the limited amount of time there is left to make a contribution to the company before retirement.

At the lower echelons, business sets store by "seniority." While it is not directly equated with chronological age, longevity on the job does lend higher status—and certainly greater job security—because of experience and skills gained. In the higher echelons, seniority —and age—does carry a preferential weight: a senior vice-president outranks a junior—as does a senior partner.

WHEN AGE IS CLASSIFIED INFORMATION

There are a number of situations in which people's ages tend to be a major consideration.

To the working person at any echelon, age can be a vital factor. Despite legislation to the contrary, people are almost inevitably affected by the age of people with whom they are dealing. Most companies accept a job applicant's statement of his or her age without question. Many young people have gotten jobs by adding two or three years to their actual fifteen or sixteen. And, of course, at the other end of the scale, men and women have assumed that their employability has increased when they've excised two, three, five, or even ten years.

Aside from reasons of vanity or personal privacy, many people prefer to keep their real age secret. The business scene traditionally has accepted euphemisms for more years than a person wants to admit:

"Over twenty-one" has been given as the answer to "How old are you?" by people from twenty-two and up—and pretty high up, too.

When asked her age, one woman executive asserts that her favorite answer is "Thirty-nine and holding." The question of age comes up on two occasions:

• *The question of age may involve some practical situation*—having to do with the company pension, for example, or qualification for a health program, or, preliminary to these, a question of employment. It's well to remember that only the accurate answer can eliminate the possibilities of complications later on.

• *One's "social age" is largely a matter of subjective feelings and what one projects to others.* There's little new one can say about age as a social factor. But three clichés still apply:

Some people are "old at forty," others "young at sixty."

For older people misled into thinking that there is something to gain by simulating youth: "Act your age."

For older people who are troubled by what they see in the mirror: "You're as old as you feel."

Finally, remember that antidiscrimination laws prohibit bias based on age, in hiring, promotion, and so on. Violations are actionable.

THE YOUNG BOSS AND THE OLDER SUBORDINATE

In general, we've been taught that age deserves consideration and respect. The individual, regardless of status, who flouts or denigrates another because that person is older is not only being unkind and inhumane but is making these qualities strongly evident.

On the workscene it is not uncommon to see a younger person— let's say, of thirty—with subordinates in their fifties or even sixties. The younger person will certainly look better to his colleagues if he or she gives age its due. This does not mean simply that the younger person treats the older with respect. It also means that within reasonable limits he or she defers to the other, asks advice, seeks the benefits of the older person's experience, and so on.

But, of course, the realities of the business situation do not always permit us to give top priority to thoughtfulness and humanity. In some cases a young boss must take issue with an older person: "I'm sorry, Bill, that you think that just because we've always handled that problem in a certain way we have to continue. On the contrary, I'm inclined to think that it's precisely because we've used that approach that we've got a problem. Let me suggest a new way . . ."

In short, business etiquette suggests that older employees be given special consideration just as is done in the larger culture outside. But where a younger person with responsibilities disagrees on a matter of policy or procedure, he or she must feel free to substitute his or her own ideas.

THE YOUNG BOSS AND THE OLD SECRETARY

The upper age brackets often contain people of higher position, more experience and status. We expect beginners to be young. But from time to time, the expectation is reversed. The person in authority is young, the experienced employee further along in years and of lower status. When this age relationship is true of the boss-secretary team, there are special considerations:

Len Hawley, newly appointed department head aged twenty-nine, has inherited Grace Greer, an experienced secretary aged fifty. As far as the work is concerned, they get along well. Hawley knows his business, and Greer is tops in her job. As long as things remain "strictly business," there is no problem. But business is seldom "strictly business." Accordingly:

Hawley treats Greer with a top-heavy formality. He's unaware of it, but the secretary is annoyed: "I must remind him of his mother," she tells a friend tartly. She would prefer to be related to in a less formal way.

Grace Greer has some behavior problems of her own. For example, she occasionally acts in a somewhat condescending manner when her experience clearly has the boss at a disadvantage. And she has a tendency to try to act younger than her age in some situations—pressing too hard to show she's up on the latest movies, current dance steps, and so on.

Another hazard of the young boss–older secretary relationship is that the latter may unconsciously develop a maternal attitude, while the boss falls into a dependent "son" role.

In this situation, being aware of the pitfalls is usually the key to avoiding any troublesome or irritating facets in the working relationship.

For some people, there may be considerable help in the idea of avoiding the unconscious temptation to role-play. The young executive may feel he has to prove his capability to his secretary by acting the *Wunderkind.* Similarly, the secretary should try to avoid trading on her years of experience, and not fall into the role of either mother hen or big sister.

THE OLD BOSS AND THE YOUNG SECRETARY

It's worth noting that the reasons for the potential hazards of the boss-secretary team of contrasting ages is the Oedipal carry-over. Admittedly the emotional hierarchy on the workscene is influenced by the heirarchical family pattern. The male boss tends to be Big Daddy. The woman executive is often seen by her subordinates as Big Momma.

In the situation where the ages are reversed from the case mentioned above, the older man who has a young, impressionable, and attractive female secretary may respond to the temptation, possibly unconscious, to be impressive as the capable, dominant male figure.

The older boss's attempt to impress may be matched by the young woman's willingness to go along with the byplay.

Again, awareness of the pitfalls can be enough to help both parties avoid pointless, even if harmless, role-playing. Regardless of status, age owes respect to youth, and vice versa. The secret in all cases is for people to behave with ordinary respect for the other person's dignity and integrity, so that age becomes just one more personal quality like height or foot size.

HOW MUCH CONSIDERATION FOR AN ENFEEBLED BOSS?

Occasionally a person, possibly due to advancing age or health problems, retains a position of responsibility for which he or she is neither physically nor mentally competent.

Such situations are obviously temporary. Eventually, from its higher echelons the organization will institute the moves that will resolve the situation. Meanwhile, what about the subordinates of the superannuated manager?

Even though the situation is fairly uncommon, it's interesting that the response from the people involved is almost always the same. What happens is that the subordinates almost automatically take up the slack created by the superior's failing capabilities. A secretary, for example, will cover for the boss, carry out such of his responsibilities as she reasonably can. This tends to be true of other people on the aging person's staff.

There is a good deal that favors such humaneness on the part of subordinates. However, there may come a point when a group, or in some cases a single individual, will feel that higher management must be made fully aware of the situation. Usually this resolve comes about either as a result of a crisis or because some near-misses have suggested that more serious consequences may threaten.

In such an event, a subordinate may in good conscience discreetly arrange for a meeting with someone in authority and describe the work problems that are arising as a result of the limited capabilities of his superior.

The acceptability of such an action is largely the result of the way in which it's done. If the case is presented matter-of-factly and with sympathy for the boss's personal problems, chances are the move will be accepted gratefully.

EXERCISING AUTHORITY

DEALING WITH THE "YES-PERSON"

Some bosses—wittingly or unwittingly—create among their staffs that robot known as the "yes-person." People like this are emotional slaves trading their freedom for the possible favor of a person of high status.

There are invariably damaging consequences from sycophancy, both to the fawner and the fawned-upon. For the former there is servility, dependence, the ever-present threat of losing favor, and, above all, the sacrifice of personal integrity. For the boss, results can be almost equally damaging. He or she is saddled with a plastic relationship, pseudowarmth, false reassurance, inflated self-assessment as a result of the yes-person's distorted levels of approval. And usually whatever creative contribution the toady might make in the ordinary course of doing his or her job is minimized.

Fawning upon authority is usually but not always done for gain. Some people are actually intimidated by the power of authority and react to it unconsciously in a self-abasing manner.

As has been suggested, the yes-person is created, intentionally or otherwise, by the person in authority. Clearly, the former could not exist without the latter's acceptance. If the person in the executive chair has any doubts about the extent to which he or she is being "yessed," a few questions can clarify the situation:

Have I made it clear to my staff that everyone has the right to dissent or present their own divergent views?

Does everyone on my staff avail himself or herself of this right?

Thinking of those who tend to side with me, would I say their agreement is sincere, or is there overreadiness to see things my way?

With individuals whom I suspect of being at least incipient sycophants, do I ask *why* they agree with my views in specific instances?

Do I challenge their thinking by suggesting that they take a line of thought further or look into reasons to support points of view opposed to my own?

And then, two more points:

Do I indicate that unthinking agreement with my views or going along too quickly with a "prevailing" opinion is unacceptable and unwelcome?

And do I praise and otherwise reward those who present original ideas, especially when they break with tradition or my own views?

Any and all of the steps suggested above help to make clear to everyone that the boss is just not interested in using status to gain approval, agreement, or flattery.

WHAT SHOULD BE DONE ABOUT THE STATUS-WORSHIPER?

"Sid is status-struck," observes one of the junior executive's peers. That's one of the nicer ways of describing his behavior. Sid's co-workers chuckle about it, but they resent him, too.

Catch Sid at a company party. He's talking to a colleague. Suddenly, along comes someone of higher status, and Sid stops in the middle of a sentence to rush over to pay his respects. And if in the course of *that* conversation someone of a still higher echelon appears, Sid will tear himself away and make a beeline for the bigger prize.

What, if anything, should be done about the Sids of the business world?

Well, there are two choices:

• *Do nothing.* This is the better choice if your organization is permissive and the idiosyncrasy is viewed as a source of mild amusement. In this case there are likely to be no ruffled feathers and no feelings of hostility to be dealt with. Time and tide—that is, the ebb and flow of Sid's own situation—will eventually resolve the situation.

• *Take action.* Anything that's done should be of a mild nature. Who should speak up? Perhaps a well-wisher of Sid's—his boss or a friendly colleague. What should be said? Something along these lines, reasonably soon after there has been an incident involving Sid's weakness: "Sid, I happened to be watching you during the break in the meeting last night. Seems to me you were giving Mr. Floyd too much of a play, being overly attentive. Some people might have thought you were polishing apples in public. At any rate, I thought you might like to have a friend's view. . . ."

SPECIAL PROBLEMS OF THE "BOSS"

Being a boss or relating to one is a central problem on the work-scene. Many people have trouble with authority—wielding it or accepting it. Here is how to minimize such difficulties:

• *Don't flinch at being a "boss."* The leader of a group not only has special authority but also the responsibility for using it wisely. For example, a boss can't act like "one of the boys" or "one of the girls." Attempts to show egalitarianism may only emphasize the fact that it just cannot be applied across the board. If you really want to see discomfort personified, watch what happens when a well-meaning executive reaches down the echelons and tries to treat an employee as an equal. The best of intentions cannot level ranks.

• *Respect knows no station.* A boss, because of his or her authority and status, can cause aches and pains or make an employee happy. It goes without saying that every person is worthy of respect, regardless of position on the organization chart. Each person owes to others a basic courtesy and a regard for individual integrity. This holds for the mutual attitudes of boss and bossed. One may dislike another person or resent him or her and yet conduct business with the person by using matter-of-fact, neutral behavior.

• *Take the sting out of criticism.* A boss may often have to criticize a subordinate for an unacceptable act. But even criticism can be administered without personal animosity. The traditional way of accomplishing this seeming paradox is simple: one criticizes the *act*, not the *actor.* Make criticism constructive by suggesting a better way.

• *Avoid playing favorites.* As a boss, you have authority over others. Implicit in this authority is the right to give orders, guide behavior, criticize unsatisfactory performance, and often, as the ultimate expression, fire a subordinate for cause.

But while a boss may apply a wide range of controls, certain acts are definitely to be avoided as unfair and hurtful. The most common lapses involve favoritism. It may sound unrealistic to proclaim the need for fairness when instances of favoritism abound in the business world. But the fact that playing favorites is common doesn't make it acceptable.

The thing that's wrong with favoritism is that it inevitably leads to unfairness: a privilege granted to a subordinate because of a boss's personal preference means that other individuals are being short-changed—with bitterness and upset a likely by-product. What the boss may view as generosity is often given at the expense of others.

STATUS AND ORGANIZATIONAL POLITICS

Every organization is political. Politics, according to the dictionary, is the art or science concerned with influencing governing policy. Politics and status meet when an individual generates influence beyond the normal expectation for his or her position.

One way or another, we are all subject to political forces. We may want to head up a movement, or we are asked to join one. And sometimes we are not sure how to respond: Is it wrong to play politics? Should one reject political alignments? How should one respond to a colleague who seeks to enlist our support for a particular cause or group?

To begin with, accept the rule that politics may be either good or bad—and it may be impossible to distinguish between them. For example:

John Jones is a capable executive, in line for the presidency when the incumbent retires. People with an eye to their own future align themselves either discreetly or overtly with John Jones. Jones is now head of a clique that helps him develop his ideas and his programs, and put them over. One instance: Jones thinks it is a good idea to open a sales office on the West Coast. His adherents do whatever they can at their level to push along this project.

If the West Coast plan is good—that is, one that will benefit the company and its employees—then support of Jones represents acceptable, even desirable, politics. Politics becomes bad when it leads to repressive, unjust, and destructive consequences.

Although the good-bad distinction can be a helpful guide to behavior in some situations, there are two complicating factors:

• *Steel fist, velvet glove.* Unlike the ordered and visible power shown on an organizational chart, political clout tends to be hidden, or disguised. The fact that a second-echelon executive is the real power in a given department may be known to only a few insiders —or those who have been singed.

• *Win-lose.* The realities of organization ordain that those who align themselves with a winning factor gain influence and status, while others tend to lose them. This win-lose climate is generally destructive to fairness and organizational harmony.

Yet, politics may not seem vicious or malicious. In some cases, people are motivated by principle rather than by the quest for personal gain. For example, an insurgent group may attack current management policy because operations are considered unsuccessful, and the good of the organization is sought.

In the battle between the ins and outs, reputations, careers, and the fate of the organization itself may suffer. And damage may result regardless of good intentions when individuals are not permitted to function according to reasoned judgment. A tradition in which the faithful rather than the deserving win the spoils is not good management, nor, being unjust, is it good etiquette.

The antidote to excessive politics in an organization must originate at the top echelons. It is only when the top echelons permit—or, as unfortunately occurs occasionally, encourage—political rivalry that it can exist. A set of guidelines for top management can help prevent the undesirable consequences of rampant politics:

1. *A policy of fairness* that eschews favoritism and influence-peddling.

2. *An avoidance of a win-lose climate.* Success should be, even must be, rewarded. As a matter of fact, increased status gained by the successful person is a substantial part of his or her reward. But the success should be earned. Accordingly, top management must be wary of—

3. *Clique formation.* It is one thing to reward the successful employee. It's another thing to permit empire-building that divides an organization into in-groups and out-groups and brings on the undesirable consequences of such divisiveness.

4. *Recognition for losers.* A whole book could be written on the subject of fair and constructive treatment of losers. In this present context, however, let it suffice to say that while it's desirable that winners be held up for public praise, it does not follow that losers should be scorned. Many a person who has lost out in the competition or failed in an effort has done so despite outstanding performance—the use of imagination, intelligence, skill, and so on. It is a generous and considerate move to recognize these qualities despite a negative outcome. And the suggestion by word and deed that those who fail do not lose face and have not lost status is the mark of a wise management.

THE POLITICS OF ADVANCEMENT

The urge to get ahead is as much a sign of life in business as breathing in the world at large. Indeed, ambition is not only acceptable, it is highly valued. It is the traditional dynamo for getting a promotion, improving one's lot and status.

The desire for advancement can do strange things to people. Obviously, getting ahead calls for a certain amount of self-assertion, even aggressiveness. And when people start the push toward the next rung on the ladder, there's the clear danger of stepping on toes and fingers, causing inconvenience and pain to others. What rules of etiquette can guide you in this combative area?

If you have an eye out for a better job or wider responsibilities, consider the virtues of avoiding the "trample" instinct. The man or woman who makes it up the ladder *without* leaving either corpses or injured feelings behind is going to arrive at the new level with a better chance of not getting a vengeful dagger in the back. Here are some of the considerations to be made by those with advancement on their minds:

To begin with, you can be sure that the end—advancement —don't justify any and all means. Getting ahead, undeniably a part of the American dream, is not to be won by a sacrifice of one's integrity or the undermining of friendships.

Certainly, one can exert one's self, seek to be outstanding, to draw attention to one's performance. But all this can be done without throwing stones at others. Don't forget, the very way you proceed can be a factor in helping or hindering progress.

ASSESSING YOUR CHANCES FOR ADVANCEMENT

What you do or don't do about getting ahead in your company depends to a large part on your situation. To put it quite simply, some people are in dead-end jobs, and almost regardless of their ambitions or what they do to further them, they are not going anyplace. Here are some of the circumstances that suggest that hopes for advancement are unrealistic:

- The only promotion would be your boss's job—and there's no likelihood that the position will be available in the future.
- There is one logical position into which you might advance, but a competitor has a lock on the spot.
- For any one of a number of reasons—your boss's disfavor, an unfortunate failure—your promotability has been undermined.

However, the likelihood that there will be strong knockout factors to aspiration is not great. More typical are a number of circumstances that you can influence:

- *Let your boss know you're promotion-minded.* In the many contacts you have with your superior, make it clear that it's your hope and intention to move forward.
- *Ask for the boss's help.* It's a logical second step. Once he under-

stands that you aspire to move ahead, seek his specific suggestions not only as to where in the organization you should look for advancement but also the preliminary steps that would lead you there.

• *Be ready for a frank appraisal.* No matter how well qualified you feel you are for advancement, or how deserving you are, listen to what your boss says when he responds to your inquiries. In his response to you, he may not only discuss your strengths but also your weaknesses. For example, one executive vice-president tells his assistant, "Pete, I really don't think you have what it takes to make it in Sales. It's a rough, tough competitive arena in which I think you'll be operating at a disadvantage. I think you're much better qualified both by training and disposition to go into Customer Service or Research and Development." Consider bolstering your weaknesses.

IF YOU'RE THE BOSS

Advancement takes on a special meaning if you're in a position of sufficient authority to make or participate in the decisions that have to do with advancement for other people. Here are some of the key aspects of the advancement situation you may have to cope with when you're the boss.

1. *Dealing with the "Askers."*

It often happens that subordinates will come to you and let you know of their interest in getting ahead. They may phrase their statements either in a general sense or let you know they have their eye on a specific job.

As a leader, you have the responsibility of reacting appropriately. Here are the three basic possibilities:

• *When the subordinate is on target.* Probably nothing can make you happier than to have a well-qualified employee let you know he or she is interested in a job opening that's a natural for that subordinate. Organizationally, this situation is highly desirable. The basic system of recognition and reward that is so important to business and public life alike thrives on the process of promotion and advancement in general.

Accordingly, you should encourage the qualified subordinate who is seeking to get ahead. Express your approval and, if you can, inform him or her of some of the constructive moves that can help.

• *When the seeker won't make it.* From time to time, an employee who is interested in advancement seeks a job for which he or she is not qualified. In addition, there may be one or more people who are prime prospects for the vacancy. In this case you can't offer the seeker any encouragement at all. There are two things that you must then accomplish:

First, you have to make the facts quite clear. Without fudging, you have to let the person know that this is one advancement he or she will not be making.

Second, you must do it in such a way that the individual will not be crushed or feel that other ambitions are necessarily affected.

A simple, direct statement delivered in a friendly or matter-of-fact way makes the first point:

"Tess, I'm glad to know that you're interested in getting ahead in this organization. However, I must tell you that the job of manager is pretty much spoken for."

And then, if suitable, a mitigating statement may be added:

"You certainly have potential that will stand you in good stead someday, but the person who is in line for that spot has a great deal of experience and actually has been more or less in training for the last six months to take over. . . ."

• *When additional effort is going to be required.* A third possibility is that the individual who wants to move ahead has a pretty good chance but doesn't quite have all the qualifications. In such a situation you may want to make the suggestions that will help the person. At the same time, make sure you don't commit yourself. Here's how one executive put it:

"Gus, I think perhaps you might qualify for the office manager's job, but frankly there are gaps in your experience and skills that would have to be filled. For example, you haven't had any management experience as yet. I would suggest that a course in supervision would be extremely helpful. I understand there's one being given at the local community college on Saturdays. . . ."

Add whatever guidance you feel is appropriate, but then, to make sure that there's no chance for misunderstanding and to keep your options open, add:

"To be completely fair about this, I think you should understand that there's no guarantee that if you take these courses (or make whatever moves have been suggested) you'll be getting that job. All I can tell you is that you'll improve your chances considerably. And, at any rate, you'll be improving your capabilities in a way that will help your chances for advancement in general."

2. Dealing with the "Also-Rans."

Don't assume that people who in your mind lost out on a promotion are necessarily disgruntled and may have to be talked to.

On the contrary, make the opposite assumption that if people don't indicate disappointment or come to you directly to voice it, there is no need to take the initiative with them.

But if people make clear by their behavior that they've been upset by losing out, or if they tell you that they are, then out of fairness as well as to remove an obstacle to their peace of mind and work performance, you should talk to them.

Here the problem is how to level without hurting them. Obviously, someone else was better qualified. And you may want to make a statement along these lines:

"Several people were considered for the job, and it was an extremely difficult choice because all the candidates had excellent qualifications. I can tell you that the person who got the job won it on the basis of the outstanding performance in his present assignment. He was able to show that he had a great deal on the ball, and the skills that made him outstanding in his old job are similar to those required for the new one."

In other words, you can take the sting out of a loss by pointing out that actually the aspirant can be praised for virtues, good qualifications, and so on. The point is that the person who did walk off with the honors had special qualifications in essential areas.

If appropriate, you might want to tell the disappointed individual where in your opinion his or her best prospects are:

"Actually, I don't think your strongest talents lie in the sales area. I think you're especially well qualified to get yourself a good job with the Service Department someday. If I were you, I'd start thinking in practical terms of how you could move in that direction. . . ."

WHEN YOU SEEK ADVANCEMENT

Those who want to move up the echelons fare best when their efforts are consciously thought out—prospects assayed, qualifications weighed, opportunities pinpointed. The individual who makes advancement a waiting game and waits to be "discovered" or for opportunity to appear full-blown and ready at hand is often disappointed and frustrated.

In the typical case, some self-assertion—even actions that

some might term "pushy"—is in order. How to put yourself forward in acceptable fashion? Use these guidelines:

• *Don't flinch at self-advertising.* Admittedly, blowing one's own horn is considered an unwelcome noise in some quarters. But the aspirant who couples capability with an approach that minimizes the brashness of self-promotion is likely to have the secret of ending an undesirably low profile and lack of progress.

• *Let your boss in on your aspirations.* This is not just a matter of telling your superior that you yearn for the heights. More specifically, it calls for sounding him or her out, moving the conversation around to specific job targets:

"Do you see a possibility of my moving into marketing?"

"I've been thinking of a shot at Paul Darcy's job when he retires. What do you think?"

Go over your experience and qualifications with your superior. Look for feedback. Are there any areas where more background or education would help? Could your experience in dealing with customers—or other untapped assets—be used in some way?

People have worked with a boss for years without getting a clear idea of how they are seen in terms of advancement potential. But one or more conversations on this subject will soon develop a pretty clear picture of what your boss thinks and, even more important, what his or her attitude is. If it's favorable, go on to the next step: specific moves you can take to get you on your way.

It's possible that your boss isn't a booster. If so, ease off tactfully. However, if your boss isn't encouraging:

• *Try someone else.* It may be risky. Says one authority, "You may win the battle but lose the war." Yet if you feel you're in a dead end, bypassing your immediate superior to get to someone else who can help you may be a realistic alternative. Some possible contacts:

Can you talk to your boss's boss? A key executive in another department? A member of the very top echelon? A friendly colleague who may be able to provide guidance because of his or her knowledge of the organizational facts of life?

Be prepared for the eventuality that your boss may confront you about your bypassing. If your hand is called, admit quite simply that you did try to discuss the matter and got little satisfaction.

What you are seeking in your other-than-your-boss contacts is a person who is willing to take a chance on you. One point in your favor: executives usually view assertiveness and initiative as assets.

• *Carve out your own niche.* Make a name for yourself in some special connection if "No Vacancy" signs seem to dominate the scene. Almost every organization has interests in areas for which no one claims responsibility. One employee made it his business to keep abreast of trade shows and exhibitions in his company's industry. Since he was up on exactly what was going on, it was natural that when the desirability of participating in one such event arose, his views were sought. Eventually he benefited substantially from the success he was able to help his firm score.

• *Consider unorthodox methods as a last resort.* Horn-blowing, like cat-skinning, is a many-splendored thing. Here is an instance in which a young supervisor made it into the middle-management echelon in an unusual manner:

She launched a "teaser" campaign—sending a series of anonymous announcements to influential executives in the company heralding the arrival of a "bright new manager." One announcement said the newcomer was "faster than a computer." Another claimed an unusual ability to "leap tall projects at a single bound."

After arousing curiosity and interest, the supervisor revealed her identity in a memo to the company president, to which she attached a résumé giving her credentials. Executives laughed and talked about her campaign for days—and she got the job she was after.

Just how offbeat a tack you try depends on your imagination and, admittedly, your audacity. Make a reasonable appraisal of "how you look" in taking an unusual line of action. You don't want to look foolish or acquire a reputation for strange behavior. However, if you're satisfied with how you see yourself, and a failure won't be too destructive—why not try?

From the viewpoint of etiquette, ambition courts the hazards of toe-stepping and elbowing, with possible inconvenience or detriment to others. This consideration (discussed below from the angle of zeroing in on someone else's job) is certainly central.

But there is also possible conflict between increased job responsibility and one's life goals and lifestyle. Soap-opera cliché or not, there may be found among us the individual who sacrifices integrity, old friends and pleasant ways for advancement that creates a mental burden and emotional drain. Thoughts of promotion should include potential drawbacks as well as benefits.

SHOULD YOU ZERO IN ON SOMEONE ELSE'S JOB?

In your mind, a perfect up-the-ladder jump might mean displacing someone who has no thought of moving. Should the fact that a colleague is holding down the job you covet deter you from taking action?

The answer given here may not win the approval of the soft-hearted, but it is in keeping with the realities of working life:

Don't *you* be the one to say whose job you're after. Your efforts as advancement-seeker should be directed at making clear your merits. However, if you're offered a job now held by someone else, you have these possible courses of action:

• *Level with the person.* Give some thought to the person involved. You might find the individual is unhappy in the job and not loath to leave it. But if you suspect that you'd get strongly adverse reaction—anything from panic to outrage—this confrontation should be avoided. It becomes, properly, your boss's problem.

• *Express your reluctance.* "Mr. Smith," says an advancement-seeker to her boss, "I appreciate you're thinking of me for the Credit job. Frankly, the person who has the spot now is a friend of mine, and I believe he'd be terribly upset if he were to be displaced without being given some acceptable alternative. I'd hesitate to take the job unless some such move were made. . . ."

BEHAVIOR AFTER WINNING A PROMOTION

In the typical case, the person who has been moved up is wished well by all concerned. And what's called for is the obvious response to congratulations: appreciation, some expressions of pleasure in the improved status gained, and so on.

Especially desirable is a backward glance: think back over the steps by which the promotion was achieved. Those who provided assistance, guidance, encouragement deserve a payment of gratitude, appropriately expressed. "Appropriately" here means anything from oral thanks or a written note (see Chapter 3, pages 134–135, for messages of gratitude) to a gift that is a "token of your appreciation." (See lists of gifts, starting on page 349.)

But let's say that you've won a promotion over other competitors. That means someone has lost out. How do you treat his or her discomfiture, particularly if it's an individual with whom you normally come in contact in the course of the work? Consider these points:

• *Try to enjoy your victory without relishing the other's defeat.* Don't be upset at the thought that the other person has lost. And don't project and agonize over what you think are his or her feelings. It's perfectly possible that the reactions to not getting the spot are shrugged off with more or less complacency. The game aspect of this situation includes not only a winner and a loser but the prospect of a more successful outcome in a subsequent job competition for the person who hasn't made it.

• *Don't overexult.* Your feelings toward a rival may not be friendly. Not only does his or her defeat cause you no anguish, it may even yield a special sense of triumph. But there are good reasons why you don't want to crow—either too soon or too loudly.

For one thing, you're punishing a person who is sensitized as a result of failure, and therefore is especially vulnerable. And poor winners—those who rub salt in the wounds of the losers—are not widely admired. It's neither good form nor good tactics to gloat over another's defeat. It's a good way to lose standing with the people around you.

If despite being competitors you and the loser are good friends, you may want to make some mitigating move. Avoid anything that suggests hypocrisy. Don't argue that your friend got a raw deal unless you really believe it. Stick to the vein of "Yes, it's too bad." Without posing as the architect of the other's comeback, you can ease matters by pointing out: "It's a single incident, not the end of the world."

HOW TO TREAT THE PERSON WHO IS AFTER YOUR JOB

If someone is casting an eye at a spot the incumbent is not ready to hand over, emotions can run high and actions can be bloody. Executives who have seen a threat of this kind have acted out their rage—or outrage—by firing the "upstart" or making his or her life a living hell. But there are other ways to respond that protect one's own tenure without vengefulness:

"I guess you'd like to take over my job," Paul Harley tells Ken Masters, "and that's O.K. with me. I think you're a bright, capable guy. But I'm not ready to leave yet. When I am ready, you're welcome to it, but if you try any power play, any change here will have to be over a dead body, and it's more likely to be yours than mine."

Of course, the situation needn't result in a "dead body" at all. More humane and just as effective is the "Siberia treatment," where an overly pushy contender like Ken finds himself transferred to a new job—possibly even at higher pay—but he's now working out of the sales office in Tierra del Fuego.

In other words, the boss doesn't squelch the would-be's aspirations. He tells him, "O.K., but when I'm ready to step down." If there is unwillingness to wait, the next move is up to the subordinate.

LOOKING OUTSIDE AS A WAY TO HIGHER STATUS

Out of a desire for improved status, the grass sometimes looks greener in almost any other organization. Should one consider job-hunting outside? Or should company loyalty and the close working relationships usually developed with colleagues rule company-hopping out of bounds?

One's first loyalty should be to one's self, one's own career and future. This is not bad etiquette, it's sound psychology and good business. After all, as paternalistic as an organization may be, it has no difficulty in drawing a line between what's good for the company and what's good for the employee. Often, and fortunately, these two interests overlap. But when they don't, the realities should take over.

WHEN YOU'RE COURTING A COMPETING FIRM. Sometimes there's a natural path for job-hunters that leads from a present employer to a competitor. If you're being interviewed by someone who seems anxious to get behind-the-scenes view of your present employer, avoid a temptation to tell tales out of school. It's not only a matter of protecting the interests of your employer and not biting the hand that's been feeding you, but self-protection and self-respect are involved. The person who has to give away secrets or please an interviewer by unfavorable references to the competitor is currying favor in a way that probably will *weaken* his or her job bid. You certainly don't want to be hired because you blabbed about your present employer. Your new job holds more promise if it was your special qualifications that won you the spot.

Ordinarily there's no problem in simply avoiding the subject of present company personalities or operations. If the interviewer presses, one might say, "I'd rather not talk about that. I know you'll understand. If the situation were reversed, you'd think better of one of your employees who resisted revealing confidential or private matters about your organization. Isn't that so?"

HOW MUCH NOTICE? If you land a new job with another organization, you'll be telling your present employers about it. But—*when* do you tell them? The answer depends on two factors: how soon your new employer wants you aboard, and how much inconvenience your leaving will create.

Make the decision that will be best for both organizations. Try, of course, to turn up at your new job when requested. But if that's sooner than your present employer wants to let you go, try to reach some compromise that will satisfy both.

GLOAT? There's a strong tendency for people who are changing jobs—and employers—to adopt an "off-with-the-old, on-with-the-new" attitude. Particularly if the new job is of higher status or pays more, there's a tendency to let your old colleagues, including your boss, know how glad you are to leave the old, rundown, going-to-seed organization, and so on.

Don't. Even if it's true, you want to avoid rubbing your colleagues' noses into unpleasant matters.

In general, you certainly come off looking better and leaving behind you a feeling of pleasantness and graciousness if you leave emphasizing the positive aspects, the pleasures and triumphs of your work there.

KEEPING THE HUNT CONFIDENTIAL. Once a person has waded through the emotional and logical problems that surround the decision to go job-hunting, there can be a sudden feeling of relief—and the urge to talk. You may want others to know of your resolve to brook the hazards of the job market. And this tendency is particularly strong if the decision to leave stems in part from difficulties you've been having. For example, let's say you've had a personality clash with your superior. Your decision to leave may represent a brave act, a declaration of your personal integrity. Nevertheless, there are sound reasons for confining the news of your job-hunting to as few people as possible. For one thing, the news is likely to leak out in a way that might be either harmful or unflattering to you. For another, some people might be upset because their feelings of job security and loyalty to the organization might be adversely affected.

BREAKING THE NEWS

When you're all set and you've been officially hired by your new employer, you're ready to let others know. The correct order of precedence is to tell your superior first.

Can there be an exception to this procedure? Conceivably. In a special case where you and your boss are strongly at odds, then you can use the very correctness of letting the boss know first be a way of expressing your feelings toward him. For example, by telling your boss's boss of your intention to leave, you clearly administer a rebuke by the bypass.

We repeat, this isn't recommended procedure, but it can help make a point if the point deserves to be made at all.

There is another courtesy you may extend to your boss if you and he or she are on good terms. He may prefer to let others in the organization know rather than leave it to you to tell one or two people and then have the grapevine spread the word.

A particularly gracious thing would be to ask the boss what his preference would be: "Would you rather I kept quiet about this until you've had a chance to make the announcement?"

Frequently, the news of such departures is formalized by a routine memo. Here are two models, one simple and matter-of-fact, the other warmer and heartier:

> This is to announce that as of June 1 Paul Miller is resigning his job as supervisor of the Supplies Division. We're sure that all his friends at [company name] wish him the best of luck.

> With considerable regret on our part we wish to announce that Paul Miller is leaving us to become Division Manager with the R. L. Farkas Company. Much as we hate to see Paul go, we're all delighted with this career development that represents an offer that he just couldn't refuse.
>
> There'll be a farewell party for Paul in the Recreation Room on Friday, May 29. You're all cordially invited to attend.

LEAVING THE DOOR OPEN

Usually, people who leave one company to join another seldom retrace their steps. Despite this fact, there are three good reasons for not burning your bridges behind you:

1. *Image enhancement.*

The steps you take to maintain ties with the "old company" are also those that tend to keep your memory bright. The lunches you have with old colleagues—and this might very well include your boss—the occasional social calls you make, perhaps birthday cards or other anniversary remembrances you send along, are all moves that maintain a favorable picture.

2. *Career and professional assets.*

Many a careerist moving from one company to another can benefit from some of the facilities he or she leaves behind. The company library, a key study, contact with a technical expert or outstanding manager may represent sources of help that can prove very worthwhile.

3. *And rehiring is a possibility.*

Don't laugh. It's a practice that takes place quite often. As a matter of fact, some companies tend to have such a large number of rehired people on the roster that it almost seems to represent company policy.

And why not? The person who has left was clearly hired in the first place because he or she had qualifications the company wanted. In many cases the company would like once again to have available these qualifications, and if in the time the employee has been working elsewhere additional skills, training, and experience have been built up—so much the better.

PUTTING STATUS IN PERSPECTIVE

Status is like music. When a tune is played softly, it provides a pleasant background against which other activity can take place. But the same tune blasting away at full volume intrudes on everything and upsets everybody.

Overconcern with status and throwing one's weight around on the basis of rank are intrusive and organizationally undesirable acts. But by avoiding its destructive aspects, disruption and injured feelings are prevented and it becomes salutary. As a constructive element on the business scene, status facilitates and guides, suggests proper lines of communication, and becomes an effective psychic reward for achievement.

6

Appearance, Grooming, and Personal Habits

THE INDIVIDUAL AND THE GROUP

This chapter on personal appearance and related matters essentially deals with the individual-group relationship. It is important to a person that he or she look good and be accepted by others, because the group's response determines the individual's role and social success. Needless to say, social success is a factor in career development. The person whose appearance grates on others' nerves or the one whose use of obscene language makes people wince has an obstacle in the way of advancement. And the question arises: What can and should be done about the interpersonal situations that are created?

It is not the purpose of this chapter to get people to live up to the ideal of a well-dressed, well-scrubbed, sweet-smelling nonentity. Life on the job is, and should be, a lot more interesting and varied than that. But the real-life working world has built-in requirements of behavior that are appropriate for it. For example:

In this section on "Habits," the matter of drinking is discussed (see page 267). Alcoholism is no mean problem. Millions of people and endless heartbreak are involved in it, and despite great efforts to find a remedy, difficulties persist. The alcoholic at work poses complications for his or her boss, co-workers, friends. What is said here attempts to avoid moralizing and to treat the subject in a way that makes constructive sense.

What do you do about a colleague who is an alcoholic? What is your behavior when the problem drinker is your boss? The pages ahead offer practical answers to these and other matters of appearance and personal conduct on the job.

PERSONAL APPEARANCE AND THE WORKSCENE

Once upon a time, a young man who combed his hair neatly and wore a clean white shirt and a gray-flannel suit was automatically thought to be corporate presidential timber. Because he dressed "properly"—that is, up to a generally accepted standard—his appearance became an asset, like the ability to speak properly or to zero in on the cogent facts of a complex report.

But the "proper-dress-and-grooming" concept has largely been superseded. True, there are still standards of proper dress. But with the spirit of liberation that the sixties brought, the "rules" of dress and grooming on the workscene are less rigid, more subtle.

While it's as important as ever to dress "right," just what that "rightness" consists of has become more difficult to identify. For example, it is this difficulty that drove personnel directors mad en masse with the advent of—for women—pantsuits, see-through blouses, the braless look, and—for men—beards, beads (instead of ties), sports shirts with two buttons open, exposing the male chest well below the neckline. And, of course, long hair worn by men caused endless controversy, lawsuits, arbitration cases.

THE THREE FACTORS THAT DETERMINE "PROPER" APPEARANCE

You can't help but notice as you go from one city to another —even from one organization to another—that prevailing clothing and grooming styles vary.

If you have any part in shaping your organization's policy on dress and grooming, here are the three main guiding factors:

1. *Company image.*

The way an organization sees itself—or, at least, the way the top people visualize the organization—affects dress and appearance. If the firm is seen as solid, stable, conservative, what employees wear will reflect this fact. If the organization is thought to be informal, permissive, styles will be influenced accordingly.

2. *Feelings of the employees themselves.*

A group has collective standards and tastes. And whatever the elements of this group think—in part, it mirrors the surrounding community—it expresses itself in acceptance or rejection of the individual appearance of group members. Often it's a reflection of this group attitude that is manifesting itself when an employee goes to his or her boss to complain of the dress or appearance of a fellow-employee.

3. *Individual taste and preference.*

Almost every individual has a sense of what is acceptable or attractive or desirable in the way of his or her appearance. If a female employee feels she looks good—or feels much more comfortable—in a pantsuit, it's going to take strong counterpressure to prevent her from coming so clad to work. Here the individual's tendency for or against conformity is a factor.

DRESS CODES AND JOB EFFECTIVENESS

The question of physical appearance on the workscene is different from that of society at large. In off-job situations, dress is a personal matter. On the job, not only is appearance a personal affair, but it affects job relationships and reflects on the organization overall. For example:

It was thought by some that the wearing of white dress shirts by IBM salesmen was a factor in that organization's outstanding sales success. A survey indicated that nine out of ten executives questioned felt that the white shirt *was* a definite asset.

In another study, an office group that had been permitted to dress without any guidelines was given a dress code that prohibited more extreme fashions. Results suggested that after some time work performance improved.

Among companies that say they have dress codes, about one-third have written regulations, fifty percent have unwritten ones, and the remainder say they have none.

CONTEMPORARY RULES FOR DRESS ON THE JOB

Here are some paragraphs from a letter received by the Research Institute of America from one of its management members:

Help! Help! An article on appropriate office dress is desperately needed. Also, pointers on how to handle those who show lack of good taste and common sense. I'm talking about the very casual pants outfits, party pajamas, bare feet in sandals, super-tight pants, blue jeans (that's right), see-through pants, very short scooter skirts and the like.

Our company has a *very* liberal dress code which is to be administered by the supervisors. However, many of the supervisors are men who do not pay enough attention or even know what some of the fashion terms mean. Besides, most of them probably just do not want to ruffle the waters so they let infractions ride by—and probably enjoy it. Even the female supervisors disregard good taste for themselves and their employees.

How in the world do we improve the situation without infringing on somebody's "rights"? How do we let these girls know that proper dress doesn't mean unfashionable or expensive?

For men as well as women, the old traditions of dress have largely crumbled. The business suit, once thought an absolute essential, often lost its top half. The sports jacket and slacks appeared, followed by the leisure suit—in which the top half looked more like a shirt than a suit jacket. Neckties vanished as though interdicted by law. Turtlenecks appeared—yes, even in executive suites—sometimes worn along with beads! And for both sexes, hairstyles went unisex. Men wore their hair long. Women's hairstyles became short.

Between dress and hairstyle, questions became common that in view of our past seem incredible: "Is that a man or a woman?" Or: "Is that a boy or a girl?"

WHEN THE RULES ARE BROKEN

In most organizations, the question of what is and isn't acceptable appearance on the workscene falls to the lot of personnel executives. The practical problem often comes to this: an organization either formally or informally decides on a rule such as: "Pantsuits may not be worn by females on company premises." Two things may happen to destroy what seems like a reasonable rule. First, pantsuits for women become widely accepted off the job, and companies with an enlightened outlook permit female employees to come to work wearing the new pants style. Soon, organizations other than the most hide-bound or autocratic have to give way.

Eventually policy on appearance in most companies jells along lines like these:

Both men and women are permitted dress of any style as long

as it is "within reason." The "reason" limit is defined in a case such as this:

A young woman newly hired into a computer-programming department turned up one day without a bra and in a somewhat transparent blouse. Some of the older men in the department, although appreciative, found the presence somewhat upsetting. As a result of comments made, the head of the department took the young lady aside and explained that although she personally had no objection to extreme styles, the workscene in general, and her department in particular, should be considered out-of-bounds for her style of dress. The employee found it easy to accept the ruling because of two things:

• *Matter-of-factness.* The department head had not moralized or accused the employee of bad taste, low morals, or made any other such judgmental statement.

• *Tone.* The tone of the interview also had been mild and nonaccusatory. The culprit was not being scolded or found guilty of anything. The point that was being made was not unreasonable.

BRINGING ABOUT A CHANGE IN HAIRSTYLE

There is another element in the limits that help determine what is and isn't appropriate. Example:

Ron Dennison was a young man with two years of college training who decided to use his skills as a typist as a means of earning a living. (You may remember that male typists became fairly common on the workscene as a result of equal-opportunity legislation and the general desexing of jobs and job categories.) Part of Ron's assignment was to take over the receptionist's job during lunch periods. Seated at the reception desk, he made quite a striking picture with his long, flowing blond hair coming well below his shoulders. But shortly after he began his receptionist's chores, a top executive passed through the reception room, was startled by what he saw, and made a beeline for Personnel. A brief conference resulted in the personnel director's having Ron Dennison come down to his office after lunch:

"Ron," he said, "what you wear or your personal grooming is obviously your own affair off the job, and, as you know, you've been working here for a month and nothing has been said about your appearance. However, anyone who sits at the receptionist's desk becomes a highly visible representative of our company, and frankly, although I have no personal objection to it, the length of your hair can be quite shocking to our customers and other visitors."

Dennison admitted that the argument made sense, and a mutually acceptable hair length was finally agreed to.

The point here is that special consideration as to appearance should be made when employees are called on to meet the public—customers and so on. Here it is perfectly proper for an organization to set specific rules for appearance according to its own concept of company image and the appearance of employees that would either help or interfere with that image.

HOW TO APPLY THE RULE OF REASON

Most organizations state that they expect their employees to dress "in appropriate business attire" or "in good taste."

Organizations that don't have written dress and grooming codes face the problem from time to time of one or more employees who their colleagues or supervisors feel are outside the limit of acceptable appearance. They have, in short, violated someone's idea of the appropriate.

Taste being the evanescent thing it is, one person's good taste may be another's idea of the totally unacceptable. How is the judgment to be made, and who is to make it?

The main point to keep in mind is that such judgments tend to be highly subjective. What is reasonable is what a person in authority *says* it is. With this fact in mind, the next item suggests a course of action to follow when you get a specific complaint.

WHEN YOU GET COMPLAINTS FROM OTHER EMPLOYEES

One of the specific problems that may arise from the appearance of an employee:

The employee's co-worker may come to you and register a personal complaint: "I think that's an outrageous dress the new girl is wearing. It may be O.K. for the beach or a vacation resort, but it's out of place in an office like ours. I must admit it bugs me. . . ."

When a manager gets this type of complaint, there are hazards that must be kept in mind:

• *Look before you leap.* Before taking action, it's advised that you personally check into the circumstance being complained about. Make your own assessment of how acceptable or unacceptable the matter is.

• *Get other opinions.* It's advisable, unless you're quite sure of your own judgment in this matter, to get reactions of other people involved. For example, after checking, you may find that the person making the complaint is the only one in the group who has even noticed or has had a negative reaction.

In evaluating the condition complained about, make the distinction between what is acceptable *in general* and what is reasonable in your own organization or department. Particular work settings have their own standards. And the professional level of the individual makes a difference. Creative people—artists, designers—are often permitted considerable latitude in casualness of dress. And a law firm or brokerage house would tend toward more conservative dress and behavior than an art or advertising agency. Remember also that contemporary attitudes toward dress are much more relaxed than those of only a few years ago. Even old-line companies now tolerate secretaries in jeans.

If your decision is to try to modify the opinion of the *complainant,* proceed along these lines:

• *Advising the complainant.* Your investigation may show that while the girl complained about is wearing an unorthodox costume, it is within acceptable limits. Then the problem is to calm down the complainant and gently make the point that his or her feelings are somewhat exaggerated. For example, you may point out that you've only gotten one adverse reaction. You might say, "Marion, I've looked into the matter you mentioned earlier. I certainly appreciate your telling me your feelings, but I must say that none of the other people here seem to feel the same way you do. Of course, this isn't to say you're wrong. Standards of dress have changed considerably in recent years, and some of us find some of the new styles rather startling. However, in this case I do feel that the thing you're complaining about is still within acceptable standards. . . ."

However, if you find the complaint is justified, then you must deal with the culprit.

• *Talking to the offender.* Here your goal is equally delicate. You want to change a person's behavior without causing future complications. Usually it's an excellent idea *not* to tell the person the name of the individual or individuals who made the complaint. You can accomplish this by intimating that it's your own sense of propriety that has been jarred. And as has been said earlier, the two points to be stressed are, first, the nonaccusatory tone in which your comments are made, and second, that the style of dress in question is not being criticized except in the sense that it is inappropriate in a work setting.

The section that immediately follows offers a summary of steps to guide you around the pitfalls that attend action in this difficult subject area.

SOME QUESTIONS TO ASK YOURSELF BEFORE TAKING ACTION

You have noted a situation or behavior that you feel requires remedy. It may be anything from extreme dress to an antisocial habit like excessive use of profanity. Before doing anything, ask yourself the questions below as a guide to action:

1. *Exactly what is wrong?*

Pin down precisely the behavior or element that seems objectionable. Avoid generalities, like "appearance," in favor of specifics, like "Tod is wearing a pair of torn and dirty shorts."

2. *Why is it upsetting?*

Tod must move around from department to department, and he suggests a disreputable appearance that might be all right on the athletic field but is out of place in the Sales and Service Division.

3. *Who is offended?*

Often there's no question. People tell you or make grimaces that show their negative reaction. However, reactions may be mixed. One co-worker may shrug off the situation, while another may respond excessively. The point is, the nature and extent of the reaction may require some investigation.

4. *Is there a minimum action that might settle the matter?*

Before thinking about action of any magnitude, consider the possibility that the whole problem might be made to disappear by a simple, straightforward approach: "Joan, perhaps you don't realize it, but bare-midriff dresses don't make it in a bank. Would you mind changing during the lunch period? . . ." However, if action of this kind fails, consider these additional questions:

5. *Would an attempt at a remedy violate the rights of the individual?*

This question is one that arises from time to time, and may have legal overtones. For example, many employees took their employers to court to contest efforts to have them choose between modifying some aspect of their appearance or quitting their jobs. Men's hair length, large moustaches or beards were often the center of these controversies. Even if there is no clear-cut answer to this question —or, especially, when there isn't—the firm's legal counsel should be consulted.

6. *Are there others in the department who are doing the same thing?*

Before acting in one case, make sure there aren't other instances of the same infraction of good taste. If there are, you might be accused of playing favorites—letting Paul get away with something that you're criticizing in Peter. Or if the circumstance is more widespread than you first thought, your evaluation of it or your approach might well be different. For example, you might be willing to accept a practice or style that is widely practiced and apparently causing no adverse reaction. Or you might decide to issue a general edict against the practice:

"It's been noticed that some members of the staff have been going about their work barefoot. This is inadvisable both from an aesthetic and a safety viewpoint. It will be appreciated if this practice is stopped. Please see me if there's any question about this matter."

7. *Any others elsewhere in the organization?*

A department or division head might run into trouble in attempting to prohibit something that is accepted elsewhere in the company. If there are instances of the practice that you feel is undesirable being accepted, at the very least you should discuss this with the managers involved or with a higher-echelon executive so as to achieve some organizational consistency. This *doesn't* rule out a manager's saying, "I don't care what they're doing in the XYZ Department. It's unacceptable here. . . ." But this is better said after thought has been given to the possible argument that other managers are taking a different view.

8. *Who should handle the situation?*

In most cases the superior of the "erring" employee is the logical person to act. But there are other possibilities to be considered:

a colleague;
head of the next-higher echelon;
personnel executive;
other?

9. *The final step: Can you minimize or dampen aftereffects?*

Properly handled, correction of an undesirable bit of behavior need not leave a personal scar or general resentment. If possible, the conversation with the offender should be confidential. No comment need be made after the fact. And, finally, the supervisor or other person should make it clear that there are no hard feelings.

The questions that have been posed are intended for situations involving unacceptable dress or appearance. They may also be applied to other types of behavior or habits that are inappropriate on the job. But some of these are of such a nature that they require a somewhat different approach. The additional considerations necessary when dealing with personal problems, such as body odor, or other problem factors are described below.

GUIDELINES FOR ONE'S PERSONAL STYLE

Aside from the group and organizational considerations, dress and grooming is an intensely personal matter. At some point, you stand in front of a mirror and make a judgment on what you see there.

The source of much of the workscene problem with appearance is that, to put it simply, many people see themselves inaccurately. For example:

A fifty-year-old secretary, newly returned to the workscene after a divorce, turns up at work in a see-through blouse. True, she still has an attractive figure. But even this asset doesn't justify the poor taste.

We've already explained how a problem of this type should be handled by the person in charge. A friendly, discreet word succeeds in making the secretary modify her ideas of personal glamour. But the question still remains: What is the problem of personal appearance, and what guidelines can be supplied to prevent major gaucheries?

First, it must be repeated that many people have distorted ideas of how they look or about what is and isn't becoming to them. One thirty-year-old executive admits, "I still can't go into a dress shop and buy my own clothes. I depend on friends to help me choose."

The semanticist Senator S. I. Hayakawa tells an anecdote that makes the point: "Mrs. Smith went out to buy herself a hat. The one she selected looked terrible on her, but it looked great on her self-image."

The matter of personal appearance can be a decidely tangled affair, involving psychological factors such as self-esteem, how one sees one's social role, one's sense of status, and so on. Without attempting to brave such murky waters, it is nevertheless possible to suggest some guidelines for making decisions about aspects of one's appearance. Three paired concepts provide limits that can simplify making a decision for or against a particular style or item of one's appearance:

• *Formality versus informality.* QUESTION: "Should I, a thirty-five-year-old middle manager, wear a turtleneck shirt to work? My wife tells me I look well in that style, but is it appropriate for the office?" ANSWER: Consider the degree of formality that exists in your work milieu. If people are generally relaxed about things in general, and there is no reason not to (such as having to deal with outsiders who might find the garb puzzling, or an antiturtleneck edict put out by management), wear the shirt. Just expect some reaction—either negative or positive—the first day or so, and be prepared to persist if that is your wish.

• *Conservatism versus flamboyance.* QUESTION: "I'm an office manager, given to wearing somber colors. But I recently bought myself an orange pantsuit that my friends tell me is quite becoming. Should I wear it to work?" ANSWER: Of course. Why not swing a little? Dress can be a source of fun and enjoyment. It enhances a person to change styles from time to time—either way; that is, for someone who ordinarily dresses conservatively to loosen up, or one who tends toward the flamboyant to go in for the appeal of the cool and quiet of conservatism.

• *Conformity versus nonconformity.* QUESTION: "My company is somewhat traditional, and clothes are generally supposed to be unobtrusive. Although I'm not unhappy with the somewhat restricted styles that we wear, I do get fed up with the monotony of it all. Would any foundations crack if I broke out of the rut? Nothing wild, mind you, but perhaps a bright shirtwaist dress heavily accessorized, for example?" ANSWER: If the style is becoming, by all means, indulge yourself—and see what the results are.

One basic rule about appearance supersedes almost all others: if your dress or grooming is "right" for you and enhances your looks, almost anything within reason goes—unless it flies directly in the teeth of firm policy.

CHANGE TO SUIT THE OCCASION

There is one recourse that can give you the best of two possible worlds: change your apparel for a specific occasion. For example:

One executive says: "Ordinarily, I wear dresses or skirts and blouses to work. But on days that I know we're going to have meetings of any length, I switch to a pantsuit, because they're more comfortable—permit slouching in one's chair, and so on."

In one New Jersey company, attire is usually informal. However, when clients are expected, a dress alert goes out the day before. Then the men who ordinarily wear slacks and shirts wear suits, and women change from pantsuits or otherwise flamboyant garb to more conservative dresses.

FACELIFTING, TOUPEES, AND OTHER ENHANCEMENTS

People often seek cosmetic guidance—anything from "Should I get a face lift?" to "Should I get myself a hairpiece?" The range of changes sought to improve appearance runs the gamut from hair dyeing to nose surgery.

The question has particular point because appearance is clearly career-related. An attractive person regards his or her looks as an advancement asset.

Keep in mind that there are two types of physical renovation. The first includes all kinds of minor effects—minor in terms of both cost and degree; hair dyeing, removal of skin blemishes, for example. The second has to do with major expense and possibly surgery: facelifting, nose reshaping, and so on.

One type of change seems to dangle somewhere in between minor and major: the toupee question for men. While it's more drastic than simply changing hair color (although "keeping the gray out" can be a crucial question for both men and women) and less drastic than surgery, it does involve a major appearance change. There is a big difference between a baldheaded man and one with a good head of hair—not simply one of looks, but with consequences for apparent age and personality.

The answer to those seeking guidance: do whatever makes you feel comfortable. Many a balding executive has gained in self-confidence by wearing a well-shaped toupee. Many an aging person—of either sex—has avoided panic and hurt vanity by covering up the advent of graying hair by appropriate hair coloring. Dewrinkling skin and having sagging facial muscles surgically lifted has helped many people feel better about themselves.

There is nothing wrong or unacceptable about the desire to improve or retain one's looks. However, there are some *practical* considerations that should be made before any but the most minor efforts are undertaken:

• *Cost.* Some appearance-improving moves are not cheap. Clearly, cosmetic surgery involves higher cost brackets. A good toupee costs several hundred dollars, and this expense may have to be repeated after a year or two—depending on how much wear the item gets. But whatever is being contemplated, be sure to investigate the expense. And remember, it's not only a matter of initial cost. Some efforts involve a repeated or continuing expenditure.

• *Permanence.* Hair transplants, face lifting, and other major transformations may decrease apparent age, but only for a time. One should get some realistic estimate of the length of time the effects of such treatment will last before undertaking them.

• *Benefits.* Don't believe the people who try to tell you that the gains from appearance improvement are all in the head. They *can* be in the pocket as well. Many a person has been able to get a job or a promotion as the result of improved appearance. Before the days of the laws against age discrimination, many people were hired who might not have been if some artfully applied hair dye hadn't substituted a youthful appearance for one of aging. And even today, well-used gray-retardant can prevent unconscious discrimination.

And yes, it's true that a large part of the benefit is psychological, in the form of improved self-confidence. But that can be an important factor influencing not only the way a person feels about himself or herself but also the image projected to others.

FOR THOSE WHO WANT TO BE THEMSELVES, WARTS AND ALL

Some individuals may have real or fancied defects that they hesitate to do anything about. For those who are tempted but would rather not, here are two encouraging thoughts:

• If one can learn to accept one's self, others will do likewise.

• Personality and manner can offset imagined or even real physical blemishes. Remember, the possessor of a face that objectively might be described as wrinkled is often seen by others as "having character."

WHEN AND HOW TO GET A PHOTO PORTRAIT

Your appearance—as far as the public is concerned—is often what a photograph says it is. There's a long-standing tradition that heads of companies have portrait photographs taken to be used for publicity purposes. In recent years, the practice has spread through the echelons. Now, almost every key person in an organization has a photograph in personnel files. One thing about photo portraits: unlike the picture of Dorian Gray, they *do* grow old. Changing hairstyles and clothes may date an otherwise fine picture. Experts suggest that executive portraits be taken anew approximately every three years. One should check on one's own portrait in organization files. See if you feel it's still satisfactory. To some extent, you judge on the basis of how the portrait might be used.

TYPICAL USES

A photo portrait can satisfy several needs for the businessman and businesswoman:

- for publicity releases to magazines, trade journals, and the newspapers;
- as an adjunct to company programs, appearances as a speaker where there are printed programs, and so on;
- for annual reports, in-house publications;
- for sales brochures and organizational promotions;
- for newspaper advertising;
- for displays in headquarters buildings or branch offices.

The new thing in the field is the color portrait. Not only are these becoming less expensive due to advances in technology, but black-and-white prints from a color negative can be used for newspaper and magazine reproduction, eliminating the need for both a color portrait and one in black and white.

The cost for a professional portrait in color starts at about a hundred dollars. Of course, the top men in the field may demand up to a thousand dollars for a portrait, but an average is somewhere around the two-hundred-dollar mark.

The traditional head-and-shoulders shot has been nudged aside in favor of the on-location photo. Here the individual is shown in his or her working environment, often full-figure. Of course, with cropping, a head shot can be obtained if that's wanted for newspaper purposes.

SELECTING A PHOTOGRAPHER

A professional photographer can help with suggestions on appropriate dress, setting, and pose. A facial expression, often a key to the effectiveness of the portrait, will be "directed" by the photographer.

In selecting a photographer for portraits for yourself or your staff, here are some helpful pointers:

- Seek out photographers who have a reputation or experience in doing portraits of business people.
- Look over his or her work in advance, and choose the individual whose style—degree of formality or informality, for example—you feel is most appropriate or most to your taste.
- You may also want to discuss fees, and if more than one portrait is involved, investigate the possibility of a discount.

HOW TO DRESS

Before the photo session starts, you may describe to the photographer the purposes to which the portrait will be put and the kind of image you would like to project (a V.P. Sales might want to seem more extroverted than a director of research, for example). If you are in doubt as to the style, color, and so on of dress that will photograph best, ask for suggestions before the photo date.

One expert in the field of business portraiture offers these tips on dress to ensure a satisfactory portrait:

FOR MEN. Follow these guidelines:

- Suits or sports jackets are more flattering. Solid colors or subdued plaids are best. Wild patterns and extravagant styles can date a photograph.

- Let your tie or shirt create a color accent.
- It's best to visit the barber or hair stylist several days before a portrait sitting so that the new-shorn look will have faded.

FOR WOMEN. Women should:

- Opt for long or three-quarter-length sleeves that flatter, no matter what the pose.
- Select dark or medium-toned clothing for a businesslike appearance. Color selection can help place the emphasis on your face in the photograph.
- Avoid busy patterns.
- Use scarves and jewelry for accents. If you normally wear glasses, be sure to have them on hand for the portrait.
- Wear your everyday makeup. You may wish to add a touch of makeup gel to your cheeks, and lip gloss for highlights.
- Keep your normal hairstyle; this is no time to experiment at the beauty parlor.

FOR TV APPEARANCES

Executives who may be called on to appear before the TV or news cameras will find the same considerations that have to do with a portrait photo also apply to the requirements of this type of situation. Here, also, garish patterns or overly flamboyant accessories tend to distract an audience. One advantage of TV appearances: the larger studios have makeup people who will give you a helpful cosmetic going over before you face the cameras.

B.O. AND ASSORTED ILLS

"Mr. Jones, I hate to bring up this matter, but . . . that new girl works right next to me, and she has such a bad case of body odor I can hardly stand it. . . ."

From time to time, executives get a complaint of this kind about an employee from a co-worker. Or it may involve a smelly pipe or too much perfume. Whatever lies at the heart of the complaint, you're faced with a delicate situation.

Consider the "bad-breath" problem. Contrary to the message of a TV commercial for a well-known mouthwash, it's usually not a good idea to try to handle the problem by leaving the anti-bad-breath product on the offender's desk. Even less realistic is the expectation that the offender will welcome the attempted assist. You're in a highly booby-trapped situation. One wrong move and somebody's feelings will be badly hurt.

The problem is usually intensified by the urgency of the complaint. As in the case mentioned above, Susie says, "I just can't stand it anymore." And the fact is, the complaining employee may come to you under the pressure of strong upset—further complicating your situation. Don't minimize the difficulties of handling this type of situation. Consider these suggestions:

1. *Check for yourself.*

There's always the chance that the complaining employee is distorting the facts. This may come about either because of hostility toward the other employee or through an exaggerated reaction. For example, an employee may complain to a manager that "I just can't bear to work next to Gary anymore. Maybe I have a thing about dandruff, but with him it's like a snowstorm, and it makes me feel itchy and creepy. . . ."

On checking, it appears that while Gary's dandruff may seem like a major problem to the complainant, otherwise it's marginal—for example, it's most obvious when Gary wears a dark suit—and is accepted as a fact of life by Gary's other co-workers.

Here you have two courses of action, recommended in this order:

• *Supply perspective.* Calm down the complainant and gently put across the message that the feelings expressed are somewhat exaggerated. For example, you point out that no other people have registered adverse comments.

• *Switch work stations.* If the complainer still balks, consider the possibility of making a slight adjustment in the work setup that will minimize contact between the two. Preferably, change the station of the person who is dissatisfied.

However, if neither of these moves is feasible and the complaint is not unreasonable, you may want to consider action that addresses itself directly to the problem; that is, the condition complained about. In this case . . .

2. *Figure out the course of least trauma.*

Once you verify the situation and feel action must be taken, your immediate objective is to act in a way that will stir up minimum fuss.

Don't underestimate the sensibilities of the individual involved.

Even the best-natured person will resent being told of his or her personal deficiencies. It's not easy for anyone to accept the fact that he or she is guilty of unknowingly offending others.

Consider, then, that you may not be the best person to broach the subject. As a matter of fact, you may seriously want to:

3. *Let someone speak for you.*

Executives in the past have discovered that their most effective approach is through a mature individual from the group. For example, in handling the body-odor problem, an executive went to one of the motherly and discreet people in the department and explained the problem to her. She agreed to talk to the offender in an informal heart-to-heart chat.

Another possibility: a good friend of the offender may also be an effective intermediary. In any case, the person who conveys the message must do it without any suspicion that you have initiated the action.

4. *Do what you can to minimize guilt feelings.*

Handling the touchy question of personal hygiene is difficult enough—but at least you can feel that you're on the side of the angels when you confront the offender. Just as delicate is the problem of poor taste in personal matters—the overpowering use of perfume, for example, an offense that is disturbing to some people.

Admittedly, there is no graceful way to tell someone that he or she is in bad taste. Translated, that means that if you *must* bring up the question of an overdose of roses, it might be prudent to make the problem the other fellow's. A white lie will be more acceptable than the blunt truth.

Something like: "Helen, your perfume is delightful. But it's making it tough for the fellows to concentrate because it's *too* delightful. I hate to ask you to wait until quitting time to dab it on. Would you mind very much?"

If Helen is smart, she'll cooperate. And if she reads between the lines, she may even be grateful that you put it tactfully.

5. *Avoid going through channels.*

One executive thought he was taking the easy way out. He got the head of Personnel to agree to talk to an engineer who was the source of trouble, in this case an overly free use of garlic in his diet. The interview seemed to go fine. The technician listened while the personnel manager delivered a well-reasoned lecture on the undesirability of eating certain foods that left aftereffects that might make others uncomfortable. He admitted that he himself had a fondness for onions, which had caused trouble, but he had become aware of the consequences and now limited himself in their use. Garlic, he added with a knowing look, was also known to offend one's workmates when eaten in excess.

The personnel manager, with the interview concluded, phoned the executive and reported that all seemed to have gone well. The executive complimented himself on his perspicacity. But the employee failed to show up the next day or any other day thereafter. Once Personnel had gotten into the act, he felt a "big thing" had been made of a minor matter—and his resentment registered itself in the form of quitting.

6. *Can you bring in professional help?*

In some cases, where the problem is not merely a matter of habit but reflects some physical condition, it may be possible to get the employee into the hands of a doctor who may be able to help. One example:

An executive noticed that his secretary had developed a skin condition that caused unsightly blemishes bad enough to make a negative impression. After weeks of hoping that the condition would clear up or that she would see a doctor, he decided that he'd better try to take some action. (Even his boss had said, "Harry, can't you get Miss Hayes to a dermatologist?")

Opportunity knocked in the form of the annual physical given by the company's medical department. The executive called the examining physician and asked that Miss Hayes's skin ailment be looked at and, if possible, treated. Now at least he felt that whatever could be done would be done.

7. *When the problem can't be eliminated.*

Offending symptoms or personal handicaps often can be eased. For example, if it's something like bad breath, intelligent use of breath sweeteners, mouthwashes, and so on will ease the complications.

But some difficulties of this category aren't easily dealt with. And where the difficulty can't be eliminated or mitigating moves prove useless, you may have to think of making more than minor changes. For instance, one manager transferred a warehouse employee, whose body odors were unpleasant, to an outside work gang. Transfers, changes of assignment can either put the unintentional offender in less exposed areas or have him or her work with less sensitive co-workers.

WHEN YOU'RE THE PURPORTED CULPRIT

The unthinkable has happened. Someone has pointed a finger at you! Whether it's bad breath or a pungent shirt, the implication is clear. *They* have the nerve to say *you.* . . .

Well, what are you going to do about it? First, hopefully, you'll cool down. Then, slowly, you'll consider the possibility that maybe— just *maybe*—it's true. Give it the benefit of the doubt, anyway. O.K. So what?

The "So what" is: be grateful. If you are guilty of offending, certainly you're better off knowing it. Maybe you don't care what this particular S.O.B. thinks, but certainly there *are* people both at work and in your life you *do* care about. And there's little doubt that any distasteful habit represents a crimp in aspirations for advancement or even for good relationships in the job. At least now it isn't everybody else's secret but yours. And since you do know, you can do something about it.

Just do whatever is necessary to be sure the offense isn't repeated. No need to make a federal case about it. Get the proper remedy, use it, and try to put injured pride behind you. The less said, the better. And you'll get high marks for personal dignity if you act as if the whole incident never happened.

DEALING WITH THE PROBLEM OF OBSCENITY

We live in changing times. Language that once might only have been whispered is now trumpeted to mixed audiences from stage and screen. Off-color words and phrases that never were heard in the office and only occasionally among factory workers now are prevalent in previously sacrosanct settings. And yet you may get complaints from traditional-minded employees who find some aspects of the "new behavior," and, specifically, the new spoken vocabulary, difficult to take. (See also "Profanity," page 153.)

"Dirty words" are not unfamiliar to the ears of working men and women. Anyone familiar with the vocabularies of lower-echelon employees knows that obscenities may be a standard part of verbal exchange. As a matter of fact, studies have been made that suggest that profanity on the workscene is a form of protest that in the guise of conversation helps relieve a certain amount of tension and rebelliousness. When obscenity is limited to the hearing of those who accept it matter-of-factly, it poses no problem. If a couple of stock clerks want to exchange profane remarks that represent both their idea of humor and self-expression, there is no need for anyone to do anything.

However, obscenity is a problem when it offends. And this can be the case anywhere—in offices, factories, warehouses, or whatever. For example:

Estelle Borden is a newly hired clerk in a warehouse office. Her desk is in a glass-walled section that abuts directly on the warehouse area. The warehousemen working within her hearing use language that makes her feel extremely uncomfortable. Her first reaction is shock, her second is one of hope: Maybe I'll get used to it in a day or so, she thinks. But after time has passed, she finds that she continues to be upset. It almost seems as though the warehouse workers step up the range of their obscenity to discomfit her. Finally, almost in tears, she talks to her boss, Sid Leavitt, foreman in charge. Leavitt's actions represent a good way to handle this kind of problem:

1. *Spotting the offenders.*

The foreman decides that instead of trying to, in effect, throw an acoustical blanket over the whole group, he will talk only to those people who seem to represent the problem at its worst.

2. *Holding a quiet, low-pressure meeting.*

Leavitt asks the three men whom he has identified as being the most foul-mouthed to stay for a few minutes after work one evening. And he quietly explains the situation:

"Some people [he doesn't identify Estelle Borden by name, although he is sure there is no mystery about who is meant] have been upset by some of the language that is being used here. Now, I know that none of you intends to upset anyone. As far as I'm personally concerned, the language could be twice as extreme and it wouldn't bother me [here the foreman is making the point that he is not reprimanding the employees because of any personal reaction, but rather that he is speaking up on behalf of others]. But since some people are being disturbed, I'd appreciate it if you'd tone it down a bit. O.K.?"

Ordinarily, the approach the foreman has used up to this point would be sufficient to get the employees to agree to go along, but let's assume that there is a recalcitrant in the group who believes that his "freedom of expression" is being unfairly limited.

He might say: "Sid, I think you're being g—— d—— unreasonable. I intend to just keep on talking the way I always have, and I don't give a —— who doesn't like it."

At this point, the supervisor must make a final statement: "I'm sorry you feel I'm infringing on your rights, but no one has the right to make a fellow employee needlessly uncomfortable. So I'm going to make it very plain. I insist that you curb your language. Any failure to do so will be dealt with by disciplinary means."

Here the foreman has made his ultimate move: using his authority to stop undesirable conduct within the area of his responsibility. (For more on how to use authority to backstop leadership, see "Discipline," Chapter 4, page 178.)

DRINKING

The word "drinking" is not synonymous with "a drinking problem." To deal realistically with both the work and etiquette problems that arise, it helps to distinguish between two kinds of drinking:

• *Benign.* For many people, and in many situations, drinking has a bright, attractive aspect. The "good" face of alcohol looks down on many scenes of happy fellowship. There is the pleasant social function known as the cocktail party; the drink with lunch that eases the tension of a tough morning, improves the appetite, and prepares one for the pressures of the afternoon. There is the cocktail hour at which the hardworking executive relaxes with his or her spouse at home. There's wine with dinner, the brandy afterward, the pleasant tradition of the nightcap. So long as all these do not follow one another on the same day, they may be benign.

• *Destructive.* And then, almost as though it involves another type of beverage, another world, and other people, some men and women drink steadily throughout the day, gradually dulling their senses and their ability to function. There is, for example, the employee who must resort to the secret bottle in a file drawer to withstand the anxieties of his job. There is the individual who loses control after several drinks and flies into rages, depressions, or maudlin self-pity.

It's because of this contrast in drinking habits and drinkers that speaking in generalities tends to be confusing and counterproductive.

To make the discussion of greatest usefulness, we will draw a clear distinction between drinking that stays within acceptable social and personal limits and the point at which it becomes a degrading or destructive habit.

WHEN DRINKING IS TO BE AVOIDED

There are some situations in which, regardless of your own feelings and your own drinking habits, one should forgo strong drink. Note that in these cases the less potent beverages such as wine or beer *may* be allowable. But this is a matter of judgment. Note these situations:

1. *When company policy forbids it.*

Some companies have a simple and explicit rule: no drinking of alcoholic beverages on company premises. The reason for this rule may be the personal or religious convictions of top policymakers. In some cases, however, the rule reflects the nature of organization activity. In units handling high-security matters, for example, drinking of any kind is incompatible with the need for alertness. Accordingly, the organization's dining rooms or cafeteria will not make such beverages available.

2. *During "working periods."*

Even in organizations in which drinking is perfectly acceptable—at lunchtime, for example—imbibing during work periods is generally frowned upon. There are few organizations—even the most relaxed—that would not find casual drinking in the course of the working day unacceptable.

There is one exception to this rule, and it usually hinges on the status of the individual. An upper-echelon executive might, in the course of entertaining a visitor, break out a bottle of whiskey or open a private bar as one of the aspects of welcome and hospitality.

The status distinction, however, is quite sharp. While it may be perfectly all right for executives to have a bar in their offices, or at least a few bottles of liquor, few organizations would tolerate any parallel practice on the part of lower-echelon people.

The distinction is made supposedly so that executives can help make customers, suppliers, and other visitors feel comfortable and relaxed.

3. When one person's drinking may adversely affect someone else.

In some situations—let's say two people are having lunch together—one person may be trying to limit drinking for one reason or another. If you're the host and your guest has turned down the offer of a drink, you should also forgo it unless you are sure that the other person won't mind or it's for some reason such as dieting, where your drinking isn't likely to cause a difficulty.

WHEN THE DRINKER'S PROBLEM AFFECTS OTHERS ON THE WORKSCENE

One of the unexpected findings in the work histories of alcoholics: sometimes they have been able to hold down jobs for years, or they seem to have comparatively little trouble in finding jobs. One alcoholic, for example, had fifteen jobs over a ten-year period.

Of course, there can be many explanations for the ability of heavy drinkers to maintain a fairly steady level of earnings. Unusual ability or job skills is one explanation. Another is that as long as the individual is able to perform at an acceptable level, anything but extreme behavior or symptoms of alcoholism can be overlooked. However, the problem of the alcoholic is often not limited to the individual alone. Co-workers are often involved, even though the problems created are upsetting. Here are some specific cases that delineate the problem and suggest what may or may not be done:

WHAT TO DO ABOUT A COLLEAGUE WHO'S AN ALCOHOLIC. Hal Jones and Bert Cooper are both on the copywriting staff of a large advertising agency. Bert Cooper has been on the job for a couple of months when Jones realizes he keeps a bottle of whiskey in his drawer that he samples from time to time during the day. Once when Jones has entered Cooper's cubicle unexpectedly, he has found the latter tapping the bottle. "Want a shot?" says Cooper. "Good for the brain cells." Jones laughs and says no, he depends on jogging to get the same effect. But actually Jones is quite upset about the discovery, and over the next few weeks he becomes sharply aware of the consequences of his colleague's drinking. At lunchtime Cooper has three martinis, occasionally making some joking reference to a toothache or some such ailment that supposedly the drinking will assuage.

After these liquid lunches Cooper is still capable of going through the motions of working. But there's a slight glaze to his eyes and his mental capabilities are obviously blunted.

One thing Jones starts to do automatically, whenever they're to have a discussion with the head of the department, is to always push for a morning meeting. And second, when he realizes that Cooper is more or less affected by an alcoholic fog, he takes the initiative and discusses their joint projects with the department head, making some such excuse as "Bert's up to his ears on the cigarette campaign," and so on.

It's hard to fault Hal Jones's behavior. He's certainly being compassionate and trying to be helpful to a friend. But in the long run Bert Cooper is going to lose his job. And while one might say that having a job for the long run may justify Hal's efforts, it's obvious that in the longer run Bert Cooper is facing a bleak future that, just possibly, a different approach might ameliorate. Here are some alternatives to the cover-up that should be considered:

TALK TO THE DRINKER. In some cases heavy drinkers may have sufficient control to be able to modify their drinking habits. For example, Hal might say to Bert: "I hope that you feel we're good enough friends for me to be open with you. I have to tell you that regardless of what you and I might think about drinking in the abstract, you've been affected in your work by the amount of drinking you've been doing during working hours. Of course, that's your affair and you're the one who has to decide what to do. I would simply suggest that you cut down as much as you can and do your drinking during the times that won't affect your work."

While this approach verges on moralizing, notice that what's said concerns only job consequences. Unfortunately, as reasonable as this approach may seem, it's not guaranteed to succeed. However, if this approach has been used and it fails, or if it's suspected that it would be ineffective, here's another alternative:

PUTTING IT UP TO THE BOSS. An action that might in other circumstances be considered a violation of friendship or sacrificing personal values to the priorities of the organization, in cases like these can be fully justified both in terms of friendship and company objectives.

There's another justification for what is about to be suggested; namely, that the situation be brought to the attention of the drinker's superior or other concerned executive. It is that in recent years alcoholism has come to be viewed as a social disease rather than as a personal vice, and the virtue of this concept is that it does make remedial action possible. The question then becomes what steps you may take. Here are some suggestions:

PICK THE PERSON WHO CAN HELP. Depending on your organization, that person may be someone in Personnel, the alcoholic's immediate superior, or possibly some higher authority.

Explain your motivation at the outset. It's important that you start to present the case by making it clear that you expect help for the individual—certainly not censure; still less, disciplinary action: "What I'm going to tell you has just one purpose, Mr. Smith, and that is to get help for someone that I feel is a capable and deserving employee."

DESCRIBE THE SITUATION OBJECTIVELY. Tell what you have observed in the way of drinking patterns and consequences. Presumably, this description should be sufficient to suggest that remedial action is desirable.

Insist that the individual make his or her own investigation. If there is to be follow-up action, it's obviously undesirable that you become a prime suspect as being the informer. No matter how pure your motives or how objective your observations, insist that separate observations and conclusions be made. You want action taken on these observations rather than your own.

Of course, you will want to make it clear that you want your name kept out of any conversations that may take place between the executive and the drinker. But there may be a slipup. You should be prepared, if necessary, to defend your actions to your colleague: "Yes, I did discuss your situation with the boss. And believe me, it wasn't easy. But I had to make a choice between doing nothing and taking an action that is your best chance for getting help. . . ." Avoid such phrases as "I did it for your good" or "I couldn't stand by and see you sinking lower and lower." These are judgmental and could be resented on that score. Certainly, implicit in your taking action is the fact that you have made a judgment. But if you're accused of "butting in" or "playing God," make the point that you care enough for the other person to want to help—even though that might seem like meddling. "I'd want you to do the same for me if our situations were reversed" could be a final thought to show your feelings.

HELP FOR ALCOHOLICS. The hopeful aspect in this unfortunate situation is that new approaches have been developed that can be effective. Especially important can be the awareness of the heavy drinker that the organization is sympathetic, is willing to help, but that he or she will be fired if the habit isn't controlled. The fact is that fear of job loss has been one of the major factors in helping individuals resolve a drinking problem.

CONTINUING YOUR FRIENDSHIP. In your association with the heavy drinker there are other practical steps you can take that can be helpful. In lunching with the person, for example, you can steer the action away from the pub-type restaurants to those that, even if they serve liquor, are not obviously drinking spots. Of course, if there are restaurants in the neighborhood that don't serve alcohol, so much the better.

And if a waiter should approach with the question: "Anything to drink?" take the initiative and assume that neither of you will be drinking.

WHEN THE PROBLEM DRINKER IS YOUR BOSS

When the boss has a drinking problem, subordinates do indeed have some pretty hefty headaches. The boss may be effective and charming when sober—in fact, this is often the case. But as the bouts with the bottle occur more frequently, so do the orders and decisions that don't make sense, the lies, the unnecessary risks blithely taken.

Yet the people who report to this sometimes irrational person depend on him or her for performance appraisals, promotion recommendations, approval of pet projects. And their fear of offending can lead them into behavior that undercuts their own best interests without benefiting anyone else—least of all, in the long run, the boss.

There are specific guidelines that subordinates and colleagues of the excessive drinker may find helpful:

• *Note the pattern.* Some people who can't handle their liquor will go for weeks at a time without hitting the bottle. Others drink daily. But almost always there's a pattern that it is useful to note.

For example, some people will invariably fall off the wagon when a major project is completed. If possible, anything important should be held until the cycle of drinking—and hangover—is finished. In other cases, mornings will be relatively sober times, and it's after the martini lunch that things begin to deteriorate. If that's so, late-afternoon discussions should be avoided as much as possible—and any orders received in the afternoon should be double-checked the next day.

• *Weigh carefully invitations to drink together.* Most heavy imbibers like company. Subordinates who are asked to "drink along" should note that there are pros and cons to both accepting and rejecting such invitations.

Aside from the fact that it's flattering to be singled out, refusing to join in "the fun" can backfire. Someone else will probably accept —and may win points by doing so.

Yet the subordinate can also become the butt of the nasty mood that so often overtakes heavy drinkers as the evening progresses. Next day, the boss won't remember what was said—but may well remember the feeling of hostility.

What to do depends on the particular situation—there are no surefire safe solutions here. But subordinates who find themselves expected to keep the drinking boss company should ask themselves fairly frequently: How much am I really getting out of this? Am I harming my own health? My career? Can I bow out gracefully by saying the doctor doesn't want me to drink or a family situation requires my getting home early? Am I willing to risk having the boss see through my evasions? Am I willing to risk having a rival take my place at the bar?

Obviously this is a trap that it's best to avoid from the start. But the climate in many organizations is such that no one realizes an executive is developing a problem with alcohol until years of drinking together have set an accepted pattern of before-lunch or after-hours conviviality.

• *Decline to play patsy.* The fact that alcoholics lie and ask others to go along can be one of the most disturbing things about working under one. Subordinates should cover for the problem drinker only if it is absolutely necessary. But one's reluctance should be shown.

• *Suppress any value judgments about the heavy drinking.* No one can argue an alcoholic away from the bottle. Lectures, frowns, scorn, pointed jokes are both useless and potentially harmful to the well-meaning subordinate. Nor is it likely that anyone except the boss's boss will be able to induce the heavy drinker to get professional help.

A situation that seems unsupportable to subordinates may arouse less concern with the boss's superiors if they have no quarrel with present performance.

Unless the organization has a program for alcoholics, going to top management can be a risky course: higher executives may resent the implication that they're not keeping track. It's usually better to let the boss's superiors find out for themselves what is going on—and to stay as uninvolved as possible. There is no point in sacrificing your own career—or even your peace of mind—in vain.

(For more on the subject of drinking, see Chapter 9, specifically the sections on "Ordering" and "When the Meal is a Test," pages 365 and 367.)

7

Meetings: From the Informal Get-together to the Large-scale Conference

MEETINGS: THERE ARE MANY SHAPES AND SIZES

When you talk of meetings in general, you have to consider many possible variations. Two people getting together to discuss some operational matter of common interest represents a meeting. At the other end of the scale is the company affair: a full-fledged get-together of large numbers of people, usually to celebrate an occasion—a company anniversary or other key event.

A practical way to categorize meetings is to say there are two types:

INFORMAL. This is the average kind of work meeting, which may last anywhere from a few minutes to several hours.

FORMAL. This type has an agenda, usually a large attendance, and if important enough, may be held off company premises.

WHAT CAN GO WRONG

Problems of etiquette arise in meetings for a reason that derives from the very nature of the process: people in groups tend to set up *dynamics;* that is, as industrial psychologist Kurt Lewin points out, interchanges having particular force and complexity because of group behavior. For example:

A common phenomenon in a business meeting is to have the group zero in on one member as a scapegoat to be sacrificed to the negative mood of the members.

Another problem that may end in hostile feelings is a tendency for such groups to *polarize*. Here an issue creates pro and con feelings, and group members align themselves with one or another view. What follows may be an emotional free-for-all in which partisanship upsets rationality and fairness.

WHEN AN ARGUMENT GETS OUT OF HAND

The meeting room occasionally is seen as an arena in which two antagonists have a chance to stage a battle to seek vindication for a viewpoint or the approval of others. It's usually up to the leader of the group to intervene in any such public airing of conflict, so it's important to watch for developments in meetings that reflect injustice to individuals or groups or represent the misuse of power by one or more individuals to punish or publicly humiliate others. Here are some possible courses of action:

• *Misunderstanding?* If the quarrel is the result of a circumstance that can be minimized or eliminated, the simplest move may be to point this out: "Claire, it seems to me that you misunderstand George's viewpoint. He hasn't suggested that we discontinue the community project, but that we stop long enough to assess it. . . ."

• *Turn a quarrel into an exchange of views.* In some cases the controversial subject is one that should be discussed at the meeting. Here your object should be to eliminate the overheated, possibly vindictive aspects while permitting the exchange of views. Explain to the principals: "It's important that we get that subject out on the table and discussed thoroughly. But let's do it in a reasoned manner. We gain nothing by making it a battle instead of a debate. . . ."

• *Table the matter.* If you feel the confronting groups or individuals cannot be curbed, then you must put a stop to the argument: "We're getting nowhere with this discussion. We'll just suspend dealing with this subject and take it up another time. Let's move to the next item on the agenda. . . ."

PROTECTING THE WEAK

Good etiquette does not suggest the need to overprotect people or to coddle the ineffective. What proper etiquette does dictate is the limiting of such educational or disciplinary acts to methods and times that minimize humiliation or unnecessary emotional discomfort to the people involved.

For ordinary participants, too, it is desirable behavior to step in and make clear their disapproval of bullying, baiting, or other abuse of one individual by another. Clearly, the logical person to undertake the intervention is the leader of the group. But if there's hesitation from that quarter, anyone aware of the painful process should feel free to take the initiative: "Gary, regardless of the merits of your argument, I don't think this is the time and place to indulge in such a highly personal approach. . . ."

PREVENTING A CONFLICT BETWEEN EFFICIENCY AND ETIQUETTE

Listen to the complaints you hear about meetings and you wonder why they're held at all: "Meetings are a waste of time." Or: "Whenever I try to get in touch with Mr. Smith, he's always at a meeting. How does he ever get any work done?"

But notice that despite the derogatory comments and feelings, meetings continue to be held in almost every company. The reason is simple: for certain types of communication there is no adequate substitute. For example, if you want to get a group's reaction to a new plan or policy, there's no more flexible or potent means than getting a bunch of people together in a room and starting a general discussion.

The *management* aspects of meetings have been dealt with at great length. Every book on general management deals with meetings in some way and to some extent. And, of course, there have been entire books devoted to the subject.

However, the *etiquette* considerations of meetings are often overlooked. This is one of the areas in which business effectiveness and business etiquette do not completely jibe. Certain procedures that may be effective from a purely management point of view may be undesirable from the viewpoint of desirable behavior. For example:

President Peter Jones is running a meeting of his staff. Old Bob Ward, somewhat failing in his faculties as he approaches retirement age, has preempted the floor. He's holding forth on the way a particular problem was handled in the good old days. Succumbing to the urge for efficiency, Mr. Jones cuts Bob Ward's somewhat rambling dissertation short and pushes briskly on to the next step. Etiquette recommends greater consideration for Ward's position and feelings—to the point that, within reason, Ward is indulged in his long-windedness. We're not giving Jones really bad marks for terminating the somewhat irrelevant discourse of an old employee. We are suggesting that there are more humane ways of dealing with people in meetings. Short of permitting Ward to talk on without interruption, Peter Jones could have limited Ward's conversation by interjecting at some convenient point: "Yes, we ought to keep in mind the important idea that Bob has just offered for our consideration. . . ." If there is some nugget of wisdom or a worthwhile aspect to Bob Ward's statement, this may be pointed out. Then the leader can move the discussion along to the next subject.

HOW TO AVOID WASTING PEOPLE'S TIME IN MEETINGS

A major affront is implicit in the meeting situation: people in a meeting to some extent become a captive audience. While possibly more constructive duties are held in abeyance, they are forced to participate in discussions that, from where they sit, may seem pointless or unproductive. One way of avoiding major wastes of time and going easy on the nerves of the conferees is to be clear on the *kind* of meeting that's being run.

In other words, *be clear on your objectives.* Before a meeting is started, the person in charge should be clear about the kind of conference it is to be. As a means of helping clarify what a meeting is about, here are nine possible types. If you know the type of meeting you're running, you're more likely to avoid the confusions and misdirection that annoy and irritate conferees:

1. *Problem-Solving.*

Here the purpose is to arrive at a solution to an operating difficulty.

2. *Policymaking.*

In this kind of conference, your objective may be to formulate a uniform rule or practice.

3. *Appraisal.*

The purpose is merely to review or evaluate a course of action that has been taken or a situation that has developed.

4. *Planning.*

The goal is to work out a blueprint for future activity.

5. *Informative.*

The sole purpose is to disseminate information—to announce a new policy or report new developments.

6. *Decision-Making.*

The conferees, acting as a group, meet to choose among a given set of alternatives.

7. *Team-Building.*

The conference atmosphere has proved effective as a means of building morale and group cohesion.

8. *Training.*

People stimulate and motivate each other to learn more and faster when they are in a group.

9. *Attitude-Shaping.*

This kind of conference is used to develop a set of common viewpoints as a background for unity of action in the future. Differences of opinion are expressed, but the net result is tolerance and mutual understanding.

A conference can have several of the above targets at the same time. But it's important that you know in advance which ones you want to adopt. And to make sure the people in the conference avoid irrelevant byways, they, too, should know your goal at the outset.

ANNOUNCING THE MEETING

A simple memo to those who are to attend is both a courtesy and a help in keeping the meeting on track. The meeting announcement should provide the following basics: time, place, subject. For example:

> Dear Grace:
> There will be a meeting of all divisional supervisors in my office at ten o'clock Monday morning, December 6, to discuss holiday schedules and policies.
>
> Cordially,
P. J. Somers

Announcements may include additional information. For example:

A list or other discussion of those who are to attend and, sometimes, those who will not be there: "I've only asked the supervisors of first-shift operations to be present, and will hold similar meetings with the other supervisors at a later date."

AGENDA. To help people prepare and prethink the subject areas to be covered, you may also want to list or describe subjects to be discussed: "Since we want to have the storage area cleared as soon as possible, be prepared to make suggestions as to how materials can be moved, where they can be stored, and so on, while renovations are being made."

A simple track for a meeting to follow can be indicated in just a few words. Here is the way one executive did it for a meeting dealing with the problem of complaints from customers about service:

> Statement of the problem: We've been getting excessive complaints.
> Description: Some typical complaints, and a tabulation.
> Analysis: Reasons for the customers' dissatisfaction, causal factors.
> Solution: How to eliminate complaints—participation from group.

With information like the above included in the announcement of the meeting, the participants can do considerable thinking in advance.

WHOM DO YOU INVITE?

You do a kindness by not inviting people to meetings in which they do not belong. There's a double benefit. First, you avoid imposing an unnecessary burden on the person—he or she does not waste time, is not bored, and so on. Second, you streamline the situation for those who do have business to transact—no deadwood in the crowd, and so on. In most cases, there is little mystery about those who should attend.

In a typical get-together, for example, those people involved with the planning or problem are obvious attendees. To these, however, you sometimes might want to add "resource" people or others who should be in on the basic planning. For example, in a meeting to discuss a major movement of materials, you might want to invite, in addition to the employees who would be directly involved, a member of the security department or safety department to make sure that these aspects of the operation are covered.

In recurring meetings for review of departmental activities and so on, there tends to be a fairly standard group—"all department heads" and so on. However, in some cases, the potential list of attendees presents a problem:

• *The person who expects to be invited, but shouldn't be.* For example:

Pauline Travis is a regular at Monday morning meetings in the division head's office. On a particular Monday, a work problem to be discussed does not involve her area of responsibility. In such a case she is owed an explanation for breaking the past pattern. "Pauline," her boss may say, "you don't have to attend our get-together this Monday. We're taking up Ed Lee's floor-layout problem, and it would be a waste of your time to have you sit in. But, of course, we'll see you at the meeting after that. . . ."

• *The person whose contribution you'd rather not have.* You are holding a meeting to discuss the problem of coffee breaks. This presents a ticklish situation because Dick Reeves feels very strongly that he has the answer. "Let's just abolish them" is his oft-repeated solution. You know this is the case, and you know that Dick's presence will only add an unnecessary controversial note, but you owe it to Dick to offer him some acceptable alternative. Something along these lines is suggested. "Dick," you might say, "we're going to be looking into the matter of coffee breaks. I know you have definite ideas, and I'd like to have you express them. I feel it would be more helpful if you and I had a meeting at which we could discuss your views in advance."

• *The obligatory attendee.* In some cases, even though you'd rather not have a person included in the roster, the complications—emotional and otherwise—of excluding him or her would present a greater problem than the inconvenience of their presence. For example, Harry Payne is retiring in several months. Mentally, he's already "out" of it. Even though he may have absolutely nothing to contribute to a problem-solving meeting, it would be a discourtesy to exclude him. You *might* be able to resolve the situation by giving him a chance to stay away: "Harry, we're going to be talking about the high level of errors in our ordering procedure. It's pretty routine and you may not want to bother attending. If so, please feel free to pass it up."

THREE TYPES OF MEETINGS THAT SHOULD NOT BE HELD

There are some meeting situations that are almost inevitably painful or unfair. Since the consequences are almost completely predictable and represent a basic discourtesy to some individuals, they should not be held at all. Here are three prime examples:

1. *The Unpleasant Surprise.*

It may seem incredible to some, but every once in a while, either through miscalculation or insensitivity, an executive holds a meeting in which an announcement is made that is a painful surprise for at least one group member present.

In some cases a misguided manager may feel that public humiliation is a desirable form of punishment—which, of course, it never is. True enough, managers from time to time do have the responsibility of informing, criticizing, or even punishing individuals for undesirable behavior. A supervisor may fall down badly on a critical job. But a blunt announcement in a meeting that the culprit is attending with his or her peers is not the place or the setting for the executive to show displeasure. A one-to-one meeting provides a much better opportunity for the criticism to be made, relevant discussions then following, without the intrusive element of an audience.

2. *The Confrontation.*

A gathering is called ostensibly to determine "how Department A can improve its working relationship with Department B." However, in the minds of the meeting planners is the intention of giving everybody a chance to see what stinkers the Department A people are—uncooperative, uncaring, and so on. But instead of providing a basis on which the rapprochement between Department A and

Department B can eventually be made, the meeting reinforces hostile attitudes. A better working relationship or even détente between Department A and Department B then becomes almost impossible.

A much better approach from the point of view of both avoiding insult and injury as well as leading to improvement in the situation is for the heads of the two departments that are at loggerheads to get together, possibly in the presence of a higher-echelon executive, to analyze the problem as a preliminary to remedy.

3. *The Snow Job.*

Management rightly uses meetings as the means by which to disseminate news, plans, intentions, and so on. Some organizations, unfortunately, misuse this particular type of meeting. They get their people together and try to make up by exaggeration or distortion the good news about past accomplishments or future plans that is lacking. The result is a snow job that's no more believable than the typical annual report. And while management kids itself into believing that morale has been raised, the result is to raise expectations falsely and leave people with a feeling of either frustration or outrage.

At lower echelons, managers also misuse the forum format as an opportunity to propound petty beliefs or gripes. Such self-serving meetings destroy the integrity of the people holding them and obviously should be avoided.

THE BEST SIZE FOR A MEETING

The effectiveness of a meeting is directly the result of the number of the participants and the purposes it is expected to achieve.

There is evidence that the best group size for problem-solving or decision-making occurs in small, odd-numbered groups (five, seven, nine). Where originality and creative contributions are desired, psychologists recommend that the group be kept small—five people is the number suggested for optimum efficiency, freedom of exchange, and cooperation. As the group gets larger, the chance for individual participation becomes smaller. Discussion becomes more difficult to focus, and the bane of many meetings is likely to arise; that is, some individuals withdraw into the crowd and don't participate at all, while others tend to dominate. The result is detrimental to group thinking and productivity.

One of the most frustrating—and, in a way, insulting—things that can happen in a meeting is when people who have something relevant and constructive to contribute don't have the chance to be heard. To prevent this situation, not only must the makeup of the group be such as to provide a serviceable forum for the subject matter and the people who have something to say, but the agenda and proceedings must permit the leader to call on those with a worthwhile contribution to make.

MAKING LIFE EASIER: THREE PROBLEM CONFEREES

Few people ever develop perfect meeting manners. From time to time, an individual will be argumentative, stubborn, hostile, and so on. It is usually possible for the group and the leader to work out these problems and to get on with the business at hand. But there are three types of participants who require special attention both for their own sakes and for the accomplishment of meeting objectives. And, of course, you want to deal with them with finesse:

1. *The Clam.*

Paul Grey sits in on meetings week after week and never speaks. Yet he may be one of your vital sources. Here are some techniques to help the stage-shy, intimidated, or nonparticipating individual:

• *Call on him for his experience or specialty:* "This is something that Jim has had a lot of experience with. Let's hear from him."

• *Tell him in advance that a certain topic is going to come up.* Ask him to prepare a comment. Then, at the appropriate moment in the meeting, feed him a cue line.

• *Pose questions he can handle:* "How does this breakdown procedure on this equipment look to you?" Or: "Did you ever run into this kind of situation when you were out in the field?"

• *Give him time to compose what he is going to say.* Try calling on one or two others in the group before calling on the clam. That way, you can tip him off and give him time to prepare an answer.

However, never cut off or put down another conference member to protect or favor your reticent subordinate; and don't wrench the conversation around to set things up for him.

2. *The Hog.*

He or she talks and talks and talks. And yet it's not because there is nothing to say. More often, it's just that the speaker takes so long to say it. In the process, others are prevented from making their contributions.

To control the monopolizer:

• *When he or she has made a point and is rambling on to another, interrupt to reinforce the one point made so far and suggest that it ought to be discussed.* Then ask others for their reactions to the point already made. Or explain to the person that you want to go around the table to ensure that everyone else gets an equal chance.

• *Once the statement has begun to ramble or become disorganized, stop it.* Explain that you are not certain you understand what has been said. Ask for clarification. If he or she persists in digressing, interrupt and call on someone else.

3. *The Victim.*

From time to time, discussion in a meeting takes a turn that makes one of the members a group target—call it scapegoating or the occasional insensitive or sadistic impulses that arise in the collective bosom. Whatever the cause, one person becomes the focus of a group attack. It may be for something that's been said or something that's been done, but all at once everyone is up in arms belaboring the outnumbered victim. To deal with this problem:

• *Stop the group in its tracks.* State in unequivocal language that the discussion has taken a destructive turn: "Let's hold it a minute, folks. We seem to have changed from running a meeting to throwing stones."

• *If relevant to the purposes of the meeting, permit the discussion to continue on the* subject matter, *but without the personal vilification and name-calling:* "I think it's proper for us to discuss what went wrong in our relations with our customers in the southwest region, but we'll get much closer to the mark if we leave out all the personal finger-pointing and discuss the situation objectively."

WHEN YOU'RE MEETING WITH AN OUTSIDE VISITOR

Many meetings are a two-person affair between an executive and a visitor from another organization or with another outside affiliation. A meeting with an outside visitor creates a number of requirements that you must take care of in order for matters to run smoothly, pleasantly, and productively:

• *Confirm time and date.* If there's any question at all, or if the original arrangement was made sometime ago, it's desirable that the appointment be confirmed, preferably the day before the meeting is to take place.

• *"Bring along material."* The confirmation should verify not only the time and place but, if there's any question, the subject of the meeting and any preparations that are required: "And please remind Mr. Mason," one secretary says to another, "that Mr. Willoughby is looking forward to seeing the plans, blueprints, and so on for that proposed structure."

• *Directions for travel, and so on.* The visitor should be given any information that will simplify either the trip or getting to the reception room where he or she will be picked up by a secretary, messenger, and so on. In some cases travel instructions should recommend preferred routes: "Mr. Willoughby suggests that Mr. Mason's trip will be more convenient if he takes the two o'clock train out of Grand Central. That's an express. . . ."

If a person is to make a trip from a bus or train station or airport, it's an especially appreciated courtesy if taxi or limousine arrangements can be made. For special visitors, the organization may want to send a representative to personally meet and greet the visitor. If this is done, make sure that the exact means of meeting—generally the two people will be strangers—are pinned down: "Have Mr. Mason wait at the information desk, which is at the south end of the station. Our company chauffeur wears a uniform with our name on it, and he'll be there waiting for Mr. Mason."

Where the offices in question are in a large office-building complex, specific instructions should be given so that the visitor can get to the proper reception area: "Have Mr. Mason take the elevator to the twenty-ninth floor and ask for Mr. Willoughby at the reception desk there."

• *The arrival.* The first few minutes after the visitor has come into the reception area may be crucial to his or her comfort, peace of mind, and general sense of the thoughtfulness and consideration being extended. If possible, have the receptionist informed of the arrival. A simple "Oh yes, Mr. Mason, Mr. Willoughby expects you" is a particularly warm and pleasant welcome for the visitor.

• *Unexpected delays.* In some cases there may be an unavoidable hangup. If so, the visitor should be informed and, if possible, entertained during this period. No song and dance, of course, but if an employee, usually your secretary, can come out and say, "I'm terribly sorry, Mr. Mason, but Mr. Willoughby is involved in an emergency matter at the moment. However, he will be able to join you in fifteen minutes. Meanwhile, may I get you a cup of coffee? And perhaps you'd like to look at a copy of our current company publication?"

Or sometimes the time can be satisfactorily passed with a brief tour of the premises or a visit with some other executive who may be able satisfactorily to fill in the time.

• *Physical conveniences.* If the visitor has a hat, coat, packages to be stored, it's a nice gesture to have him or her assisted with putting these in a convenient spot. The offer of coffee or other beverage is also a pleasant and appreciated courtesy.

• *A welcoming manner.* There's one factor that can make all the difference in the way visitors feel as they set foot on your premises. This is the attitude of the organization's personnel. It's highly desirable that everyone along the line, whether it's a building guard, elevator operator, or receptionist, be pleasant and helpful. If your representative—a subordinate, assistant, or secretary—is at the head of the list of welcomers, their pleasant and friendly manner can also make a major difference in the warmth of the welcome. If you have any reason to doubt the performance of these key people, it may be worth your while to observe or check on just how visitors in general are welcomed in reception areas. Many organizations understand correctly that a well-trained and pleasant receptionist is an extremely important part of the company front or image. At any rate, your immediate subordinates, who may be involved in such greeting activities, should have the benefit of your review and approval of their methods.

THE MEETING SITE

Usually if what's involved is a one-to-one get-together, your office is the proper site. Executive offices being what they are these days, many have both a working area (desk) and a "social area"—a grouping around a coffee table, for example. If your meeting is a working one and requires sitting at your desk, then that's the best place for your conversation. Otherwise, the informality and the relaxed manner that the coffee-table setting makes possible is more desirable.

But whether you meet in your office, the organization's conference room, or some other area, keep two things in mind:

• *Prepare.* Ordinarily, it's a courtesy to your visitor to feel that the meeting and his or her status warrant steps being taken to arrange for a neat and serviceable place. For example, escorting a guest into a messy meeting room with everything from chairs in disarray to butt-filled ashtrays is undesirable. Any indication that you've anticipated the visit ("I had that small table brought in for the model you want to set up") will be most welcome.

• *But don't be overly apologetic.* It's wrong to transfer the standards of home neatness to the workplace. It's quite usual—and acceptable—for a visitor to be escorted into an office that is partially in disarray. The simple statement "Sorry things are so messy" takes care of the situation. If your meeting then moves on smoothly, physical appearance will be accepted as one of the small and common realities of working life.

KEEPING THE ATMOSPHERE PLEASANT

If your meeting runs long, your consideration for your visitor may include additional offers of a beverage, a washroom break, or perhaps even the interjection in your conversation of nonbusiness subjects —any appropriate small-talk item will do, from the weather to a current news headline.

Meetings of any kind are best concluded in a positive way. You may want to summarize what has been said, repeat a final decision or agreement, and so on. The final sendoff is also a factor in the way the visitor assesses the experience. A personal word, a firm handshake, and your attention to such details as the visitor's being helped to retrace his or her path—everything from getting out of your building to making a travel connection—will reinforce a pleasant impression.

HANGUPS AND DISRUPTIONS

Most meetings tend to proceed reasonably well to their objectives. But in some cases—and particularly with an outside visitor— certain potential complications should be taken into account. Here are some of the kinds of things that can upset the applecart:

• *Telephone interruptions.* They're bad enough at any time, even worse when your visitor has come a long way to spend a comparatively short time with you. Make sure that your secretary takes all calls. If a secretary isn't available and your calls can't be held back, explain briefly to anyone who does call you: "I'm in the middle of an important meeting. I'll call you back later on."

• *The emergency.* You may be entertaining an outside caller and a major matter arises. If you really must break away, explain at least in general terms what the problem is, make your apologies, and, if possible, arrange to have the visitor entertained or at least taken care of by a subordinate or colleague. In some extreme cases, of course, the meeting will have to be cut short regardless of how far a distance the visitor has come, or even regardless of the importance of the meeting.

Fortunately, it does not happen often, but in one plant a fire in the operating area required the presence of a front-office executive in the course of a meeting with one of the firm's customers. Knowing the emergency would not be over quickly, the executive made his sincere apologies, explained the nature of the emergency, arranged to have the visitor taken to lunch by a colleague, and assured him that the date would be reinstated as soon as possible.

WHAT TO DO WHEN A GUEST SPEAKER DRAWS A SMALL AUDIENCE

There is a classic situation involving a meeting group that may cause considerable embarrassment:

Esther Masden has been invited by an organization's management club to come to its monthly meeting and give a talk on report writing. Ms. Masden teaches technical writing at a local university and has a reputation for excellence in her field. At the appointed hour Ms. Masden is escorted into the auditorium by her host, Hank Gardner, president of the organization.

There is a small handful of people on hand, and Gardner apologizes: "Some people always come straggling in at the last minute. . . ."

But ten minutes after the announced starting time sees the addition of only two or three more people, making a total of about fifteen, who only flyspeck the expanse of a hundred seats.

After the fact, it's easy to explain what's happened. The program chairman has scheduled the evening because a number of people have told him they'd like to have a speaker on the subject of report writing. But the chairman has overestimated the amount of interest. And even some of those most eager to attend for one reason or another have been hung up on other matters.

Two types of action can mitigate this kind of development:

• *Try to "verify" the audience.* The people making the arrangements for this type of meeting must take the steps that will give them a pretty good idea of the attendance *in advance.* It's unsafe to depend on advertising, or even past attendance figures. Some individual should be given the responsibility of taking a "reading" of intentions to attend. A helpful report: "Of the twenty people I canvassed, three said they'd definitely attend, five are probables."

If on the basis of the survey it is likely that you're not going to have a satisfactory turnout, further moves are indicated:

• *Try to increase attendance.* "We've got to increase the number of bodies" is the way one experienced meeting chairman puts it. Best move is to enlist the efforts of the program group or, indeed, the membership of the sponsoring organization. There are many precedents for such audience-building moves: one group does it by having each member go all out to bring a friend or colleague (this worked very well for an engineering group). In another instance, attendance of nonmembers of the organization was solicited.

• *Should you cancel?* Occasionally, the least of the possible evils is to scratch the meeting. If this is done, the speaker should be notified at the earliest possible time. What explanation should be given? You or your program people have a choice—from a simple statement of the fact: "We failed to get a registration large enough to justify your appearance," to some reference to circumstances: "the flu season" or "a competing event."

The speaker should be thanked for the offer of his services, and if a fee is in question, he or she should be compensated wholly or in part, as seems appropriate.

• *If you want to carry through.* Despite the disappointing size of the group, you may want to hold to your announced schedule. There are a few things that can make the situation somewhat pleasanter:

• *Don't lose your cool.* Both speaker and audience will take their cues from the program chairman, organization officers, or master of ceremonies. Even if you're dismayed, put the best possible face on the situation.

• *Absolve the speaker.* Make it clear in what is said to the speaker and to the audience that the unexpectedly small attendance is no reflection on the speaker in any way: "I guess we didn't get the word around early enough" or some other such statement.

• *Regroup.* A disaster may be turned into a highly successful meeting. One management group that had invited a well-known authority to address its regular quarterly meeting decided to transfer the site of the meeting from the large auditorium to a conference room, which the thirty-five-member audience filled nicely.

The master of ceremonies, in introducing the speaker, suggested that the new meeting setup made greater informality and a freer exchange between speaker and audience possible. Since this is exactly what happened, the audience was delighted at the opportunity to participate more fully in the proceedings. "Best meeting we ever had," commented one pleased attendee, to which there was general agreement.

ARRANGEMENTS FOR A WORK MEETING: A CHECKLIST

Some group discussions of work require little preparation. Three or four people get together, perhaps even on an impromptu basis, to discuss a current and immediate problem—how a particular order is to be handled, what to do about some particular emergency such as a major equipment breakdown, large-scale absenteeism due to transportation difficulties, and so on.

More typically, work meetings can be scheduled in advance and require a certain amount of planning. The checklist below covers key requirements:

1. *Who Will Run the Meeting?*

Two or more people may take turns with this responsibility. But the leader(s) should be definitely designated and, preferably, should participate in all the planning.

2. *Who's to Be Invited?*

In part, the answer to this question depends not only on the subject matter but also on the scope of the meeting. A full-fledged discussion of a major matter clearly requires a larger group than a top-level coverage where basic policy or other such considerations are to be made by upper-echelon people. Three test questions:

• *Does the individual have anything to contribute to the meeting?*

• *Will anything be dealt with that he or she should learn about firsthand?*

• *Are there any reasons other than purely functional ones* such as status or sentiment (the subject may be one of special import to an employee who may have no current contribution to make) that would make attendance a good thing?

3. *Which Is the Best Setting?*

Time and place should be arranged according to what's proper and convenient. A small office is usually better for a two- or three-person conference than a large board room, for example.

4. *Physical Arrangement.*

Once the place has been designated, it's important to ensure that it be made ready for the use to which it's been put. Here are some of the specifics involved:

• *Temperature.* Air conditioning, heating, whatever will make for physical comfort.

• *Lighting.* Adequate for all needs—writing, darkness if a film is to be shown, and so on.

• *Seating.* Enough comfortable chairs to go around.

• *Table and other furniture.* If the group is not too large, it's generally best to have it seated around the table. A lectern may be desired—either one that will stand separately or one that will rest on the table.

• *P.A. system.* If a microphone and amplifiers are to be used, they should be installed and pretested before the actual meeting time.

• *Blackboard, easel charts,* equipped with proper writing implements.

• *Audiovisual equipment.* If a slide projector, film projector, or videotape is to be used, the equipment should be installed and pretested.

5. *Service People.*

Particularly if you have equipment that can conk out or act up, it's desirable to have someone capable of making repairs or adjustments on the spot, or at least readily available.

• *Muscle men.* If in the course of the meeting furniture or equipment will have to be moved, don't depend on volunteers unless the changes are very minor. Preferably appoint a group that will know in advance what has to be done and can plan to do it with a minimum of fuss.

6. *Flexible Crowd Size.*

In some cases the size of the group may not be known in advance. It's wise to keep seating plans flexible in case a substantially larger or smaller number of people shows up.

7. *Substitute Leader.*

In some cases a meeting can't or shouldn't be postponed simply because one person can't make it. However, if that person was to have run the meeting, it's desirable to have a substitute ready to pinch-hit for key people who may be unavailable at the last moment.

8. *Agenda.*

The conference leader should be prepared with a list of discussion points. In an informal meeting, just a few notes will suffice. In some cases copies of the agenda should be circulated to the conferees in advance—to make it possible for them to prethink the subject, and so on.

9. *Planned Participation.*

In addition to the conference leader, in some cases other individuals may be expected to contribute to one or another part of the discussion. If possible, these should be briefed and given the opportunity to prepare just what they want to say and do.

10. *Rehearsal.*

Some particular piece of business to be taken care of in the meeting may be either complex, delicate, or unpredictable. It's unwise to undertake this on an impromptu basis. For example, one conference leader had the responsibility of demonstrating a proposed new item. It had to be partly disassembled to be adequately demonstrated. He practiced the disassembly procedures to avoid time-wasting in the meeting itself.

11. *Cleanup.*

Usually it's thought that the meeting ends when the last conferee quits the meeting room. Most of the time, however, there's another step required; that is, the cleanup and straightening out after the meeting. Where you have maintenance people whose job this is, there's no problem. But if this is not your happy situation, the people responsible for the meeting must attend to the final chore of seeing that the impedimenta and leftovers of the conference are removed. The main thing to avoid, of course, is the assumption that a secretary (or in some cases it may be the female members of the group) will "naturally" attend to such details. This problem is important enough to warrant separate treatment:

• *Who does the cleanup?* One of the signs of new ways in the world of business is the questioning, and often the changing, of some patterns expected in the past. In the bad old days, an executive secretary was expected to act pretty much as an office wife. Her duties included everything from preparing coffee to sewing buttons on her boss's coat.

But the new order of things that followed the social changes of the sixties and the Women's Liberation Movement obsoleted many of these customary practices. Accordingly, the question of who cleans up the meeting room when the meeting is over may be only a detail, but it could also go to the heart of the roles and relationships that exist in an office, department, or entire organization. Perhaps your secretary is the logical person to empty the ashtrays, wipe off the tabletop, and discard the empty plastic coffee cups. But he or she may not be, and no matter how large or small the meeting, it is suggested that careful consideration be given to the question of who takes care of the final steps of the physical straightening out. If you have a subordinate who is available and really doesn't mind the chore, there's no problem.

But the least that should be done in such a situation is that the employee be made to understand that this is a service above and beyond the call of duty. You're not likely to find a job in any category that includes such cleanup unless it's for a cafeteria worker.

(Parties are a kind of meeting that require special formats and planning. See Chapter 8 for such items as "The Office Party," page 298; "Invitations," page 301; "Guidelines for Planners," page 304; "Selecting the Date and the Place," page 325.)

8

Parties, Celebrations, and Other Occasions for Gift-Giving

Most managements are aware of the vital role of nonwork activities in unifying an organization, improving its morale, and enriching the working life of employees.

Accordingly, organizations make a point of observing a large range of events that are not directly related to work. These events may involve just a small group in one department or the entire company.

Birthdays of employees are recognized by a variety of observances, typically flowers for a female employee, a small group lunch for males, with a large number of additional ceremonies available.

Anniversaries of the day an employee started with the organization are another, and possibly the more widely observed, event. While most anniversaries get at the very least a smile, a handshake, an expression of good wishes from one's boss, fifth-year anniversaries, tenth, twenty-fifth, and so on are time milestones getting special attention.

How does an organization appropriately mark a long-time celebration such as a key employee's twenty-fifth year with the company? Should there be a gift, and, if so, who should select it and what would be appropriate? Who should make the presentation, and, for that matter, who should be invited to the celebration and who should not? All these questions must be properly answered for these vital organization events to assume their full meaning and achieve full effectiveness.

Christmas parties require special attention. Over the years, the organization Christmas party has undergone basic changes. The traditional, much-whispered-about "wild" Christmas parties are largely behind us. But how does one observe the holiday, make it an occasion for real conviviality, a reinforcement of group unity? The etiquette of such occasions is crucial.

Finally, an area in which guidance can be particularly welcome is that of gifts and gift-giving. The considerations that guide one to make a happy choice, as well as a series of gift suggestions covering a broad range of what's available for every taste, will be found on pages 348–359.

THE OCCASIONS FOR CELEBRATION

Milestones in the passage of time are noted as much in the business world as on the outside. Kept within bounds, such observances add a highly desirable note to the business scene. Out of hand or mishandled, such occasions can make the most easygoing executive wonder how he or she ever got "roped in."

Depending on the local customs, some or all of the following can be cause for on-the-job celebrations:

- birthdays;
- wedding anniversaries;
- anniversaries of the day on which the employee joined the company;
- "founding day" (the day or year in which the company was founded).

In addition to these general time milestones, some firms honor dates of an even more esotoric sort. For example:

- the day on which an executive assumed some notable position— became president of the company, head of a division, and so on;
- the day on which a particularly esteemed subordinate—a secretary, for example—came on the scene—not necessarily started to work for the company, but for the particular executive.

In addition, there can be the "good-bye–and–good–luck" type of event that you may find yourself celebrating because some kind of ceremony seems to be expected:

- a subordinate's retirement;
- an employee's transfer;
- an employee leaving for another job;
- an employee leaving to get married or to have a baby.

For people of sentiment, any of these celebrations—or the ignoring of them—can be of major importance. Since both sensibilities and crucial psychological factors are involved—recognition is perhaps the greatest noncash reward people find on the workscene—what you do or don't do becomes an important part of the organization's ritual observances.

ACCEPTABLE WAYS OF CELEBRATING AN EVENT

You have a wide range of options to choose from in marking an anniversary, birthday, or other notable event:

VERBAL RECOGNITION. This can vary from the sincere first-thing-in-the-morning greeting—traditionally a hug and kiss where the relationship is friendly enough.

A CARD. The greeting-card industry has made it very easy to recognize anniversaries. And as anyone who has visited a card store knows, you can find sentiments ranging from the almost obscene to the most exalted and sentimental. Obviously, the card chosen will be most effective when it satisfies two criteria:

- It is "handpicked" for the taste and personality of the recipient. One person will be delighted with a humorous card. Another would be either puzzled or put off by humor if sentiment is his or her preference.
- *It reflects the particular relationship between the giver and receiver.* For example, an anniversary card with a message that reflects the shared hard work or loyalty of the person may be particularly suitable and therefore especially effective.

And in some instances, card-givers prefer to "roll their own." If you have a knack for versifying or a good hand with a sketching pencil, a handmade card may be a sign of special esteem. And, of course, even if a card is bought, it will hit the mark better if you personalize it with an addition of a word, a sentence, or a message of your own.

A MESSAGE FROM THE TOP BRASS. A birthday or anniversary greeting from the president of the company always has special impact, even if the employee is quite far down the ladder and may have little direct contact with top brass. His or her immediate superior may be able to arrange for such recognition.

FLOWERS. There are few occasions in a female employee's working life in which flowers are not appropriate and won't be welcome. Men have still not yet been liberated to the point where flowers are equally acceptable, but potted plants seem to satisfy male taste and ego.

One of the reasons flowers are so happily received is that they are a public, visible proclamation of the anniversary. The clerk who has been given a dozen roses for her birthday will almost always proudly display them on her desk. Four out of every five people who pass by will comment on the floral display, eliciting further recognition and good wishes for the occasion.

CANDY, CAKE, AND SO ON. A box of candy, cake, cookies, and so on has some of the virtues of flowers. If you give a box of candy to a subordinate, invariably this will be opened and set on the desk for all to partake of. Here again, this gift tends to have the virtue of a public recognition of the event. As the candy disappears, almost piece for piece will come questions about the occasion, who the donor was, and so on.

One executive gave a subordinate two boxes of chocolates—one for the office, the other for home consumption, a particularly thoughtful gesture.

GIFTS. They come in all sizes, shapes, and prices. (This kind of recognition is dealt with under the heading "Gifts and Gift-Giving," page 335; and pages 348–359 for specific ideas.)

THE "GATHER-'ROUND" OBSERVANCE. In some situations it may be desirable to have the group recognize the event without quite going to the extent of having an outside lunch or dinner affair. An acceptable compromise can be one in which you arrange for wine and cake, coffee and cookies, or some similar eating-and-drinking observance. Typically, these preparations are made undercover. While the "surprise" is seldom actual, the intent is generally appreciated by all. At any rate, the sudden gathering at the desk of the guest of honor with the tools and materials for the celebration suddenly whisked out of closets and cabinets creates an impromptu festive air.

Closely related to the coffee-and-cake observance is the *drink-and-canapé* party. There is generally a sharp distinction made between the celebration that includes liquor and other types of eating-and-drinking affairs. Usually, if cocktails are served on the office premises, the timing is usually at the end of the workday. If the person in charge isn't included or can't attend, it's a good idea to check out arrangements in advance.

LUNCHES AND DINNERS. For the employee who is retiring from the company or one who is leaving to have a baby or to get married, group off-the-premises celebrations are common. The crucial problems of who, when, and where, of course, must be settled—and light is shed on these matters in Chapter 9.

THE OFFICE PARTY: ON AND OFF THE PREMISES

When people who work together suddenly find themselves in a nonwork situation, relaxation and a changing of roles can lead to new and enriching ways of relating to one another. For example, when the junior accountant is appointed official party bartender, he'll find himself meeting people face-to-face with whom heretofore he's had only a nodding acquaintance. But whether this turns into an opportunity or a trauma often depends on preparation.

Successful parties are marked by conviviality, individual and group pleasure, a feeling of closeness, and the sharing of a memorable occasion. The unsuccessful party may suffer from many ills—from being perfunctory, so that people leave wondering why they bothered to come in the first place, to that truly disastrous event that as a result of poor planning occasions discomfort, irritation, and embarrassment. The rewards of a successful party can be so substantial that it's worth making the effort—and usually this can be minimal—to see that it goes off well.

ORGANIZING THE PARTY

Here are the factors you have to consider:
• *Someone in charge.* Whether it's one person or a group, primary

responsibility for all arrangements should be clearly given. Simple arithmetic suggests the wisdom of one or two people for minor events, a larger committee for more ambitious ones. If you have a large group, parts of the task can be delegated to specific individuals. One essential: if there is a special guest of honor, at least some, and preferably all, of the people involved in planning the party should know the individual who is being honored. This is vital for a variety of decisions ranging from the selection of a gift to the type of celebration that's planned.

HANDING OVER THE RESPONSIBILITY

• *The experienced party-giver.* In every community you find one or more people who have a natural gift for party-giving. Because of their skill and experience, their parties are almost always highly successful and invitations to them are sought after. Most organizations—for that matter, almost every group of people—include individuals with a social flair. They go about their party-giving the way artists create. They have a conception of what is to be accomplished. They have the imagination to develop their concept and the skill to take care of the practical details.

There are just two pitfalls to having the "naturals" among your hosts and hostesses take on the party planning every time:

• *Overload.* The individuals may enjoy the distinction up to a given point. Beyond that, they may feel they're being taken advantage of. And they may even become tired and bored, particularly if the assignment is repeated too often.

• *Rigidity and resentment.* No matter how good a party planner the person is, his or her events will eventually develop a sameness. Also possible is the fact that there are individuals in the group who may want to try their hand or may simply resent what amounts to being permanently excluded from the planning effort. A good idea is to start the change by asking a new hand to work with the old-timer.

Executives will be aware that participation in planning gives individuals an "in" feeling. Accordingly, it becomes an effective means of giving recognition to people outside the ordinary work context. In a direct sense, they have been selected for a special, and what is usually seen as a pleasant, duty. Whether or not executives use this kind of assignment—although it's usually given on a "request" or "volunteer" basis—it would be an oversight not to be aware of the implications and effect of this type of move, and it should be used constructively.

APPOINTING A PARTY COMMITTEE

Women's Liberation aside, the female of the species tends to have more experience, more skill, and more imagination in the way of handling some types of social functions. However, depending upon whether the party involves an outside lunch, it is an inside cocktail party, or whatever, try to choose people who are familiar with the scene, regardless of sex. And before you turn the responsibility over to a committee of two or three people, be sure they represent the group as a whole.

It will be helpful if you supply some guidelines—the amount of money to be spent, the general nature of the celebration you have in mind, and so on. In some cases you may have to supply a brake that will keep the planning within reasonable limits: "It's true Wilson's is an awfully good restaurant, but it's out in the next county and will take a lot of time to get there. Don't you think we can find a satisfactory place that's closer by?" However, if you use the committee approach, it's wiser to have decisions on what they will do come out of discussion rather than by laying down firm guidelines. "Just carrying out orders" makes the operation a chore instead of a fun activity—which is what it should be.

WHOM TO INVITE

When it comes to rounding up a group for a particular event, the question often arises as to who should and shouldn't be invited. Here are some of the rules for inclusion and exclusion:

• *Include everyone who works directly with the employee, especially his or her boss.*

• *Ask the employee whom he or she would like to have at the celebration.* To avoid the "Invite everybody!" answer, you might ask the question in connection with a specific number of people: "We were thinking of having a group of ten or twelve people at your promotion party. Whom would you like to have in that group?"

• *If the occasion is important enough—for example, a key employee's anniversary—stress the organization's regard by inviting members of top management.* In some cases an especially important individual to be included is the employee's boss's boss—as a sign of the esteem in which the guest of honor is held.

Worth special consideration are individuals who ordinarily would be invited but who for one reason or another have a poor relationship with the guest of honor. Generally, these people should be invited, leaving the choice of whether or not to accept up to them. Such invitations, when accepted, have been the occasion for the reestablishment of good relations. When the hostility is well known, the tentative nature of the invitation may be indicated by the host: "Greg, we're having a little party in my office for Charles on the occasion of his fifth anniversary. Of course I'd like you to be present if you care to come."

Office politics and special relationships should be taken into account before the lists are closed. If the head of a neighboring department is included, omitting his or her opposite number from another adjacent area might seem like an affront to the latter. If two managers are of equal status and are in some kind of competitive situation with one another—for example, both bucking for a promotion to the same spot—it might be taken as favoritism if only one is invited. If the guest of honor overlooks anyone who the party-giver feels should attend, suggest that person and explain the reasoning behind the suggestion, leaving it up to the guest of honor to make the final decision.

If the party is made up of a specific group—the order-processing group, X Department, old friends of the guest of honor—keep in mind that the presence of anyone outside the group, except for a good reason, may cause resentment among other outsiders who might feel left out for discriminatory reasons.

Finally, not to be invited are people who represent the favored of the party-givers who are not similarly regarded by the guest of honor. Such a selection fuzzes the purpose of the occasion and makes it less one for the individual for whom it is presumably given than a party to satisfy the whim of the givers.

INVITATIONS TO MEETINGS AND GET-TOGETHERS

To make sure people show up, send a written invitation or announcement. If a verbal announcement has been extended, the written message serves as a reminder.

Most business invitations are for informal events—a work meeting, a business lunch, a cocktail party after hours to celebrate some matter of work-group interest.

In general, the invitation should match the nature of the event to which it refers and its degree of formality or informality. For example, here is an invitation typed on a preprinted interoffice form summoning people to an after-hours event:

From: Henry Ellis

To: Al Baker

Subject: Celebration of an Outstanding Event

Dear Al:

A group of us are getting together after work next Wednesday, November 26, to celebrate Jane Boswell's promotion. Time: 5:30. Place: Billie's, 35 North Central Avenue.

I assume the party will end before the dinner hour. Please let me know whether you can come.

Henry

Some invitations may be even more informal and, if so, can be sent out just a day or two before the event itself. The following message was handwritten on a plain sheet of paper:

Betty, Four or five of us are getting together for a surprise lunch for Nancy. As you know, she'll be leaving at the end of the week. We haven't picked the restaurant yet—depends on how many people can make it—but let me know whether you're available.

Ellen

FORMAL INVITATIONS

When the organization itself sponsors an event, invitations tend to be more formal. Here are some examples:

The Spring Picnic Committee of the J. H. Smith Company
requests the pleasure of your company
at our Annual Spring Picnic
to be held on the lawn behind the Main Building
on the afternoon of Saturday, the ninth of May
at twelve-thirty

The invitation below is sent out on behalf of the management of the company.

The Management and Staff of C. B. Maxwell and Company, Inc.

invite you to be present at

the Annual Christmas Dinner Dance to be held at

The Crocodile Club

on Tuesday, the twenty-third of December

at four o'clock

R.S.V.P.   C. B. Maxwell, President

(For more on invitations, including additional samples, see Chapter 3 page 136.)

RESPONDING TO INVITATIONS

In most cases an oral response, either in person—if you come in contact with the individual doing the inviting—or by phone, is acceptable. However, in some cases you may want to reply in writing:

> Dear Mr. Maxwell:
> Thanks for your kind invitation. Of course, I accept. I've always enjoyed attending your annual Christmas get-together and know the affair will be the great success it always is.

TURNING DOWN AN INVITATION

The informal note reads: "We're giving a farewell party for Ruth in the Rec Room at five o'clock on Friday. Please come." And it's signed by department head Fred Toan. Now if you can't make it because a previous appointment interferes, you have two obligations:

• *Express your regrets to the sender.* Either in writing or otherwise, tell Fred Toan: "I'm awfully sorry, but I won't be able to attend because of a previous arrangement."

• *Get your message to the guest of honor.* If Ruth is a friend of yours, you want her to know you regret not being able to attend her party. If you're sure it's not a surprise affair—that is, that Ruth knows about the party—then you can call or write her a note that expresses your regret. And it might be in order, if your relationship is friendly, to suggest a personal farewell—lunch or something similar. However, if Ruth doesn't know, you surely don't want to spill the beans. In that case tell Fred Toan: "Please be sure to tell Ruth how sorry I am that I couldn't attend. . . ." Then contact her *after* the event to repeat the message personally.

To formal invitations, especially those that request a response, reply as suggested. If there is a phone number, call and let your intentions be known. If an address is given, write and say whether you will or won't attend. If you plan not to, make your statement brief but gracious: "Very sorry that I won't be able to attend the anniversary dinner." Then add your excuse or explanation: "Unfortunately, I plan to be abroad at that time." Or: "Personal business of considerable importance makes it impossible. . . ."

GUIDELINES FOR THE PLANNERS

No matter who does the actual planning of the event, it's desirable that a series of helpful guidelines be provided. Here are the major elements to be covered:

• *What it's all about.* In most cases there is no question. The party is for Donna Miller's tenth anniversary. Or it's a "department warming" to celebrate the group's moving into new quarters.

In one young company the office manager thought it would be a nice idea to celebrate the thousandth order the company had received. Further mileage would be gotten from the event, she thought, if the spotlight were to be on the efforts of the office staff. Accordingly, Lynne Hart, the clerk who had processed that order, became the focus of the celebration. The party then was given for Lynne as "the person who had handled that achievement milestone, the company's thousandth order."

• *Scope—and, of course, expense.* The planners must start with some idea of the size of the celebration. This takes in everything from the approximate number of people who will be invited to the amount of space that will be required.

And somewhere along the way, specific amounts of money will have to be mentioned. Obviously, it will make a big difference whether the budget for the event is to be ten dollars or a hundred. Don't leave your committee in the dark about the budget.

WHO'LL AUTHORIZE THE TIME OFF?

It's a practical matter but one that can't be overlooked when toes may be stepped on and resentment needlessly aroused. For example, supervisor Fay Smith has backed a lunch for Helen Kendall, who's just been engaged. The occasion is happy, the lunch is a huge success, but the group comes trailing back to the office some two and a half hours after leaving. And that very afternoon the big boss gets a complaint: "Fay Smith sure is setting a lousy example. The other departments have never taken advantage like that. . . ."

If you have enough authority to be able to stretch the rules a bit for celebrations, you *may* want to use it. But if there's any question, you'd be wise to clear matters with your boss in advance. That will keep both of you out of trouble.

KEEPING THINGS WITHIN BOUNDS

We've already pointed out the need to have the celebration suit the event. What's involved here is not only cash expenditure and a balance between the current event and others like it, both past and future. The proprieties are also involved. Company Christmas parties have acquired tarnish in business lore due to excesses of the past. Similarly, too much of anything can spoil an otherwise happy event. Too much noise, too much disruption, too much liquor, the consequences of preempted business activity—all can sour a good thing.

In most cases limits can be clearly set in advance, But there are two additional precautions that should be taken. One is the anticipation of obvious danger spots. If J.P. has a tendency to drink too much, a word in advance to a pal of his will at least see to it that he is under friendly surveillance. The second important arrangement: be sure that there'll always be one or more people of responsibility who can be counted on to keep things running smoothly and to cope with emergencies, whether it's an argument that springs up between two employees or what to do if the liquor runs out.

PROS AND CONS OF THE "OFFICE COLLECTION"

One of the side consequences of celebrations is the collection of funds to further the event. Obviously, this calls for an initiative by someone. Usually a well-wishing peer of the celebrating employee starts the ball rolling. But it's up to the immediate superior to suggest —or permit—that funds be gathered if there is to be a celebration on the premises or a purchase of gifts. Here are some of the do's and don't's of office collections:

Do:

- make sure that only one "authorized" collection takes place;
- see to it that either you or a committee sets up some kind of guideline to keep the amounts of money within reasonable limits;
- see to it that everyone who might possibly be interested is given the opportunity to contribute;
- be sure that whoever does the collecting makes it in such a way that people who don't want to contribute may say no without either feeling guilty or causing a ruckus.

Don't:

- have the fund-raising done by one or more people (who will then go on to spend the money for a gift) who have notably bad taste—many a pleasant office ceremony has come to a bewildering or disappointing end because the object bought or the nature of the observance was out of keeping with the employee's expectations or own taste level;
- have the actual collecting done in such a way as to become a nuisance—possible in situations where work pressures are high.

(For more on this subject, see Chapter 10, especially "Collections, Charities, and Contributions," page 425.)

WHEN NOT TO HAVE A PARTY

There are certain situations that signal a no-go for celebrations. In some cases a development outside may suggest the no-party decision. In other cases events within the company militate against celebrations. Here are some of the possibilities:

• *National upset.* If you had a dollar for every company celebration that was canceled on November 22, 1963—and properly—you'd be rich. A nation downcast, depressed, or in tears over the loss of one of its leaders offers an unsuitable background for celebration. Plans that are cast in dismal shadow by outside events should be canceled or at least postponed.

In some cases the implications or effect of an outside circumstance may be unclear. In one Midwest town, for example, the mayor's home had burned to the ground and some family members known personally to many workers had been injured. A twenty-fifth-anniversary celebration scheduled for the following day had taken weeks of preparation. The president of the company wasn't sure whether the upset caused by the mayor's personal tragedy warranted canceling the celebration or not. He resolved the question by checking with a few of his executives, some of the managers at lower levels, as well as a number of rank-and-file employees. The consensus was that the mayor's personal catastrophe was unfortunate but wasn't likely to cast any pall of gloom on the company event—which was forthwith held on schedule.

If the party/no party question does arise, and you're in doubt, it's best to get reactions across the board from people involved. Of course, if the partying group is small, everyone can be canvassed.

• *When the offsetting event is internal.* Sometimes a development within the organization makes the fun and gaiety of a party seem improper. The death of a top executive or even a serious illness of someone directly connected with the partying might suggest a postponement.

• *Poison in the air.* Developments within an organization may not center on individuals. In one company the loss of a major customer was deemed enough of a joy-killer to change a birthday party planned for a popular executive into a postwork couple of drinks with his boss and one or two colleagues at a neighboring restaurant.

And there are still other kinds of things that can happen that interfere with party spirit to the point that celebrations held are almost inevitably soured and doomed to failure. In addition to "bad business" as exemplified by the loss of a big customer, these include:

• *Labor-management friction.* An organization that is in the throes of acrimonious negotiations or conflict is not a happy context for celebrations of any kind.

• *Layoffs.* An organization going through a severe shakedown in which people lose their jobs and a climate of uncertainty hangs heavy is also one in which any major kind of celebration will seem out of place.

The best way to go in situations where for one reason or another the organizational climate has turned bad is not necessarily to suspend all celebration but simply to scale it down as in the case mentioned above where a party was converted into a friendly drink at a local bistro. But give careful thought to the way the "disinvitation" notice is handled. In most companies this should warrant high-level and/or personnel department consultation to ensure that a touchy situation doesn't set off an unhealthy chain reaction.

YES, YOU CAN HAVE A PARTY WITHOUT THE GUEST OF HONOR

Every once in a while that most unfortunate of developments takes place—the person for whom the party is being given cannot be present. The reasons may range from sudden ill health to an overriding business situation that requires his or her presence elsewhere. In some such cases the individual urges that "after all the trouble you've gone to" it would be too bad to disappoint everyone. And so birthday parties, anniversary celebrations, and so on have taken place, and the graciousness of the missing guest of honor has been duly noted by a speaker to the group: "It was really great of Avery to urge us to have this gathering without him. We certainly appreciate his thoughtful generosity. . . ."

Although the guest of honor may be absent, it doesn't mean he or she can't participate. In some cases the absentee may send appropriate sentiments—the kinds of things that would have been said in the speech that was to have been presented in person. One consultant who had gotten an emergency summons from a European client arranged to make a long-distance phone call that was put on over an amplifier to the assembled group.

In these days of videotape, one executive recorded his image and sentiments, which were then played on a video monitor to the delight of those assembled.

But if the principal can't be there, do try to make amends with a memento—a piece of the party cake, a program or menu autographed by all attendees, photographs of the occasion inscribed with some sentiment about how much he or she was missed.

WHEN THE PROSPECTIVE GUEST OF HONOR SAYS, "PLEASE, NO PARTY"

From time to time, a prospective guest of honor will say, "If you don't mind, I'd rather there be no fuss or observance of any kind."

There may be no recourse from such a stand. If after a certain amount of persuasion and coaxing the verdict is still "No celebration," you usually have to go along. But clearly it's desirable to find out the reason for the negative verdict. Of course, it may be the individual's shyness. But there are other possible explanations that are worthy of consideration.

Some individuals may have developed an antagonism toward the organization. The reason may include anything from a disenchantment with career progress to disagreement with the organization's policies.

The point is that the disinclination of an individual to become the guest of honor at his or her own party is a sufficiently significant aberration to warrant some thought and investigation. What is learned may be of sufficient importance to require some organizational remedy.

There are two follow-up actions that should be taken, in any event:

• *Some recognition.* The individual who says "No party" usually doesn't mean to say "And nothing else, either." A gift, a small gathering, some special mark of the occasion by the organization—time off is sometimes given—is still in the cards.

• *Informing others.* Colleagues and others who naturally are puzzled by what seems like an oversight or a slight should be told informally: "May Lever said she didn't want a party of any kind. But her boss took her to lunch, and the company gave her a camera she's been wanting. . . ."

PARTY CHECKLIST

1. *Responsibility.*

Are there people in charge to do the planning, make all the arrangements, and continue to watch over things until the last guest has departed, the last light put out? If there seem to be any matters not getting adequate attention, should you see to it that someone in the planning group is given this specific responsibility, or should people be added to the group for this purpose?

2. *Invitations.*

Be as plain or as fancy as you like, but be sure that the place, day, and hour of the affair are clearly given—and *double-checked*. Amazing how often invitations are either misprinted or basic information omitted. And if you want a reply as to acceptance, provide the name and address of the person who should be notified.

3. *Place.*

Are the quarters *large enough* to accommodate the number of guests? Have you planned for a percentage of unexpected additions—relatives of some employees, retired employees who may show up? And can you make step-down moves if bad weather or other circumstances cause large cuts in the expected group size?

4. *Lighting.*

If the quarters may be lit in a number of ways, you may want to consider the possibilities so that you can select the kind of lighting that will give you the atmosphere you prefer for the kind of party you want to run.

5. *Heating.*

Guests have been frozen and roasted. To avoid either eventuality, make a point of checking the temperature controls that will be available and specify the temperature you want. (If there's to be dancing, you may want it to be several degrees cooler.)

6. *Hat and coat checking.*

The one detail of clothing checking—overlooked—can sour an otherwise splendid affair. Departing guests who have to stand in long lines or battle one another to get at an undermanned counter won't leave in a pleasant frame of mind, and a major objective can be damaged.

7. *Washrooms.*

The more convenient they are to your party area, the better, but also be sure that washrooms are newly cleaned, fully stocked with hand towels, and so on.

8. *Service people.*

To cut down on the expense, you may want to have your own organization's volunteers take care of the bartending, food-dispensing, and so on. However, if this is not the case, make sure there is a clear understanding as to the number of service people provided to take care of your needs.

9. *Conflicts with other parties.*

An otherwise perfect party can be ruined by having someone else's affair in an adjoining area impinging on it. For example, you may have no music and they may have a roaring rock-'n'-roll band. Gone is the serenity of your affair. Try to ensure that you have adequate privacy and are free of anyone else's partying if and when you rent outside facilities.

10. *Food and drink.*

Someone must make a decision about the kind of menu or what kind of beverage preparation is to be made. If you're planning a cocktail party, then the kinds of drinks you want should be specified and the details of the payment per bottle of whatever it is you're ordering should be agreed on. Whether you're going to serve beer and pretzels or cavier and champagne, the specifics as to quantity and quality of food should all be understood to avoid the possibility of argument later on.

11. *Music.*

You have a range of choices from large live bands to a tape recorder playing in the background. Whatever you end up with should be the result of a conscious choice of your planning committee. Of course, the music as well as every other aspect of the event should reflect the kind of atmosphere you want for your affair. And don't overlook local talent—someone in the group who plays a musical instrument or sings well enough to perform in public. Avoid those who have more willingness than skill. You may schedule just one or two numbers for the home talent. Let the group call for encores if they're wanted.

12. *Special decorations.*

If you plan to have them for the walls, tables, and so on, make sure they'll be put where you want them.

13. *Door prizes and so on.*

Some gatherings are enlivened by door prizes, raffles for everything from a live kitten to a color TV. Make your decision to have them or not, but it's a point to consider.

14. *Special people, special arrangements.*

One member of the planning group should take on the assignment of arrangements that may be necessary or helpful for some people. For example, an elderly or infirm person arriving by air perhaps should be met at the airport by a company representative or chauffeured limousine. Or a guest coming to the affair in a wheelchair should be given either assistance or instructions as to how to bypass stairs to get to the party area.

15. *Hosts, hostesses, guides, and so on.*

You may want to appoint your more sociable people, either on a formal or informal basis, to break the ice that sometimes mars party start-ups, or even assign them on an individual basis to newcomers or those who tend to be shy.

16. *Tipping.*

If possible, arrange for all gratuities to be taken care of in advance by the planning group. And be sure to let your attendees know what the arrangement is—no tipping necessary, some tipping has been taken care of (for hat and coat checking, for example), other services not covered—or the guests may be on their own for all tipping decisions.

BIRTHDAY CELEBRATIONS

YOUR SECRETARY'S BIRTHDAY

Of all the natal day remembrances in your organization, your secretary's is probably the most crucial. He or she is the one you've worked with most closely, the one with whom your working relationship has the most personal aspect.

Most secretaries are in a position to know not only the details of your work but also the many facets of your moods and methods, your hopes and aspirations. In many cases they're tapped directly into your off-the-job life, whether it comes in the form of being a phone pal of your spouse's, or taking messages from your kids or your broker.

Because of the closeness of this working relationship, a birthday gives you a special opportunity to express recognition or gratitude, perhaps for favors above and beyond the call of duty. Even if your working relationship has been strictly confined to the work, a birthday provides a good opportunity to show your recognition of him or her as a person and a colleague. Consider, however, that some executives ignore their secretaries' birthdays, celebrating their hiring anniversaries as the equivalent.

It will help the effectiveness of what you do if your hand is not forced by seeing a pile of greeting cards on the desk or by other visible tokens from other well-wishers.

"Oh, is it your birthday today?" is certainly a less welcome opener than your being first in line. Clearly, this calls for a reminder to yourself, and it's a wise move to mark your desk calendar each December when you get a new one with the key anniversaries you'll want to recognize during the coming year. Your secretary's birthday is clearly one of these.

Which one of the forms of overt recognition you choose for the occasion depends on your feelings and the tone of your past relationship. If you and your secretary make a close and friendly team, then a birthday lunch may be most appropriate. If your relationship with your secretary is very formal but satisfactory, a small gift—a scarf or a handkerchief if a woman, a belt or tie for a man—can be an acceptable token. Here again, local custom may dictate your choice. You certainly don't want your secretary to feel less well treated than others in the company. Nor do you want to create a competitive race. A little off-the-record agreement among peers can help set guidelines. (See also page 336, on "Gift-Giving from a Boss to a Secretary.")

YOUR OWN BIRTHDAY

When your own birthday shows up on the calendar, your secretary or other subordinates have a problem. How are they going to react to this situation? To some extent, the answer lies in your hands. For one thing, the way you've accepted previous moves on their part can either reinforce or extinguish a particular kind of recognition. If you've been taken to lunch and it's been a happy experience all around, you set the stage for happy repetitions by your pleasant response.

And, of course, you'll be sending out a very clear signal if as your birthday approaches you make a casual reference to the previous celebration. But if for one reason or another you're averse to the lunch, the group gift, or whatever method was used, a word to your secretary or other key subordinate will get the word around: "That was an awfully nice gift I got last year, but frankly I thought people spent too much money on it. . . ."

It's perfectly in order for one of the would-be celebrators to go to the celebratee and say, "John, I see your birthday's coming up next week. What do you think we ought to do in honor of the big day?"

WHEN IT'S YOUR BOSS'S BIRTHDAY

It always seems to come as a surprise that bosses also have birthdays. But it shouldn't be such a surprise to realize that, being human, they'll appreciate some recognition of the occasion. The danger is in overdoing—since any excessive expense or fuss might cause more embarrassment than gratitude. But don't go to the other extreme and pretend to ignore the event. It's worth the effort to find an appropriate, comfortable middle ground that shows you recognize the human side of your boss. This isn't to sound a maudlin, "pity-the-poor-boss" note, but it *is* to suggest that a boss can derive just as much satisfaction from being wished a happy birthday or the equivalent as a subordinate does.

Again, let the nature of your relationship help you decide on an appropriate form. But whether it's a card or an after-hours drink, consider it in terms of your relationship with your boss rather than on the basis of what other people may or may not be doing. No need for you to be limited by other people's ideas—or by their insensitivity or narrow vision.

ENGAGEMENTS, SHOWERS, WEDDINGS

There are some events that involve an employee's personal life —engagements, showers, weddings, and christenings are examples, although the list doesn't end there by any means. In some tight-knit groups, employees may suggest a celebration that is not for a colleague but for the employee's kin—a child's sweet-sixteen party, a boy's bar mitzvah, a son's or daughter's wedding, and so on.

How far should you go in recognizing these off-the-workscene events? What obligations do you have? And should you foster these or try to minimize them insofar as they involve company personnel?

To answer the last question first and quickly, company policy had best set guidelines. Left to their own spontaneous impulses, employee decisions may be made on the basis of status or the popularity of the principal. This can involve the company in a totally unnecessary kind of complication. Where one highly sentimental group, for example, insists on marking the birth of a colleague's grandchild, the supervisor would be wise to urge that the celebration take place after hours and off the premises. Best move is to minimize the organization's or its representative's participation. Let colleagues, as individuals, do as they wish.

INVITATIONS TO EMPLOYEES' PRIVATE FUNCTIONS

Another question that often arises for an executive or other official is whether you should—or must—attend off-premises celebrations—such as the wedding of an employee's son or daughter, for example. Two major factors help you make this decision:

First, your closeness to the employee. If you're on friendly terms and the relationship is one of long standing, this is a positive factor for acceptance.

Second, the fact that executives as representatives of the company traditionally have certain ritual responsibilities. Attendance at employees' weddings, funerals, and so on is one such responsibility, and usually the question simply comes down to who it is who will represent the company. In most cases, the employee's immediate superior is the proper person.

In short, most companies, even those that are not necessarily paternalistic, are aware of the importance of showing an interest in employees as people. Accordingly, at significant personal moments such as an engagement or wedding, the company in the person of the employee's superior, if invited, should certainly put in an appearance unless there is a good reason not to. And if the immediate superior cannot attend, he or she may seek a suitable substitute, possibly an assistant, but not without discussing it with the employee involved.

CHRISTMAS PARTIES
(See also "Company Affairs," page 319.)

Office Christmas parties have given office Christmas parties a bad name. Of course, it's the excesses that have caused the trouble. Nevertheless, business as a whole has taken the past very much to heart. The statistics show that the office Christmas celebration reached its somewhat wild heights in the 1950s. From smashed furniture to pregnant secretaries, the record made it fairly clear that things *could* go wrong. With the wisdom of hindsight, Christmas affairs are planned to be quieter, less hectic, less alcoholic—and more enjoyable and more suited to the occasion.

There is no formula for an ideal Christmas celebration. Organizations vary. What would be suitable and desirable in one instance might be altogether inappropriate in another. In short, each organization must plan according to its own needs and preferences. Here are the checkpoints where good judgment and good taste must be applied:

THE PLACE

The basic choice is between the organization's own premises and "outside"—which may mean a nearby hotel, a caterer with dining facilities, a local hall, and so on.

Generally, if you view the Christmas celebration as being an unpretentious occasion for the company to give its employees a chance to get together and wish each other joy of the season, the company's own meeting room, cafeteria, and so on, are most desirable if large enough.

The question of size of the company facility also bears on another crucial point. Do you plan a single get-together for the entire roster, or do you run separate gatherings for different divisions, departments, or other organizational units?

Here are some of the considerations:

• *It's inadvisable to have groups get together that have had so little contact with each other that you have a mixture of strangers.* It's not easy to have the warm good-fellowship that is a desirable objective in this type of observance with large numbers of people who literally may never have met each other.

• *On the other hand, some people see the Christmas party as being the occasion for members of the same organization who don't know each other to meet,* thereby enlarging their view of—and possibly their respect for—the place where they work. But if this is the intention, special efforts might be in order. For example, hosts and hostesses must be appointed who will introduce guests to one another, see that the people who feel uncomfortable because of their newness in the group are talked to, coaxed over to the refreshment tables, and so on. Mechanical aids can also help improve matters. Tags on which people can write their names, job titles, and/or department affiliations can help. If some of the departments represented are from different organizational premises, large signs welcoming them: "Merry Christmas to the Sales Department," "Welcome to Our Warehouse Colleagues," and so on will add warmth to the party. And if any speeches are to be made, the keynote speaker might well make a point of "my pleasure at being able to finally get under one roof all these different departments," and so on.

• *Some companies, however, may not have adequate facilities for any kind of Christmas party,* or the meeting areas available may be unsuited to the purpose. Once you consider going outside, you're faced by the fact that it's a pretty large world out there. Most cities, for example, have a range of hotels or other party facilities available; that is, they *may* be available, but in good years bookings for this space grow rapidly. If there is a facility that's a natural for you because of its location, size, and degree of elegance, you may have to make your reservations well in advance to make sure you get the kind of space you want.

ARRANGING FOR AN OUTSIDE PLACE

In any event, if you're going outside, it's essential that whoever has the responsibility for selecting the space arrange to meet the hotel representative or other individual through whom arrangements are to be made, to avoid disappointments or misunderstandings. It's essential that you see the quarters that you're considering and then, with the assistance of the facility representative, check on the dozen and one details involved—the adequacy of the quarters for the number of people you're planning for, the coat-checking arrangements, possibly even the temperature of the room. And it goes without saying that who is to supply what in the matter of food and drink, how many service people will be made available, and so on must also be covered. (You'll find a checklist of items like these on page 309.)

And now, getting back to the matter of:

SPEECHES: YES OR NO?

Unless the group is very small, it's desirable for the organization's top people, perhaps two or three of them, to make some comments appropriate to the occasion. To have no speeches at all does seem to miss an opportunity to improve the warmth of the occasion and to give the organization the chance to strike a blow for its own selfishly benign purposes.

The guidelines for such talks are simple. They should be given by the president, vice-president, or other top-echelon individuals. They should be brief. At all costs, they should avoid any areas of unpleasantness, indeed any subject not related to or in the spirit of the occasion—for example, this is not the time for one executive to take a verbal shot at a political opponent.

It's not the time for the treasurer to tell the celebrants how bad business is.

In short, it's not a time for any remarks or information that will interfere with the Christmas spirit.

Here is an outline of a simple speech designed to avoid undesirable or risky areas:

- Welcome: To employees, relatives of employees, special guests if any.
- A continuing tradition: "We at the X Company have been getting together at this happy season for the last fifteen years, and it's great to be able to get together on this happy occasion."
- If there are favorable things or developments: "This has been a very good year at the X Company," and so on.
- Wishes for a pleasant time: "We hope you enjoy the festivities."
- Credit to the planners: "We want to thank Bill, Jane, and Ed for the spendid job of planning they've done. We certainly appreciate their efforts on our behalf. . . ."
- Closing: "And so, our best wishes of the season to all of you. . . ."

COMPANY AFFAIRS

The average organization plays host at a number of occasions—meetings, picnics, anniversary parties, dinners. Conducting a company affair (not the kind that suggests romance—for that subject, see Chapter 11) provides your organization with an important occasion for self-advertising, a chance to look good to an important public—employees, customers, and so on.

Strangely enough, even though organization get-togethers would seem to be group matters in which the individual would be submerged, the fact is that individuals tend to be "alone in the crowd." Putting it another way, the participants in a company party retain their individualities and needs even when the group seems most unified and homogeneous. Many a person has been badly shaken, disappointed, even insulted by oversights or misjudgments resulting from inadequate planning or foresight.

A mismanaged affair *may* produce more anguish than joy and cost more than it is worth. But despite the potential pains and problems, the benefits of the company affair are most attractive. And so they continue to be held because of what they can contribute to organizational solidarity, group spirit, and sundry other objectives. Just as one can't be against the human race because it produces occasional undesirable specimens, it's inadvisable to stay away from celebrations because they sometimes turn sour.

Planning with an eye on the subtleties and opportunities can create good feelings that leave worthwhile results in their wake. There's no one best way to plan or organize an event. What is essential is a systematic approach that covers all the details. Here are some key points:

GROUNDWORK

For a special event, especially one that's new to your company, allow six weeks for planning. (A really big affair might call for six months!) Four weeks is tight, twenty-one days the bare minimum. Start with a preliminary meeting at which are discussed the objectives to be accomplished:

Prestige?
General enjoyment?
Better community relations?
Spreading of information?

Employee goodwill?
Publicity?
Awards for deserving employees?

Of course, you may have two or more purposes. But it is essential that the aims be matched against the arrangements being made to ensure that you achieve what's wanted. For example, if it is publicity you want, invite the press, arrange for photo coverage, and so on.

PLANNING COMMITTEE

A key to the success of the affair is the group that takes on the responsibility both for the planning and for the implementation of the plans. Since there may be countless details to be taken care of, suit the size of the committee to the scope of the affair. For example, a dinner dance at a luxury hotel for "all employees" should have about six or eight planners. This makes it possible to divide up the planning job—everything from picking the place to deciding what kind of music there should be and who should supply it.

Make sure that your planners are among your most capable people—people of good judgment and preferably with some experience in putting together the ingredients of a party and running the program from beginning to end.

Should you appoint one person to take charge, or leave it to the planning group to organize itself? The latter course is generally desirable. Most people like to feel they're really taking over, that it's their baby. But if you have available the services of an outstanding person whose very presence will be an attraction so that you'll get people happily volunteering, consider appointing the leader and asking others to serve along with him or her.

The group will tackle points like these for starters, and may be directed along these lines:

• *Pick your "working" team.* These are the people who will officiate at the party—hosts, hostesses, and so on. Those selected—preferably willing volunteers—should include both "officials" and their assistants. The committee should select people with horse sense. Plain common sense is the best answer to the innumerable crises that arise. Give preference to informal group leaders. They'll add to the success of the occasion.

• *Make assignments.* Assign specific responsibilities. Be sure everyone understands with crystal clarity what's expected. Provide information and leads for questions that arise in connection with assignments. Set deadline dates on which progress is reported.

• *List "points to watch."* Have all the people involved list every conceivable detail and question that they foresee. (See "Danger Points," page 323.)

• *Report on progress.* The planning team should get together frequently enough to keep everyone on top of developments. Don't neglect the last-minute roundup. The day before the event, or as close to it as possible, hold a final meeting in which all unanswered questions, final assignments, last-minute arrangements and re-arrangements can be taken care of.

PROGRAM

The purpose of the event determines the program. For example:

If your company is having an annual get-together and the goal is goodwill and improved interemployee relations, the program may feature humor, perhaps group singing, and speeches in a light vein.

If the meeting is to mark the launching of a new product, a primary objective may be to kindle the enthusiasm of your people. In this case, speakers will select such ardor-building subjects as past company successes, the hard and imaginative work that went into the new product's development, awards for the developers, and so on.

Keep the objective clearly defined. Avoid the pitfall of using the occasion for items outside the main objective. A neglected elder statesman of your company may need recognition, but inappropriately dragging him into the spotlight may alter the tone, get your audience off the track.

Allocate agenda time according to importance. Consider the selection of speakers carefully. For example, Bill Reed, president is . . .

• *The main speaker.* His talk must strike most directly at the theme of your meeting. He merits the top spot, usually last on the agenda. Twenty minutes is a good length for his contribution, certainly no more than thirty—unless there is special justification.

He may be helped by suggestions: effective visual aids, demonstrations, props. Usually there's little trouble with a main speaker. As the main attraction, he probably has had considerable experience. It will help if he can provide a draft of his talk in advance.

• *Supporting cast.* The other speakers, who precede the featured guest, should be guided on matters of subject selection and time allotment. You don't want anyone to steal the thunder of the chief speaker by covering his topic or by talking at greater length.

Select people you can depend on so that you know in advance what they will do. Don't schedule an inexperienced speaker whose nervousness will set everyone on edge.

Be firm about time allowances. Keep the number of events down within the limits of the purpose of the meeting.

A successful program depends on style, cadence.

How are these qualities achieved? By:

- action—a toast to an event, a personality;
- change of pace—in the length of introductory remarks, a short item on the program alternating with a long one;
- change of mood—a moment of silence, an introduction or speech that produces laughter, contrasted with a dramatic introduction or talk.

OFFICIALS

The people who run the event may not parallel regular company officialdom. In some cases the person in charge may not even be in the executive group. (We're talking here *not* of the planners and policymakers but those who will supervise the actual proceedings.)

Here are some of the hurdles facing event-runners:

• *Person in charge.* The program coordinator—usually the head of the planning committee—must be capable of quick and decisive action. On the day of the event especially, he or she has to make decisions instantly—right or wrong—and take the risk of making the wrong one.

He or she must be available during the entire proceeding to handle emergencies. He or she should be armed with a list of events and activities to be able to follow the program, speed it up, slow it down, or juggle items.

• *Staff.* The actual running of the affair is a one-man job. But the person in charge should have an adequate number of assistants to whom he or she can delegate details—everything from getting extra chairs to escorting a speaker to the washroom.

These people must know three things:

- overall plan of the day—agenda, speakers, and so on;
- physical layout of the scene of operations;
- who the senior officials are, especially those equipped to handle emergencies.

DANGER POINTS

Early in the game, everyone in on the planning should make up a list of details, problems, critical points that must be settled. Pre-thinking emergencies is the best way to avoid them. Here's how to gather items:

• *Let each person think up every possible contingency imaginable.* Think through every step of the affair, decide what will be needed.

• *Visualize each item on the agenda, each guest (or group) entering the room, and follow through from moment to moment.* What's he or she apt to do? What difficulties will he or she encounter? What information will he or she need to avoid getting lost?

Most important is to have alternatives to crucial arrangements:

• *What can be done if the featured speaker fails to show up?* One company arranged to have a standby telephone set up whereby the main speaker could address the assemblage by phone if necessary.

• *What if the master of ceremonies can't make it at the last minute?* Best insurance here is for the M.C. to get up a minute-by-minute agenda, clearly written out. Then a duplicate can be handed to a stand-in.

• *What about individuals who have assigned roles in the event?* This applies to everyone from guides to speakers. The answer is to rehearse everyone until he or she is letter-perfect.

A partial list of points to check, worked up by one anniversary-meeting coordinator, highlights what's involved:

Will timetable provide enough time for printed material to be prepared?

Make sure printer knows to which ballroom to deliver programs if they're not in our hands in advance.

Can hotel management suggest best parking arrangements?

Get outside agency started on announcements.

Discuss with Personnel amount and type of internal publicity.

Schedule conference of executives to get their ideas on agenda.

Select key color to identify all internal correspondence on meeting.

Meet with treasurer to discuss cost limits.

Liquor.

Outside guests? Who and how many?

Unlimited number of family members for individual employees?

Special arrangements for our six handicapped employees?

What part does president want to play?

Mementos of the occasion?

Should employees participate in planning?

Who's the biggest man we can get from the community?

Get all files on past anniversary celebrations.

Get opinions on well-received and poorly received events in past.

How ambitious should we make our P.R. play?

Invite suppliers?

Invite customers?

Invite prospective customers?

Whom can we award what, for the occasion?

If complications arise despite the best-laid plans, quick and decisive action must follow:

• *The food hasn't arrived.* The supplier must be called at once, and a clear-cut answer received. If the delay promises to be too long, a last-minute switch to another source must be considered.

• *The programs haven't arrived.* The printer must be contacted. The first lot off the press must be delivered by the fastest means, the balance brought by special messenger as soon as available.

The "show-must-go-on" policy is a good one to adopt. It's usually better to continue with improvised means than to cancel at the last minute. Announcements of changes, if made in a cheerful way, will be accepted in the same spirit. After all, most people won't know what was planned, only what is finally offered.

ATMOSPHERE

Conscious effort must be made to produce and sustain a mood or spirit suitable to the occasion. For example, a picnic may call for informality and good-fellowship; an anniversary meeting, for dignity and restraint.

Many elements contribute to the mood of an event. A chief factor is the demeanor of top officials. An unmistakable mood of informality and friendliness is set by the company president who appears in slacks and sport shirt at a company picnic and chats his way through the group.

Whatever the occasion, determine in advance the appropriate mood and keep it in mind in planning the program, decor, and so on. Key individuals must be let in on the decision so that they know what will be appropriate in the way of speeches, dress, and general behavior.

PUBLIC RELATIONS

The affair may be planned for its public-relations value. At any rate, public-relations side benefits are desirable to build the company's reputation, increase goodwill, and so on.

If your company has a public-relations department, of course the P.R. person should be in on the affair from the beginning.

The P.R. representative will be able to make recommendations for publicizing the event, and will be able to suggest features that will make it more newsworthy and ensure better press coverage.

In the absence of professional P.R. advice, check with local news or trade publications to get their suggestions as to what they might use—photographs, types of publicity releases, and so on.

Don't overlook the community relations angle. Including local officials or community leaders as honored guests will increase local interest as well as improve relations with specific individuals.

SELECTING THE DATE

Once the program is tentatively set and it's been decided where the event will be held, choose the date. Avoid special days such as the day before a holiday, special religious days, and so on.

Watch out for conflicting events—conventions, meetings, and so on. In larger cities, convention and meeting-list services will check dates. In smaller communities, this type of information may be obtained from hotels or other regular meeting places.

What day of the week is best? If outside people are to be invited and your potential audience is made up of commuters, avoid Mondays and Fridays. Wednesdays for evening events are generally inadvisable because many people plan to go elsewhere. Best bets are Tuesdays and Thursdays.

There are generally fewer problems choosing a luncheon date than one for dinner.

THE PLACE

Should the event be held on company premises or outside? If it's customary to use a given site, it may be advisable to shift, just for a change of pace. One company that always held annual meetings in the company cafeteria successfully switched to the main ballroom of a local hotel for its fiftieth anniversary.

In selecting a place, ask:

What is the most advantageous section of town?

What is the reputation of the place—for food facilities, service, cooperation of the staff?

How well suited is the place to the objectives of your event?

How well suited is it to the atmosphere aimed at?

• *Special note on dealing with outside staffs:* In using a hotel or outside restaurant, make a point of enlisting the cooperation of the service people. Once the monetary arrangements have been made, spare no effort to make the management realize that yours is a good group to work with and that the meeting is going to help their business. Once their goodwill has been won, they will do hundreds of little things quickly that otherwise might overload your team.

ROOM SIZE, AND SO ON

Particularly for an event involving outsiders, pick a room, meeting hall, auditorium that will look well-filled but not jammed. If possible, get one that can "stretch." Then a certain number of guests will adequately fill the main section. A larger number can overflow into additional space that nevertheless seems to be part of the main area.

A "flexible-dais" arrangement is also advisable. Being able to place the speakers' table at one end or the other and to increase or decrease the seating capacity at the head table helps avoid inappropriate seating. At a key point, check:

size of room and number of exits;
public-address system;
lectern;
lighting;
acoustics;
location in building;
folding chairs and tables (for unexpected guests);
adequacy of attendants—waitresses and so on;
rest rooms;
other (add your own) ——————————————— .

Don't take anyone's word for any of the above. In the case of the lighting and acoustics, for example, someone should sit down in the room, have the lights turned on, and judge the effect.

Use people whose experience and judgment can be counted on. If possible, inspection should be made during some other group meeting. At that time, listen to the P.A. system. It may sound quite different during a session than in an empty hall.

MENU

When it comes to food, decisions must be made, keeping in mind the nature of the group and the occasion as well:

What to serve?
Where to serve it?
When to serve it?
Who is to serve it?
How to serve it?

No matter what else you have on the program, your menu is the most susceptible to criticism and, fortunately, to praise as well. Many a dinner has been made a resounding success by one tasty dish—or wet-blanketed by one tasteless one.

It is not simply a matter of what goes into the pot. Hot dishes that arrive lukewarm will be denounced along with poor service or small portions.

Some companies find the best way to avoid 50 percent of the problem is to serve buffet-style. The guest who helps himself from a well-filled serving table isn't likely to complain about the size of the portions, the service, or the fact that the soup is cold and the ice cream hot.

PROTECTION

If the affair is being held in a hotel or other such place, the premises are probably covered by liability insurance. Check in any case, but especially if the location is one not generally rented out to the public. Consider security: personal as well as personal belongings.

If the affair is outdoors, is rain insurance obtainable?

It may be advisable to have the company's executive in charge of safety survey the place, rule out-of-bounds all hazardous areas or activities.

INVITATIONS OR ANNOUNCEMENTS

No matter what the occasion, standard questions always arise: "Can I bring friends or relatives?" "Are ex-employees invited?"

"How about children?" "Is there a charge? Same for employees as for others? Lower for children?"

FORM OF THE INVITATION OR ANNOUNCEMENT. Before the printer lets his presses roll, someone should make a final check to see that all relevant information is on the invitation: name or title of the occasion; date, time (start and finish); place—with some simple directions if necessary ("one mile north of Main Street"); type of dress suggested; features of the occasion; R.S.V.P.

Decide whether a return postcard or tear-off form for acceptance should be part of the invitation or announcement.

If the group is asked to reply, provide the name and address of a specific individual to whom acknowledgments should be sent. That way there will be less confusion of letters going all over the lot or ending up on the desk of a busy executive not directly involved in the proceedings.

CLOTHING

Prevent embarrassment by suggesting to attendees what you consider to be appropriate dress. Unless you do, people will turn up wearing their Sunday best at informal picnics, or sloppy outdoor casuals at a formal dinner.

For recreation events, your announcements might read: "Bring bathing suits if you plan to swim." Or: "Temperature drops below 40 after sundown, dress accordingly."

FIRST AID

Accidents are infrequent, but lack of preparation may be serious.

If no doctor is available, minimum protection is a first-aid kit with a qualified person who will take over the responsibility of doling out the adhesive bandage, burn ointment, aspirin, and so on. (See "Protection," page 327.)

TRANSPORTATION

If the affair is off the premises, you'll want to make sure that adequate transportation facilities are available for those who are planning to attend.

Does this mean chartering of buses or limousines? It may. In the average case, car-pooling arrangements are adequate. However, where there is an unusual situation, check to see that "special" cases are taken care of.

PARKING

It may be a key problem. Benefit from the experience of one company president. He decided to have a company outing on his newly purchased estate. Overlooking the parking difficulty, he spent the first two hours shooing employees' cars off the lawn, unblocking the driveway, and breaking up the traffic jam on the street outside his house. This problem may merit one person's entire attention.

SEATING ARRANGEMENTS

Assigning seats is one thing to put off to the last possible moment. The difficulties are compounded fivefold once changes are made.

Begin by laying out a facsimile of the room. (The layout should clearly indicate location and seating capacity of tables. Many hotels furnish this type of floor plan.)

Now consider all those who will be present, and group them in categories:

people who must sit at the same table;
those who merit the choice locations;
those who may be assigned the least desirable spots;
the in-between (and most difficult to assign) group.

Allow some room up front if there is a chance that last-minute important guests may show. This should be done even at the risk of having these remain empty if they prove not to be needed.

A formal meeting, especially if it is a lunch or dinner meeting, will usually have a celebrity or top-executive table. Decide early in the planning what kind of special guests are wanted on the dais. Who is seated where depends on the nature of the function and the guests.

• *If the list includes government officials and representatives of other countries,* you might want to go so far as to check seating arrangements with the State Department in the United States or the Department of External Affairs in Canada.

• *If the list is made up of businessmen,* decisions must be made on the basis of who are the most important ones in the community. Work from there to the ones who are less important.

• *If the list is made up of nongovernment and nonbusiness people*
—civic organizations, community groups, and so on—the size of the
group is often a rough measure of priority of importance.

PHYSICAL PROPERTIES

When the gold watch can't be found at the moment of presentation, it can be very annoying. A single individual should have responsibility for props that will be required during the event. Aside from
the standard items such as the lectern, ashtrays, and so on, possibilities are:

projection screen;
projector;
tape recorder;
pads and pencils for each guest;
blackboard;
flip chart;
special exhibits, blowups, charts, and so on;
awards or gifts.

There's no limit to number or variety, and a single item may be
crucial. To avoid misfires, be sure to check with speakers, particularly, to make sure their needs will be met.

HANDLING THE PRESS

It's a critical element in the publicity results you'll get.
• *Seating.* Place them where they can see and hear.
• *Guidance.* Have someone on hand to answer their questions,
and, if possible, have someone at each press table who can either
answer questions and feed them *facts* or knows how to get someone
to the table who can.
• *Help.* Assist in getting the story. Slip in the facts from time
to time, but don't try to *sell* the newspaper people on the importance of the event, the organization, and so on. Remember that
they are there because their publications feel the occasion merits
a story.
• *Material.* See that they are provided with handouts—mimeo-
graphed or typed background information.

RECEPTION FOR SPECIAL GUESTS

A brief reception before festivities:

• *Provides a convenient meeting place for special guests and assures their presence on time.*

• *Gives them a chance to get to know one another and thaw out.* (There's nothing so depressing as a guest table full of strangers.)

• *Gives the company an opportunity to recognize and cement relations with special groups*—customers, suppliers, and so on.

How the reception is run is flexible. But make certain that someone in the reception room will know the guests who haven't arrived and can get this information to the M.C. or the program coordinator. Last-minute absences create the need to remove a chair, change place cards, make other adjustments.

MEETING THE GUEST OF HONOR

The arrival of the guest of honor must be under control. Best bet is to arrange to have the guest met and picked up. Then, if something goes wrong, a representative can telephone full details of how long a delay there will be, and so on.

If the weather is apt to interfere, arrange, if possible, to set up alternate routes. If the trip was to be by air, can new arrangements be made for train? Car?

Have someone on hand at the entrance to the building or reception area to escort the guest to an agreed-upon point. If there are several entrances, it might be wise to post a watcher at each one. It is helpful to provide a personal guide. Someone in the organization acquainted with the guest of honor would be a logical choice.

DECORUM AND DISCIPLINE

One individual out of line can sour the entire affair. Handling violations of decorum or disciplinary problems is touchy. The coordinator may wish to make a mental note of three or four people who can be counted on. Enlist their aid in advance by telling them their help may be required in case of emergency.

It's important that a responsible official appear early on the scene if a disciplinary problem arises. The well-meant attempt on the part of one or more individuals to take action or to move in before it's really necessary may be worse than the original situation. Milder measures should be tried before lowering the boom.

THE PROBLEM GUEST

It's unfortunate, but occasionally one or more appear:

• *Problem Guest 1: The Seat-Jumper.* How do you spot him—and get him back where he's supposed to be *before* trouble brews? Station people around the room to spot the maneuver when it begins and who will get the offender to go back to his assigned seat. They have to be persuasive, friendly, and firm. Kidding—gentle ridicule —is their most effective weapon.

• *Problem Guest 2: The Griper.* Sometimes he's justified, sometimes not. If he's got a basis for his complaint, take whatever steps will give him satisfaction. But if he's decidedly unreasonable and wants to make an issue of his claims, refer him to the "bitch" table. This most helpful device should be located *outside* the meeting area. Your most clearheaded and persuasive person should be put in charge. He'll handle all unresolved complaints, make on-the-spot judgments.

• *Problem Guest 3: The Overdoer.* He or she eats, drinks, or dances too much. Result: illness. If this is at all a possibility, arrange for a "recovery" room, with one or two "nurses" to get the unfortunate person into the rest room and taken care of. To avoid embarrassment, have two "rescue" teams, one male and one female, to tend their own.

WHEN THE EVENT IS OUTDOORS

When the Treasury Building in Washington, D.C., was dedicated as a national historic landmark, the goofs that developed during the ceremony represented an excellent "how-*not*-to-do-it" example for managers involved in planning large meetings, conferences, and other company events.

Everything from Freud to the weather seemed to conspire against the Washington event. The first speaker began by welcoming everyone to the "historic equation." (The speaker, an official of the U.S. Treasury Department, explained the Freudian slip by saying he had been preoccupied with revenue formulas.) The second speaker, whose job it was to introduce the guest of honor, got the name wrong. (It was the familiar case where the individual had two "first names" —such as James Paul—and the speaker reversed them.) And, finally, flags and banners provided to brighten the occasion fell like autumn leaves due to brisk winds.

An historic occasion on which the great outdoors proved deleterious was the inauguration of John Fitzgerald Kennedy: the bright sun glared on the sheets of paper containing a special poem written for the event by poet Robert Frost, whose efforts to get his weak eyes to perform were painful to behold.

You're not expected to keep a bright sun from glaring, but for outdoor-event planners, a checklist that takes into account some of the special requirements of this type of affair can minimize the chances for disaster:

• *Program.* As you plan, keep in mind the physical situation with which you're dealing. If the setting for your event is the open lawn in front of your plant, this may suggest problems of seating that may be minimized if you're using the local ballpark. And program items must be considered as to their appropriateness for the place. For example:

A magician with a stack of trick cards up his sleeve may be very effective in a small indoor auditorium, but hard to see in a large outdoor stadium. By the same token, consider problems of hearing and visibility. Avoid like the plague any idea of using a public-address system as the means for broadcasting a long speech. The blasting, low-fidelity of such systems is unsuitable.

And the physical comfort of the audience is a factor. Comfortable, theater-type seats can keep an audience happy for a two-hour program. Benches or other backless types of seating—which might be fine for sports fans—would cause a plague of restlessness in a less involved crowd.

• *Meeting-place preparations.* Whether your meeting is to be held in a stadium or in an open field, an individual or team must have the responsibility for having it in readiness. Lighting and acoustics must be checked. Seating, audibility of speakers, and so on must be planned. Traffic control and parking facilities, where these are a factor, are absolute musts.

• *Double-check assignments.* Pin down responsibility for *everything.* If you're hiring an outside concern to set up tents, pavilions, chairs, and tables, check to make sure you're getting what was agreed on. If you're using home talent, see that matters are progressing according to plan—from the kegs of beer you've ordered to the expert who's going to put on a fireworks display after dark.

• *Prop control.* If your program calls for equipment of any kind—from tables and chairs to sound equipment—someone should be put in charge of procuring and properly deploying such items.

• *Rehearse speakers.* Your program chairman or other individual must make sure that whoever will be called on to speak knows in general what he is to say and how long he has to say it. If you have a master of ceremonies, he should have a final version of your program, including all the notes he needs to introduce the speakers by name, title, and qualifications, as called for.

• *Substitutes.* If you have invited two hundred to three hundred people to an event, it's desirable to have substitutes on hand to pinch-hit for key people who are unavailable at the last moment.

• *Guides.* Events attended by large numbers of people must have the equivalent of a traffic-control group, ushers inside, people to facilitate car-parking, and so on.

As a special part of your "guide" service, consider having people available to greet your speakers or other special guests, welcome them, guide them to their seats, and so on. It's not only a desirable courtesy, it can also prevent the kind of near-catastrophe that occurred at a large formal dinner at which the guest of honor got lost in the hotel, making the crowd restless and almost giving the sponsors heart-failure.

• *Muscle men.* If there's any moving of furniture or equipment involved, don't depend on volunteers from the audience. Appoint a group of people who will know in advance what they're supposed to do, and then plan how to do it with a minimum of fuss.

• *Flexible crowd size.* In some situations, you may not know in advance how many people will turn up at your affair. It is wise to have alternative plans in case a substantially larger—or smaller— number of people appears. You don't want to use a five-hundred-seat auditorium for fifty people; and you don't want to crowd a hundred people into a small conference room.

• *The weather factor.* If you're planning an outdoor event, wind, rain, darkness, or cold can wipe out an otherwise successful program. Upshot: disaster. As an alternative, indoor quarters are obviously one way of offsetting an unexpectedly bad turn in the weather. You may want to set a rain date if the weather becomes impossible.

• *Cleanup and toilet facilities.* Especially if you're dealing with larger crowds, both trash disposal and the availability of toilets become important considerations. In each case, check to make sure that facilities are adequate. If not, you should take steps to supplement whatever is available. In the case of trash, for example, unsightly accumulations of paper, garbage, and so on can ruin both the aesthetics and the tone of your event. And as for toilet facilities, when nature speaks, we must heed. You don't want guests to be made uncomfortable or otherwise discommoded. Portable units are available in most areas on a rental basis.

(If your outdoor event includes the serving of food—as for a picnic, for example—see "The Company Picnic," Chapter 9, page 391.)

GIFTS AND GIFT-GIVING

Gift-giving is one of a small group of ceremonies that add a humanizing element to the world of work. However, gift-giving, like many other things, has two sides—one all whipped cream and cherries, the other somewhat sour or bitter. To function satisfactorily in this area, one must know both aspects. Certainly, knowing the seamy side can help avoid moves that might pain others or damage relationships.

Looking at the positive aspect first, a gift conveys a message from giver to recipient—one of admiration, respect, regard, esteem, goodwill. The happy aspects of giving a present appear when the gift is appropriate to the occasion and the recipient. A well-chosen gift delights both the person who receives it and the one who gives it.

But a gift may bring the opposite of pleasure—it may be ill-suited, given in the wrong way at the wrong time. Specifically in the business context, a gift may look like a bribe—even though it was not so intended. Or a small gift is given as a token, and the recipient feels slighted because it suggests low esteem and a mean spirit on the part of the giver.

To give completely foolproof gifts is almost impossible. But if you have your second thoughts in advance and enlarge your view of the possibilities by consulting some of the guidelines as well as the sample lists of gifts toward the end of this section, you will be able to gain the advantages of gift-giving and avoid the pitfalls.

OCCASIONS FOR GIFT-GIVING

The world of work offers a number of occasions when the giving of gifts is appropriate. But whether or not you may *want* to give a present on a particular occasion depends on a number of factors: the occasion; your relationship to the recipient or principal in the case; the other person's expectations; the past pattern of gift exchanges within the company.

And if you do decide to give, the nature of the particular gift you may want to select depends on still other considerations: the state of your exchequer at the moment; the degree or intensity of your feeling; and—though some people may scoff at this idea—the comparison of your gift with gifts others will give (you might want to make a point of giving more *or* less).

Here is a list of events that may trigger the gift-giving impulse:

birthday;
anniversary with company;
engagement;
wedding;
wedding anniversary (especially the 5's and 10's);
hospitalizing;
recovery from a serious illness;
promotion;
special feat or accomplishment;
consolation prize—for a defeat or failure;
gifts at unexpected times—just for the joy (or hell) of it.

FROM A BOSS TO A SECRETARY

Bosses may be either male or female. Ditto secretaries. But to simplify the discussion here, let's assume the most common situation, that of a male boss and a female secretary. One further assumption; that is, that the gift-giving is in the context of a good working relationship, one without any hidden animosities or, for that matter, any special emotional ties.

WHEN TO GIVE AND WHEN NOT TO. There are many possible occasions for gift-giving in the boss-secretary relationship. Your secretary has just completed a job over and above the call of duty, and you want to express your gratitude. Or she has a birthday, company anniversary, or wedding anniversary. Any of these are legitimate occasions for gift-giving. This is entirely your decision and should reflect your honest feelings. One executive points out: "I have two secretaries and four other people on my staff. Obviously, this matter of recognizing anniversaries could get out of hand. Accordingly, I've developed a practice of taking staff members out for lunch on the day of their company anniversary. On other anniversaries or similar occasions, I either send a card or convey my wishes, congratulations, and so on verbally."

A good starting point is to first be aware of:

• FOUR GIFTS YOU SHOULD NEVER GIVE YOUR SECRETARY. There are certain types of presents that are inappropriate—unless the boss happens to be female, too! For example, no matter how friendly a man is with his secretary, an intimate gift such as lingerie or stockings is in questionable taste. Somewhat less offensive but equally out of line would be the gift of a ring—unless it had some special justification. For example, if your secretary put great store by American Indian jewelry and on a Western trip you happened to come across an unusually nice turquoise-and-silver ring, then the ring gift could have some possible excuse. But even here—why not seek out a pin? Avoid ambiguous gift categories. One seeks to please, not to mystify.

Similarly, "gag" gifts usually turn out to be violations of good taste for either a male or female boss. No matter how funny it might seem in the store, a sheer black nightie embroidered with red hearts will not seem like a good-natured joke in the office. This is not to suggest that humor of itself is an unacceptable adjunct to gift-giving. On the contrary. But, certainly, tasteless humor is bound to boomerang. A good rule here is "When in doubt, rule it out!"

Another type of gift to avoid with some secretaries is the one that is strictly utilitarian. Utilitarian gifts are fine for occasions like showers, weddings, or if you're looking for a housewarming gift. Otherwise, especially if your secretary is obviously not the home-body type, consider something that indicates a little more personal thought.

Particularly recommended for the younger secretary, especially one who shows a keen interest in dress, is a high-fashion item such as a scarf or a handbag. But be sure you know her taste. Best bet is to enlist the help of another employee who is keyed in to the same wavelength.

If your secretary is a music lover, tickets to a particularly hard-to-get musical performance may be welcome. But be sure you're swayed by *her* taste, not yours. Opera tickets can be an awkward gift if your secretary is a jazz buff.

Perfume is on the borderline. It may be just a bit too personal in the average case. On the other hand, if you know your secretary well enough to know that it would be well received, perfume or cologne is fine—but never bath salts or other items that are essentially deodorants.

These years male bosses may have to be particularly aware of the sensitivity of some women to the possible male chauvinism of a gift. You would be well advised to avoid the feminine cliché gift—such as the perfume—if your secretary tends to be somewhat militant about her female role.

The overly expensive gift is also best avoided. A gift that departs too strongly from the "token of one's esteem" and is obviously expensive cannot be adequately justified, even on the basis of generosity. To put it simply, no one could give a secretary a mink coat or diamond tiara without raising eyebrows. Exactly what point on the dollar scale begins to exceed the bounds of good taste, again, is generally a matter of place and individual relationships. In ordinary circumstances it can be said that a gift under twenty-five dollars should be able to convey the full measure of your good wishes and not violate the taboo of costing too much.

GIFTS TO A SUBORDINATE

The considerations above apply generally to female subordinates, whatever their function. With male subordinates, relationships and expectations may differ:

If you are male yourself, minor occasions may best be celebrated not by a gift but by the kind of friendliness and camaraderie shown by a warmhearted "Let's have a drink after work tonight in honor of your birthday"—or whatever. Picking up the tab at a leisurely lunch will probably leave everyone feeling fine.

If you are female, the sex of your subordinate may suggest some do's and don't's. In general, if you concentrate on the *relationship* and forget about the sex difference, you'll probably find the problems disappear. Here again, an invitation to lunch often works out well. Many women executives find a credit card solves all awkwardness over the check.

A book on a subject you know is of interest goes gracefully from female boss to male and/or female subordinate. Ditto a desk accessory or a leather wallet or key case. Just keep it small and neat.

FROM A SECRETARY TO THE BOSS

Some companies—wisely—have a policy of discouraging up-the-line gift-giving. In most cases a subordinate runs more risk of embarrassing a boss than pleasing him with any sort of gift other than the merest token. But since the generous impulse cannot always be stifled by mandate, here are some rules for minimizing gift-giving headaches.

To simplify matters again, let's assume that we're talking about a female secretary and a male boss, although the same considerations generally apply to all subordinate-superior situations. As a starter, let's point out the taboos, the kinds of gifts that cause problems and raise more doubts than you want to deal with.

THREE TYPES OF GIFTS TO AVOID. While an overly expensive present is inadvisable in any situation, it's especially out of place in an "up-the-line" situation. For one thing, a boss knows exactly what his secretary's salary is, obviously less than his own. And a gift that strains the secretary's budget can only be an embarrassment to her boss. If gifts going the other way should stay within the twenty-five-dollar limit, then under ordinary circumstances a secretary's gift to her boss should not exceed ten or fifteen dollars.

And as with the boss's gift to his secretary, the gift should not be overly intimate. Apparel for a man, strangely enough, tends to be even more personal than for a woman. While it's conceivable that under certain circumstances a boss might buy his secretary gloves, for a secretary to buy her boss shirts—or even gloves or a belt—is usually too personal.

Also under this heading come such items of jewelry as cuff links. Traditionally, personal items of this kind are bought by wives. The secretary shouldn't seem to be preempting wifely prerogatives.

A third and final kind of gift to avoid: one that's likely to become a white elephant. Of course, this hazard exists in any gift-giving situation, but for a boss whom a secretary sees practically every day of his working life, the gift he never uses can be a burden on the working relationship. For example, if your boss isn't the kind of person who's intrigued by the cute and clever, stay away from figures of Snoopy, "darling" little animals, and, for that matter, even greeting cards with cloying sentiments.

Recommended for bosses are work-related items for which there is an evident need. An inexpensive pen-and-pencil set, for example, or other desktop tools—ashtray, pencil holder, paper-clip container, and so on—may be just the thing. In most cases, he may really be happiest with a card and a birthday cake that can be cut and consumed at the morning coffee break.

THE TOKEN GIFT

In a general sense, all gifts are tokens. They represent a feeling of gratitude, esteem, goodwill, and so on.

However, there is a more specific sense in which a gift can be a token. And the phrase—a cliché but a necessary one—used so often in presenting a gift, "Accept this as a token of our esteem," tells the story precisely.

It is this "token quality" that explains the popularity of the nonutilitarian gift—the plaque, the "certificate of achievement," and so on. It's because these items are not utilitarian that they tend to symbolize more clearly the sentiment of an occasion. The employee who's given a congratulatory letter from the president of the company—nicely framed—can show it off to friends and colleagues and have the nature of his achievement and its appreciation more clearly marked than if he were given a power drill for his home workshop.

There is one danger, however, in the token gift, and that is the expectation of the recipient. Some people are less sentimental than others. Accordingly, while they will be pleased by the recognition, they might prefer that it be shown in a more material way. For these people the token will be better received if it does have other than sentimental value. For such people the power drill *is* a better "token of esteem." A leather handbag for a deserving assistant, if she's in this category, would be more welcome than being taken out to lunch. Well-established company policy that sets a pattern for such occasions can take the guesswork—and, therefore, the pain—out of it for all concerned.

WHEN IT'S WRONG TO GIVE A GIFT

As we've said, gift-giving is essentially an act reflecting friendliness and warm feeling. The spirit of giving, then, may sometimes come into conflict with situations that ordinarily call for a gift. For example, a person with whom you are on indifferent, even unfriendly, terms has been promoted. This turn of good fortune favoring an "enemy" may summon up no warm feelings whatsoever. On the contrary. Nevertheless, it's a generous and therefore desirable thing to send, either by a brief written message or verbally, moderately stated congratulations. A gift clearly would be hypocritical.

And in some cases a gift represents an overreaction to a situation, and the gift-giver comes off as being overly effusive. In other words, an occasion that calls for best wishes or "Many happy returns of the day" may be adequately observed in those terms. Anything more would be too much. Also, if the relationship of the giver to the recipient is not particularly close and there has been no tradition of gift-giving in your organization in similar circumstances, then a gift should not be considered.

In general, any time a gift risks the reaction of bewilderment ("Now I wonder why he sent me that!"), gift-giving is clearly not called for.

WHEN IT'S WRONG NOT TO GIVE

In some rare cases it's advisable to give a gift even though it's done with little enthusiasm. For example:

A colleague with whom you're definitely not friendly is going to be married. A collection is taken up—everyone's being asked to contribute three dollars to buy a group gift. It's advisable not to be a holdout. You're making a choice between a slight bending of personal principle—not giving a gift when you don't really feel like it—in favor of the inadvisability of adding a sour note to an otherwise pleasant occasion. In other words, you make the decision that it's better to lean over backward to be a "good guy" rather than spoil things or dampen them slightly for others.

Another time when it's wrong not to give: when a precedent has been established. Let's say you've always given some service person in the organization—it could be anyone from the janitor to the mail boy—a token of your gratitude for special services rendered. It's inadvisable to break the precedent unless you do it intentionally. In other words, don't disappoint the expectations of people who rightly or wrongly come to depend on the kind of recognition represented by the gift.

WHEN IT'S WRONG TO ACCEPT A GIFT

It's always inadvisable to accept a gift that has an ulterior motive. No matter from what source, if you have any reason to feel that the intent behind it is to corrupt your fair-mindedness or to exact special favors, any gift should be politely returned or rejected.

Another reason for refusing a gift: its cost. If you feel that either through misjudgment or some similar reason a colleague, client, or customer has given you a gift greatly in excess of what the occasion demands, the gift should be returned with a simple explanation: "I'm deeply grateful, but I'm afraid in this case generosity has exceeded reasonable limits. I just can't accept anything this expensive. . . ."

PERSONALIZING A GIFT

It may seem like a small matter, but personalizing a present can yield a major return in terms of pleasure and appropriateness. One possibility: consider putting the recipient's name on the gift. For example, a silver plate can be engraved with the legend:

To Ellen Gray
On Her Promotion to Director
June 6, 197—

Inscriptions have been put on metal pens and pencils, loving cups, and wall plaques. But an object doesn't have to be made of metal for this kind of treatment. An employee was given a wood-and-leather tobacco humidor that was just a so-so present. But he prizes it because his colleagues attached a small bronze plate that reads:

20 Wonderful Years 20
David Lee at P. Antrim & Co.
August 9, 197—

WHEN GIFT-GIVING BECOMES A SMALL NIGHTMARE

Gift-giving can become an annoyance, a bother, a time-consuming irritation. While the initial impulse to give may have been prompted by genuine warmth, it can often lead to a "duty" to continue on the basis of precedent rather than feeling: "The department gave Hal Farley a birthday present last year and the year before. He'll feel hurt if we don't come through this year."

Or, another factor that spoils things is the out-of-hand escalation:

The first year, Kate Drury gave Gale Rorick two handkerchiefs for Christmas. Gale gave Kate a scarf.

The next year, Kate upped the ante and gave Gale a piece of costume jewelry. Gale gave Kate a two-record album of the current musical hit.

The third year, Kate gave Gale an expensive bottle of perfume. Gale gave Kate a signed sketch by Chagall—a steal at seventy-five dollars, but it seriously dented her already Christmas-shrunken cash supply.

The fourth year, jingle bells jangled both Kate's and Gale's nerves. How were they going to continue their gift-giving in the unfortunate style to which they had become accustomed, without going broke?

Since gift-giving can go haywire and boomerang in the close-knit workscene, consider these self-regulating steps:

• *Don't start something you won't want to sustain.*

• *Pick peak occasions.* (You may want to recognize a fifth anniversary or a tenth, and not necessarily all the single years in between.)

• *Terminate exchanges, if you want to, by mutual consent.* Call the department together and suggest they all agree not to exchange Christmas gifts. Or set a firm limit on the amount to be spent.

HOW TO BREAK OFF GIFT-GIVING THAT HAS BECOME UNDESIRABLE

Let's face up to the situation just suggested—the case where you've traditionally given a gift but for one reason or another *would like* to halt the practice.

To make the break without some sign to the other person would suggest thoughtless oversight on your part and would cause feelings of questioning and self-doubt: "What have I done that has caused this change?" Another possibility: feelings of resentment.

Some action is called for. What can it be? Here are some choices:

• *A direct—but tactful—statement.* As one executive put it to a subordinate: "Ginny, I know we've been having [*not* "I've been taking you to"] lunch together on your birthday for the past few years. But I must confess I have the feeling that it's become kind of routine. I guess I've been getting older, too, but I just can't bring the fresh spirit to the occasion that I used to. But I do wish you the happiest of birthdays—and I don't care who knows it. . . ."

• *Provide a substitute.* If you've been giving gifts, you can tell the recipient you'd like to take him or her to lunch. If it's been an after-hours drink, you can make it lunch or a small gift. Any change will have the virtue of breaking what has come to be a meaningless, repetitive act.

• *End on an upbeat.* An executive had been giving a clerk in the shipping department a cash gift of twenty-five dollars each Christmas. It had started when the clerk had three or four times during the year wrapped or shipped personal parcels. But for the past two years the executive had not asked for such favors and yet had felt impelled to maintain the gift-giving practice. But in the third year the illogicality of the act became clear. And so the executive gave the clerk the usual envelope with the twenty-five dollars, and a box of the man's favorite cigars. And he added an oral message: "Tom, I certainly appreciate your help in the past. You've been great. But things have changed, I haven't had to impose on you, so I want to show my gratitude this last time. . . ."

This is one situation where your own feelings are likely to be much more sensitive than the other person's. Just remember that the pressure on you in discontinuing arises from your own embarrassment or fear that the other person might resent your action, rather than from any other source. Recipients are likely to be both under-standing and realistic.

GIFTS FOR FAILURE

Happy events—a promotion, the achievement of some major work objectives—are traditional and welcome occasions for giving gifts. However, people do have failures, both in life and in business. The recognition of such situations makes it possible to demonstrate an empathy that can be particularly effective and gracious. Note this example:

Rose Taylor's boss is an avid sailboat racer. All through spring and summer, he keeps her informed of his progress in the regattas held at the yacht club of which he is a member. He's sailing a hot boat and is very competitive. Then comes the big race of the season, which he enters. He places poorly, fourth in a field of ten. He's quite depressed. Shortly thereafter, he comes into the office to find on his desk a silver plate, a gift from his staff, on which Rose has had en-graved:

> . . . the race is not to the swift
> nor the battle to the strong . . .
> but time and chance happeneth to them all.

The impulse to give a gift, some small token of esteem, needs not so much an occasion as a sentiment to be expressed. Alice, of Won-derland fame, devised the Un-Birthday. As Lewis Carroll pointed out, you can give only one birthday present a year, but there are 364 occasions for an *unbirthday* present. While gifts are usually given for accomplishment, you can give a gift that recognizes persistence or a hard-fought battle, even if it did not end in success.

GIFTS AS AN APOLOGY

An oversight, a misunderstanding, an unintended hurt may call for an apology. Usually one thinks of such an expression of regret as being either oral or written—and you'll find the act of apology cov-ered in Chapters 1 and 2.

However, there is a third way to express one's regrets, and this is by means of a gift. Usually such a gift is given in connection with a verbal apology. Here are some possibilities:

• *Saying it with flowers.* Gary Loomis, head of one of the departments of the Lane Company, has an argument with Lois Adalon during a staff meeting: "You don't know what you're talking about," he asserts hotly, after a remark by Adalon. "You haven't been around long enough to really understand . . ." (referring, in part, to her recent ascent to supervisory ranks). After the meeting he's surprised to have his boss tell him that his remarks were poorly worded and quite out of line. "You owe Lois an apology," he's told. When he recounts the incident to his wife, she suggests that in addition to the note he plans to write, he send a small bouquet of flowers. He acts on the suggestion, and when Adalon calls to thank him, he has the feeling that his regrets have been fully accepted.

• *Dinner for two.* The personnel director of a publishing company invites all the secretaries from one of the departments to a business lunch. To her chagrin, she realizes that due to an oversight she has failed to ask one of the group—who just happened to be out the day the invitations were extended. She explains the reason for the slip and says, "Jane, I've arranged for you to have dinner at Whitby's at company expense. The arrangement is for two, and you can make it anytime you like. . . ."

The purpose of the gift, as an adjunct to the verbal apology, is to emphasize the giver's concern and sincerity. There are many token gifts that are appropriate for this situation, of which the two examples are suggestive. The lists of gifts at the end of this section provide other possibilities.

One additional point about gifts as an apology: they should *not* be given when there is some doubt as to whether the apology itself will be accepted. In such a case, they seem to take on the appearance of a bribe.

GROUP GIFTS

Group gift-giving is a tradition in organization life. As a matter of fact, it has become the subject of endless jokes and cartoons: "If there's one more birthday or engagement in the department, I'll be broke for the rest of the week." "Of course Miss Smith can't get her work done. She's much too busy collecting for the boss's birthday, two people who are retiring soon, and Helen's baby shower." The person who is in charge of a department or organization unit has the management responsibility for keeping collections for gifts within reasonable limits.

However, gift-giving does have a role in organization life: creating a climate, heightening morale and pleasure. Therefore, as a manager, you may find yourself in a situation where instead of limiting group collections you want to see that special ones are not overlooked. In other words, if you're aware of a gift-giving occasion coming up that you feel your staff would recognize, you may want to discuss the occasion with two or three of your key people and get one of them to start a collection going.

Whatever you do, take precautions to guarantee that the matter is handled properly. It may not be enough just to get a volunteer to collect the funds. In some cases there are a number of other elements involved:

A SELECTION COMMITTEE? If someone in the department is to be married, for example, the range of possible gifts can be very wide. Should the gift be something utilitarian, like a kitchen appliance? Should it be decorative, like a glass bowl or vase?

Obviously, there is no absolute scale of values for making such judgments. All kinds of variables have to be taken into account, such as the money variable, the tastes and the values of the recipient, and so on. The point is, whatever is done will require judgment. The decision may be put into the hands of one person—preferably one who is in a position to judge what the recipient will really approve —or you may even want to appoint a committee. Whatever approach is used, clearly the result will be happier if the selection is not rushed.

Finally, unlike an individual gift, group gift-giving generally calls for some kind of ceremonial presentation. This calls for special and separate consideration. . . .

PRESENTING THE GIFT

Generally, when a group has chipped in for the purchase of a gift, the contributors would like the satisfaction of seeing it presented. These presentation ceremonies for the most part are very simple, but they also can be quite elaborate, depending upon the occasion. For example, when a top executive retires from a company, it may be sufficiently noteworthy to call for an ambitious ceremony. The details for such an occasion are covered in Chapter 2 on pages 39–40. In our present context, we're talking only about a presentation of modest proportions.

For ordinary purposes, then, here are the things that must be prepared:

PLACE. Usually the departmental area itself is adequate. In some cases there is available a conference room, lunchroom, or other recreation area that may be somewhat more festive.

TIME. A favorite time setting is toward the end of the day, perhaps at quitting time if the presentation will be brief, or a little before quitting time if it may run on for a while. In addition to the circumstances of work, of course, the convenience of the attendees should be taken into account. For example, if a top executive has been invited to attend as a special guest, his availability may have to be a prime consideration.

FOOD AND DRINK? If the person in charge so desires—and this will depend on judgment as to what's appropriate—the presentation may be made without benefit of anything edible or potable. But starting from nothing to eat or drink, the choices may range anywhere from cake, cookies, and soda pop, to beer and pretzels, to a full range of alcoholic beverages with canapés and possibly a buffet. This takes planning and a firm budget.

THE PRESENTATION SPEECH. Someone should be designated to make the actual presentation of the gift. It should be someone of prominence in the group, and the recipient's boss is a natural choice. However, there are alternatives. The person who bought the gift, for example, may be recommended for the presenter's role for the same reasons that qualified him or her to select the gift. Or a special friend in the work group may warrant the assignment. Whoever is selected should be notified well enough in advance to be able to compose the "speech," whether brief or otherwise.

THE SPEECH. There are certain shining virtues for the words that precede the actual giving of the gift. One is brevity. Since the occasion is obviously one not suited to long-windedness, usually the shorter the better. There is one exception. If there is a person who is sufficiently well-spoken and witty who can add to the occasion by his humor and warmth, certainly the opportunity should be taken.

"THANK YOU." The recipient should be given an opportunity to respond to the presentation, even if it's just a brief expression of gratitude. The choice is entirely the recipient's. A final question that sometimes arises:

SHOULD THE GIFT BE OPENED? The answer almost always is "Yes." Usually the only person who has seen the gift is the person or people who have selected it. Since many other people in the room will have contributed, they have a natural interest in seeing what's been selected.

Of course, the gift is not always physically presented. Sometimes a delay in delivery interferes. In other cases the gift itself may be of such an unwieldy shape or size that it's a kindness to have it sent directly to the home of the recipient.

In such cases the presenter simply announces what the gift is, tries in a sentence or two to describe it to the satisfaction of the group.

Otherwise, it's traditional for the recipient to untie the ribbons and bows, remove the wrappings from the gift to the assorted oohs and ahs of the group so that all can share the surprise.

MONEY, FLOWERS, AND CANDY

Some kinds of gifts are given so generally and frequently that they deserve special consideration. You may want to consider these—three in number—at the beginning of a gift selection, or at the end, when an examination of an interminable list of items from an antique Japanese fan to an Art Deco lamp and a blur of things in between has left you groggy.

MONEY. It can be just the thing. It's always the right color, it has great utility, and you can be sure it will never end up in someone's white elephant sale. However, it has drawbacks:

• *It's impersonal.* Whatever other qualities it has, it lacks the one that will show the recipient you understand his or her taste and have combed the marketplace to get just the thing that rings the bell.

• *Ten bucks is ten bucks.* There's no disguising the actual worth of the gift. It is what it is. Money does run into a "price" problem. The color may be just the right shade of green, but unless the amount you're giving is really adequate, it may seem like a paltry present. You have to gauge the recipient, his or her tastes and expectations. If the office gang can chip in a large amount for an about-to-be-married colleague—plus a small token or gag present—the cash may be the ideal gift. Weigh the person and the occasion against the dollar figure to see whether money is your best bet.

FLOWERS. For many people, the most thoughtful gift is a colorful arrangement of flowers—especially if funds are limited. And for certain occasions and from particular donors—boss to secretary, for example—these make a most acceptable recognition. However, there is another consideration: in these days of heightened sensitivity on the part of some women to female-role stereotypes, flowers may seem to be a "sexist" gift. "Would you give flowers to a man in my position?" a recipient might ask, and resent the gift and the flowers if the answer were negative. However, these days liberated men might also consider flowers as a suitable gift for an anniversary. And some people like to give flowers as a partial gift and follow it by something else—a table radio, a book, and so on.

And, of course, there are flowers and there are flowers. A single blossom—usually a rose is chosen for such a gift—can be as effective as a horseshoe arrangement. You must gauge the occasion, the recipient, and the sentiment you want to express.

Traditionally, florists have claimed there is a "language of flowers." For example, red roses are supposed to express love, daisies innocence, dahlias pomp, violets modesty, and zinnias thoughts of an absent friend. These associations have been largely discarded. What remains, however, is a sense of taste that suggests that flowers do have individual feeling. Some, like daisies, are bright and cheerful, orchids are exotic, roses feminine. These qualities make certain flowers more appropriate than others in given situations. For example, you'd send daisies or a similar bloom to a hospital patient rather than orchids. And if you did want to send flowers to a man, chrysanthemums rather than roses would make the better choice.

And then, just to move a slight distance into an adjoining area, there are plants, potted simply or elegantly, and in great variety.

CANDY. Although dieting and weight-watching have reached great prominence in today's culture, candy continues to be popular as a gift. In considering candy as a possible gift, a few guidelines:

• *Individual taste.* Try to learn the recipient's preference. Some people love sweet chocolate, others prefer it less so. Some like milk chocolate, others like it dark. And as for the filling, maraschino cherries delight some people as the ultimate taste sensation, others won't touch them. And, of course, there are dozens of other types. When in doubt, get an assortment.

• *Cost.* Most boxed candy can be purchased inexpensively, which is fine if that's what you have in mind. But some manufacturers put out de luxe chocolates in supremely elegant packages that can be a smashing gift—for the right person. But we're talking now of the difference between a five-dollar gift and one at fifty dollars.

• *Diet.* Candy is a proscribed item for some people for health reasons. It's a knockout factor not to be overlooked.

Just in case you think the rules of business etiquette have pared your choices down to an unimaginative few, the following lists will dispel your fears.

Check the basic guidelines set out in this chapter first and then browse through the possibilities for an appropriate item. Gift-giving will never be a problem again!

ITEMS OF USE IN THE OFFICE

DESKTOP GIFTS

ashtray
clock—electric or otherwise

desk-blotter holder (leather)
desk calendar
desk lamp
desktop gimmicks (they abound in specialty shops—anything
 from an "executive timer," which is a small hourglass, to an
 "executive pushbutton," which activates nothing)
desktop thermometer
dispenser of 3 x 5-inch scratch paper
holder for pencils
letter opener (these can be elegant)
paperclip holder or dispenser
paperweight
pen, pencil, and stand
radio
small sculpture
standing picture frame or frames
TV—miniscreen-size
work-organizer—a gadget with pockets for various categories of
 papers and so on

OFFICE WALL DECORATION

antique rifle
antique saber or sword (pair)
art photo (according to special interest—yachting, sports, rural
 landscape, urban landscape, industrial scene)
curio (African mask, and so on)
picture, framed print
wood or bronze plaque—commemorating a particular achievement
woven material—small tapestry, wall rug, unusual woven fabric
an item made up of donee's special-interest object—anything
 from a framed copy of his first order (sales executive) to a
 framed copy of a business or professional group's citation or
 award)

FREE-STANDING ITEMS FOR THE OFFICE

bookends
coffee maker
desk chair (particularly where a good one can offset a back problem)
items inside a display case—collections of coins, antique dolls, and
 so on

lounge chair
models—ships, trains
piece of sculpture—in keeping with the general office decor
plants—they come in all sizes, colors, varieties, including those
that hang
special piece of furniture—coffee table, occasional table
vase or urn—for flowers or other uses

EXECUTIVE "TOOLS"

attaché case—of appropriate size and shape for the donee
calculating machine
dictating machine (pocket size or deskside models)
minicalculator
pocket notebook (possibly combined with leather wallet)

FOOD AND DRINK

brandy
candy
cheese
fruit-of-the-month
jellies and jams
specialty foods—caviar, gourmet cocktail snacks, ice-packed seafood (clams, lobsters, and so on), prime beefsteak
liquor
wine

KITCHEN ITEMS

HOUSEWARES

bar tools—for those who entertain a lot
dishes—service for four, six, eight, twelve; individual pieces (plat-
ters, pitchers)
cooking utensils—apron (not a utensil, but . . .); carving or other
knives; pads; pots, pans, coffee maker; spoons, scoops, ladles
cutlery, dining utensils—special patterns, materials
food mixer
mixing bowls
pepper and salt shakers

punch bowl and glasses, ladle
spice racks and dispensers
steak knives
trivets, tiles

LINENS

bathroom towels
kitchen towels
sheets and pillowcases
tablecloths, napkins

GLASS AND CRYSTAL

cut-glass pitchers, serving dishes, and so on
figurines
handdecorated plates
vases
wineglasses, tumblers, and so on

RUN BY ELECTRICITY

can opener
corn popper
electric knife
electric pot, pan, hot plate, coffeepot
food slicer
rotisserie
toaster
waffle maker

MISCELLANEOUS HOUSEHOLD ITEMS

CERAMICS

bowl
cups and saucers
pitcher
plates
pots (for cooking)
trivet
vase

PICNIC AND PATIO

apron
garden tools
gloves
hibachi
lawn mower
outdoor furniture
portable, movable grill
skewers

MAJOR APPLIANCES (This type of gift might be given to colleagues starting up a new household)

clothes dryer
deep freeze
dishwasher
radio
refrigerator
vacuum cleaner
washing machine

LAMPS

floor
special conversation items (ship's lantern, and so on)
table
wall

SPECIAL-INTEREST ITEMS

OPTICAL GOODS

binoculars—field glasses, opera glasses
camera and related equipment—lenses, carrying case
instant-picture camera
movie camera and projector
slide projector
sunglasses
telescope

BOOKS

art book
Bible

book of photographs
cookbook
current bestseller
dictionary
encyclopedia
first or rare edition
leatherbound classic—single volumes, sets
poetry
special interest of donee—hobby (anything from stamp collecting
　　to antiques), crafts (how to make, how to build), and so on

ART

etching
lithograph
oil painting
membership in a local museum
pencil, charcoal sketch
print
reproduction
seriograph
shadowbox item
wallhanging collage, montage
watercolor

SCULPTURE

copy of classic
copy of contemporary work
mask
original by local artist and so on
primitive—Eskimo, African, and so on

MUSIC

records—from the latest popular recording to a ten-disc full-
　　length opera—vocal, orchestral, instrumental, show music, spe-
　　cialty records, and so on

FUN AND GAMES

backgammon
bridge accessories—cards, card holders, scoring pads, table and
　　chairs
checkers—pieces and board

chess—pieces and board, in almost limitless design
executive "toys"
jigsaw puzzles
Monopoly and similar board games
playing cards—poker, pinochle, bridge
poker table
pool table

ANTIQUES

For people who are especially interested, there are a million and
one items ranging from a milk bottle, circa 1890, to a
Stradivarius violin.

LUGGAGE (Styles, colors, and materials cover a wide range from
the utilitarian to the ultrasmart. The trick is to match the recipient's
tastes)

attaché case
borsetta (man's pocketbook)
overnight bag
over-the-shoulder bag (man's or woman's)
suitcases—all sizes
trunk or chest
vanity case

SPORTING GOODS

There are countless games, and a mystique and array of equipment for each. The list below is just by way of example:

bicycles—including folding models
boots—hiking, skiing, hunting, riding
decoys—water and land
fishing gear
golf—clubs, balls, club carrier, cart, and so on
model boats
picnicking items—many choices, from complete basket with
    utensils to ice chest, chairs, tables, and so on
ski equipment—skis, boots, clothing—before, during, and après
tennis—rackets, balls, clothing
water sports—everything from surfboards to diving equipment

SPECIALS

a gift made for the recipient, anything from a table lamp to a
 beach robe
company's product—in a special version or mounted in a unique
 way for a top executive—the desk used the first day on the job
 (probably to be hauled out of the warehouse and cleaned up)
handmade afghan
old photos of the recipient at work
other mementos of his or her early days on the job
painting commissioned for an occasion—portrait, recipient's
 house
photo portrait
wall hanging—crocheted, knitted, woven, and so on
gift certificate

ELECTRONIC AND ELECTRIC ITEMS

COMBINATIONS

radio-phonograph
radio–phonograph–tape recorder
tape decks or recorders

HI-FI

Complete systems or components—speakers and so on

RADIO

console
portable
special shapes—from "telephones" to hanging spheres
table model

TV

black-and-white
color
console
portable

VIDEOTAPE

playback monitor
video camera

PERSONAL GIFTS

Men

CLOTHING

boots
gloves
handkerchiefs
jeans
muffler
necktie
shirt—dress, sport
shoes
sox
sports coat (sheepskin, and so on)
sports jacket
sweater

ACCESSORIES

belt
borsetta
over-the-shoulder carrier—bag
wallet

JEWELRY

cuff links
money clip
neck decoration, pendant
ring
tie clasp or pin
watch—wrist or pocket

TOILETRIES

after-shave lotion
electric shaver
razor
shaving kit
travel kit—combination for shaving, powders, lotions, and so on

FOR SMOKERS

ashtray
cigars

cigar holder
cigar trimmer
cigarettes—by the carton, exotic brands, and so on
cigarette holder
cigarette lighter
pipes—in many shapes and materials, but smokers have shape
    preferences
pipe cleaners and reamers
tobacco

Women

CLOTHING

belt
blouse
boots
handkerchiefs
raincoat
scarf
skirt
sports coat (sheepskin, and so on)

ACCESSORIES

belt
handbag
over-the-shoulder bag
wallet, purse

JEWELRY

bracelet
cuff links
earrings
necklace
pendant
pin, brooch
ring
watch

TOILETRIES

bath soap
cologne

perfume
toilet water
combinations—including body powder, bath salts, and so on

A GIFT OF SERVICES

Usually we think of things or objects when we think of gifts. But there are services we can give that are less frequently thought of but may be all the more welcome because they are unusual. The following list is meant merely to be suggestive, since this category is in a way so vast—the child strapped for cash gives his mother "six trips down to the supermarket" for Christmas, for example. A gift of services can be particularly apt and welcome when it's imaginative and satisfies a special need or desire of the recipient. As we said, the following brief list is meant only to be suggestive:

theater tickets
tickets to a concert, opera
diaper service (for a mother-to-be)
a trip—with spouse?
weekend at a name hotel
limousine service—for an occasion, day, week
tickets to a sporting event—ballgame, hockey, basketball, and so
on

9

Dining: Deskside to Company Picnic

WHEN FOOD AND BUSINESS MIX

The dining table is almost as common a place to do business as the office. In some industries—publishing, for example—the business lunch at which editors and authors discuss everything from book ideas to book jackets is traditional.

Of course, eating incorporated into business-related matters does not confine itself to the three normal meals of the day. After-hours cocktails and canapés are a common way of marking a business event—retirement, promotion, and so on. And nights on the town are a way of entertaining customers that involves not only a restaurant but everything from a supper club to after-theater pub-crawling.

On all occasions in which meals and business mix, there are many situations in which plans must be laid, choices made, protocol and people's expectations given consideration. This section deals with situations you should know about that require special attention.

Some of the do's and don't's are fairly obvious. For example, it's not generally desirable to entertain a good customer in the local diner. At the same time, that same good customer might have difficulty hiding his fretfulness if he were taken to an elegant restaurant when his main interest was to grab a fast snack and get out to the airport. As usual, *it all depends,* as Alice observed so wisely in Wonderland.

DESKSIDE DINING

Whether it's the rising prices at restaurants or the pressure of business, an increasing number of people find themselves eating lunch at their desks these days. This practice raises questions of both etiquette and efficiency:

• *Is deskside dining proper?* One executive says, "I wouldn't use my living room at home to wash in. Why should I eat in my office?" This is a minority view, but certainly for people with such feelings, deskside dining should be ruled out. However, in general, it can be said that eating at one's work place is a perfectly acceptable practice as long as certain abuses are avoided. For example:

• *Does it look bad?* "I don't think a top executive eating a sandwich at the desk does himself or herself any good," says one dim-view-taker. Occasionally you'll find an individual who feels that eating at one's desk somehow lowers one's status. But this is seldom the case. As a matter of fact, the manager eating at the desk creates an atmosphere of dedication to the work—of which he or she seems to have just a little more than a fair share—an appearance that would work to one's advantage rather than otherwise.

• *Does it smell bad?* An executive asks his secretary to heat a stew on the office hot plate that was ordered earlier from a neighborhood restaurant. The entire room soon fills with an onion odor that is not only disconcerting in the business setting but hard to take for individuals with a particular aversion to onions. Clearly, then, one must avoid foods that might assault the olfactory organs of others.

• *Does it sound bad?* Some people like to listen to music or the news while eating. If one's office is acoustically insulated—for example, if a closed door successfully bottles up the sound—fine. But otherwise, co-workers shouldn't be bothered by radio programs that go fine with the diner's lunch but badly with others' work.

• *Does it create an unwelcome chore?* If the diner himself or herself prepares the lunch and cleans up, there is no problem. Too often the burden falls on a subordinate, particularly a female secretary. These days, with greater awareness of the undesirability of converting a co-worker into a housewife, the traditional practice of having the secretary order the lunch, serve it, and then clean up afterward should be appraised. Even if a subordinate is willing, you may properly decide it is a service that shouldn't be asked. And don't be guided altogether by the past. Even where this kind of duty has been accepted for years, it's quite possible that changing times and attitudes will mean that a subordinate called on for these chores would now rather not do them.

INSIDE VERSUS OUTSIDE DINING

Far from producing indigestion or ulcers, many people find deskside dining affords serenity, time-saving, smaller cash outlay, and less food intake. And some, because it creates a relaxed atmosphere, combine a deskside lunch with small group meetings with colleagues.

As far as the menu itself is concerned, there need be little limitation. Most restaurants have an outgoing-order service, and where the competition is strong, eating places tend to vie with each other to do a good job. Hot dishes are insulated and, incredibly, arrive hot. Salad plates are made up as attractively for the outside as for the inside customer.

However, outside dining, aside from a greater range of menu choices, does provide a break in the workday and takes you out into the fresh air.

DESKSIDE DINING WITH A GUEST

You may have a visitor in your office when lunchtime comes around and may wonder about the pros and cons of inside versus outside dining should you want to extend a lunch invitation. Or sometimes you have a lunch date with a colleague or visitor. Is a meal at deskside desirable? Again there is a minority view, summed up by one executive: "Having someone in for lunch in your office makes you look like a cheapskate." This suggests that a meal at the desk is somewhat insulting to the status of the visitor.

Few people hold this opinion, but there are advantages and disadvantages to playing host at a deskside meal.

A top-heavy schedule for either host or guest suggests the time lost getting to a restaurant and the usual delays encountered there make the convenience of lunch in the office outweigh other considerations. As far as the quality of the food itself is concerned, given the choice available at most restaurants that send food out, you should have no trouble finding something to a guest's taste. And, finally, there is a decided virtue in the relaxed atmosphere and the informality of eating at your desk. In some cases executives have found a new level of communication—one that is friendlier and more open—possible as a result of the informality of the situation.

However, if you want to underscore the esteem in which a visitor is held, a restaurant, particularly one that is attractive and offers fine cuisine, makes the point. You have the opportunity to be the generous and considerate host in a way that is not otherwise possible. If you feel these qualities are more suited to your relationship with a guest than the informality of the office, the restaurant locale is the one for you.

PEOPLE YOU MAY NOT EAT WITH

In these days of relative social freedom, it may seem old-fashioned to even consider the idea that it would be *verboten* to be seen in public with some particular person. While this may be true in general, in specific instances other than *general* considerations may be involved. For example, in a given case, company tradition and practice may be a factor you should consider. At any rate, here are some of the combinations of people that, in some cases, are inadvisable to be seen together in a public eating place. You may deplore the chintziness that such prohibition suggests, but to avoid making people feel uncomfortable and the possibility of an undesirable aftermath, these questionable pairings are worth weighing in the balance:

A BOSS AND SECRETARY. It may be a male boss and a female secretary or vice versa. In some milieus such a pair would represent no problem. In other cases it would occasion considerable talk and would lead to complications. We're not saying don't have lunch with your boss or don't have lunch with your secretary. We are saying if you're contemplating doing so, give a moment's thought to whether this might not be unacceptable behavior in your particular circumstance and milieu.

PURCHASING AGENT AND SALESMAN. Here again there's no intention of asserting any prohibition. The fact is, in many cases salesmen customarily take the buyers of customer companies out to lunch or dinner. Just make sure in your case that policy or tradition does not frown on the practice.

"BIG BOSS" AND "LITTLE EMPLOYEE." Contrary to general opinion, people in the upper echelons can't do as "they damn please." This isn't because they don't have authority or status. On the contrary, because of their authority and status, being seen in a public restaurant with a lower-echelon employee might create problems, not for the executive but for the worker. Rightly or wrongly, the employee might be kidded, resented, and possibly even harassed—in certain situations. If you're a top executive and feel in some expansive moment that you would like to have lunch with that interesting young college graduate who works in the shipping department, just make sure that the result of your best intentions won't have undesirable consequences for your young dining companion.

Just in case you think that cautions about public dining are unnecessary, consider a recent news item. In one small town a middle-management executive was recently fired because he was seen dating (that is, having dinner with) a young female colleague. The reason for management's anger: the man's wife had died just six weeks previously, and company officials felt his behavior represented callousness and irresponsibility.

HOW TO PICK A RESTAURANT

Business lunches are of all kinds. Therefore, there is no such thing as *a* proper dining place. In making a selection, what you're after are surroundings appropriate to the kind of business meal you're having. Here are some of the considerations that can lead you to make the best possible choice:

DEGREE OF ELEGANCE. Consider the nature of the meal you have in mind. If you and your guest—let's say it's a customer—agree that all you want is a fast lunch so you can get back to the office, a local bistro that serves edible food quickly may be just the thing. On the other hand, if you are taking your staff out for a celebration lunch, the occasion is best honored by a place of some elegance. And one, incidentally, that will give you a table that will seat your group comfortably.

In some cases your aim may be to impress your guest as well as to show your high regard. Such occasions may call for a name restaurant, one known for its cuisine, and so on. Every big city has half a dozen such places. Even small towns have one or two eating places that are highly regarded, or at least that people consider the best. You select these under the circumstances mentioned—where your purpose is not merely to ingest food but to eat in style.

CONVENIENCE. Another consideration has to do with the comfort aspects of your choice. One such factor: the ease of getting to the restaurant. If two restaurants of approximately equal appeal are available and one is across the street and the other across town, the closer is clearly a wiser choice.

Another aspect of comfort has to do with the material aspects of the table available to you. Two physical considerations here: one is its location. Everyone tries to avoid the table near the swinging doors to the kitchen, for example, or out of the main flow of traffic. Another point: what's the noise level in the restaurant? Particularly if the space around the tables is small, any attempt to have a serious discussion of business matters is likely to fail if you are surrounded by other diners. Your own conversation then is bound to be blended with theirs, interfering with audibility. Results in such a situation are almost always irritation and frustration.

The obvious way to avoid such an annoyance is not only to pick the restaurant in which this is not likely to happen but also to make a reservation well in advance so that either you can specify the table you would like to have or make it clear to the person taking your reservation that you want a table sufficiently secluded to make easy conversation possible. If you're talking business and tables are too close to others, it might be embarrassing if someone you know or even a competitor is sitting nearby.

COST. In some cases the price of the meal may literally not be a consideration. If it is, it's unwise to take your guest to a restaurant whose price ranges you don't know. You want to avoid creating the situation in which you're handed a menu on which the prices indicated are so much higher than you intended to pay that it influences your food choices or makes you anxious about the price of the items your guest will order.

ORDERING

Is there any problem about what you order? Why should there be? Presumably, whether you're ordering a sandwich and coffee to be sent in or selecting dishes from a sumptuous menu, you just pick what you feel like eating and drinking. Right? Well . . . not necessarily.

Here are some of the complications that may require you give special consideration to the food-and-beverage selection process:

• *Should you try to match the other person's drinking habits?* Whether you're host or guest, it can be a problem. For example:

Peter Paul is taking Hank Billings, a supplier's service engineer, to lunch. The waiter approaches: "Anything from the bar, gentlemen?"

Billings says, "I'd like Scotch on the rocks."

Paul would rather not drink, but when the waiter turns to him he says, "Tomato juice, please." He explains to Billings, "I'm drying out a bit this week," and the conversation turns to other things.

Paul's behavior has been exemplary. First, he's not left Billings to drink alone. And second, his light remark explaining his nonalcoholic beverage order cancels out any suggestion that he disapproves of Billings's drinking habits.

Here's another situation that may develop (since we've got Paul and Billings comfortably settled at their table, let's continue to use them to dramatize our problem):

Again the waiter approaches: "Drinks, gentlemen?" Host Peter Paul turns inquiringly to Hank Billings. Billings, in this case, can either take it or leave it, so he says, "I will if you will." Good tactic. This leaves the drink–no drink decision with the host.

Here's a slight variation: Billings says, "I'll pass it up today." Then Paul has to make a decision. If he decides he doesn't care for a prelunch cocktail, either, there's no problem. But if he wants one, the conversation might go like this: "Mind if I have one, Hank?" Billings is most likely to say, "Of course not." Paul may then say, "Would you like anything—soda or tomato juice?"

Needless to say, if one or the other diner knows that his companion has what's referred to as a drinking problem, it's desirable that he not order a drink. People who have had difficulties with alcohol and have solved them are usually prepared to meet the drink-at-meals situation by ordering a nonalcoholic beverage. (For more on the drinking problem in general, see "Drinking," pages 267–273 in Chapter 6.)

• *The appetizer problem.* If you order the businessman's lunch or other table d'hôte meal, the question of an appetizer is simple. If it's part of the fixed-price meal, you simply have to decide whether you feel up to it or not. But if you're ordering à la carte, several considerations arise:

If the other person orders an appetizer, should you? Answer: Yes, just for the sake of making the lunch a more equally shared experience. This may seem like a pretty esoteric reason for a somewhat mundane activity. But when one person orders an appetizer and the other doesn't, an awkward moment or two arises as the eater is engaged and the other person must mark time. And sometimes a waiter will serve the main course to one diner while the other is tackling a fruit cup or pâté—another way in which diners may get out of phase. (Of course, it's not suggested that if you have an antipathy to appetizers in general or nothing on the menu interests you, you should force yourself.)

Two other considerations—both suggesting that at lunch, which many people consider a sparse meal, having a course before the entrée would seem like overindulgence:

COST. These days, the price of an appetizer is sometimes as much as an entire meal one or two decades back.

OVEREATING. Having a big lunch may seem like self-pampering —and so, not too attractive.

ONE-UPMANSHIP AT TABLESIDE

"I hate it," says one executive, "when some business contact gives me the gourmet bit."

What he's getting at is the practice some people make of going beyond casual ordering. For example, George Smith orders a martini and adds half a dozen sentences that specify the brand of gin, the amount and brand of vermouth, and what the temperature should be—usually, "Very cold."

The same judiciousness may be used in ordering anything from the salad dressing to the ingredients of the bouillabaisse. Should one, or shouldn't one?

The answer is: If you're ordering and you have particular tastes, give the instructions that will get you what you want. However, the person who is tempted to do this to show off his or her sophistication might consider trying to make an impression by other, more meaningful means.

If you're the host, it is desirable that you aid and abet your companion, making it clear that you want him or her to be completely satisfied.

WHEN THE MEAL IS A TEST

In some cases the dining situation is used as a kind of proving ground. The guest—often a job applicant—is not only being taken out to dine. His or her behavior is being carefully noted and evaluated to add an additional dimension to previous interviews and other kinds of assessments.

Such tactics are usually used only for upper-echelon jobs or those in which the applicant is being considered for a job that involves frequent contact with customers or other outside people. In these cases an individual's conduct at the dining table is not irrelevant and does provide some basis for judging general deportment and social behavior as well as what is generally thought of as "table manners." If you're the person on the spot, here are some of the considerations to be made:

REMEMBER YOU'RE THE GUEST. This simply means that you more or less let the host set the tone of the meeting, everything from choosing the dining place to creating the conversational climate— which may be anything from jolly and jovial to pleasant and relaxed.

BUT DON'T HESITATE TO BE YOUR OWN PERSON. As a matter of fact, your degree of self-assertiveness will probably be one of the points on which you're judged. Certainly don't feel you have to go along with your host at every turn. If he orders a martini and that's your taste, by all means: "Make it two, please." But if you prefer a glass of wine, beer, or water, say so.

Since you're being weighed in the balance, you should know the kinds of cues and clues the assessor will be looking for:

• *How much to drink.* Unless the ability to put down three double Scotches is a requirement of the job you're angling for, keep your drinking within modest limits, even if your host imbibes freely and urges you to do likewise.

• *How hard to hit the menu.* It's also inadvisable for the person in this situation to order everything in sight. If there's an appetizer you're particularly fond of, no reason not to ask for it: "I'm very fond of oysters and I see they have them on the menu. If you don't mind, I'd like to order them as an appetizer."

As your eye roves over the entrées, you won't be able to avoid the common question: "Should I let my choice by affected by the price?" A lunch menu may offer eggs Benedict, lasagne, or a special broiled lobster that costs twice as much as most other items. Should you have the lobster if it's your favorite? In general, it's recommended that you try to satisfy your appetite with some dish in the middle range. Fairly or otherwise, your host will make assumptions based on your choice. If you pick a simple, inexpensive dish, it suggests an abstemiousness that your host may feel is a questionable virtue for certain types of jobs—such as selling. "Unfair and ridiculous," you may say. "Stereotyping," you may add. All these are true. But you take advantage of the odds by playing the game in this way.

The *amount* of food you eat may also be a judgment factor. Here again we're not talking about fairness but common prejudices. The person who is assessing may find it questionable if the guest, after ordering the full five-course table d'hôte meal, adds to it by ingesting three or four rolls and three glasses or beer.

The one case where the moderation counseled above might be set aside is that in which the host sets a style of eating and drinking and expects you in a spirit of camaraderie to keep pace. If you're so inclined, do so. But make sure to stop at *your* limit.

WHO PAYS?

Usually, when the host and guest roles are clearly defined, the host pays, and that's it. But there are other possible arrangements, of course, and it's helpful to be aware of them both to divide the burden, particularly if the host pays out of his or her own pocket, and to offset the status implications that may result when the guest doesn't share at all in the expense. Here are some alternatives:

• *Going Dutch, or Dutch treat.* Here the expense is shared. There are two possible ways to do this. One is to divide the total of all costs by the number of diners. Another is for each diner to pay for the items he or she has ordered. In this case, where the diner's company will be charged eventually and a bill is necessary, it's highly desirable to tell the waiter *in advance* that you'll want separate checks. It's a lot easier to keep the charges separated at the beginning rather than have the waiter try to go back over the items ordered and to allocate them properly.

• *Items the guest may pay for.* In some cases the guest may like to share the expense, at least in part. Even as a symbolic gesture, it may be appreciated by the host. Accordingly, the guest may offer to:

leave the tip;
pay for the drinks or wine;
tip the person at the hatcheck counter.

PARTICULAR RELATIONSHIPS THAT DETERMINE THE HOST-GUEST ROLES

A so-called business meal may involve two or more people in a wide range of possible relationships. Since it's the relationship between the diners that usually determines who pays, a number of factors must be considered in the decision as to who is the host, who the guest. Some of the relationships are traditional, and the host-guest roles practically predetermined. In other cases, you have to play it by ear:

WHO INVITES WHOM? Usually the person who has suggested the occasion should take on the host role.

WHOSE TURF? Certainly, if a meal is eaten on company premises —either in the company cafeteria or where the food has been ordered from a nearby service to be eaten deskside—the "home" person should pay.

WHO WILL BENEFIT? Amy Miller says to Susan Glenn, "I'm about to start a new project, and I'd like to get your ideas. Do you have about an hour or so to spare in the next few days?" Glenn thinks a moment: "I'm free for lunch tomorrow. How would that be?" Here, even though Glenn has suggested the lunch, presumably the occasion is an assist to Miller. It's up to Miller, then, to *offer* to pick up the tab. Her colleague may suggest sharing the cost. Then it's up to

Miller to accept the counteroffer or to insist on paying, depending on how she assesses her relationship with Glenn. If they are good friends, Glenn would probably not want to be "paid" for her assistance by being treated to the meal. If Miller wants to underline her sense of obligation, she should persist in her resolve to pick up the check.

THE STATUS FACTOR. In some cases, status becomes a major element in answering that sometimes slippery "who-gets-the-bill" question. When a boss takes a subordinate out for a meal, and particularly if it's work-related matters that the conversation centers on, the boss should pay.

There is an exception to this resolution of the question. In some cases the higher-status person may want pointedly to waive the appearance of superior status. If so, he may not want to stick the subordinate with the check, but he may be willing to accept the subordinate's suggestion that they "go Dutch."

In some industries there tends to be an established relationship between common pairs of dining-out people. In publishing, for example, editors and authors often make a lunching twosome. And tradition has it that the editor pays for the meal. The basic assumption is only partly that authors are indigent, and editors, bankrolled by the company treasury, are well heeled. On a somewhat more elevated level is the fact that publishing firms consider author relations as a function that deserves both continuing effort and appropriate expenditures from time to time. Occasionally an author who has struck it rich or who wishes to express particular appreciation to his editor will grab the tab.

THE SALESMAN-CUSTOMER DUO. Salesmen often have an expense account to which entertaining customers is a natural charge— deductible by the company, as a matter of fact, as a business expense. So the salesman will invite a purchasing agent or other influential customer-company representative out for anything from a prestarting-time breakfast to a night on the town. From the guest's point of view, questions may arise: Does company policy permit acceptance of such favors? Even if there is no policy involved, can the individual in clear conscience go along with such goodwill-fostering tactics— particularly if there is no intention to buy from the salesman? But even if the company is a good customer and, indeed, the guest makes or shares in the buying decision, should the salesman's desire to play host be viewed as a form of payola? These are ethical questions, and the invited person must decide for himself or herself whether or not to accept; and if the invitation is accepted, a second choice: to permit the salesman to pay, or to offer to share the bill.

Some executives courted by salesmen feel they may accept an offer to be taken to lunch or dinner, but they like to make it clear that this generosity cannot and will not influence their buying decisions. They justify letting the salesman pay on two grounds: first, there's always the chance that changes may occur that will justify their giving the salesman an order; and second, if the meal talk deals with business matters, there can be some benefit to the salesman in information or ideas that help in his or her selling.

THE JOB-SEEKER. One category of person is almost always an automatic guest in a business-meal situation. This is the person who is job-hunting. The automatic host may be an ex-colleague, an acquaintance who is offering suggestions or leads, or a possible employer. The host may make the check-cadging more gracious by saying something like "I'll pay for this one, Helen, but let's agree that when you get a job, we have a celebration meal that you stand for."

TWO COLLEAGUES. When co-workers dine out together fairly often, the simplest arrangement is to divide the check. The "this-one's-on-me" practice may be all right if the meetings are infrequent. But even here, the "now-it's-my-turn" situation may become confused: Who hosted last time? Will this tab be much more—or less—than the previous one? And so on. Divide and concur.

THE EXPENSE-ACCOUNT SITUATION

Many business lunches are underwritten by the host's organization. This is a business fact of life that involves expense-account living, of which further note will be taken elsewhere (see Chapter 10). The expense account relates to business dining, naturally enough, but the context varies, depending on whether you're host or guest. Here are some of the things that can happen:

• *The host:* "Come on, let's have another drink. The company's paying for it, anyway." This bit of camaraderie is not very amusing as humor, and is seriously detrimental to the host's personal integrity. It's unfortunate if a company representative actually feels this degree of irresponsibility in regard to his or her employer's finances. But to use it as a basis for personal indulgence is inexcusable.

Of course, the host's disregard for company interests may be less blatant but equally clear. Lunch or dinner at a superelegant, superexpensive place when the occasion really doesn't warrant such extravagance is equally revealing of a low level of integrity.

• *The guest.* Any suggestion of the idea "Let's live it up because your company is picking up the tab" is in poor taste and also is bad ethics. Two other acts of a guest get across an undesirable message, without the idea being expressed in 'words:

The guest is asked to suggest an eating place and picks the most expensive spot in town. Unless there's a special reason—the guest may just have placed a ten-million-dollar order with the host's firm—you head firmly for a less costly site for the meal. Then, the guest goes hog wild in ordering. You may tolerate such behavior and say nothing, or show your displeasure: "Is there a famine in your part of the country, Hank?" Not genteel, perhaps, but you don't always have to be.

SUPPORTING TRAVEL-AND-ENTERTAINMENT EXPENSE DEDUCTIONS

Every person in business knows that to support a tax deduction for travel and entertainment expenses, the U.S. Treasury Department requirements are that you have evidence of the amount spent, the time and place, the business purpose and business relationship of the entertainee.

Caution: even though a taxpayer produces a blizzard of bills, chits, and other paper, plus witnesses to prove that sums were spent for valid business purposes, *that's not enough.* To support claims for deductions, what's needed—for each separate expenditure—is evidence of each of the elements of time, place, and so forth.

HOW TO BE A GOOD GUEST

A guest should give consideration to the host's situation. Naturally. This consideration, in practice, involves matters like these:

IF YOU'RE ASKED TO SELECT AN EATING PLACE. If your host is gracious enough to ask you to choose the place, accept if you can. Of course, if you're a stranger in town and don't know the restaurant scene, you may want to beg off on that account. But there's no reason for you not to cater to your own preferences and put your choice conditionally to your hosts: "Do you like seafood [or French cooking, or Greek, Chinese—whatever your taste]? Then how about. . . ."

It's assumed that you try to find out if your host has any attitudes that may influence your choice. For example, if you learn that he or she is a vegetarian, you would want to avoid a steak-and-chops place in favor of one with a varied menu from which a vegetarian-style meal might be selected.

If the occasion is in the evening and it's less a matter of business discussion than one of maintaining a social contact, factors other than food may be involved. You may hanker for a nightclub atmosphere, entertainment, and so on. If your host is like-minded and the cost is not likely to exceed acceptable limits, O.K., you're in for a fun evening. But watch your host's reactions to your suggestion, and if you don't get obvious acceptance, tailor your second choice accordingly.

And if time is short and you have specific matters to discuss, the suggestion "How about having food sent in?" can be most welcome —even though your host, seeking to be hospitable, has implied a desire to dine out.

A considerate guest is as prized as a gracious host. So:

MAKE IT EASY. Show regard for your host's time and convenience. For example, in choosing a restaurant, you may want to suggest one that is equidistant between your location and his or hers so the burden of travel isn't one-sided. And once the place and time are set, arrive promptly. If there must be a delay at your end, have your secretary phone and suggest a change in line with your needs. If the delay comes at the last minute, the call should be made to the restaurant, and a message given to the maitre d' or the manager.

As experienced business diners know, there tends to be an unspoken rapport about wrapping up the occasion. It's rare that one person will linger over the meal while the other pushes to finish. But if there's any question, don't hesitate to ask: "Tom, do you have the time for us to continue our discussion [or to have another cup of coffee, or whatever]?"

EXPRESS YOUR APPRECIATION. If you can say something complimentary about the ambiance, the quality of the food, service, and so on, don't hesitate to do so. And of course "Thanks for lunch"—or whatever—is in order.

HOW TO BE A GOOD HOST

A good—meaning gracious, considerate, possibly generous—host on the business scene shares some of the same virtues that distinguishes the successful host in general. But there are some aspects of the business setting that require additional attention. Here is a list of exemplary elements:

THE GUEST'S WISHES ARE CONSIDERED. His or her time availability and preferences in everything from atmosphere to type of food are inquired into. Even if the host is eager to show off "the newest spot in town," time pressure may suggest a quick visit to the company dining room as most desirable to the guest.

IF POSSIBLE, MAKE THE MEAL AN OCCASION. Business people will tell you: "One of the highlights of my visit was the dinner Mr. James and his wife took me to. Mrs. James learned that I love Creole-style cooking, and they reserved a table at. . . ." And so on.

APPLY THE LIGHT TOUCHES THAT MARK THE THOUGHTFUL HOST. If restaurant dining is involved, some minor but effective bits of behavior can comfort and please the guest:

As you're being seated, you let your guest follow directly behind the maitre d', preceding you.

Ask whether the location of the table is satisfactory.

Give your guest a choice of seats.

Ask what the guest desires from the menu and convey this information to the waiter. If the group is three or more people, the waiter should be permitted to take the orders of each person, the host last.

Suggest specialties of the house if you're familiar with them, inquire as to whether he or she would like wine with the meal, and otherwise show your interest in furthering the guest's enjoyment.

WHOM TO TIP AND HOW MUCH

For some types of dining, you are faced by a large number of service people. While there may be no question about tipping the waiter, there tends to be some confusion as to what should be done with regard to others. The following will help clear some of the fog:

Waiter—15 percent of the bill. Add another 5 percent for unusually good or extra service.

Wine steward—15 percent of the wine bill.

Bartender—If you and your party have had a drink at the bar before the meal, 15 percent of the bill as you leave the bar.

Busboy—no tip.

Checkroom—thirty-five cents for each coat and hat. If you check a parcel or package, add a nickel or dime.

Washroom attendant—a quarter if service is rendered, a towel offered and so on.

Cigarette girl—a quarter or the change left over from a dollar if that is a little more.

Musicians—tip if you or your party requests a number. Two or three dollars. Five dollars if there are two or three players or if more than one number is requested.

Parking attendant—thirty-five cents when your car is brought around.

SHOULD YOU TIP THE HEADWAITER?

Of all the service personnel, the headwaiter usually poses the biggest question mark. Should he be tipped at all? And how much? The same considerations apply, whether the title is headwaiter, hostess acting in that capacity, or maitre d':

Generally, no tip should be given if all the headwaiter has done is to take your reservation and seat you. However, if any special service is rendered—providing a preferred table, cooking or preparing a dish at your table, and so on—from two to five dollars is appropriate, slipped into his hand as you leave. The actual amount depends on the type of restaurant, size of your party, how helpful he has been. In a particularly elegant place, where you've gotten special service ten dollars would be about right.

TIPPERS INTERNATIONAL

In recent years an organization has been formed born out of the discontent and injustices of tipping waiters and workers in restaurant and hotel locales. The organization, Tippers International (P.O. Box 2351, Oshkosh, Wisconsin 54901), was formed to institutionalize common discontents—for example, self-annoyance when one tips an inattentive waiter or waitress or slips a few dollars into the hand of the headwaiter who has done nothing more than look coldly aloof. For a ten-dollar fee, people may join and become a part of the organization's activity. This consists of sending back to TI's headquarters evaluations of hotels, motels, and restaurants that are then broadcast to membership through a monthly newsletter. Both negative and favorable comments are forwarded to the establishments involved. Members are also given yellow complaint cards on which they can register their decided dissatisfaction with service either in lieu of a tip or to explain the small amount that's been left.

Remember that this organization grew out of the resentment experienced by salesmen and traveling executives who routinely add 15 percent to the check for a waiter or waitress and then leave grumbling about the injustice of an undeserved tip.

You don't have to join an organization to register dissatisfaction. But if you're timid, it may help to feel you're part of an organization that will back you up, for the average person's tips should be considered an acknowledgment of services rendered. Where the services have been inadequate, a tip can be pared down; or, for extreme ineptitude, nothing can be left at all.

(For more on gratuities, see "Tipping Within Your Own Organization," pages 430–432.)

A "FAVORITE" RESTAURANT AND MEMBERSHIP DINING

If you or your company does a fair amount of hosting that requires a place for outside dining, it can be very helpful to patronize a local dining place. Of course, it should be one with suitable facilities. Your continuous patronage will get you both the special attention and service that can be everything from a last-minute reservation to the "quiet corner table" that makes for easy conversation and a relaxed atmosphere.

In many towns and cities there are available special dining facilities that are more or less private. These include the college or university club or the private club.

Many university-related facilities have flexible enough prerequisites for joining so that it may not be necessary for you to be an alumnus, just a good, dues-paying contributor.

If you have not already made such an arrangement, it might be worthwhile to have someone in your organization make a brief survey of the kinds of organizations, nature of facilities, and quality of the food service available. A company membership may make it possible for any company representative to use the facilities—including, of course, the restaurant. The club type of dining room usually offers what its name implies—a comfortable, relaxed atmosphere with service people who know the names of most of the "regulars." When you take a guest to such a place, the serenity usually not found in a public restaurant is conducive to business discussions.

One caution: some clubs, in their effort to maintain an appearance of relaxation and noncommercialism, frown on "paper activities" at the table. A polite waiter or manager might discreetly ask the club member who has pulled out a blueprint or a batch of papers not to proceed with such matters in the dining room but to save them for the waiting room outside.

A benefit of being a favored patron at a restaurant or being a club member is that you're known, greeted by name, and so are assured of better than casual treatment. When you and your party are welcomed by a friendly maitre d', the entire occasion rises a notch or two and certainly gets away from the too frequent appearance of disinterest that one finds in ordinary restaurant dining.

MAKING THE RESERVATION

If the meal is to be at a restaurant, it's usually desirable to assure a table at the place of your choice by making a reservation. There's no intention of making a big thing of a minor matter, but it's amazing how an oversight can needlessly confuse matters and ruin what might otherwise be a pleasant occasion. Here are some of the checkpoints to cover:

AGREE ON WHO IS TO MAKE THE RESERVATION. It sometimes happens that each party assumes that the other will make the arrangements. When the time and place for the get-together is agreed on, don't conclude the conversation before either you or the other person says, "I'll take care of reserving a table."

Remember, some restaurants—in high-traffic dining areas—don't take reservations, particularly at lunchtime. If you select such a place and don't want to stand in line, it's best to arrange to meet before the rush starts.

IF POSSIBLE, SPECIFY THE KIND OF TABLE—OR THE LOCATION —YOU WANT. You may be arranging for a lunch meeting for a group of five or six. In addition to making the number of diners clear, you may be able to ask for a private dining room or a table in a corner where your discussion won't be interfered with by others, and vice versa.

LET THE OTHERS KNOW THE NAME IN WHICH THE RESERVATION IS MADE. The person making the reservation may not be the official host—who may be a senior executive, company president, or what have you. In this case, the reservation may properly be made in the name of the top executive. Letting the other diners know this fact in advance will prevent the confusion you sometimes see when a diner asks for "Miss Smith's table" and the maitre d' can't find it because it's Mrs. Jones whose name has been used.

ARRANGE IN ADVANCE FOR ANY SPECIAL SERVICE. If the occasion is a birthday lunch for the boss and you'd like a cake complete with candles—well, perhaps just a small symbolic cake with one candle—ask the manager to prepare the surprise. Most restaurant managements like to supply these touches as a sign of their personalized service. Of course, if you want a large cake, that will be supplied also—a fact you'll find duly noted on the bill.

Special dishes, desserts, beverages—these also may be requested, appropriate to the capabilities of the restaurant staff.

WHEN THE HOST DOESN'T NECESSARILY GUIDE THE CONVERSATION

Business dining involves two major elements: eating and talking. The eating part requires no special consideration here. It's not within the province of this book to inveigh against soup-schlurping or eating with the fingers. The eating, then, will have to take care of itself. But there is an interesting and relevant relationship between the conversation and the host and guest roles.

The point is, despite assumptions to the contrary, the person who guides the discussion does not necessarily pay the piper when the meal is over. This situation becomes clarified when you visualize a group of three or four people having a business lunch. The individual who steers the discussion may be an outsider—not an employee of the X company as the others are. In other words, it is not necessarily a prerogative of the host to control the conversation, and both guest and host should understand this point.

HOW MUCH SHOP TALK?

Should there be any limitation to the amount of time devoted to talking business? Ordinarily, no. Most business people discover that business and dining can mix very well. What's good for business can also be good for the digestion.

The only qualification here is the way in which the invitation has been extended. If it's been suggested that the purpose of the meal is entirely social, then business subjects may seem out of place.

Ordinarily there's no question of the propriety of talking business with business contacts at meals. It may be advisable, however, to acknowledge the social aspects of the situation by interspersing nonbusiness subjects—anything from the latest news sensation to the talk that starts with that old chestnut "Read any good books lately?"

AVOIDING THE CHECK-GRABBING SITUATION

You see check-grabbing in nonbusiness dining, too, but business or otherwise, it's embarrassing, ludicrous, and unnecessary. Here's a typical scene:

Two people have been dining and chatting, and eventually the meal is over and the waiter places the bill on the table. There's a grab for it. Then the altercation starts. The person with the slower reflexes demands that he or she be given the check that the other person is now holding. The one holding the check declares that "It's my treat." Eventually, of course, the flurry dies down, the argument is settled. But has the "right" decision been reached? Is one or the other individual's feelings—and sometimes both—ruffled by what's happened? (The person paying may be a wry victor, annoyed that he or she has been "stuck" with the tab.)

It's wise to forestall this classic contretemps. Here's how it can be done:

• *When the date is made.* The host should make clear his or her acceptance of the role: "I'd like to take you to dinner. . . ." Or: "I'd like you to be my guest. . . ."

• *On approaching the restaurant.* As host and guest are walking to the dining-spot door together, the purported host may say, "Of course, Mr. Greene, you understand that this is my treat. . . ." Then, if Mr. Greene sees it differently, he may argue the statement, but at least the matter can be resolved before they are seated. Remember, sharing the cost—usually splitting it down the middle, regardless of who orders what—is a common method of resolving the problem.

• *When the menus are offered.* When you're looking at the menu, you usually have an idea of the cost to be incurred, and the question of menu choices comes up. It's logical that the question of who is to pay should arise if the question hasn't already been settled. The would-be host may use this appropriate time to say, "Remember, you're my guest," "It's my turn to stand the gaff," or whatever phrase is used to make the offer clearly and firmly.

Finally, if the meal is approaching an end and the "who-is-to-pay" question hasn't yet been settled, the would-be host may then indicate his or her intention to pay. This can be followed up by the host's signaling the waiter for the check.

INVITATIONS TO BE DECLINED

Generally an invitation to a business meal should be accepted. (For exceptions, see earlier, "People You May Not Eat With," page 363.) As has already been made clear, it should be a felicitous occasion, one that can promote rapport and provide an atmosphere conducive to discussion as well as an extension of friendly relationships among people. However, there are some invitations that certainly should not be automatically accepted, and that, as a matter of fact, you may have to refuse:

1. *The "bribe" meal.*

People who make buying decisions are often the target for solicitations that are either subtle or outright means of ingratiation. Within limits, this common business practice is perfectly acceptable. For example:

Hal Boyd has been selling metal wire to purchasing agent Glen Roth for years. Every month or two, Hal takes Glen out to a fairly plush lunch. Glen accepts for several reasons. First, he and Hal devote a large share of their conversation to shop talk. Second, Glen enjoys Hal's company; actually, they're good business friends. And third, Glen's company has no policy that prohibits such fraternizing —or even accepting a "gift" that the lunch might constitute. However, the Boyd-Roth situation can be altered to where the invitation to the meal should *not* be accepted. Here are the factors that change it:

A company rule that forbids acceptance of any kind of gift from suppliers.

An invitation from a salesman to a purchaser when the latter has absolutely no intention of buying. Perhaps one such invitation may be accepted. To continue to accept the largesse—usually offered with the understanding that the salesman is "getting somewhere" with the buyer—is misleading and to some extent taking advantage of the other person.

Of course, this need not be an all-or-nothing situation. An invitation of this kind might be accepted; for example, the prospective customer may have a personal liking for the salesman or be interested in discussing one or another aspects of business. In this case the invitation might be accepted with a "Fine, let's have dinner, but I want it clearly understood that we'll be going Dutch," or some such phrase to suggest equal sharing of the expense.

2. *When you're out of your element.*

In some cases an invitation is extended by a person or a group with whom the invitee has no particular affinity. Sometimes an invitation in this case is made as a courtesy, possibly with the hope that it will *not* be accepted. For example:

"A bunch of the boys" at the office are having dinner out. They've done it two or three times before and had a rollicking good time. When plans are being made, Wally Hayes happens to be within earshot and one of the group says, "How about joining us, Wally?"

Well, Wally is sixty-four, and his idea of solid comfort is to have dinner at home. The average age of the rest of the group is under forty. Wally makes a wise choice: "Tell you what, Bill. I'm tied up tonight, but why don't I join you down at the bar for a drink?"

In your own case, if you feel it's advisable to eschew even Wally's compromise, a simple excuse can get you off the hook.

The situation changes somewhat if the invitation is not impromptu. The excuse "I'm tied up" doesn't suit as well if the invitation is for next week or some later date. In this case the problem becomes one of making an excuse that doesn't seem to reflect unfavorably on the person extending the invitation, or on the occasion itself. Using the Wally example, he might respond to an invitation at a later date: "Frankly, Bill, I think you people are too far out for me. If you don't mind, I'll pass this one up. But why don't you and I have lunch together one day. . . ." Incidentally, change or mix the sex of the people in the example above, and you have exactly the same situation—and the same recommendations for action.

3. *When you don't want to be involved in a political ploy.*

In some cases the invitation may represent a tacit bid for your support of a political group in your organization. If you're aware of this fact and are interested in learning more, obviously the invitation presents you with such an opportunity. If, on the other hand, you don't want to commit yourself, you avoid taking the first step toward such a commitment by refusing the invitation.

4. *When you're being buttered up.*

The salesman-buyer situation is sometimes paralleled within an organization. A colleague may invite you out "as his guest." If you're aware of the nature of the ploy and don't want any part of it, a refusal with some mild put-off excuse can avoid misunderstandings or complications.

5. *When there's confrontation in the air.*

Sometimes the solicitation to the convivial atmosphere of the table may veil an implicit power struggle. Of course, this same kind of array of forces may show up in the conference room or other type of arena. But if you're invited to lunch or dinner and you know from the lineup of other people involved that warfare is intended, you may stay out by turning down the invitation. For example:

Audrey Bell invites Janet Kinney to join her and Sue McDowell at lunch. Janet knows quite well that Bell and McDowell are at loggerheads over a job matter. She knows the question will arise and she'll be expected to side with Audrey Bell. Since she really disagrees with Audrey Bell's viewpoint, she'd rather not be pushed into this confrontation under the guise of a friendly lunch. So she begs off.

DEALING WITH THE "NO-SHOW"

Occasionally one is involved in an appointment contretemps: a person doesn't show up at the agreed-on place and time. It can be a disconcerting experience. The following example suggests some aspects of the problem:

Chuck Gridley is an account executive for an advertising agency. A friend calls and suggests that he get in touch with the director of a small airline. "They're not satisfied with their present agency," the friend says. "You may be able to land the account."

Gridley phones the advertising director, who indicates some interest in switching her firm's business. They agree to a lunch meeting.

Gridley arrives on time, the director doesn't, and eventually it becomes clear that she won't appear at all. Back at his office, Gridley calls the woman to find out what happened. "Something came up," the director says, "and I couldn't make it."

Gridley has no doubt that the airline executive had intended to put him down. Obviously, she could have phoned in advance to his office, or even called the restaurant.

What to do about "no-show"?

• *Don't be of their number.* It's an unattractive rudeness for which there is seldom an excuse. If there *is* an excuse, it should be made in advance of the meeting time or as soon thereafter as possible, with an appropriate apology.

• *Drop the contact.* If the slight appears intentional, as in the Gridley case, phone to make sure that an accident or misunderstanding hasn't taken place. But if the explanation seems weak, let that be the end of the relationship. It doesn't deserve to be continued.

WHEN THE HOST IS A HOSTESS

The "freeing" of women that started in the 1960s has considerably changed the role of the woman executive. The tradition of the man in a business-meal situation with a woman—automatically paying everything from the taxi fare to the checking fee—is obsolete in most areas. Nevertheless, women report that there are still some bastions of male privilege and attitude that have to be taken into account. Some of these are notably in the business-meal situation when a woman is the host and the guest is of the opposite sex. Here are some of the problems and solutions when sex considerations become a factor:

SHOULD THE MAN BE PERMITTED TO ACT LIKE THE HOST? One female executive reports: "Occasionally I have a problem with a male client in a restaurant. It's not that he objects to my picking up the check. The problem is that it seems to be expected that I'll remain demure and passive while he goes about being the traditional male host. He insists on my preceding him down the aisle to our table, pulls my chair out for me, gives my order to the waiter, and so on."

This executive has found a simple solution: "I have found that, if properly handled, this consideration remains a problem only for one meal. If I break through the rut, I establish a precedent that resolves matters thereafter." What she does, then, is refuse to accept the traditional female role. She signals her "liberation" by beating her male companion to the punch. With fancy footwork she sees to it that he precedes her to the table. While she doesn't pull his chair out for him, she does take care of her own briskly. Then, depending on how strongly she wants to make the point, she will either ask her guest what his choices are and indicate these to the waiter or will tell the waiter directly what she wants to order.

Of course, some of the male-female distinction depends on the waiter. For example, if a bottle of wine is ordered, who will test the first mouthful? Usually the waiter will offer the man this privilege, and possibly the woman may feel that she can give up this much to tradition. But if she is known at the restaurant, she may by one means or another let the waiter know that she intends to assert her prerogative as host and be the one to taste the wine. In other matters of service, the woman tends to be served first. Here, if the woman objects to this tradition—even though ordinarily it's a harmless enough convention—it's best that she patronize a restaurant where her preferences in these ways are made known.

A major sticking point tends to be the paying of the bill. Some men will feel uncomfortable when a woman—with what he mistakenly thinks of as ostentation—pulls some bills out of her purse to take care of the check while the guest tries somewhat vainly to appear at ease and looks off into the distance to show his lack of interest.

Some women executives who do a considerable amount of tableside entertaining arrange to eat at a restaurant where they establish credit, sign the bill, and have it charged to a company account, or they use a credit card.

THE BOSS AT YOUR HOME DINING TABLE

Bringing the boss home for dinner is a time-honored custom. Since this situation involves considerations other than those involving dining, you'll find our treatment under the heading "Making the Boss Feel at Home in Your Home" on page 204.

DINING WITH OVERSEAS VISITORS

From time to time, the occasion arises when you play host to a visitor from a foreign country. It's a special occasion, clearly different from having lunch with a co-worker or other business people from your own locality.

The problems you're confronted by are basically:

• *Uncertainty as to their tastes and interests.* For example, would a Japanese businessman prefer Japanese cuisine; a Yugoslav, Yugoslavian?

• *Not knowing which aspects of your city or town to display.*

• *The multiplicity of cultures that may confront you, and your uncertainty as to what they represent in terms of your hospitality.* For example, you're entertaining a Pakistani who you know is a Muslim. Accordingly, you understand that there is a restriction against alcoholic beverages and the eating of pork. Or you may play host to an Israeli engineer. Does this mean you are limited to restaurants that observe Jewish dietary laws?

In trying to answer questions like these, there is a tendency to fall into stereotypical thinking: "All Russians like vodka and caviar" —and so on. You're not entertaining all Russians, but an individual from Moscow. There are as many variations among other nationals as there are among Americans. To avoid gaffes:

1. *Consult the visitor.*

As soon as possible—to show your hospitality and make clear the warmth of your welcome—contact the individual and make preliminary plans that are mutually convenient. It may be a limited engagement, or you may want to go all-out. At any rate, in addition to the simple fact of meeting, you will probably want to arrange to dine together. Say: "I'd like to take you to dinner. Do you have a preference as to the kind of restaurant we go to?"

Typically, if you pose this to a Japanese, you'll be asked to make the selection. Here there's one misapprehension to avoid. If you live in a city that boasts Japanese restaurants—New York City, for instance, has scores in midtown alone—you note that a large percentage of the patrons are often Japanese. Ah, you may think, Japanese prefer home cuisine. But the Japanese you have observed usually are *permanent* visitors working in the area. The new arrivals will be grateful to try something new. People who have played host to Japanese visitors say a frequent preference is Continental cooking, which means a good French or Italian restaurant.

2. *Offer specific choices—including "American."*

Best move is to suggest a range of places available to you. And, if possible, include in the list one or more restaurants that feature American cooking. Admittedly, this type isn't easy to define—hence the quotation marks above. But to some visitors, hamburgers, frankfurters, fried chicken, or regional styles—Creole, for example—are intriguing. A visitor from Italy may well find a thick New York–cut sirloin a hearty improvement over the thin steaks served at home.

3. *Drinking.*

Be prepared for differences in drinking habits. English are still strong for Scotch, and vodka is usually the Russian drink of choice. *But*—most Europeans do not drink as much before meals as many Americans do. And if they do, it's more likely to be sherry, vermouth—sweet or dry—or other aperitif wines. Wine or beer with meals is common. You may want to offer an after-dinner drink—cognac, a liqueur. But don't press alcoholic beverages at any time. You may get acceptance against the guest's better judgment—or even desire—in order to be a good guest. And there may be uncomfortable consequences.

4. *Time and timing.*

The custom in many foreign cultures is to take longer to dine than we do. This suggests avoiding any eating place, no matter how choice it may otherwise be, in which you're put under pressure to eat and leave. And in many countries—especially South American or indeed most Spanish-derived cultures—the evening meal is taken late—at nine or ten o'clock, for example. Let your guest suggest the preferred time if there is any question.

5. *Display American customs?*

Some styles of American dining are unique. Few nationalities duplicate our weekend combination breakfast-lunch called brunch —and foreigners accordingly have been delighted with this novel meal. And cookouts. While picnicking is widely practiced abroad, the backyard barbecue may also intrigue your visitor.

This last recommendation implies that you take the visitor into your home. Should you—when in most foreign countries business acquaintances are rarely welcomed across the threshold of a host's domicile? The answer is part of a larger answer: don't try to emulate or duplicate the style or customs of your guest. When in Chicago, do as Chicagoans do; when in Los Angeles, do as the Angelenos do.

Your visitors are likely to want to see our country and its customs as they exist *au naturel.* You can make the meal a cultural exchange as well as a culinary event.

NIGHT ON THE TOWN

The business-related occasion that can run a full-scale test of your hosting capability is one covered by the phrase "night on the town." This need not necessarily mean a wild night on the town, but it does suggest something other than the simple business dinner. To cover this situation in some of its more varied and common aspects, let's assume that Lester Birch, one of your company's good customers, has come to visit your city and you plan to entertain him—and his wife— for an evening and to include your own wife to round out the four-some.

FLEXIBLE GROUND RULES. To begin with, understand that there is no one right or best way to proceed. At the heart of these decisions lie such questions as the age, interests, and disposition of Les and Helen Birch. A related factor is obviously your and your wife's tastes and preferences. There's no reason, for example, to include a visit to a sports event—basketball or hockey, let's say—if either you or your wife would be bored stiff by such an event. And exactly the same thinking would apply if the event under consideration were the opera or a serious play. The only exception to this rule would be one where you know for a fact that your guests have a raging passion for one or another type of entertainment. In such a case, in the role of considerate host you might be willing to accept the burden of two or three hours of boredom for your guests' sake. Otherwise, as has been suggested, feel free to program an evening in such a way as to provide maximum enjoyment for all.

WHAT WOULD THEY LIKE? If you don't already know, don't hesitate to ask your guests direct questions: "I know you don't get into town very often. Is there anything you'd especially like to see or do—any restaurant you're particularly interested in having dinner at?" And so on.

THE UNACCEPTABLE REQUEST. Occasionally your guest, either on being asked or volunteering on his own, will suggest an activity that's out of line with your own sense of propriety or even safety. Almost every town or certainly every city has areas whose streets may not be safely trod. It would be foolish to go along with a guest's request to "see" some gang-ridden high-crime area just for the thrill of it, or to have dinner at some restaurant that is the known hangout of an undesirable element.

Another possibility is that your guest, responding to the upsurge of prurience to which even the best of us is occasionally subjected, may suggest some activity involving highly off-color entertainment or activity. (This is even more likely when the guest is an unattached male.) It's undesirable, even under the prod of wanting to be a gracious host, for you to submerge your own aversion and attempt to satisfy the request. Aside from any question of morality, the fact is that such adventures often leave a bad morning-after feeling, and business relationships, instead of being cemented or improved, can sometimes be irretrievably ruined. Don't hesitate, therefore, to offer some explanation or excuse that will clearly put this request out of bounds: "I'm sorry, Les, but I don't really think that would fit into our schedule. As a matter of fact, I've already made plans that I think you and your wife will very much enjoy. . . ."

ANY PRELIMINARIES? There may be some pleasant gesture you want to make before the evening starts. For example, you may want to arrange to have a basket of fruit or some flowers delivered to your guests' hotel room. Or you may want to have a corsage delivered to Mrs. Birch, finding out, if you can, the color of the dress she'll be wearing that evening and relaying this information to the florist. Of course, if you go the corsage route with Mrs. Birch, it would be appropriate to do the same for your own spouse.

TRANSPORTATION? Particularly if your guests are unfamiliar with your town—and desirable in any event—you want to minimize any problems they may have in keeping the date. This can mean you and your wife picking them up at their hotel or engaging a limousine or taxi that will get them from where they're staying to where you'll be meeting.

SHOULD HOSPITALITY BEGIN AT HOME—YOUR HOME? Of course, the whole evening may be spent with the visiting couple as guests at your home for dinner and so on. But if you prefer going out, it might still be a pleasant way to start an evening by having drinks at your place. This gesture sets a tone of friendliness and hospitality that can get your evening off to a particularly strong start.

WHAT SHOULD THE PROGRAM INCLUDE? We're assuming that it's your intention to spend the entire evening with Mr. and Mrs. Birch. This may be pared down to dinner at a pleasant restaurant—and that's all. But if you want to make the plan more elaborate, here are the kinds of elements to consider:

COCKTAILS. These can be at a place other than the restaurant if you prefer. The bar in the guests' hotel itself sometimes can be a convenient as well as attractive place to meet. Of course, the cocktail hour can be a good party-starter if you and your guests enjoy a social drink. An aversion to alcohol on the part of any of the foursome might suggest that it not be played up as a separate part of the evening but simply included as a predinner libation at the restaurant.

DINING. Some of the considerations about the selection of restaurant and so on have been made elsewhere in this section (see specifically page 364). Here is a series of questions geared not so much to general questions of dining as more specifically to that aspect of it suggested by the phrase "night on the town":

HOW ESOTERIC SHOULD YOU GET? Unlike ordinary business dining, when you give over an entire evening to your business friends, you have a much wider latitude in the choice of dining places. For example:

Would they like to sit on the floor and eat with chopsticks? (Some of the more elegant Japanese restaurants encourage this type of dining.)

Would they enjoy smorgasbord dining? Some people like the Scandinavian-style buffet where a wide range of food is set forth to excite the diners' imagination and appetite.

How about the "in" place? Almost every city, town, and community has one or more restaurants that are also showplaces. Would your guests appreciate this kind of setting for their meal?

Or are they the kind of people who would prefer the small hideaway, the little gem of a restaurant known and appreciated only by a few, but where the food, the service, and the ambience are unique and memorable?

MUSIC? In certain cases a choice that would be appreciated would be a place with music either for dancing or as part of a program of entertainment.

ALSO TO BE CONSIDERED. An evening in a so-called nightclub. The term "nightclub" itself has become somewhat obsolete, but what is suggested here is the large restaurant with full-scale entertainment including well-known stars, a chorus line, and so on. For some people this kind of experience has little appeal. On the other hand, there are those who equate a night on the town with precisely this kind of setting. If your guests fall into this category, they might consider any other kind of dinner situation as a letdown.

A RANGE OF ENTERTAINMENT POSSIBILITIES

In conjunction with dining and as part of the evening's program, you may want to consider a number of possibilities:

SPORTS EVENTS. Larger cities may offer basketball, hockey, or other such spectacles.

THEATER AND OPERA. Anything from the commercial theater to little-theater productions are of interest to people who like "live" performances. Even if your community doesn't boast regular theatrical offerings, you may want to check to see if there may not be some performances that may be of interest. And opera can make a grand occasion for people with a developed taste in this medium.

ORCHESTRAS AND SO ON. If the people you're hosting are music lovers, local performances, either orchestral or individual soloists, may be of interest.

THE DANCE. Ballet and modern dance have had a great revival in recent years. Dance programs by local or traveling groups may make for an unusual and happy choice—for the type of guest who would appreciate this type of entertainment.

MOVIES. These come in great variety. Limiting factor, of course, is the number of movie houses in your area. But a real movie buff, eager to see a particular film, will find happiness in your local movie theater if it's showing a film he or she wants to see.

SPECIALS. And then every community has special events from

time to time. It can be anything from an art show of local painters to a display of handicrafts by people in the community.

As we've suggested, it is the proper linking up of what's available to the interests and susceptibilities of your guests that makes the wisest choice.

HOW THE GUEST MAY RECIPROCATE

Let's say you're the beneficiary of a host's thoughtful and pleasurable night's entertainment. In theory, you may still be his guest—in the sense that you will continue to be in his town and will be continuing to pursue your mutual business interests during the day. But if you are to see him another evening—or this can be arranged—you may like to take on the role of host. You may want to do this to show your gratitude or to keep the hosting responsibility, or even the expense, from being so one-sided. Here are some things you can do to even things up, show your appreciation, and so on:

• *"Tonight's on me."* Whether there are just the two of you or spouses are included, you may extend an invitation to an evening that you plan. Keep in mind that this gesture must be made in such a way that there is no suggestion that you're attempting to outdo your host's hospitality in any way. If this issue is in doubt, you can make your intention clear. When you're being thanked for "a lovely evening," you may respond with, "I hope you enjoyed it as much as I enjoyed last Wednesday night," or whatever way you want to refer to the occasion he or she hosted.

• *Send a gift.* You have wide latitude here (see Chapter 8 on "Gifts and Gift-Giving"). And of course the gift need not be business-related or even given to him. It can be a personal item sent to his home and may be for the home, for his wife, or even for one of his children. You might consider this latter course if you visited the host in his home and met the child. For example, a visiting executive sent the son of his host a book of photographs of vintage automobiles, since this had come up as a subject of conversation between them.

• *An invitation in kind.* If it's a likelihood that your host will be coming to your town, invite him to let you know well in advance so that you can arrange to be free to entertain him. If you don't hear soon, you may repeat the invitation in a letter. This message may be included in a communication that is otherwise devoted entirely to business matters: "And Tom, don't forget that you have a standing invitation to spend at least one evening with me next time you come to Chicago. Please let me know when you're due for a visit."

A minimum move is to send a personal letter of thanks to your host when you get back home. This may be on either personal or business stationery. If you use your business letterhead, however, do not include any business matters along with your thank-you. This missive should be entirely given over to expressing your gratitude for hospitality received.

THE COMPANY PICNIC

The outdoor picnic, supposedly one of the most informal and freewheeling of events, usually hides a high and serious purpose: it is designed to put the organization's best foot forward with employees and guests. It gives the lower echelons a chance to hobnob with the higher-ups, and vice versa. Properly run, it is an effective reminder of the organization's interest in having employees enjoy themselves, and of being viewed as a human and friendly employer.

While the affair may not primarily concern food and dining—sports events, other entertainments usually rate high—there's no doubt that the food-and-drink factor is important to its success, as the attendees see it. The considerations involved in serving food and drink to a group of picnickers—numbers may vary from a small group to infinity—may be viewed under headings like these:

1. *Planning.*

Perhaps an unplanned picnic with serendipity on your side can make for a pleasant event. But don't count on it. You have a much better chance for a happy outcome if all the major aspects get careful consideration from the people doing the planning. They should make judgments starting with the question: "What kind of a picnic do we want to have?" Don't jump too fast to the mental picture of how your picnic is going to be. Believe it or not, such an outdoor event can be fairly sedate—let's say where older or unathletic people are involved. In this case the kicks come from an unusual setting, a chance for togetherness, and the charms of nature, whatever they happen to be. The program of the "quiet picnic" may be modest. Easy-to-serve food, some speechmaking, entertainment, and croquet for the adventurous. However, where the group contains a large number of active younger people, the program should reflect this fact—with greater emphasis on athletics, for example.

2. *Deciding on some basics.*

To prevent your planning from misfiring, to minimize the possibility of misunderstanding, there are some questions that you have to answer, and then publicize the answer to all your invitees. Here they are:

• *Who's invited?* Some organization picnics are family affairs. Some are for employees only. In some cases employees may bring nonfamily friends. If friend-bringing has created difficulties in the past, you want to make it clear—either in your announcement by specifying clearly who is invited or through your supervisors if you want to put in a discreet word that will prevent the introduction of strangers who may even without any overt activity pervert the nature and makeup of the group.

If among those who are "also invited" are children of employees, and these are likely to turn up in any appreciable number, it's a kindness not only to the children but to the parents to have some elements of your program designed for them—the traditional three-legged race or potato race may seem old hat to you, but they are activities still capable of interesting and exciting the younger set.

• *How to dress.* Don't assume that "everybody knows how to dress for a picnic." Groups that have had no guidelines have had members turn up for a day in the outdoors in street garb; that is, men in suits and jackets and women in street dresses, for example. And at the other end of the scale, women have turned up in bikinis and men in abbreviated shorts—somewhat to the distress of their elders. You prevent such inappropriate attire by explaining in your invitation under the item "dress": "anything that's comfortable for an athletic day in the outdoors." A discreet reminder to "wear dress that will give you some protection from the sun to avoid sunburn" will make the point for the bikini crowd. Suggest that people bring bathing suits if there's swimming, and games and athletic equipment—a football, for example—if this is appropriate for your program and there are sports facilities.

• *Transportation.* Making it possible for your guests to reach the picnic area and then to get home with a minimum of difficulty will be a most appreciated bit of your planning. In some areas where most people are car owners, there's little problem. You may simply have to help a few individuals without cars to be picked up by others. If this is not the case, you may want to organize car pools, supply company cars, or have vehicles rented especially for the occasion —anything from taxicabs to buses.

An important part of the transportation consideration: make sure that directions for getting to the picnic area are available to all. And, of course, make sure the directions are easy to follow. A map showing people how to get from well-known thoroughfares to service roads and finally to the specific place will be much appreciated.

• *What about food?* The menu is always a major planning item. General considerations: should you go for the traditional frankfurters, hamburgers, and beer—or perhaps a notch higher, to fried chicken and corn on the cob?

If seafood is available, successful picnics have been built around a menu consisting of fish or clam chowder, boiled lobster, and so on. Or how about steaks? There are also all the possibilities of a buffet made up of casseroles—everything from pasta dishes to stuffed grape leaves—available when you ask the picnickers to contribute the dishes they cook most expertly. Or simply cold-dish attractions—deviled eggs, different kinds of salads, cold meats, and so on.

Basic questions about your menu: Will the food be procured from a local restaurant or caterer fully prepared? Or should the makings be bought and prepared at the picnic site? Or should the picknickers be asked to bring items—on an assigned basis? You may properly choose this latter course, not out of cost considerations but to more incisively make the picnic the picnickers' own affair.

• *Drink.* What is to be provided in the way of beverages may also largely determine the nature of the event. In some areas a picnic without beer is practically unthinkable. As a matter of fact, the event is essentially a beer-drinking party, with everything else subordinated to this basic activity. Whether or not you have beer, you may want to include other types of beverage, from those which are alcoholic to fruit juices or carbonated drinks.

3. *Serving.*

Special attention should be given to selecting the people who will prepare or set out the food and drink. When this part of the operation is done smoothly and efficiently, you avoid the mishaps that can cause irritation and cloud the success of the event. If possible, select those people who have had experience in food-handling and in serving large numbers of people. In many organizations this group remains the same year to year, picnic to picnic. But don't hesitate to add some younger people to the group just to prevent the stigma of "more of the same" or "the same old thing" from being justified.

4. *Eating facilities.*

A minimum situation is one where the food is served from the tailgate of one or more station wagons, and picnickers are expected to find their own seating arrangements on the ground or other natural "furniture." At the other end of the scale is the sit-down meal where the food, usually already prepared, is brought in by a catering service that also provides the waiters and waitresses to serve the diners. The point is that whatever kind of meal you have, don't neglect the question of the physical facilities required, whether it be one or more serving tables or tables and chairs for the guests.

5. *Washing and toilet facilities.*

Many picnic areas are equipped with toilet facilities that are fully adequate to your needs. Where this is not the case, you may have to make other arrangements, either with a service or the manager of the picnic area, to provide for the physical comfort of your guests.

6. *Safety and first aid.*

Be sure some person is prepared to supply instant bandages and deal with other minor emergencies. The larger the group, the more likely a mishap. For very large groups, you might want to arrange for a nurse. If you have a medical staff, be sure to get one or more members to agree to attend both as guests and as standby medics. If there is to be swimming, be sure you have adequate water protection—qualified lifeguards and so on. And, somewhere along the line, warn of hazards—poison ivy, and so on.

7. *Cleanup.*

The picnic has been great, a howling success, everything clicked right along, and a great time was had by all. You don't want to spoil the effect by leaving picnic grounds that look like a battleground fought out with paper plates, orange and banana peels. Usually all that's required is the spotting at strategic places of large-capacity cartons or trash baskets. And to complete this phase of your planning, assign the responsibility of policing the area, picking up the occasional stray beer can or paper napkin, and then having the receptacles removed to a garbage-disposal site.

10

Money and Ethics: Hazards on the Workfront

MONEY IN BUSINESS

Business is a money game. Almost everything that happens in the business world involves cash. However, there are money factors in job life that may or may not involve the organization but *are* of direct interest to individual employees. And many of these raise questions of propriety—to the individual personally, and, for those in authority, professionally as well. The money matters dealt with in this section are:

- expense accounts;
- kickbacks and bribes;
- gambling;
- petty dishonesty and pilferage;
- salaries and raises;
- collections, charities, and contributions;
- tips and tipping.

Each of these subjects involves areas of interest and hazard that can be crucial to an individual's career situation, and also poses profound questions of personal choice.

It is difficult to discuss matters such as these without being negative. In the matter of workscene gambling, for example, one can state that gambling is undesirable, is usually proscribed by company policy, and should be avoided. Ditto, shady expense-account practices.

Nevertheless, an effort has been made to point up the positive aspects of these subjects. For example, you'll find recommendations on how to resist pressure to join others in expense-account abuses, how to refuse a bribe offer, and so on.

Even such ordinarily virtuous activities as soliciting funds for charitable purposes take on special meaning—and raise questions of proper conduct—on the workscene. If you've ever been puzzled by enigmas like "How do I turn down a colleague collecting for a cause of which I don't approve?" the pages ahead offer useful guidance.

In general, it may be said that the emphasis you'll find is on how to keep money from being the root of evil.

THE EXPENSE ACCOUNT

The expense account is an arrangement by which debts incurred by employees in line with their business activity are eventually paid for by the company. For example:

Tim Mayo is a salesman for the J & B Office Equipment Company. His job activity requires travel, meals, overnight sleeping accommodations. His hiring agreement with his company stipulates that these and related expenses will be reimbursed.

Employees in almost every category may have expense accounts or incur expenses from time to time that their employer eventually squares. A company executive who takes a customer to lunch or dinner will have the cost of the meal paid for by the company. A secretary who uses her own funds to buy special office supplies will be reimbursed, either through petty cash or by filling out a purchase order for items above a given amount.

The expense-account *theory* is simple enough. However, in practice, abuses may and do occur. It is the potential for misuse of the expense account that creates problems of conduct for individuals. To understand the problems of propriety in the expense-account area, it is essential to understand the emotional underpinnings and contradictions of what is basically a muddy ethical and psychological situation.

TEMPTATION: THE DEVIL'S ADVOCATE

Superficially, the explanation for expense-account low-jinks can be given in one word: temptation. Since people have the chance to rip off organization funds—and usually without penalty—they do. As a result, "expense-account living" has become a recognized, and in some cases lamented, tradition.

Think about the situation for a moment, and you see the individual employee's problem: "Many people cheat on their expense accounts. Why shouldn't I?" Social pressure is added to other inducements: if others are indeed "doing it," then to follow suit is to become a member of the group, to refrain is to be a loner, an outsider.

THE COMPANY DOLLAR VERSUS THE EMPLOYEE DOLLAR

One of the contributing causes of expense-account abuse is the difference that is perceived by some employees between an organization's wealth and an individual's. This perceived difference shows up in the attitude "It's on the company, so let's spend freely." The same big-time spender who will pay out organization funds with relish is likely to part with his or her own cash for personal expenditures most reluctantly.

RIPPING OFF THE ORGANIZATION

In dealing with the expense-account situation, either for yourself or subordinates, it helps to deepen one's understanding of just what is involved. The fact is, the phenomenon of expense-account living and its fairly widespread abuses is somewhat puzzling. We have already pointed out the distinction an employee may make between two "different" kinds of cash—that belonging to himself or herself and that which is the organization's.

And there is an even more startling contradiction: People who are the soul of probity, who wouldn't steal a nickel from another person, will, without the slightest qualms, mulct their employer out of as much as they think they can get away with. How come?

One common explanation: "The company can afford it," says the EA double-dealer. Another view that is used to justify EA dishonesty suggests *revenge* as a motive. Conversations with people who are willing to confess their actions in private reveal this feeling: "The organization doesn't pay me what I'm worth, so I make up the difference by a little tricky arithmetic." In short, resentment against an employer for a real or fancied reason may also be a causative factor.

Of course, dishonesty for whatever reason or however rationalized is still dishonesty. But people do appease their sense of guilt in a number of ways. . . .

A FEW PRACTICES THAT "REALLY AREN'T CHEATING"—BUT ARE

Some of the things people do to make their expense account yield a profit is to charge the company for a more expensive item or service than one actually paid for. For example:

Individuals using a company expense account typically find themselves in circumstances where they must make choices: Should they travel first-class or coach? Should they eat in the most expensive restaurant or one that charges average prices? Should they rent a car for a day in order to cover a twenty-mile distance, or use a bus?

In some cases, the half-honest employee will use the cheaper service and charge the organization for the expensive one; for example, charge for first-class and go coach, then pocket the difference. The conscience-quieting rationale is that if he or she is willing to put up with the inconvenience of lower-class accommodations, that deserves a little extra cash! Unhappily, this circular reasoning is only a flimsy pretext for petty theft. And some people are even able to cheat despite the usual requirement to send in bills.

Some organizations insist that their employees in transit fly first-class or have the best train accommodations. When the company itself suggests an expected level of spending, then the employee or executive will do well to abide by company policy.

Some executives may find company rulings on a particular type of expenditure unsatisfactory. They may indeed prefer to fly first-class rather than economy—which the company suggests. In that case, they make up the difference in the cost of a plane ticket or other such service from their own personal funds.

WHEN THE ORGANIZATION WANTS YOU TO SPEND MONEY

In some cases, people have mistaken the organization's attitude toward spending. One example:

An editor, new to the staff of a business publication, failed to turn in bills for business lunches as his colleagues did. His boss, noting this deficiency, asked him whether he took business executives and other interviewees out to lunch. The editor said that he did.

"Then why don't you put in for expenses?"

"We always go Dutch," the editor explained.

His startled boss simply said, "Bert, the company *expects* to pay for business lunches. When you take a business contact out to lunch, pay for both meals and turn in the bill."

Sometime later, the editor turned in a bill for $12.50. The boss, who knew it covered a lunch for five people—Bert had been conducting a group interview with four junior executives—asked whether he had paid for all the lunches.

"Yes," said Bert.

"Why is the amount so low?"

"I took them to the quick-lunch place on the corner," Bert said—to his boss's horror.

Bert eventually came to understand that as part of the company's public relations, as part of its corporate image, it was important to treat company guests to a somewhat more elevated fare than a hamburger and beer.

The point here is that occasionally you do find people who transfer their own penny-pinching attitudes to their business spending. Of course, this behavior can be as undesirable as overspending.

A GENERAL PROCEDURE FOR DEALING WITH EA ABUSERS

Getting people to observe desirable behavior is largely a matter of removing expense-account dealings from the realm of the abstract and the fanciful. It should be made clear that expenditures involve real money for which an accounting must be made.

To explain how this can be done, start with the fact that in the average organization there is a two-stage review of expense statements turned in by employees:

• *Bookkeeping.* An accountant, internal auditor, or other business-office employee verifies the mathematics and other mechanical aspects. This person may disallow items not considered reimbursable or request documentation or explanation. (Organization requests that expenditures of twenty-five dollars or more be backed up by a receipt are not arbitrary. This is required by federal tax law.)

• *Higher-level inspection.* Once the business office has recorded and approved, the account goes to another person—in the case of salesmen's accounts, for example, to a sales executive. This person's focus is more general—comparison may be made between total expenditure and benefits supposedly derived, whether an entertainment item is justified, and so on.

In most cases, this is the person who will spot an unwarranted or questionable pattern of payout—or claims thereof. Let's say that, in a given case, this individual has decided that in the course of policing an employee's account, some remedial move is required. Caution is desired for several reasons:

It's not desirable to accuse a valued and otherwise honest employee of theft, even if it's taking place. (Of course, if the depredation is so serious that firing is in order, that's a separate consideration.) Further, other people may be equally guilty, and there is an obvious unfairness in "making an example," cracking down on one person while others escape any punishment. Here is a suggested procedure:

1. *Select the proper person to confront the EA double-dealer.*

Who should talk to the employee about a questionable expense sheet? In most cases, it should be the person's boss. But in cases where it is felt that such a confrontation might damage a working relationship, a treasurer, personnel director, or other staff executive may be a better choice. If this is indeed a major confrontation rather than a matter of one or two items, the questioner should be a person of higher status than the questioned. And, of course, confidentiality must be maintained.

2. *Make it low-pressure.*

At the very start, minimize the matter. Let the person feel that you're dealing with a problem or misunderstanding that can easily be remedied.

3. *Suggest that the one meeting will cover the problem.*

Whoever conducts the interview should signal the fact that the problem will be expected to disappear once current matters are rectified.

4. *Monitor the account.*

Subsequent checks should establish that the objectionable practices have been eliminated. If this is not the case, then clearly a second interview is required, where a warning suited to the seriousness of the transgression should be delivered. Continuing difficulties may call for punishment—some revocation of expense-account privileges, perhaps, or even dismissal in extreme cases.

BROADFRONT MOVES TO CONTAIN EA COSTS

To minimize abuses in general, and to prevent the necessity for questioning individual accounts, management has available steps like these:

Company officials are informally cautioned by the treasurer to evaluate reasons for client dining and entertainment more carefully. They are reminded that money spent must represent an eventual benefit to the company. When outlays seem to be getting out of hand, those having expense-account privileges are told directly: "Keep expenditures down." And, finally, the matter of accountability is essential—receipts, bills, records of payment must be available.

WHEN IT'S UP TO YOU TO DEAL WITH EA ABUSE

From time to time, company executives find themselves confronted with an instance where the expense-account privilege seems to have been abused. How do you handle such a case? You may want to minimize the shock to the individual, but even more certainly you want to stop an undesirable practice. The guidelines below should help get the result you want with the minimum of tattered emotions and aftereffects.

• *"I'm doing the same as everyone else."* If the wrongdoer can truly make this statement, you must think twice before you act. It may very well be that the expense-account abuses that you have discovered in one employee's practices are indeed generally practiced throughout your organization. If this is so—and you may have to make an investigation to verify—it's suggested you avoid the "making-an-example" tactic. Aside from being basically unfair, it may not stop the malpractices, but lead people to seek more skillful ways of circumventing procedures.

• *If possible, have hard evidence before suggesting to an employee that anything out of line has taken place.* You should have some means of backing up your assertions. In one case, an executive learned that one of his assistants had turned in a bill for dinner for two people. The dinner had taken place, all right, but the executive learned that the other person, not his subordinate, had paid.

• *Decide in advance what you want the confrontation to accomplish.* If you feel that the inflated or false expense-account item represents a degree of dishonesty that justifies dismissal, then your meeting with the subordinate should be planned in that context. However, you should also be prepared for explanations from the subordinate that may make you reconsider or even decide to give the individual another chance. For example, in the case above, the employee may say that it was a terrible oversight! "Yes, of course, Mr. Thomas paid the bill. If you notice, the date on that goes back a month. I guess the details slipped my mind." Whatever the excuse or explanation, you'll have to decide whether you want to accept it as a mitigating circumstance. You may decide to accept the employee's statement and warn against a repetition.

However, you may simply want to reprimand your subordinate and warn of dire consequences if such practices continue. If this is the nature of the confrontation you have in mind, it is suggested that you be firm and matter-of-fact in your presentation. Scolding, moralizing, proclaiming bitter disappointment at the misbehavior is not desirable. Your calm assertion that any repetition will end in dismissal is more to the point and more suitable to the situation.

WHAT SHOULD AND SHOULD NOT BE CHARGED

Employees, particularly those of long tenure, sometimes slip into the habit of adopting an almost proprietary attitude toward company funds. Putting it simply, they don't draw a sharp line between company expenditures and personal expenditures. Accordingly, you'll find an individual going to a stationery store to buy some items needed back at the office. "And while you're at it," he may say, "put in an extra dozen number-one pencils and a three-hole punch."

Everything ordered up until this point has been entirely for company use, but the purchaser has remembered that his two school kids have asked for soft pencils, and the older one, who uses a three-ring binder, has asked if there happens to be "a spare punch" down at the office that Daddy could bring home.

As a result of a kind of self-deceit, the most upright individuals will assure themselves that there is nothing dishonest in fudging a bit and adding personal items to a company purchase. However, such behavior is definitely wrong, and to keep matters straight, the best procedure is to avoid having personal items made part of a company bill. Specifically ask for two separate bills whenever some of the items purchased are not for company use.

There is another instance where personal charges can get fudged onto a bill to be paid by one's organization. An executive traveling for the company stays at a hotel. Typically, the hotel bill and related expenses—meals, travel, and so on—will be paid for by the company. But what about personal phone calls? What about extra drinks at the bar—a nightcap, for example? Before making a decision, it's a good idea for the individual involved to check with his or her superior or perhaps even the company treasurer to find out just what the company practice is. Some organizations expect to pay for small personal items like extra phone calls and so on. If so, these can be added with a clear conscience. If not, including such personal items is certainly not recommended behavior and must remain entirely a matter of conscience for the individual.

THAT MYSTERIOUS CATCHALL—"MISCELLANEOUS"

One of the banes of expense accounting from the point of view of the treasurer's office is the item "miscellaneous" that often turns up on an employee's list of expenses. There is a classic story that shows the immense possibilities in this item. The actor John Barrymore was told by a Hollywood studio that hired him that his expenses during a particular trip made for publicity purposes would be paid for by the company. "All we expect, John," said the producer, "is that you let us have an accounting." The actor affably agreed, and when he returned a week later, his expense form read as follows:

Cigar for trip to airport	$ 3.00
Miscellaneous	$5,000.00
Total	$5,003.00

Few executives will go quite as far as the great Barrymore. Nevertheless, people in organizations who take care of out-of-pocket expenses by their employees will tell you that miscellaneous items over a few dollars are very poorly received by them.

However, there are certain types of items that qualify for that "miscellaneous" designation. A traveling executive who purchases a pack of cigarettes, three magazines, a couple of paperbacks, has a Coke, and buys a couple of candy bars should not be expected to list all these items individually. And it is desirable—because it prevents hassles after the fact—to reach an understanding with those who supervise expense accounts as to what items, if any, qualify for the "miscellaneous" label and how large the amount may be.

WHEN YOUR EXPENSES ARE QUESTIONED

Every expense-account user has had the experience. The phone rings and a voice at the other end says: "Mr. Haines, this is Mildred

Weill in the business office. I have a statement of yours on your recent trip to London. You included some of the bills, but there doesn't seem to be one for the hotel for the three days you spent in New York, and you say you hired a car, but there is no verification of that. Can you help us out?"

Two things not to do in this instance. One is not to bully the clerk or accountant who has called—even though you may be a top executive. Nor should you ignore the request. Of course you realize, as a company executive, that the call is a sign of efficient monitoring of company expenditures. The fact that the request may be personally annoying or embarrassing is unfortunate but must be discounted.

You have several courses open to you. If, among your effects, you can find the missing records, track them down and send them to Ms. Weill. If the missing records can be duplicated—that is, if you can write to the hotel, the car-rental service, or whatever, and have a duplicate bill sent—then this information should be relayed to Ms. Weill.

If for some reason you cannot satisfy the request for verification, you may simply have to leave the matter at that. In such a case, to simplify things for the clerk, send along a memo addressed to her that she can show to her superior for consideration. The memo probably will simply be your statement that these expenses were made but documentation is unavailable. What you'll probably get from Ms. Weill's boss is a call or a note to "please remember we do need original bills on these matters," and unless the items are unusual, the case will be closed. But the lesson learned should be a reminder to collect bills for every item that is going to appear on your expense account, with the possible exception of the nickel-and-dime items. And remember, federal law requires documentation for expenditures over twenty-five dollars claimed as tax-deductible.

DOCUMENTING T&E DEDUCTIONS

The U.S. Treasury Department requires evidence—that is, receipted bills, statements on the stationery of the supplier or service organization—for business travel-and-entertainment expenses claimed as deductions. If your organization claims the deduction, it must have from you such evidence.

The thing to remember about the "evidence" is this: a ream of bills, chits—even witnesses who will aver that sums were spent for valid business purposes—*won't* do the trick. *To be allowed,* each separate expenditure must be backed by documentation indicating:

amount spent;

time and place;

specific business purpose;

business relationship of the entertainee.

RESISTING THE PRESSURE TO JOIN THE SHARPERS

A choice people may have to make—particularly new employees —is whether or not to go along with expense-account shading practiced by one's colleagues. These considerations may clarify what's involved:

• *Individual choice.* Keep in mind that the individual is judging for himself or herself. It's what *you* think, your sense of right and wrong, that is involved. Every other person in a group being a wrongdoer does not justify or excuse the individual from not doing the right thing.

• *Be willing to resist group pressure.* Don't underestimate the power that a group can exert on individuals to conform to its pattern—for bad or good. Depending on just how the confrontation takes place, you may have to, with more or less self-assertiveness, face the opposition and maintain your privilege to act as you see fit.

• *Avoid being judgmental.* You have made a point—and a strong one—by making clear your intention to tread the straight-and-narrow path. There's no point in moralizing for the benefit of less highminded colleagues, or arguing the wisdom of your choice over theirs.

• *Expect compartmentalization.* People who are familiar with the expense-account world will tell you that what people do or don't do about their personal money dealings with the organization usually has no effect on any other job behavior. There is a kind of matter-of-factness about a good deal of expense-account wheeler-dealing that keeps it from rubbing off in other areas. In short, the person who plays it shady on the swindle sheet may be exemplary in every other aspect of the work. This may be a helpful thought in adjusting to a new work group to which you've been assigned or into which a new job takes you.

A SIMPLE EXPENSE-ACCOUNT PROCEDURE

Most organizations tell employees exactly how they want expenses reported. Others are less explicit. But in either case you may want to use the points below either for comparison purposes or as a guide that will make it possible for you to provide the accounting department with the data needed and will help skirt some of the hazards:

1. *Follow organization requirements.*

Go along with the procedure set up by your organization. However, if you have any questions or disagree with any parts of the system, discuss these matters with an appropriate authority—your boss, the treasurer, and so on.

2. *Avoid "miscellaneous."*

Many organizations disallow this item. At any rate, unless it is for a number of small amounts, the outlay covered deserves being spelled out. For the cost of newspapers, local phone calls, postage, and other nickel-and-dime items, reach some agreement with the office on how these should be handled.

3. *Keep records of expenditures as they are made.*

This practice makes it unnecessary to pad the items you do remember in order to end with a total that represents sums actually spent because you've forgotten some outlays.

4. *Develop an acceptable level of spending.*

Arrive at a level of expense (and standard of living) that is a good compromise between what you are used to at home and what the organization expects of you.

5. *Get approval in advance of doubtful items.*

By getting a decision about a contemplated expenditure, you prevent later argument. Examples: Is a spouse's travel expense O.K. for a specific trip? What about entertainment plans you may have for entertaining a customer? You're traveling across the country to attend a son's graduation. Yes, you did spend a day with one of your suppliers. But how much of the tab will the company pick up?

Some companies are willing to accept small expenses incurred in the course of a business trip—things like cleaning and pressing of clothing, the cost of magazines and paperbacks to help pass the time, and so on. Again, any expense in doubt—hotel prices, per-diems, incidental items—should be questioned and agreed on in advance. This is the best means of staying on track and preventing misunderstanding.

6. *Don't even pay lip service to expense-account sharping.*

There is an air of sleaziness in the manner of a person who, even in jest, refers to an expense report as a "swindle sheet" and suggests that expense accounting is just "one big rip-off." Accept and treat expense accounting for what it is—a business transaction between employee and organization—and, as such, as demanding of honesty as any other business matter.

KICKBACKS AND BRIBES

One of the strongest reasons for the tarnish on the business image involves a practice that has been described as "payola" or "kickbacks." What's involved is the payment, either in money, goods, or services, to individuals in a secretive way—sometimes called "under the table."

As with other questionable practices, our intention here is not to moralize. However, in seeking to set forth prescriptions, standards, and limits of good and bad behavior, the kickback practice poses difficult and puzzling situations for which other sources seldom provide realistic answers.

It's easy enough to say that people should not be unethical, nor should they cheat or lie. But the fact is that the business world has developed certain practices and traditions that are unique to it and perhaps should not be judged in the black-or-white terms appropriate for the teaching of moral principles to children. Again, it must be repeated that the purpose here is not to condone anything that is illegal, unethical, or immoral. But as any experienced businessman knows, the question of kickbacks and related practices does not lend itself to simple treatment. Consider a problem like this:

Allen Holt is the owner of a film-editing service. Its customers are advertising agencies and other groups that produce films for TV commercials, educational purposes, and so on. The business that Holt is in is extremely competitive, and as is often the case when services are sold in a difficult buyer's market, the service company must cut corners to find and hold onto customers. As a result, there is a whole range of things that Holt and others in his business do under the heading of "improving customer relations":

Customers are taken to expensive lunches and dinners.

They're given presents at Christmas time whose lavishness depends on the "size of the account."

The customer's representative—purchasing agent or other representative—is given birthday presents, special gifts when there's a new baby in the family, and so on.

It's a fact that some organizations have strict rules forbidding their purchasing agents and other representatives to accept gifts of any kind from suppliers. In some cases this rule is modified. For example, the purchasing agent may accept an occasional meal or wedding present up to a value of fifty dollars, and so on.

But people on the inside of this type of practice know very well that the kickback racket can involve much larger sums and can spread from the goodwill gesture to the cold-blooded rip-off. Let's get back to Allen Holt.

Holt is approached by a representative of an advertising agency in charge of producing a series of TV commercials. This man says, "You can have my business, but I want ten percent on every bill." Now Holt has a serious problem. If he refuses to go along with the kickback request, he doesn't get the business—and he can be pretty sure someone else will. His propositioner represents a large account and a large income for him. His profit margin is so small that he has to scramble for survival. To put the situation into perspective, let's even say that if Holt were to make it a strict rule—"no gifts, no entertainment, no payola"—he might well be forced out of business.

Now what happens in case Holt and other suppliers go along with the kickback request is that the customer eventually has his bill padded in a way that will give Holt the additional margin he needs to pay the kickback.

One executive who is particularly embittered by the whole kickback situation says: "In my business, individual customers sometimes go completely wild. Would you like to know what I've done for one purchasing agent recently? I paid for the redecorating of his apartment, bought two color TV sets—one for his home use and one for his girl friend—bought all the liquor for a recent housewarming, and, finally, believe it or not, paid one year's tuition for his son."

What can the businessman with a normal sense of what is right and ethical do in such a situation? The answer seems to be to seek a middle ground. To make a basic rule "not to spend a nickel for customer goodwill," including such traditional gestures as a business lunch or dinner, tickets to a sporting event, and so on, may mean to be put out of business by competitors with a somewhat less stringent view.

But neither is the other extreme acceptable. Those who are familiar with the ways of payola know that requests and exceptions can get completely out of control. What can be done realistically, then, is to have a policy based on two points:

1. *Make the expenditures and gestures that are appropriate both in terms of your own personal standards and those in your industry.*

This may include everything from Christmas gifts to occasional dining and entertainment.

2. *Learn how to say "No."*

Somewhere along the way, particularly with especially avaricious or unreasonable customers, you have to be able to draw the line.

HOW TO TURN DOWN A BRIBE

The person who wants to turn down a would-be briber may be in a delicate situation. For one thing, the person offering the bribe may be someone whose goodwill or even friendship the target of the offer may want to retain. Even if this is not the case, the question of just how to respond, and what subsequent action to take, if any, must be settled. These considerations can help meet the situation:

HAS A BRIBE REALLY BEEN OFFERED? First thing to be sure of is to clarify the exact nature of the proposal. This may not be as simple as you might think. For example:

David Roper, head of a production division, is called on by a service manager of the company that supplies heavy-duty machines Roper uses in his department. Lunchtime intrudes on their discussions, and the service manager says, "Come on, Dave, let me buy you lunch. There's a great restaurant on the other side of town. . . ."

Now, according to ordinary business practice, most people would agree that the lunch offer is perfectly acceptable. But consider two modifying circumstances:

The manufacturer is eager to get Roper to buy some new equipment. In this case the lunch could be regarded as a move to buy not only Roper's goodwill in general but to win a favorable view of the purchase. To extend the point a bit: instead of a lunch offer, let's say dinner at a swanky restaurant is involved—with the service manager giving strong "expense-be-hanged" signals. One more turn of the screw: add to the dinner the invitation to a big-name nightclub. Somewhere along the way from a simple lunch to a night on the town, the dividing line between acceptable customer relations and bribery has taken place.

A good rule to observe: where there is an immediate issue where goodwill is not general and long-range but involves an advantage the proposer is seeking, the target of the offer should courteously turn it down—yes, even a lunch. "Sorry, I'm tied up for lunch" or "All right, if we go Dutch" will keep the situation pure and simple.

Second rule: where expenditures for entertainment—whether a meal or other attraction—seem excessive, the effort should be made to keep such expenses within reasonable limits. This might mean saying, "The dinner was fine, but anything more would put your firm in the red with our account. So why don't we call it an evening. . . ."

SAYING "NO." In the case where there's no doubt that what's being offered is meant to buy your influence or partisanship, your statement can be simple and direct: "I'm sorry, but I can't accept your offer."

What else you say depends on how you feel about the situation and the person involved. Here are some choices: "I don't like the way you operate. I'm afraid we no longer have any reason to continue to do business with each other." Or if you aren't the person who can make the decision to sever relations, you might say, "I intend to talk to my boss about this. . . ."

If you're considering legal action, remember these difficulties. An accusation without proof can be futile, particularly in a bribe situation, where the individual can claim his intentions—or even his actions—were misunderstood.

If you have no witnesses and no evidence, you might want to make a written record or submit a written report to your superior or other authority. This move is for the record so that if there is ever any question raised in any quarter as to what happened, your statement reporting the facts—everything from time, place, date, circumstances of the meeting, and the conversation, verbatim if you recall it—can go a long way toward protecting you from misrepresentation.

GAMBLING

Gambling, as everyone knows, is both legal and illegal, a vicious vice and a pleasurable pastime. Gambling in all its ambiguity becomes an even more problematic entity when it appears on the workscene. The reason is that in addition to all the questionable aspects it has in general, gambling at work poses special difficulties. Here's one way to consider the overall situation:

• *"Gambling" that's acceptable.* There are some forms of gambling that have organization approval. As a matter of fact, in some cases the organization itself sponsors the event. A raffle for turkeys at Thanksgiving, even door prizes at a Christmas party represent a form of gambling about which there can be little objection.

Actually, the forms of acceptable gambling may vary from locality to locality, company to company. In some businesses the baseball pool or football pool run by an employee or a supervisor is accepted as a matter of course, and it may actually add wholesome fun and excitement to life on the job.

And in other organizations anything from the sale of Irish Sweepstakes tickets to a raffle on a car to raise money for a local hospital comes in under the wire.

• *Gambling that is verboten.* There are certain manifestations of gambling for money that no organization should tolerate. Card-playing and crapshooting on company time and company premises, for example, should be firmly stopped and clearly ruled out to the full understanding of the culprits. This type of activity is inadvisable for two reasons: first, it is an obvious misuse of working time, and second, such practices tend to have a demoralizing effect and lead to a general letdown that can cause serious work problems. And, of course, these activities are usually illegal as well, and an organization conceivably could be prosecuted for permitting gambling on its premises.

"GAMBLING" YOU SHOULD OVERLOOK

There are some kinds of activity that technically are gambling but may be ignored because they are usually isolated incidents and no threat to morale. It may even be said that for a representative of management to take corrective action against such behavior would mean making a crisis of an unimportant matter. More harm than good would be the likely result. Here's an example of the kind of thing we're talking about:

Supervisor Larry Ranger suddenly rounds a corner in the corridor and comes across two mail boys who, while waiting for the freight elevator, are pitching pennies. As far as Ranger knows, penny-pitching is not a common time-wasting practice. He smiles and says, "O.K., men, none of the Las Vegas stuff on company premises," and keeps right on walking. The comment has the effect of a gentle reprimand—which is sufficient under the circumstances. A second incident might call for a sterner warning, a third might lead to Personnel and a warning for the record.

Another type of "gambling" that may be ignored is an impromptu bet: one employee bets another on a prizefight, or whether it will rain over the weekend.

Remember, a distinction is being made here between organization-approved activity—approval may either be explicit or tacit —and minor and mostly spontaneous betting that is not likely to recur.

PETTY DISHONESTY AND PILFERAGE

Pilferage has become a major source of loss in the business world. Company property is filched in ways large and small; for example, an employee makes off with a box of paper clips for home use. It's not really "stealing." After all, the company "won't miss it," and after all, isn't he part of the "company family"? Of course, as the items taken increase in value and as the motivation changes from casual, unthinking "borrowing" to out-and-out stealing of company property for cash sale to others, the nature of the act becomes more serious.

There are two points of view about company property:

• *Strict and uncompromising.* Some people say, and feel quite strongly, that absolutely *no* item of company property should be taken for personal use, not a paper clip, not a pencil or typewriter ribbon.

The people who advocate this view have a strong argument in their favor. They say, "If taking a single paper clip is acceptable, how about two paper clips? How about ten? Or a gross? Where do you draw the line?" But there is another point of view, and its supporters are people who see themselves as realists.

• *If it's small enough, it doesn't matter.* The defenders of this behavior say, "Of course it's all right to take inconsequential things for one's personal use." And so, many people who consider themselves both loyal and honest have over the course of the years brought home an occasional ball-point pen, a scratch pad, a roll of Scotch tape. Certainly there's been no major harm done, and the consequence has been simply to make the firm somewhat like an indulgent, if unwise, friend or parent.

It is our view that either of these two approaches to company property is acceptable. As a matter of fact, the second, more liberal attitude is both widespread and traditional. But as we pointed out, there must be limits to the value of the items taken and to the frequency with which it is done; and, in a way, the act should be for a constructive purpose. The executive who brings home a mechanical date stamp that's being discarded because one of the months no longer registers can justifiably feel good about giving his grade-school kid a gadget that the youngster is entranced by. One bit of behavior that's observed and is objectionable is the systematic taking of office supplies that simply accumulate unused in a dresser drawer.

And certainly pilferage for profit is clearly unacceptable behavior and should be proclaimed so by all responsible employees.

SITUATIONS INVOLVING PETTY DISHONESTY AND PILFERAGE

It would be an easier world to live in if problems were simple and clear-cut. Consider the matter of theft, for example. One might say, "An act is either honest or dishonest." In short, one cannot compromise on honesty. Nevertheless, we recognize the fact that a father who steals a loaf of bread for his starving family has not committed the same kind of act as the person who embezzles money to live the high life. Even in law there is a consideration that modifies the nature of a crime and its punishment. This is represented by the phrase "extenuating circumstances."

As in the world outside, theft on the workscene must be considered in context and dealt with accordingly. The need to deal with it becomes accordingly more complex, but that is the nature of justice. Here are some typical situations:

DEALING WITH THE "PENCIL AND PAPER-CLIP STEALERS"

Employees find themselves surrounded by items belonging to the company for which they have some personal use. This may involve anything from paper clips to file folders. One employee takes home used typewriter ribbons to give to his typewriter-owning high-school age son. Another "liberates" an old desk stapler that has been replaced by a newer one.

This type of petty pilferage is practically universal. Everyone from the janitor to the company president, strictly speaking, might be found guilty. Occasionally one hears of a person going to extremes to avoid encroachment on company property rights, and this of itself makes the case for a relaxed view. For example:

Joe Garcia is a bookkeeper for a large chemical company. He keeps two pencils in his pocket—one for personal notations, the other for company work.

Such bending-over-backward behavior does seem to verge on the ridiculous. A more realistic alternative would suggest that an organization permit a certain amount of cost-little borrowing. The problem then becomes one, essentially, of keeping such appropriations at a low level. People found exceeding this acceptable limit should be reprimanded. If within a given department or area items are disappearing at an undesirable rate, the point should be made to the entire group and warnings issued as to possible punishment of the culprits.

SHOULD A SECRETARY BE ASKED TO TYPE PERSONAL MATERIAL?

Steve Popper occasionally would ask his secretary, Grace Beck, to type a letter for him involving personal business—a complaint to the gas company, a letter to the Internal Revenue Service explaining a deduction he had made on his tax return, and so on. Gradually, however, the practice took on a larger dimension. The item that finally broke the camel's back—that is, Grace Beck's acquiescence—was a request from her boss that she type his son's high-school term paper.

The question of whether a secretary should be asked to work on personal projects has no absolute answer. No question that it is a form of pilferage, a misuse of an employee's time, which belongs to the organization. It helps to hew closely to basic guidelines to avoid either improprieties or unreasonable demands:

• *The quality of the work situation.* In an office of strong work pressure, any unnecessary additions to a work load should be avoided.

• *The secretary's attitude.* Some people like to do favors for others. On the other hand, there are some who take even a minor request as an imposition. You have to decide in which of these two categories your secretary belongs in order to move intelligently.

• *The amount of work involved.* Few secretaries will react negatively to requests of a minor nature. For example, being asked to address twenty or thirty Christmas cards "at your convenience" can be taken in stride. A list of two hundred becomes a major project and is likely to seem an imposition.

• *What's been the policy on the secretary's own personal business?* Where a superior has objected to a secretary taking care of his or her own personal business on company time, it's contradictory and perhaps even hypocritical to ask that the "rules be broken" on the executive's behalf.

If an executive does have personal typing of any sizable amount, he should consider offering to pay the typist to do it on his or her own time at a rate that compares favorably with regular earnings. One secretary reports: "My boss does a considerable amount of writing for trade journals. I've arranged to spend several hours a week doing this work on my own time. He pays me from his personal checkbook. This way, his work and the company's work don't compete for my time."

PROTECTING PEOPLE AND THE ORGANIZATION FROM PILFERAGE

The stealing of corporate assets either by sneak thieves or as a result of carefully organized gangs costs the business world hundreds of millions. But there is a kind of theft that breaks out from time to time almost like a disease. This is the stealing of office equipment —typewriters, calculating machines, and so on. Somehow a clever thief has figured an angle, has developed a plan whereby one or more people, sometimes disguised as messengers, for example, can get into the company premises and walk off with a valuable piece of equipment. Sometimes criminals working inside or outside an organization have been able to include maintenance people in their gang and have had such equipment taken out with garbage or mixed in with other outgoing shipments.

Losses of this type are unsettling to company personnel, both in a personal and a general way. Most people are shocked when, however distantly, they're victimized by theft. And then there is the direct interruption of work to be considered also. The protection of such assets is a primary organization concern. Every firm must be ready to develop a plan of security, from the employment of guards to the permanent fastening-down of equipment to prevent such losses.

One of the most common and upsetting thefts on the workscene is that of an employee's wallet or pocketbook. In some offices where security is poor, sneak thieves come in from outside. And these can be almost miraculously efficient. A secretary's handbag, for example, is taken from the top of her desk or from a desk drawer. ("And I was only gone for just a few minutes.")

One of the difficulties is that when this type of theft occurs, one can't be sure whether it's an inside or an outside job. The best protection—and it should be insisted on by supervisors—is that everyone maintain a continuing guard. Women, for example, should be told that their bags should never be left behind, even if it's only for a visit to the washroom or to deliver a message down the hall. As a matter of fact, people who will be leaving their work station frequently should be provided with a special means of protecting valuables, whether it be a locked metal cabinet or some other type of physical protection.

If there are one or more thefts and it's suspected that the criminal is an employee, it's a good idea to take up with higher authority the question of both prevention and apprehension. This type of crime can be highly demoralizing and can unsettle an entire organization.

• *When one employee steals from another.* Sometimes thefts, however petty, become more serious. For example, in a shop one mechanic may have a micrometer stolen. Even if it's company property, this type of theft is compounded by the victim's reaction.

In such a case the supervisor must act. A strong attempt must be made to find the missing item and the culprit. Such losses may represent a real hardship for an individual—on which more will be said shortly.

There is one traditional way of resolving this question. Presumably the supervisor will have indicated the seriousness of the act by publicized efforts to recover the missing item and at the same time find the thief.

If preliminary efforts do not succeed, the supervisor may assemble the group and say, "Jerry's micrometer is missing and it's pretty clear that it's been stolen. We can't tolerate anything like that in our department. I want that item returned within the next twenty-four hours and there'll be no questions asked—this time." This approach frequently serves its double purpose—first, to recover what's been stolen, and second, to serve clear notice that such thefts will not be tolerated.

A further step that may be taken: the theft may be reported to one's boss or the personnel or security department. The follow-up actions made by this higher authority will further spell out the seriousness with which the theft is viewed, and should act as a deterrent.

WHEN SOMEONE SAYS, "LET'S TAKE UP A COLLECTION AND REPLACE THE LOSS."

Occasionally, when an individual has been ripped off, colleagues have the impulse to chip in and make up the loss. What should the supervisor or executive in charge do? For example:

Linda Dowd just gets back from cashing her paycheck and breaks out into hysterics. "My wallet's been stolen! There must have been a pickpocket in the elevator!" Kim Tanz, Linda's colleague, goes to Mr. Jefferson, the department head, and tells him the news. "Don't you think," she says, "we ought to help Linda out? She just can't afford to go without that money. I know."

There are three basic moves Jefferson may make. And they suggest, in general, the possibilities for those in a similar situation:

• *Full support.* Jefferson may say, "I think that's an excellent idea. Please start with me. Here's ten dollars [or whatever the amount]." Jefferson might give two suggestions to the fund-collectors: first, give everyone in the department a chance to contribute, but exert no pressure, it must all be voluntary; and second, keep the amounts contributed secret. It's no one's business how much another person has given.

In addition to the department head's personal contribution, where the case is clearly one of need, the personnel department may be contacted to see whether the organization itself might want to contribute, to bring the sum—if it fails to come up to some respectable level—up to a desired point.

• *Partial support.* Jefferson might respond, "I think that's a generous impulse, Kim, but it might set a bad precedent. Feel free to proceed if you like, but it will have to be without any help from me. I'm sure you can understand my position in this."

• *Prohibition.* Conceivably, Jefferson might feel the idea is a poor one and should be discouraged. There may be several reasons for this conclusion. Here are two:

Linda's may not have been the only personal loss. Another employee may have suffered a loss through theft in which no attempt at restitution was made. To do so now in Linda's case might seem like playing favorites.

For one reason or another, Jefferson might question the circumstances of the loss or its extent. An overcoat may have been stolen, worth, according to the employee, a large sum of money. But Jefferson suspects, realistically, that the value placed on the coat represented an original cost, long since depreciated. He properly feels it would be unfair to have well-meaning colleagues, in a sense, cheated out of the funds they might contribute. Another kind of questionable circumstance: an employee may lose something out of carelessness and claim it is stolen. The fact certainly changes the nature of the situation.

In cases such as those mentioned above, the department head might say to Kim Tanz, the well-meaning colleague: "I can understand your wanting to help, but I don't think it is warranted. I suggest that you don't do anything." If the message is received reluctantly, the injunction might be added: "If you insist on going ahead, please don't do it on company premises or on company time."

PROTECTING DEPARTMENTAL ASSETS—STAMPS AND THE PETTY-CASH BOX

Almost every office or department that has its own supply of postage stamps and keeps a supply of petty cash on hand runs the hazard of theft. It's essential that the first and strongest protective step be physical security. Stamp boxes and petty cash should be under lock and key. The smallest number of people should have access. Removing temptation will greatly decrease chances of loss.

Despite all precautions, however, sometimes there are losses. Regrettably, in some cases the people who have been trusted to protect the valuables may themselves be involved. Here's a typical case:

Division head Ted Swayne is out at the front door when he remembers he's forgotten a book he intended to take home. He goes back to his deserted department. There he discovers supervisor Chris Donner taking money out of the petty-cash strongbox. "What's going on, Chris?" the manager asks. Donner, visibly shaken, utters a few incoherent sentences, the sense of which is that he was "borrowing a few dollars" for carfare home.

Conceivably this explanation might be true. It's up to Swayne to evaluate Donner's statement on the basis of his knowledge of the man. If Swayne believes he's being told the truth, he may do one of two things:

He may accept the explanation and let matters rest there, although perhaps future checks on petty-cash funds should be more stringent.

Or, even if the explanation is believed, Swayne may say, "I'm not going to judge the act, Chris, but from now on, if you need any petty cash, you'll have to come through me."

WHEN YOU CATCH SOMEONE IN A DISHONEST ACT

Where an act is definitely theft, which of the two courses available is used depends on your own personal judgment.

ANOTHER CHANCE. If because of the long tenure of an employee and his otherwise clean record you feel the depredation is not likely to recur if the employee is "put on probation," you may say so: "I'm willing to forget this incident, Betty, but it's up to you from now on. . . ."

PUNISHMENT. Here, and again depending on circumstances, the punishment may range from transfer to another and logically less desirable job to dismissal. Remember the problem of proof, however. You must be able to make a clear-cut case. Whether or not the police will be called in and legal action taken depends on company policy. Companies generally act on the basis of the nature of the theft. If small amounts are involved, punishment is usually dismissal. If the crime involves larger amounts or attendant objectionable circumstances—breaking into a locked cabinet, related vandalism—it's usually made a police matter.

DISHONESTY THAT INVOLVES A FRIEND

There's a special situation that sometimes develops—the person perpetrating the theft may be a personal friend of the one who discovers it. For example:

Pete Erickson walks in on his friend and colleague Jeff Winters. To his surprise, the latter is in the process of stuffing into his attaché case a secret model of the company's newest product. Erickson knows that there would be no logical reason for his friend to be taking the model off company premises. Winters's red-faced silence confirms the nature of the act, and he quickly confesses, "I needed money, Pete, and the competiton is willing to pay a good deal. . . ." Regardless of friendship, Erickson cannot make the offer "I'm willing to forget all about this." An extenuating circumstance might possibly be that Winters is in desperate need of funds for family reasons. But even if this were true, someone in Winters's situation need not have chosen this particular road.

Erickson has two choices. He can say, "I'll agree to keep this quiet, Jeff, but I expect you to start looking for another job tomorrow and submit your resignation by the end of the month."

Or he can simply say, "I'm terribly sorry, Jeff, but I'm going to have to tell [a higher-echelon executive, head of Personnel, and so on] about this. It's really out of my hands."

BORROWING

"Can you lend me ten bucks until payday?" In some places that's a day-before-payday battle cry. Some people just have trouble paying their way from one pay period to the next. And, of course, there's nothing bad about borrowing per se. If it's overdone, of course, it just becomes a darned nuisance. However, troubles can arise from borrowing. Here are the complications and how to handle them:

• *When a boss borrows from a subordinate.* Since in our country personal equality—aside from status and authority situations—is taken for granted, there's no more reason why a boss shouldn't borrow from a subordinate than vice versa. But the borrowing boss must be scrupulous in paying the debt and also keeping the borrowing, both in frequency and size of amount, within reason. Further, in general it's a good idea for a person in authority not to borrow from a subordinate if it can be avoided. It simply becomes a complication, adds a tension factor in what can be a somewhat strained relationship in any event.

• *When the borrowing is forgotten or denied.* People can be forgetful, and the fact is that where a borrowing pattern has been established—that is, sums have been borrowed and repaid over a period of time—the borrower may honestly confuse a previous payment with one that has not been made. And so an argument may be started, tempers may flare. Unfortunately, all the supervisor has to go by are two opposed statements by two vociferous people.

Of course, a sensible arrangement is for the borrower to write an I.O.U., which can be torn up after repayment. This simple procedure is usually thought to be too formal for small loans between co-workers, however.

The "rights" in this situation favor the presumptive borrower. If he or she continues to maintain that the debt was paid or never made, for the matter, and there's no proof on either side, a person in authority will simply have to say that there's nothing that can be done. (Of course, if the sum involved is large enough to warrant it, the purported lender might want to take the case to small-claims court.) Here are points to consider in the whole matter of borrowing on the workscene:

• *Persons in authority should stay out.* A supervisor or executive whose subordinates are indulging in the borrowing game has no jurisdiction. This is completely between two individuals.

However, as a matter of good supervision and out of concern for a subordinate, you might want to have a friendly discussion with an employee who is "always borrowing money." If there seems to be real financial hardship or even an inability to manage funds, you might want to check with Personnel to see if some kind of financial counseling can be offered. It's strongly recommended, however, that the immediate boss of the addicted borrower not get personally involved. This situation can become extremely sticky and completely subvert the ordinary superior-subordinate relationship.

If you can, suggest to either lenders or borrowers that they keep a record. It's desirable that *both* people do this to avoid the statement "I don't care what he's written down on his desk calendar, I never borrowed that money. . . ."

• *Protecting the new employee.* A special case deserves consideration. Some departments have people who may almost be thought of as "professional borrowers." These individuals tend to view new employees—those who don't know the borrower's reputation—as easy victims. If you are aware of the existence of such people and realize the hazard, you should warn the potential victim: "Rita, I wouldn't be too quick to lend Jessica money. Borrowing is a habit with her, and you'd be wise not to get involved. If she makes a request again, I suggest that you simply say you're out of funds yourself, or make some other excuse."

SALARIES AND RAISES

SALARIES: THE SECRET REWARD

The salary or wages that people get have a special place in their thinking. Attitudes toward earnings, if misunderstood, can cause severe problems. A key aspect is that almost everybody wants the size of his or her paycheck held in strict confidence. Of course, in some cases secrecy is impossible. For example, the salaries and earnings of executives of publicly held corporations are generally known, and for some types of jobs—those for which salaries are stipulated by contract, for example—if not the exact amount, at least the range of earnings is known.

But aside from these exceptions, employees at all levels consider their earnings their own personal business. In some countries this may not be the case. In some cultures, for example, individuals are quick to establish their status with a stranger by telling what kind of work he or she does and the nature of the emoluments that go with the job.

However, in our country, because of the general attitude, it's important that an employee's superior—who usually knows to the dollar a subordinate's earnings—not reveal this information to anyone. Of course, the boss's boss may be given this information as part of the discussion of performance or another aspect of the individual's career. But it would be highly undesirable for this information to go to anyone else in the organization except when there is a specific need to know. For example:

Grace Henley and Barbara May, department heads, are comparing work and compensation of similar jobs in their respective units. One executive might give precise earnings figures of her subordinates. The understanding here, however, is that the information would not be passed along.

One obvious hazard here is the discretion of payroll clerks and other individuals who may work with payrolls. These should be made to understand through their own supervisors that all payroll information must be considered top secret.

HOW TO ASK FOR A RAISE

There comes a time in every employee's working life when a request for a raise seems to be in order. Of course, some organizations have policies and procedures that make such requests—except under unusual circumstances—unnecessary. A system of periodic increases or regular merit raises can be the established means of satisfying employees' desires for increased earnings.

However, in an organization where there is less regularity or rigidity, an individual may want to speak to a superior about a salary increase. What is proper and what is improper, what is effective and what is ineffective behavior in this situation? Consider:

Management experts, in offering guidance, make a point of specifying that the person making the request time it optimally—that is, at a time convenient to the boss—and try for a setting—usually the boss's office—that is quiet and likely to minimize interruptions.

Such considerations are clearly helpful. But from the viewpoint of the etiquette of the situation, which focuses on the feelings and proprieties, additional preliminaries emerge:

BE AWARE OF YOUR FEELINGS AND ATTITUDES. In some cases, either from a sense that there has been unfairness, or resentment at being put into an importuning position, the person requesting the raise will feel and act hostile. Even if this attitude is justified, it should not be reflected in word or deed. After all, one continues to be courteous even to those who, in a strict sense, may not deserve it.

AVOID THE USE OF INTIMIDATION. Just as it's wrong for a person in authority to throw his or her weight around, it is undesirable for the person seeking a raise to inject a bullying note. Even if you hold trump cards, these shouldn't be used as weapons. Such behavior, aside from being undesirable in terms of etiquette, also tends to be self-defeating and leaves scars that may permanently spoil relationships. Bosses too should be treated with consideration.

BE MATTER-OF-FACT. The tone most suitable is one of simple factuality. You're conducting a negotiation. You have a number of reasons or factors that favor your claim. These should be advanced in a logical sequence.

CLARIFY THE BASIS FOR THE REQUEST. Asking for a raise should have a better rationale than "I haven't had a raise in X months." There are good reasons and poor reasons for a raise request. The lists below make the distinction:

GOOD REASONS:

- I have taken on additional duties.
- I have improved in my abilities.
- I have done an outstanding job with notable special achievements.

POOR REASONS:

- I need more money.
- I've been here longer than anybody.
- I understand my co-worker just got a raise.

The person making the request will strengthen the demand by having available specific facts to back up assertions; for example, reminders of special achievements, descriptions of additional responsibilities, evidence of improved skills. Some people write better than they speak, so a written request may be made. But this would be only the opening move. Eventually it is desirable for the sake of good communication for you and your boss to discuss the matter face-to-face.

Admittedly, discussions of wages can become highly emotional. They involve not only the practicalities of level of living and life-style but also deep ego feelings and feelings about company fairness. The ego feelings come in as the employee identifies the raise with recognition and appreciation for individual contributions, dedication, loyalty, and so on to the organization.

It's up to both parties to keep the discussion as friendly, open, and matter-of-fact as possible. This will be the case if the person asking for a raise avoids emotionality as far as possible, bases the request on performance, and recognizes the position of the person to whom the request is addressed. This person, as well-intentioned and favorably inclined as he or she may be, always has some limitations on freedom to act in this money area.

What both parties should be seeking is fairness of treatment.

WHEN YOU HAVE TO TURN DOWN A REQUEST FOR A RAISE

The individual who is being asked for a raise must keep several factors in mind. If the raise can be granted and the amount is satisfactory, then presumably both parties will be satisfied. But in some cases the employer or representative cannot grant the raise:

• *The reason for the request is unsatisfactory.* An employee may offer reasons that are not persuasive.

• *Salary-review schedules may make the request inopportune.* Some organizations review salaries at specific times of the year. If there is no basis for the request being considered as an exception, the employee should be reminded of the time when the increase will be dealt with.

• *A business situation, temporary or otherwise, may interfere.* "We cannot give wage increases to anybody for the next six months," the president of an organization tells his executive staff. "We're in a real fight for survival. . . ." When this type of restriction forces a denial of the request, the employee deserves to be given some explanation that mirrors this fact.

MAKING A REFUSAL CONSTRUCTIVE

It's never advisable to respond to a wage request with a blunt "No." And this is true even if the request seems unreasonable.

As a matter of fact, in some cases a wage request is consciously or unconsciously intended as a feeler. The employee expects to be able to learn from the way the request is received just where he or she stands in the opinion of the superior.

If the answer is to be "No," the executive should make this an occasion for helping the employee clarify not only the question of where he or she stands with the employer but also for providing targets for future efforts:

• *If possible, suggest objectives that will win a raise in the future.* "Tony, if you improve the quality and quantity of your work—and I'll be keeping a close check on that from now on—we'll resume this discussion in three or four months and see how things look then."

• *If money is tight.* In most cases it's advisable to level with employee: "Matt, I can't disagree with your feeling that you deserve a raise. I must tell you, however, that the organization is in no position right now to increase anyone's salary. However, this is a temporary situation and I'll be happy to reopen this discussion as soon as that situation improves."

If in the course of the discussion the employee intimates an immediate need for cash because of special circumstances—an operation for a family member, for example—a suggestion may be made as to how a loan might be secured. In some cases organizations have a policy of underwriting such loans to expedite them from a bank or other lending institution.

COLLECTIONS, CHARITIES, AND CONTRIBUTIONS

Fund-raising is a fact of life in most organizations. Whether it is the girl who goes around taking up a collection to buy a wedding gift for a colleague or the fellow who thinks everybody should give to his favorite charity, where there are employees there are collections.

Company policy may simplify the problem of office solicitations. Some companies have a simple blanket rule: no funds may be solicited for any reason whatsoever on company premises. Others modify the policy: no solicitations without express permission of management. But this leads to problems of discrimination and decisions that most managements would like to avoid.

Many organizations maintain flexibility by having no specific policy on fund-raising on their premises. As a result, an organization that clearly prohibits the sale of raffle tickets or other kinds of "solicitation for gain" may still blink at the collection for an orphanage, a health research organization, or even the selling of chances for a prize, the proceeds of which go to the local hospital.

In thinking about or making decisions about collections, one must start with a consideration of the points made above: What is organization policy? And perhaps a more helpful question: What is its practice and tradition?

COLLECTIONS—YOU HAVE TO JUDGE BETWEEN THE GOOD AND THE BAD

Few organizations are completely free of collection activity. Anne's birthday, Peter's anniversary, Sal's retirement—these and similar events, if celebrated at all, are often marked by the presentation of a gift paid for by funds donated by colleagues. (For more on gifts and gift-giving, see Chapter 8, especially "Collections," page 306.)

The giving of gifts to colleagues from colleagues is usually an innocent and even heartwarming kind of sentiment. And the worthiness of charitable donations is usually beyond question. But difficulties arise:

• *Too many.* "One more collection," complains one junior executive, "and my lunch money for the month will disappear." Yes, the collection and gift-giving fever can get out of hand. An outbreak of engagements, marriages, and childbearing—to say nothing of organization-related anniversaries—can create a top-heavy schedule of collecting that becomes not only a financial drain but also a nuisance.

• *Doubtful purposes.* Not all charitable causes are equally worthy. Eventually one comes across one or more that are questionable, either because of the nature of the charity or the motives of the people doing the collecting.

• *Controversial causes.* Occasionally a collection threatens to precipitate a confrontation between pro and anti forces. Someone wants to sell raffle tickets for an event or organization toward which some people have strong antipathies. Permitting the sale of the tickets suggests that the supervisor or the organization is taking a favorable stand. Of course, this is undesirable as it suggests either partisanship or unfairness, or both.

DEALING WITH SPECIFIC COLLECTION PROBLEMS

Representatives of an organization at all levels must be aware of collection activity and be prepared to take constructive (this may mean repressive) action. Consider problems like these:

You permit the selling of raffle tickets to raise money for clearly good causes—a local orphans' home, a hospital, perhaps even a theater or art foundation. But along comes an employee who starts selling tickets for some unknown charity. You may even have reason to suspect the funds raised will be pocketed largely or altogether by the fund-raisers. Yet there are few organizations that can undertake to examine and evaluate the worthiness of various charitable causes. What's to be done?

An organization can take three tacks:

First, you may ban the selling of any raffles or chances of any kind.

Second, you may set a requirement that every would-be fund-raiser must get permission from Personnel or some other department in order to operate.

The third possibility, and one definitely not recommended, is that the organization tacitly permit almost anyone to solicit funds. This last course is inadvisable because it violates a basic tenet of organization life. Organizations do have an obligation to protect the health and well-being of employees. Permitting sharpers of one kind or another to operate on company premises and presumably do employees out of their hard-earned wages is to abdicate responsibility.

HOW TO SAY "NO" TO A COLLECTOR

"Mr. Smith, I'm selling raffle tickets to raise money for the Jack-knife Sports Club. They're a dollar apiece. How many would you like to take?"

The person making the request may be a subordinate in your own department or an employee that you know well enough to nod to in the corridor. Here what's involved is not your judging the individual's right to make the collection but your own personal response to his request.

If you are favorably inclined toward the cause for which the funds are being raised and you know that your organization has no objection to the fund-raising, you may buy one or more tickets, either as a way of contributing to the fund or because you hope to win the prize—or the usual combination that motivates most people.

But let's assume that you want to refuse. And you may want to do so for several reasons. For example, one is that you aren't favorably inclined toward the organization sponsoring the fund-raising. Or you may feel you don't want to make a donation in any event.

However, if you feel that the fund-raising activity itself is suspect, you won't hesitate to say something along these lines: "I'm sorry, Bill,

I don't want to buy any raffle tickets. But may I ask, did you get approval for raising these funds from either your boss or Personnel?"

If you are the employee's boss, you may want to take a more direct line: "Bill, I know you haven't gone to Personnel to get approval to sell these tickets and I know you don't have my permission. I'd like you to either go to see Mr. Hall in Personnel and get written approval from him or else stop selling your tickets on company premises."

EXPLANATIONS FOR REFUSAL TO CONTRIBUTE

As an individual employee, you should feel free to participate or refuse to do so for any kind of collection. And you needn't feel answerable to anyone. For example:

Ann Markham is asked to contribute to a farewell gift for a departing colleague. Since she and the colleague have been on the outs for some time, she simply turns the solicitor down.

However, the manner of refusal can make the difference between an acceptable response and one that leaves bad feelings in its wake. An explanation makes the turndown gentler. Of course, the most used, or overused, refusal for donations is "I gave at the office." What can you say *at* the office? Some possibilities, involving charitable donations: "My wife [or husband] takes care of our contributions." Or: "I concentrate my giving on just a few charities." Or: "I've already exceeded my charity budget for this period."

In some cases you may want to voice a specific objection to a particular charity. Should you? Obviously, making such a point may trigger an argument. Nevertheless, if you feel strongly about the matter, you could say:

"I'm sorry, but I can't go along with the policies of that organization." Or: "I've heard that the administration costs of that organization are so high that only a relatively small percentage ever gets to the people who need the help."

When you'd rather not give and you'd rather not give your reasons, a smile and "I wish I could. . . ." make an acceptable turndown.

COLLECTIONS FOR INDIVIDUALS

Sometimes the collector who knocks at your office door represents not a charitable organization but a personal fund—anything from a Christmas present for the boss to a gift for a colleague who is soon to have a baby.

Here you have two decisions to make. First, should you or shouldn't you? In general, unless you have strong negative feelings, it's a good idea to go along with the group's decision. The second question is *how much* to give.

"How much are others giving?" is a simple way to develop a quick guideline. If the answer you get is "Mr. Jones has given twenty dollars" and the collectee is Mr. Jones's secretary, a reasonable donation from you might be about five dollars. If the collector gives you an average figure, you can duplicate that.

In some cases it's unwise to be overly generous, since this not only runs the risk of making other people feel uncomfortable but could also set a precedent for you that might be regretted in the future.

WHEN THE BENEFICIARY IS SOMEONE SPECIAL

Special feelings, special moves. It's possible that the person for whom the collection is being taken is a special favorite of yours. Perhaps he or she is someone with whom you have worked closely or been especially friendly with. In that case you may want to hand over some cash for the collection but also shop for a special gift to show your appreciation as well. Unless there is a clear-cut policy against it, there's no reason not to give your own gift. But in any event you'd be wise to present it privately.

EXPLAINING A "NO" AFTER A "YES"

One of the problems that can arise, particularly in offices where collections tend to get somewhat out of hand, is the matter of justifying a turndown after you've contributed to another cause. For example, if you made a donation to the Red Cross, can you say "No" to multiple sclerosis?

There are two alternatives to this situation. One is to give a similar but small amount to every request. And the gesture can be explained: "This is the amount I give to all such collections. My other charitable donations are made in other ways."

Yet you can say "Yes" to one charity and "No" to another if you have some special feelings about them. Certainly the benefits to a loved one from a charitable organization would predispose you to contribute in one case, while lack of contact or interest in some other charitable or health organization might find you disinclined to contribute. This experience or feeling might be reflected in an explanation to a collector—if you feel one is necessary.

TIPPING WITHIN YOUR ORGANIZATION

The tipping situations *outside* your organization—that is, involving restaurants, taxicabs, hotel personnel—are fairly standard. In some cases the question may boil down to: "to tip or not to tip." For example, in countries like Spain and France where restaurant bills have the service charge added in, there's no problem (though in both countries, small additional amounts are sometimes left to show special appreciation).

At one time *Fortune* magazine published a scale of tips listing countries from Argentina to Switzerland. Even on this broad front, the average range of tips to cabdrivers and waiters went from 10 to 20 percent, with by far the most frequent figure being 15 percent. Conclusion: in most situations where tipping is practiced, the 15 percent amount will be adequate.

PROBLEM ON YOUR OWN DOORSTEP

But for people in business, the difficult aspect of tipping is *intra*-organizational. Do you tip a mail clerk who has from time to time given you personal service—helped you post a personal package, delivered a rush memo from you to your boss, and so on? And how about cleaning or maintenance people? Or the lunchroom manager, who has always given you V.I.P. treatment—even brewed a special pot of coffee for you when the regular supply ran out?

The problem hinges largely on one point—the expectations of the other person. But it's not clear-cut. An individual may be very helpful to you without any idea of being "tipped"—that is, rewarded—and yet be pleased with a material sign of your gratitude. Or, a person may render relatively minor services and be miffed if Christmas comes and goes and you have failed to offer material recognition of what is thought of as past favors.

But that's not the end of the complication. The stickiest part of the problem occurs when you tip someone and find you have perpetrated an offensive act. In short, they are deeply insulted because of what they see as your patronizing, superior attitude. *To them, you are a co-worker*—regardless of the difference in rank.

FIVE CONSIDERATIONS ON TIPPING WITHIN YOUR OWN ORGANIZATION

To avoid the reefs of this touchy area, think through points like these:

• *Is friendship involved?* In some cases the act or service has been done out of friendly feelings. Accordingly, tipping becomes an affront, since it suggests that the service was performed for reasons of gain.

But even if you're friendly with the person, you may still feel the service deserves recognition. The *manner* used may make the difference. Note a special "explanation": "Helen, I really appreciate your doing all this personal typing for me and I'd like you to accept this small token of my appreciation. I'm giving it to you in the form of cash because you have such excellent taste and can select something for yourself much better than I could. . . ."

• *Money—or a substitute?* If there is a doubt in your mind as to how acceptable a cash gratuity will be, consider giving something else. One executive for whom an elevator starter had done a number of small services gave the man a gold tie tack on one occasion and several months later a leather wallet. But then, getting the impression that these gifts were not going over as well as he had hoped, at the next appropriate time (and "appropriate time" is usually a matter of feeling) he gave the starter cash—in this case ten dollars and said, "Frank, I'd like you to take this and buy yourself a cigar." This was both a joke and a way of suggesting the giver's realization that the amount involved was relatively small. However, the downgrading statement—suggesting that the ten dollars was the price of a cigar—had the curious effect of *enhancing* the amount.

• *Can you check with others?* Other people may already have solved the problem. For example, one executive had received a number of favors from the cafeteria manager—preparation of special dishes when she had to work overtime, for example. Came Christmas and she wondered about a gift.

The executive went to one or two of her colleagues and described the problem. She got several different answers, all of which helped her to decide on her own course. One colleague said, "I've been giving Jane ten dollars each Christmastime for the past several years." Another said, "I send her a personal Christmas card in which I express my thanks." A third stated, "I get her a gift, such as a scarf or handkerchiefs."

The executive then decided to give *both* a small gift and cash. Having learned that the cafeteria manager was interested in gourmet cooking, she bought her a paperback on French cookery and enclosed a small check and a note that expressed her appreciation.

• *How big should the tip be?* Everyone wants to avoid the hazards of undertipping, which suggests that you're a cheapskate, and over-tipping, which suggests that you either have an inaccurate sense of the value of money or of the services rendered.

For some people there's a simple solution to the question of how much. They just let themselves be guided by their *feelings*. Then, whatever the answer, they can be satisfied with the decision.

But if in a particular situation this "feeling" fails to materialize, you have to fall back on a more rational process. To arrive at a tip size that seems proper, here are some factors that apply:

Exactly what is the nature of the services rendered? It may be that if you pin them down, you'll find that they are either considerably less or more than your offhand recollection would suggest.

Does the recipient *expect* a tip? Not an easy question, but there are two sources that can suggest an answer. One is the experience of others on this same matter, which you can get by asking. The other is the behavior of the tippee. A pro-tip stance isn't that difficult to spot. Sometimes it's negative—a post-Christmas coolness suggests one answer. But if the services continue to be given willingly, even gladly, consider that it may be done out of a friendly feeling and nothing more is expected.

Can you use an "hourly rate"? Consider the personal-typing-by-a-secretary situation. Approximate the time spent at a reasonable hourly wage. You may want to go above or below the total figure you get, but at least you have one more basis for your estimate.

• *Will you be setting a precedent?* There's one thing you have to remember about tipping within your own organization—as opposed, for example, to tipping a cabdriver or someone you'll probably never see twice. Once you have decided to tip, *ceasing* to do so may seem to suggest either forgetfulness or a cessation of gratitude.

This consideration should be kept in mind *before you tip for the first time.* Just remember that, once started, it may be difficult to stop without arousing hard feelings—or puzzlement.

11

Sex on the Workscene: The New Look

THE AREAS OF SEX IN BUSINESS

The sections in this chapter are largely devoted to two aspects of the sex considerations in business:

1. *Vestiges of the past.*

Many of the problem situations that pose questions of behavior for people at work derive from our past—and now somewhat passé —attitudes. But in refusing to disappear altogether, they create difficulties. Here are some examples:

MYTHS OF MALE SUPERIORITY. These include old ideas such as "It's a man's world," and "Woman's place is in the home."

PERSISTENCE OF MANNERS. Manners that hark back to "the age of gallantry" include such things as hat-tipping and the automatic assumption of the host role by the man in a mixed-couple situation.

DOWNGRADING OF WOMEN. This occurs on the basis of the stereotype of the "helpless, emotional female."

2. *Sex as a workscene factor.*

Differences between the sexes and behavior that is sex-related pose problems. It's not necessary to get involved in a discussion about whether women's emotional makeup is different from men's, or if that is the case, why it should be so. The plain fact is that sex differences do create problem situations that must be dealt with. For example:

ADJUSTING TO A FEMALE BOSS. As the number of women executives increases, more men are in the position of having to learn to function in the role of subordinates to them. For some, it isn't easy.

ROMANCE ON THE JOB. When a man and woman discover a mutual attraction, that's romance. When the principals work in the same organization or department, that's a problem.

SEXUAL HARASSMENT. Some things change, some things remain the same. While in the past women have had to suffer the interest —sometimes unwanted—of male colleagues, our greater open-mindedness today has not completely eliminated this problem and the question of what to do about it. And women may make passes at men.

It's possible that a future edition of this volume will be printed with this entire section deleted. But for today, the material you'll find in the pages ahead represent treatment of an important area of business behavior.

READJUSTING TO THE NEW SEX MORES

A Pennsylvania court recently ruled as follows: a husband cannot sue for damages if his wife leaves him for another man because a woman has the right to choose her sexual partner.

The presiding judge explained, "This ruling is to acknowledge what we consider to be a given fact in the evolution of our moral and sexual mores."

To mark just how much of a change the ruling reveals, consider that the outdated common-law principle that heretofore applied was that a husband has the right to "the services, fidelity and body of his wife."

A final paragraph in the judge's written opinion adds an additional insight into the nature of the sexual revolution we have experienced. He said that to allow a spouse to sue for money damages because of "his spouse's voluntary . . . sexual activity with another person is abhorrent and repugnant to modern standards."

Another indication of the *speed* with which sex mores are changing: the head of a business library goes through the vertical file under the heading "Sex in Business." On all items—clips from a broad range of business and general publications—from more than a year earlier, she circles the date and notes: "Obsolete."

HOW BASIC STANDARDS AND VALUES ARE SET

Organization managements, possibly buffeted by conflicting social trends or even by a conflict of views among their own personnel, may wonder by what means they can devise a rational set of standards for such basic matters as dress, permissible conduct between men and women employees, and so on.

There is one fact that should be the core of top-level thinking on this matter of standards of behavior. It is that every organization tends to be a world in itself, and in this world it is the top executive and his or her immediate group of policymakers that may dictate any standards they want to—within reason.

Consider the matter of dress, for example, You may remember that one of the styles of the last decade that caused considerable excitement—and some panic—in many organizations was the abbreviated garment called "hot pants." In many organizations these were ruled out as permissible garb for female employees, although there was a certain amount of discontent and rebellion among those women who felt their rights were being abrogated.

In some cases the "stuffy" image of the organization that emerged may later on have been regretted, but the company rules were usually abided by. However, in companies that had a somewhat more liberal view of the range of employee dress that was acceptable, hot pants were accepted and, after a brief and startled reaction in some quarters, became a matter of course. As style trends changed in the world at large, these short shorts took their place in the museums of women's dress along with the hoopskirt and the bustle.

The point is that the main requirement for behavior and appearance standards in an organization is top management's clear thinking. It more or less comes down to this: whatever top management says is good taste is in good taste, and whatever is ruled unacceptable is so.

Nevertheless, with the power to set these standards, top management must understand that there must be flexibility in thinking to accommodate to new ways and new values. It's as necessary for an organization to grow in terms of its own culture as it is to do so in its business operations.

SEX MATTERS THAT ORGANIZATIONS ARE CONCERNED ABOUT

Most organizations—although many are unaware of the fact—have standards by which they judge employees' behavior that involve sex considerations. For example, an executive who maintains that his organization "doesn't make judgments or policy" in matters relating to sex, in the next breath will reveal and defend a policy that prohibits husband and wife from being simultaneously employed by the company.

While it is true that much of the conduct code relating to the sexes is implicit rather than written, here are some of the areas to which organizations knowingly or otherwise respond:

> any overt signs of two employees courting on company premises —anything from long phone conversations on the intercom to smooching in corners;
>
> interest of one employee in another who is married;
>
> dress—especially the body-revealing styles of young women;
>
> grooming (for example, beards and long hairstyles for men caused more of a flap than the far out women's styles);
>
> the "suitability" of fiancées of higher-echelon executives (in paternalistic organizations, some choices would be considered "bad for the company");
>
> the behavior of women in terms of its being "ladylike";
>
> homosexuality—not necessarily in terms of job behavior, but merely designation.

ADJUSTING YOUR ORGANIZATION TO THE NEW MORALITY

Many companies make unconscious adjustments to the changing world of which they are a part. But for those that may not be sure of just where their organization stands, the steps below can help reveal the basic rules and, still more important, the attitudes and standards that exist in a given organization:

1. *Review the record.*

In making a review, don't be content just to "think back" over the last few years. This approach may represent a surface inspection that hides as much as it may reveal. Make the survey as much as possible one of events and incidents:

Was anyone recently fired for "unbecoming conduct"—for example, either partner (or both) "guilty" of an office affair?

Was anyone reprimanded for "immoral behavior"—for example, a woman exhibiting what some people considered "oversexy" behavior at a company party? (This might mean anything from wearing a low-cut dress to trying to seduce the company president).

Are rules of dress reasonable, rather than "bluenose"?

Does a marriage between two employees mean one must quit?

2. *Hold a meeting.*

It's advisable to have all managers updated on just what company attitudes and standards are. If you feel there is not a general and common understanding from front-line managers (supervisors) upward, it's advisable to have meetings at which people have a chance to listen to your policies and ask for clarification.

Of course, it's quite possible that some of your people are further along the road than the company is. For example, supervisors may be completely permissive in terms of amorous exchanges in their departments during lunch periods and so on. If your company is not (yet?) in the position of condoning sex breaks, this point perhaps should be made. It may require company authority to thaw old attitudes.

3. *Highlight the changes.*

Any changes of policy or the rules that your organization is making should be stressed. After all, these are likely to be the points at which judgments must be made. The manager who is told that the latest extreme style in clothing—male or female—is no longer reason for corrective action is in a better position to deal with the matter of dress.

The field of sex mores has major areas—everything from the matter of antidiscrimination to "separate-but-equal" washroom facilities. In addition, there are many other questions of behavior that are sex-related. It is to some of these sometimes crucial, often damaging matters that the balance of this section is devoted.

WHAT RULES OF THE SEX GAME SHOULD YOU LIVE BY?

There's little question that our moral values and attitudes have changed greatly since the 1960s. Everything from language to appearance reflects a freer, more open climate. Nevertheless, this "new world" of social behavior does not solve all problems. On the contrary. In some ways the bygone days made life a good deal simpler. Men knew that when they were in an elevator with members of the opposite sex, headgear was to be removed. Now in some milieus such an act would be considered ostentatious and might even lead to accusations of being a male chauvinist.

As a result, there can be no simple and general rule that determines behavior either for men or for women. Obviously, the rules have changed for both sexes. While men who rely on the old ceremonies become suspect, so do women. A female executive going to lunch with a male colleague might find her failure to offer to share a lunch bill upsetting to the other person.

Here, then, are the circumstances that affect what will be considered good or poor behavior when "good fellows"—both men and women—get together:

• *The community factor.* Every organization, no matter where located, can't help but be affected by the mores of the community of which it's a part. For example, informality seems to be most prevalent in the western part of the country. The old traditions seem to hang on more strongly elsewhere.

• *The climate of your organization.* Organizations have character and personality. These may not be as easy to "read" as those of a human being, but such dimensions as formality or informality, liberalism or conservatism, flexibility or rigidity, may be approximated. Behavior on company premises or in matters involving the company must be decided on with current organization values and attitudes kept in mind.

• *Personal values.* In addition to the two external factors described above, the individual must be expected to make choices based on individual taste and preference. Even if one works for a conservative-minded organization, there are upper and lower limits of that conservatism. Accordingly, one may make a decision as to which point in the scale of acceptable behavior he or she wants to aim at in terms of behavior between the sexes or judgments made that involve sex considerations. This covers everything from the need for washrooms for women in areas where they have recently become accepted members of the work force to the problem of making a choice between a male and female employee both equally qualified for a promotion.

HELPING EMPLOYEES UNDERSTAND THE DIFFERENCE BETWEEN WHAT'S O.K. ON THE OUTSIDE BUT UNACCEPTABLE ON THE JOB

Organizations have a particular problem that arises when so-called advances of sexual enlightenment are injected into the business scene. For example:

Jane Newhouse is a new, young, and somewhat belligerent typist. Shortly after she's hired, she brings in a four-color picture of a male nude, which she pastes on the wall next to her typewriter.

When her boss, Mr. Lee, suggests that it might be a good idea to remove the picture—"It's fun to look at once, but it's really not a good idea to leave it up permanently"—Jane Newhouse says, "Have you been in the mail room? They have female nudes all over the place."

Mr. Lee has a problem. He can resolve it simply by ordering the typist to remove the offensive print, if a jollying suggestion is not followed. The supervisor feels this is a last resort and hesitates to do it, even though it is highly unlikely that Newhouse might threaten to protest to the anti-discrimination office.

The supervisor realizes that persuasion and education are more suitable, and so he talks to Newhouse and makes three points:

PERSONAL LIBERTY IS RESTRICTED BY THE RIGHTS OF OTHERS. "Jane," the supervisor says, "we all believe that people should have their full share of personal freedom. But in case you aren't aware of it, I want to tell you that some of the other people on the staff find your picture offensive. Without getting into anything deeper than democratic rules, I have to tell you that you're outvoted. . . ."

THE PRIVATE WORLD OF THE ORGANIZATION. The supervisor would then continue by making a distinction between what people may do on the outside and what they're free to do on company premises: "There are many things that people may care to do in their own homes which are perfectly O.K. there. But every organization, including this one, has its own rules and standards, and everyone in the organization from top to bottom is expected to abide by these."

PIN DOWN THE VIOLATION. Finally, the supervisor must make clear the specific objection. In the Jane Newhouse instance, for example: "There's no rule against putting up pictures or other kinds of decoration at your work place. The objection is to the particular nature of the item you've selected."

This point should be self-evident except that in another instance there might be a company policy against employees' putting up pictures or decorations of any kind. It is the policy being infringed that should be stated clearly.

It's true enough that in some cases what's involved is the question of good taste. And this is obviously not an easy concept to impart to others. As a matter of fact, if the concept *can* be gotten across easily, this may solve the entire problem. It's when it doesn't work that the efforts recommended above should be substituted.

MYTHS AND MISCONCEPTIONS THAT UNDERLIE MALE CHAUVINISM

People must understand the background of sex relations and sex attitudes in business in order to work harmoniously and make wise judgments in matters involving the sexes.

While most managers agree that equality between the sexes is a desirable objective, the deep-rootedness of "the-female-is-inferior" thinking stands as a difficult barrier. At the base of such attitudes may be found one or more premises understandably acculturated into men, particularly those maturing in the 1950s or before. If these can be undermined or undercut, less biased attitudes may result. As spelled out in a General Electric study on women in business, one of its Business Environment reports, here is a list:

"IT'S A MAN'S WORLD." Perhaps. But the antidiscrimination laws make it illegal to act on that premise in business.

"WOMEN WOULD REALLY LIKE TO BE MEN." It may have been part of the bygone days' attitude. But the Women's Liberation Movement and increased awareness have aroused many women to new self-confidence and a sense of equality.

"WOMAN'S PLACE IS IN THE HOME." Motherhood and wifeliness still attract many women. For those who prefer work at home to work in business, fine. But business statistics show an increasing number and importance of women at work.

"WOMEN ARE INTELLECTUALLY UNSUITED FOR PROFESSIONAL WORK." A Department of Labor report shows that two-thirds as many females as males among eleventh-grade students tested have engineering aptitude. This fact suggests that cultural attitudes rather than aptitude dissuade women from pursuing professions for which they may have potential equal to men's.

"WOMEN ARE PHYSICALLY UNSUITED FOR MANY JOBS." Individuals should be barred from jobs from which they are disqualified because of physical limitations, regardless of sex.

"WOMEN ARE EMOTIONALLY UNSUITED FOR EXECUTIVE WORK." Professional opinion is divided on this point. One authority points out: "Whether you experiment with animals in the laboratory or simply observe everyday life, males invariably go to pieces faster than females. Their endocrine and central nervous systems just don't stand up as well under strain."

Another authority suggests that in a society that is genuinely committed to equal opportunity, work schedules "could be adjusted to the realities of female experience and not wholly to the male-oriented workweek and pattern."

Since one can find authorities on both sides of the issue, and some could be found to support any viewpoint one chose in this area, a simple suggestion is made: select women executives, give them responsibilities, and judge them according to the same standards used for men.

"WOMEN AREN'T SERIOUSLY ATTACHED TO THEIR JOBS." Women have often been barred from positions of responsibility on the basis that they will leave to get married or to have a baby, or that they are more apt than men to change jobs or that they leave when husbands are moved to another location.

There are endless statistics that suggest that, on the record, women are at some disadvantage in this area. But the fact is, most of these figures relate to women disproportionately represented at lower-echelon jobs. Further, they represent the past, when the role of women had not yet felt the influence of the two major change factors of the Women's Liberation Movement and antidiscrimination laws. For the future, it would seem that when women are given jobs to which it pays them to be attached, they will respond the same way—statistically and otherwise—as their male opposite numbers.

SIGNS OF VESTIGIAL SEXISM TO BE MARKED FOR EARLY ERADICATION

With centuries of tradition pointing us in the opposite direction, completely nondiscriminatory thought and action concerning the equality of the sexes may show something less than 100 percent purity. As an assist to organizations that want to see how far they've come or how far they still have to go in order to get closer to the goal of nondiscrimination, you'll find below some indications of sexism that are so subtle and ingrained that they will be found even in organizations that honestly consider themselves completely liberated from the ways of the past. The situations described show up in business meetings where past formalisms tend to hang on:

OPENING REMARKS. "It's nice to see that there's a lady in the group," says a speaker. While in general it's all right to give special welcome to particular individuals, why invite the men to stare at a lone woman as if she were some kind of oddity?

SEXIST HUMOR. A speaker addressing a group often feels the need to inject humor from time to time. Those speakers who have not changed with the times tend to haul out the old turkeys—everything from the traveling salesman and the farmer's daughter to the one about the lady in Congress. The speaker should not be surprised if such jokes are no longer considered very funny and, further, that they may be taken as an insult.

THE OLD COURTLINESS. The leader of the conference asks for questions from the floor. A number of hands go up, and the leader says, "Ladies first, of course," and acts accordingly. As the woman executive later observes, "He could have called on me or not as he preferred, but to do it on that quaint basis sure took me back to the bad old days."

APOLOGY FOR LANGUAGE. "Men in my company occasionally do a bit of swearing," says a woman employee. "I don't mind the language, but I do resent its user turning to me to apologize. Finally I said, 'Look, I don't give a —— what kind of language you use.' That stopped the apologies."

FLIRTING. We're used to thinking of flirtatiousness as a female proclivity, but one woman reports, "I'm sick and tired of men, under the guise of good-fellowship, complimenting me on my knees, legs, and other parts. They certainly would be astonished if women treated them in the same meat-on-the-hoof way."

CONDESCENDING COMPLIMENTS. A saleswoman in a regional meeting is asked to give the new sales presentation that the group has been working on. She does, and the sales manager says, "Wasn't that beautifully done? That should make you men look to your laurels." Despite the good intentions, the sexism is blatant.

HOUSEWIFING. This is a hangover from the "women-are-menials" type of thinking. If coffee is to be served, if the debris of a lunch is to be cleaned away, women in the group are automatically shunted into the roles of servitors. Some women are guilty of perpetuating this problem either by volunteering or by moving into the activity automatically. "I make a point of avoiding such activities," says one department head. "When I'm asked, I say, 'Sure, I'll be glad to if I get some other volunteers from the males in the group.'"

Don't be surprised if despite your belief in your organization's dedication to equality between the sexes, you find practices like the above hanging on. At the same time, do keep in mind that until they vanish from the workscene an organization is still justifiably labeled as sexist—with equality as a goal rather than an achievement.

THE HIGHLY VISIBLE PROBLEM OF ELEVATOR BEHAVIOR

What people do in elevators is mostly stand at attention for a few seconds between the floor at which they've entered and the one at which they depart. As to elevators on the business scene—both in large office buildings or in company buildings that are tall enough to require elevator systems—the matter of behavior deserves attention because a considerable amount of intersexual ceremony takes place there.

And the elevator, believe it or not, is a major focus for some of the changes in behavior between the sexes, most notably in the last few years.

You get an idea of the problem by considering some of the points at which proper behavior becomes a question:

• *Getting on the elevator.* Do men stand back and permit ladies to enter first?

RECOMMENDATION. In keeping with the relaxation of behavior between the sexes, it's suggested that the traditional "ladies-first" practice be observed unless to do so would be awkward. For example:

There is a bank of three elevators. One door opens, and there is a solitary male figure standing right by it. Some distance away are both men and women, who now start heading for the open door. It would be ostentatious for the man to stand back and let the women in the group enter first. He should simply step in and move to the rear of the elevator.

• *In the elevator.* Are men still supposed to remove their headgear?

RECOMMENDATION. Even in the olden days, men in crowded elevators were not expected to remove their hats because there wasn't room to either lift their arms or to hold their hats without having them get crushed.

In cases where there is more room, it is recommended that men *not* remove their hats as a sign of deference to the opposite sex. They may remove them for other reasons—for example, the hat may be a heavy one intended for the cold outdoors, which would weigh heavily in the warmer indoor temperature. But otherwise, hats would stay on for the same reasons that would explain why a woman would not remove her hat in similar circumstances.

• *If a man and woman are both getting off at the same floor.* Should the man stand back even though he's closer to the exit?

RECOMMENDATION. If when the door opens it's the floor at which a man at the front of the elevator wishes to alight, he should do so—directly. What if a man and a woman are equidistant from the door and both are ready to alight? Strict equality would mean that neither deferred to the other. But all else being equal, it's suggested that the woman may exit first. This course is suggested in preference to one where the man bolts in order to beat the woman to the exit.

This gallantry in reverse is still inexcusable. Better to err on the side of old-fashioned traditionalism.

• *Alone together.* The elevator is moving between floors with two passengers—one male, the other female. Let's assume they're strangers. Does the physical proximity suggest that one or the other may start a friendly conversation? Or does the opposite implication apply—that since the proximity is enforced, there is a stricture against either person's starting an impromptu conversation since it might be suspected of being a verbal "pass"?

RECOMMENDATION. It's inadvisable for either person to start a conversation simply because they are fellow voyagers. There is an exception, however. The element of eye-contact comes in. If eye-contact is not established, there's no problem about each person observing an uninvolved silence. But if eye-contact takes place for whatever reason, it's a small enough courtesy for one or the other person to nod, smile, and perhaps essay a brief item of small talk: "Isn't it a beautiful day?" or some such comment. However, the talk should be kept both small and at a minimum and left hanging. This makes it unnecessary for the other person to respond unless he or she wishes to do so.

• *Door-holding.* There is an element of elevator behavior that, strictly speaking, is not sex-related. But it is a point at which wholesale discourtesy is practiced under the guise of samaritanism. This is the practice of holding back an automatic door for the benefit of a would-be rider.

RECOMMENDATION. Acceptable behavior is a matter of split-second timing. Yes, if the person requires just a second or two to get into the elevator, then door-holding is O.K. But it is a wholesale discourtesy to others in the elevator to be kept waiting while a would-be rider blandly finishes a conversation with someone while the passengers stand by without recourse.

WHEN A FEMALE EXECUTIVE FEELS DISCRIMINATED AGAINST BY A COLLEAGUE

Executives at the higher echelons may get a complaint from a manager: "Ever since I became head of the department," says Helen Mattley, "Bill Sloane has resented me. I don't mind his hostility—much. But when it shows—he's kept me waiting weeks for a report—then something should be done. . . ."

What should an executive do to satisfy Mattley's charge?

If Bill Sloane is indeed flouting Helen Mattley because of her sex, then he is guilty of both improper conduct and poor management. Yet even if Helen Mattley is correct in her assumption, the executive to whom she is complaining should look before leaping.

To begin with, for her boss to act might suggest that Helen Mattley can't fight her own battles—possibly confirming the "weak-woman" stereotype.

Second, intervention would call attention to the Mattley-Sloane confrontation. Polarization might take place, with possible division along sex lines—a serious organization schism.

Aside from avoidance of hasty intervention, there is a procedure that can maintain peace, equality of the sexes, and do justice to both parties:

• *Unearth the facts.* You may have to dig into the situation to ascertain the whole story. Certainly you'll get closer to the truth by talking to both people involved—and possibly others familiar with the situation. Refrain from any action that suggests fault-finding. Be objective, calm, and weigh what you learn against your own observations. For example, if Sloane has worked well with other women managers, it is less likely that he would show sudden bias in dealing with Mattley. Problems other than sex may account for their difficulties.

• *Supply guidance?* For example, you may suspect a woman manager is too quick to see slights where none is intended. Without labeling her "oversensitive," minimize the situation. If you feel it's a case of overreaction, suggest that she "bear with it a while" to see how things develop.

Even if you agree that she is getting a raw deal, you may suggest that she handle it herself: "I do get the impression that Bill isn't being as cooperative as he might be. What do you think of the two of you having a meeting and trying to get to the bottom of the trouble?"

Whether you think the man or the woman is at fault, or that both are out to keep the battle going, don't try to change attitudes. You want a change in *behavior* so that both can keep their attention on their work, not their emotions.

• *When should you intervene?* You may have to step in if the conflict has gone on too long and proved too disruptive. A woman who feels discriminated against because of sex might bring charges under the antidiscrimination laws. If she is being treated unfairly and higher management fails to intervene, she might have a case.

But the executive in authority should step in if prejudice and unfairness are involved. If it's obvious that the man is out to cause trouble because he is prejudiced, he should be told plainly his behavior is unacceptable and could provoke a legal complaint.

Final consideration: even if the woman's promotion was due to pressure for affirmative action (or even favoritism), factors other than merit alone can, and do, win promotions for men, too. It's just a situation men have to learn to live with.

WHEN MEN WORK FOR FEMALE BOSSES

The movement of women from lower-level jobs to those on the higher rungs has become an accepted part of the workscene. It has been more marked in some organizations than others. Certainly, compliance with antidiscrimination laws has been one factor. And as women move forward in management, the situation may require a psychological adjustment that many men find difficult.

"Women's Liberation," says a male manager, "has created a new minority, and I'm part of it. Who are we? We're males who have female bosses. And like most any other minority, we have problems. . . ."

Don't think, though, that the "working-for-a-woman" problem is limited to men. One organization reports the case of a female secretary who literally could not take dictation from a woman. The few times she was asked to, she became sick to her stomach—a symptom of psychological trauma.

REACTIONS TO FEMALE BOSSES

While the overreacting secretary is a rare case, she does suggest the turmoil that may result from what some people see as a reversal of the natural order of things. Here's how one male employee sees his situation as subordinate to a woman executive: "Mostly I was puzzled," he reports. "I didn't know what to expect. I had a nodding acquaintance with Theresa when she was assistant to the V.P. of Sales. It's very different, though, knowing someone that way and then one day finding out she's going to be your boss."

Some men take the news they will be reporting to a woman by threatening to quit. Others demand a transfer. Sometimes the resentment is more covert. They hang on, but usually at the cost of job satisfaction. Their relationship with their boss will usually be strained.

Even if a man has no strong negative reaction, he may find that his family and friends do. In fact, some men confess that what troubled them most was having to tell their wives they were now reporting to a woman.

ADJUSTING TO A FEMALE BOSS

The laws against discrimination mean that more women will enter into management in the future. This increases the likelihood that at some time in a man's career he will be reporting to a woman boss. Here is the best way for him to proceed if it happens:

• *Accept actual feelings.* Unless a man works in an organization where women have traditionally been managers, there's going to be some kind of reaction. And it is far better for a man to be aware of any feelings of hostility than to deny them and have his dealings with the new boss colored by disturbing, below-surface emotions.

• *See the real problem.* It is a mistake for the male subordinate to see his problem as being sex-related. The real problem is: "How can I learn to work most productively with this particular individual?" It is when the subordinate stops seeing himself as confronting wide-ranging social change, but rather sees the goal as one of working out a modus operandi, that the solution is at hand.

Even then, feelings of uncertainty or of attempting to undercut the woman are just as great as they would be if his boss were a man.

• *Develop a positive relationship.* Expect to go through three phases:

PHASE 1: OPENING GAMBITS. It is best to let a new manager provide the cues as to what she expects and how she will exercise her leadership.

The subordinate, however, does have some options. He may choose to remain passive and leave it entirely up to his boss to determine the pattern of their relationship. Or he may register a pleasant, accepting attitude—after all, the woman is probably expecting, and dreading, resentment from some of her male subordinates.

Or, going a step further, he can show friendliness. One manager reports he greeted his new boss by saying, "I want to congratulate you on your promotion. I'll give you any help you think I can give. . . ." He wisely did *not* offer to help her learn the ropes but decided to let her ask him if she so chose.

PHASE 2: TESTING. Will the new boss be formal or informal? Will she run a tight ship? How, and how much, will she delegate? How much initiative does she expect from subordinates? And, key question: Should I treat her "like a lady"? This includes everything from helping her on with her coat to offering to pick up the lunch check.

The answers to these and related questions come through day-by-day contact. The subordinate usually gets the message automatically. But the more awareness he brings to these contacts, the faster and better he'll understand what's expected.

Obviously, individuals alter cases. Since generalization is impossible, it becomes necessary to test out one's own feelings as well as the boss's by trial and error.

PHASE 3: OPTIMIZING. After some time has passed, the subordinate is in a position to size up the situation between him and his boss by thinking through the answers to specific questions: What are the satisfactory areas of our working together? What areas (if any) are unsatisfactory? Why are they unsatisfactory? What can be done to minimize or eliminate the difficulties? (Here the question might be reworded: If my boss were male and I had the problem, how would I get rid of it?)

With these rocky spots out of the road, the way is prepared for a good working relationship. The three phases of developing it are, in fact, those any subordinate should expect with *any* boss. For the secret of adjusting to a woman boss is to regard her, and treat her, as an executive. Whether the approach succeeds depends utlimately on the individuals involved—not on their sexes.

HUSBANDS AND WIVES ON THE SAME PAYROLL

Some organizations have doubts, others misgivings about the propriety of married couples as employees. Their concerns focus on four areas:

• *Awkwardness.* A husband and wife, if called on to work together, either in a superior-subordinate relationship or even as job equals, may find that their private feelings intrude on work procedures.

• *Favoritism.* Where one of the couple is in an executive position, there is the possibility that influence will be used to favor the spouse in such matters as assignments, promotions, salary considerations, and so on.

• *Confidentiality.* If husband or wife is in a position of trust, where confidential matters may be involved, it is feared that marital intimacy might cause the communication of such information.

• *Resentment.* Suspicion on the part of co-workers that because of special influence one or the other spouse is benefiting—even if this is not the case—may lead to complications.

There is a strong tendency in the direction of forgetting these traditional fears. To help considerations in this area, it's advisable to cast a backward eye on earlier practices, when many companies had policies against employing husband and wife. This rule often had these two results:

• *Deferred wedding bells.* Two marriage-minded people working for an organization that frowned on employing husband and wife would not marry if they wanted to stay on. Of course, this did not bar some other arrangement, inconvenient or extralegal though it might be.

• *Secret ceremony.* In some cases the man and woman would marry in secret. This obviously might cause complications, particularly if they moved in together. How to keep this from the attention of the "gang at the office"? And if the woman became pregnant— —and being purportedly single—she had some explaining to do.

Usually what happened in cases where a marriage took place was that one or the other partner accepted the need to either stop work or seek other employment.

However, there is a strong trend away from this rule against employing husband and wife. In an article that made this point, The New York Times headlined it: WHEN LOVE BLOOMS AT THE WATER COOLER, FEWER FIRMS THROW COLD WATER ON IT.

To understand what is involved in this matter, it will help to note some of the finer points:

• *Echelon considerations.* One bank had a policy prohibiting a husband-and-wife couple from being on the roster. Later, this was modified, as long as neither was a vice-president or in personnel. The reason for this restriction is clear. The spouse in either of these two situations might be unable to keep confidential information from his or her mate or might actively try to advance the latter's fortunes by undue use of influence.

• *Separation.* A power company will employ husband and wife but insists that they not work in the same building. Many banks will assign husband and wife to different branches.

The purpose of the separation is to minimize the possibility of conflict between personal and on-the-job considerations. For example, there would be obvious problems if a person were supervised by his or her spouse.

In addition to conflict of interest is the possibility of complications resulting from resentment of other employees or colleagues who might feel some advantage is being won by either husband or wife. But the increasing democratization of the workscene also means less arbitrariness and more fairness in decisions and actions. The easing of rules against husband-and-wife employment is the result of this trend. The justification lies in the experience of organizations such as one New York bank, which reports: "We don't keep track of married couples in our employ. That means they aren't giving us any trouble. If they were, we'd be counting them."

WHEN A WOMAN EXECUTIVE MISTREATS FEMALE SUBORDINATES

Gail Fenner is in her early forties, a buyer in a department store. Her boss, the head of the department, says she's "marvelous, terrific," and certainly she seems to be very good at her job, as measured by results. But people who work with and for Gail Fenner seldom like her, and even her admirers tend to be somewhat wary. Ms. Fenner's modus operandi is strikingly sexist. She is brusque, curt in most of her verbal exchanges. She gets along fairly well with male colleagues and subordinates, but no young girls can work for her because she quickly destroys them by a fierce impatience and unreasonable demands.

One explanation for her behavior is that she resents what she is not. In her childhood she was never the cherished darling. Incapable of using feminine wiles herself, she detests obviously feminine individuals. (This kind of explanation is found in psychological texts —and is used here for illustration only.)

What can one do to protect the people victimized by bosses with quirks like Ms. Fenner's? To begin with, there are some things that definitely must *not* be done:

Under no circumstances should a colleague or even a superior, despite the best intentions, undertake to "psychoanalyze" an individual who displays this kind of behavior. True enough, she has a problem, but it's not going to be eliminated by any approach such as "I'd like to tell you what's wrong with you."

Another temptation to avoid: do not try to "prepare" new employees for service under Ms. Fenner by giving a psychological explanation of her manner. You may want to say, "Ms. Fenner is a forthright person," or go as far as to say, "Your new boss may be a little difficult to get along with at first. . . ." But leave it at that.

Here are some moves that may mitigate the harmful effects of the Fennerlike supervision:

Try not to assign young and attractive women to her staff.

When assigning older women, keep in mind that those who are mature and emotionally stable as well as self-confident in their capabilities will fare best.

Males of any age should have little special difficulty.

Gail Fenner's boss should be sufficiently alert to keep an eye on her operations. Any obvious instances of bullying or unfairness should be treated with the same type of reprimand you would give to any supervisor in a similar situation: "Gail, it seems to me you're being unnecessarily harsh with Janice."

WHEN ROMANCE BLOSSOMS ON THE JOB

There's little surprise these days when romance between two employees erupts on the workscene. Some women make no secret of the fact that one of the purposes of their working—in addition to earning wages—is to go hunting for husbandly timber. And for many men, the women they see about them in their own organizations become no less attractive because they both draw paychecks signed by the same company treasurer.

However understandable the romance and however rewarding it may be to the two principals involved, there are problems of behavior that may arise. If these problems are satisfactorily dealt with, then the situation is likely to be a happy one for all concerned. But if matters get out of hand—in any one of several possible ways— there can be considerable ill feeling and disruption. Both the exigencies of the workscene and the sensitivities of other people are involved. Here are some of the considerations:

FOR THE EMPLOYEE. The major thing for the two romantically inclined people to keep in mind is that, first of all, they are in a place of business. Presumably their services are being paid for by the organization, and so any behavior that represents an interference or interruption of regular procedures is undesirable. Under the heading of questionable conduct would come such matters as:

long conversations on the interoffice phone;
visits of one of the couple to the other's work station not required by regular procedures;
any "acting out" of feelings that might make others uncomfortable;
hand-holding, embracing, kissing, while normal behavior for lovers, is not normal behavior for people in a place of business.

FOR EVERYONE ELSE. A certain amount of understanding and compassion is called for. True enough, the couple should use discretion in their behavior. But co-workers and others should be flexible enough to take unostentatious displays of affection in stride. If the organization has a cafeteria, for example, it's likely that the couple might prefer to lunch together—indeed, might even do so every day. Such interest and devotion tends to be resented because in the minds of some it is a "closed corporation" from which everyone else is ruled out. Accordingly, some people see in it a kind of affront. But without going into psychological interpretations of such reactions, it should simply be understood that while such fraternizing is undesirable, if not done to excess, it is still forgivable in the name of romance and individual susceptibility.

WHEN YOU GET A COMPLAINT

A perfectly fine romance may become a matter of contention if people for one reason or another find it objectionable. When a complaint is brought to a person in authority, however, it's important to avoid premature judgments. The fact is that there can be people of a sour disposition who react negatively to situations that others may accept as a matter of course. If it's at all likely that what you're getting is either an overreaction or possibly even a neurotic backlash, the most you should commit yourself to with this person is a statement that you'll "look into the matter."

If after doing so—and only minimum investigation is suggested— nothing questionable is uncovered, it's suggested that you let the matter drop. Leave it up to the complainer to come to you a second time. If there is a second interview, give the person a chance to tell you again what the objectionable behavior is, whether it's continuing, and so on.

Early on, you can explain that you've looked into the matter and see no cause for action. Try to get the individual to talk long enough to clarify the question of motive—why is the complaint being made? If the behavior described is relatively unassailable but the reaction is very strong—"Why, they stood out there on the steps and held hands for all to see, kind of showing off!"—then it's not unreasonable to assume that you're getting the reaction of a person who for one reason or another is oversensitive to romance in even its mild aspects.

In this case simply thank the person for bringing the matter to your attention, but suggest that even though the behavior described may seem to be in questionable taste, there is really no reason to interfere. You might add a comment to the effect that "You know, these days people have a somewhat freer idea about what's permitted in the way of personal conduct."

However, if on the basis of what you have gathered some kind of remonstration must be made to the people in the romance, go on to the next step. . . .

WHEN THE BOUNDS OF PROPRIETY ARE OVERSTEPPED

In some cases, either because of immaturity, unawareness, or perhaps even a desire to show off, the two lovers may have to be called to account. The supervisor or executive in the position to do this is the one who must take the initiative.

WHO SHOULD SPEAK UP? Preferably it should be the manager in the higher echelon as between the man's or woman's immediate superior. The reason for this is that since the behavior involves the two people, the higher-echelon executive should be the one to judge whether in fact there has been some impropriety and should be the one to act on a positive judgment.

To avoid an appearance of bluenosing, the executive should, of course, be sure of the facts. It would be most desirable if he or she witnessed the conduct in question. The next best thing would be to get a description of the behavior from several different sources, all confirming the basic situation.

THE SETTING. Since the entire tone of the admonishing interview should be low-key, formality should be minimized. For example, it's inadvisable to set up a meeting for the encounter. Better an informal contact where the executive can simply say, "Pete"—or "Alice," as the case may be—"may I talk to you for a moment?" And then in a quiet and private place the manager should say his or her piece.

WHAT SHOULD BE SAID? In essence your message can be summed up in the phrase, mildly spoken, "Cool it."

Here's one version: "Pete, I hope you'll forgive me for raising a question of personal behavior. It's about you and Alice, and your obvious interest in each other. Personally, I'm pleased, and my major message is more power to you. However, people are saying that some of the behavior that has come of this involvement is questionable. I certainly don't intend to make any judgment one way or the other, but I think you'll agree that if people are talking, first, you'd want to know about it, and second, I guess you'd want to stop giving them something to talk about. . . ."

You may have to be prepared to face a reaction or an argument. Some individuals may resent being approached on such a matter regardless of what is said. If you do get an argument—which basically doesn't contradict what you have said but shows resentment that "evil-minded individuals" are overreacting—it's best to agree and simply repeat that nevertheless the simplest way to resolve the situation is just to save the "heavier stuff" for outside or off company premises.

HOMOSEXUALITY ON THE WORKSCENE

Among the problems and considerations that have to do with sex, the matter of homosexuality tends to be a thorn in the side of some organizations. Since sex and sex-related problems are often dodged or covered up, homosexuality would obviously rate high on the "let's-not-discuss" list. But according to the observers of the business and executive scene, we have now reached a point where almost any medical and biological phenomenon can be openly broached and dealt with.

Dr. Harry Johnson, a widely recognized authority on organizational health and mores, points out that historically there has been an ambivalent attitude toward homosexuality. While the ancient Greeks accepted it as normal, other cultures made it an offense punishable by death.

But in our time, attitudes toward homosexuality have developed from the hush-hush stage to one where well-known individuals have publicly admitted their homosexual interests and pressure groups have been formed to win equality for male and female homosexuals. Recent legal decisions and statutory guidelines suggest that authorities are trying to catch up with public opinion.

COMMON PROBLEMS RELATED TO HOMOSEXUAL EMPLOYEES

Dr. Johnson, in treating a broad cross-section of executives, reveals that about 5 percent of them revealed that they were homosexuals. This figure suggests that in most organizations there is a small minority of people who have this sexual preference. The organizational questions that come up in connection with members of this group are as follows:

Does the organization show bias against homosexuals in hiring?

Of course, in some industries—everything from the theater to fashion—homosexuality tends to be accepted as a matter of course because there does seem to be a relationship between this sexual tendency and a development of interests, sensitivities, and so on that are fostered in such areas.

Would a homosexual be fired by the organization if for one reason or another that had nothing to do with the individual's performance his or her proclivity became known?

Would the organization fire an individual against whom a statement that he or she was a homosexual was made as an accusation by an employee? Here again, there would have been no question of performance or unacceptable behavior on the job.

Are you prepared to cope with a homosexual clique? Any common quality—religion, university background, even a sports interest —may serve as a basis for the formation of a workscene clique. One of the characteristics of such a group is that it attempts to become a power source and, as such, self-protective and self-enhancing. One might have to make the same moves with a homosexual group—prevent it from becoming a destructive element in organization life.

Questions like these are raised to help organizations and individual executives think through this somewhat perplexing question. If an actual situation or case in point presents itself, the comments above will be of help in clarifying the issue.

SEXUAL HARASSMENT: WHAT TO DO ABOUT IT

It's difficult to say whether actual instances of sexual harassment have increased or decreased on the workscene. Certainly, in the "bad old days," when labor exploitation was rampant, sexual demands made on female employees with threats of punishment ranging from supervisory displeasure to firing for noncompliance were widespread.

On the other hand, two factors hold for the contemporary business scene that explain why harassment still persists:

• *Less fear of embarrassment.* Back some twenty or thirty years, an executive supervisor or even a co-worker who made advances that were brought to the attention of a higher executive might find his job in jeopardy. Nowadays in a similar situation the offender might be advised to "Cool it," "Save that kind of thing for after hours," and so on. Many managements ignore such situations, expecting them to "take care of themselves."

• *Relaxed moral climate.* Since the "rules" regarding sexual conduct are less rigid, people are more likely to respond to the biological urge. The male eye attracted by one or another aspect of a female employee finds it a simple matter to make some overt precourting move. If accepted, fine. If rejected—well, no harm done.

IS SEXUAL HARASSMENT A TWO-WAY STREET?

Harper's recently printed an amusing piece by one of its staff labeled "An Ardent Plea for Sexual Harassment." The woman writer set out to maintain the conceit that ". . . a lot of women would feel deprived without a reasonable quota of sexual harassment per week." And, as is also pointed out, to speak of unwanted sexual advances as being the lot only of females continues the stereotype of women as weak and defenseless.

While the description of women as natural victims may be unjusti-fied, certainly to suggest that men are equally open to sexual harass-ment in the same sense is less likely. And yet, regardless of what the future may hold for sexual equality, management and individual executives should proceed on the assumption that men as well as women may be objects of sexual advances that because of their job situation can be difficult for them to deal with. In considering the matter of harassment, these points are worthy of consideration:

• *Protection.* It's essential that employees be as safe as they want to be from molestation. No matter how high the echelon of the misguided aggressor, any complaint that an investigation reveals to be well founded must be acted on, possibly discreetly but certainly without equivocation. Whoever is in a position to reprimand the offender should be given the duty to do so.

However, one must be realistic enough to foresee possible conse-quences. Just beating down the advances of a harasser, however successfully, may leave an open-ended situation difficult for both people involved. In most cases, depending on the individuals, it may be possible to say to both, but separately: "Now the situation has been taken care of, I'm sure it will be quickly forgotten by all concerned. . . ." However, if there is a likelihood that the aggressor is not likely to take his defeat lightly, special thought has to be given to a satisfac-tory outcome for the victim in the case. For example, it will not be a satisfactory adjudication if the woman is forced to give up her job in the face of the harasser's ill-will. Nor will it help her if she is transferred to another but less desirable job.

These consequences must be taken into account. Not to be ruled out, of course, is the possibility that where the offense has been blatant the harasser may be either demoted, transferred, or fired.

Of course, this action would be justified only when the offense has been extreme. There are few executives who will be unable to con-trol their future conduct when a reprimand has been blunt and to the point. And in such a case, a word may be added that suggests a course of future conduct that must be followed: "Of course, Ms. Smith will continue in her job. And it's going to be up to you to see to it that nothing is done to suggest the slightest punishment or ill feeling."

SEX AND THE CHRISTMAS PARTY—IS IT STILL A PROBLEM?

As people experienced in business know, Christmas parties tradi-tionally have had a somewhat tarnished aura. In some quarters any reference to an "office party" is accompanied by smirks.

A survey of a thousand companies of all sizes, and across the board in all types of industry, asked some blunt questions about their office parties. Those who checked off the questionnaire: "We don't approve of office parties," went on to answer the question "Why?" with: "They turn into drunken orgies." Another typical answer: "Mixed sexes and liquor cause problems."

The need to blow off some steam that so many Christmas parties seem to satisfy does seem to have largely subsided with changing and possibly more enlightened times. However, organizations that are still concerned about parties in general, and particularly holiday celebrations in the Christmas season, may want to consider these mitigants:

• *A liquorless event?* Some organizations have been able to have a Christmas celebration without liquor. The tone is set by the top executive who shortly after the group gathers—and has been turned loose on soft drinks, canapés, sandwiches, and so on—gets up and announces: "Dear colleagues, it's a great pleasure to see us all gather together again at this holiday season. Those interested in more volatile drinking will want to save your capacity for a celebration off the company premises. We're gathered together here in good-fellowship to spend time with friends and colleagues, and we hope you all enjoy the occasion. Merry Christmas and Happy New Year. . . ."

• *Limit the time?* One organization follows a policy of making the Christmas get-together brief. Drinks are served, there is a background soundtrack of holiday tunes. But at some reasonable point after the appropriate "remarks" have been made by top executives, "quitting" signals are sent out: key people begin to leave, the music is stopped, and the word goes out: "Time for your last drink before the bar closes."

• *Chaperones?* It may sound like a retreat to the Dark Ages, but when some individuals or groups tend to want to "orgy-ize" the affair, it's not inappropriate for more mature people to intervene discreetly to keep matters calmed down. For those intent on biological activity, what takes place after they leave the premises is their affair—with one exception. The organization has a moral responsibility—and possibly a legal one as well—for what happens after the party if, for example, excessive drinking has taken place and individuals leave partly or largely inebriated. It is both wise and helpful for people in charge to see to it that those who are not in control of themselves are assisted home or, if more practical, are permitted to "rest up" to regain their self-control before leaving.

(For a discussion of the general aspects of company party-giving, see Chapter 8, especially page 298, "The Office Party.")

DEALING WITH THE BOSS-SECRETARY ROMANCE

"Executives don't always have affairs with their secretaries, but if the chemistry is halfway right, it's difficult to avoid entanglement," says a personnel executive who has had numerous office romances brought to his attention.

A recent book dealing with the subject of sex in business reports the words of an experienced personnel director of one division of a large corporation: "A sex problem in the office? Certainly we have one. . . . Did you ever see a time when girls were more attractive, sexy, and exciting looking than today? If we *didn't* have a sex problem I'd be terribly worried we had a homosexual problem among our men. The trouble arises, of course, in the distraction it may cause. . . ."

The top executives of business organizations will be able to proceed most effectively in the touchy area of boss (male)-secretary (female) relations by understanding some of the underlying factors involved:

• *Proximity.* There's no doubt about the fact that boss and secretary work closely together, are together in a closer relationship than often may exist between the executive and his spouse or the secretary and hers.

• *The "Look-Good" Factor.* The executive is often a male, which means that he is a wielder of authority, which means that he can be assertive, even flamboyant, makes him an attractive example of Charismatic Man.

And the secretary, usually female, in the role of helpmate, burden-easer, a source of comfort and favorable partisanship, tends to acquire an appeal that can be extremely powerful.

While the above may not be the typical situation, it is sufficiently prevalent to suggest it to those in authority as a potential problem worth anticipating.

Company policymakers may want to consider the suggestions below as a means of minimizing either the problem or the consequences:

• *Try not to feed the chasers.* If you're a personnel executive and executive X, with a lively reputation for lady-killing is in line for a new secretary, look for an individual who will not in any way be a defenseless sacrifice. This may even mean suggesting a male secretary, or putting someone in the spot who you know is perfectly capable of taking care of herself.

What to do if the executive objects? Of course, the executive may object to any efforts to circumvent his own personal interests. If this is the case, it should be possible to explain exactly what's going on without making him feel uncomfortable: "We've been interviewing people for your secretarial spot, James, but frankly, on the basis of past experience, we know the pretty young ones don't seem to last very long. . . ."

Of course, executives usually have the final word in selecting their own secretaries. But if the record is indeed bad—that is, marked by a parade of young women who make no secret of their dissatisfaction—this point may be brought to the executive's attention, with the suggestion made that perhaps someone from Personnel with "more experience" might be able to select a secretary with "more stamina" and should be able to "avoid hiring job-hoppers."

• *Use job performance as a basis for judgment.* It is seldom proper, nowadays, to blow the whistle on a romancing couple on moral grounds. Regardless of our own standards, we no longer feel it is appropriate to lecture people on their personal behavior. There is one exception—and a major one. When personal conduct or preoccupations interfere with the work, then a representative of management may step forward.

Of course, it must be emphasized that work interference may be of two kinds: direct and indirect. If the principals in the romance are performing poorly because of their interest in one another, then the executive's superior is justified in playing an admonishing role. Or, if the work interference shows up in less obvious ways, action may have to be taken: "The whole office is upset about Mr. Smith and Marge," reports a junior executive. This voyeur-caused inefficiency, strictly speaking, is not the sparking couple's fault. The executive in charge has the option of suggesting to the distracted employees that they mind their own business, or of hinting to the principals that, unknowingly or otherwise, their behavior is causing trouble and would they please alleviate matters by easing up on the more visible aspects of their romance.

Of course, as long as their conduct is O.K., and so is their work, they might refuse to be intimidated by the criticism of others. If you get this response, then the logical move is to go back to the complainers and give them the usual "it's-a-free-country" speech and the reminder that the couple is doing nothing culpable.

In any case, it's important that the person who intervenes do so quietly, and without being judgmental. As long as the comments are directed to the necessity of keeping work up to standard—"What you do on your own time is your own business, but we're all paid to do a job"—the discussion can be kept in constructive channels.

THE SEXIST USE OF FIRST NAMES

One of the problems in achieving sex equality on the workscene is that the old ways often seem so natural and unexceptionable. For example:

The boss comes into the office to start the day. "Good morning, Mr. Smith," his secretary says. "Good morning, Beth," he replies.

What's wrong? The consciousness-raised woman has no trouble in answering: "Beth Lewis should be addressed as 'Miss Lewis' for the same reasons that make 'Mr. Smith' proper."

One might argue that in part the names used in the example above are as much a designation of rank as they are of sex. But this explanation may be unacceptable to those who feel that such hierarchical distinctions are old-fashioned and out of place in today's more enlightened world.

One finds the first-name problem in another typical setting. Talk to women job-hunters and you'll find this common situation: "I hope you're favorably impressed by my résumé, Mr. Jones."

"It looks fine, Lois."

And it's notable that the interviewing male will use the woman applicant's first name almost regardless of the level of the job involved.

There's a simple method of handling this first name–surname situation. One recent job-hunter says, "Whenever a male interviewer addresses me by my first name, I do the same with him."

In established job relationships this same pattern may be followed: a woman being called by her first name may, if she feels it inappropriate, request that her surname be used. Or, if she prefers, that she have the privilege of using the man's first name.

"MISS," "MRS.," "MS."

The 1970s brought in the use of "Ms." as a designation for a woman who prefers not to have her marital status signaled by a "Miss" or "Mrs." For treatment of this usage, see "When and How to Use 'Ms.,'" in Chapter 5, page 212.

UNCONSCIOUS SEXISM—SEX STEREOTYPING

One of the ways in which inequality of the sexes is perpetuated is by actions that force women into a traditional stereotype. Here are a number of practices that reveal an unconscious bias against which organizations and executives may want to take some neutralizing action:

PHYSICAL SEGREGATION. When a business group of men and women travel, women are often segregated, housed in separate buildings if this is possible. Some women resent such efforts: "I've been allowed out by myself since I was eighteen," says one woman, "and I certainly don't need anyone 'protecting' me."

OVERPROTECTION. The same type of "protection" leads one pharmaceutical company to omit home phone numbers from the business cards of their female salespeople, although these are included on the men's cards.

Complains one woman sales representative: "The men get calls at home having to do with business matters. Apparently management thinks I would have trouble handling an obnoxious phone call."

TOKENISM. Even when women are permitted into management, actions are taken to cancel out any real transfer of power. One tactic—similar to that used for handling failing male executives—calls for the following treatment: the woman is given a title, an office, perhaps even a secretary and a good salary, but then her assignments are kept "harmless." As one male chauvinist put it: "Keep her away from operations. Let people see her, but make sure she doesn't do anything."

SPOUSE PARTICIPATION. Some of the attitudes spill over into career areas. For example, some managers consider that wives are obliged to participate in the social activities associated with their husbands' careers. To a much lesser degree is career support expected from the husbands of working women.

TIME—THE GREATEST CHANGE AGENT

Early in this chapter the point was made that subsequent printings of this volume will omit this section as being obsolete. Certainly, attitudes and values do alter with time. One stays current by inviting the developments of the world at large into the workscene. After all, the two milieus are intimately related.

INDEX